CRISIS MANAGEMENT IN TOURISM

Edited by

Eric Laws

James Cook University, Australia

Bruce Prideaux

James Cook University, Australia

and

Kaye Chon

The Hong Kong Polytechnic University, Hong Kong

www.cabi.org

CABI is a trading name of CAB International

CABI Head Office
Nosworthy Way
Wallingford
Oxon OX10 8DE
UK

Tel: +44 (0)1491 832111
Fax: +44 (0)1491 833508
E-mail: cabi@cabi.org
Website: www.cabi.org

CABI North American Office
875 Massachusetts Avenue
7th Floor
Cambridge, MA 02139
USA

Tel: +1 617 395 4056
Fax: +1 617 354 6875
E-mail: cabi-nao@cabi.org

A catalogue record for this book is available from the British Library, London, UK.

A catalogue record for this book is available from the Library of Congress, Washington, DC.

ISBN-10: 1 84593 047 9
ISBN-13: 978 1 84593 047 9

Typeset by Columns Design Ltd, Reading, UK
Printed and bound in the UK by Athenaeum Press, Gateshead

Contents

Contributors

Dagmar Abfalter, *Department of General and Tourism Management, University of Innsbruck, Austria. Fax: +43-512-507-29, E-mail: dagmar.abfalter@uibk.ac.a*

Barbara Anderson, *Senior Research Fellow, Quality Use of Medicines and Pharmacy Research Center, School of Pharmacy and Medical Sciences, City East Campus, University of South Australia, GPO Box 2471, Adelaide SA 5001. Tel: +61 8-8302-1369, Fax: +61 8-8302-1087, E-mail: barbara.anderson@unisa.edu.au*

Awangku Hassanal Bahar Pengiran Bagul, *Victoria Management School, Victoria University of Wellington, New Zealand. Fax: +64 4-4635180, E-mail: hassanal.bagul@gmail.com*

David Beirman, *Director Struan & Associates, PO Box 345, Bondi NSW 2026, Australia. Tel: +61 2-9369-2141, E-mail: David@aicc.org.au*

Mike Berrell, *RMIT, City Campus, 124 La Trobe St, Melbourne, Victoria 3000. Tel: +61 7-4781-4019, Fax: +61 7-4781-4019, E-mail: mike.berrell@ rmit.edu.au*

Graham Brown, *Foundation Professor of Tourism Management, School of Management, City West Campus, University of South Australia, GPO Box 247, Adelaide SA 5001. Tel: +61 8-8302-0313, Fax: +61 8-8302-0512, E-mail: graham.brown@unisa.edu.au*

Kom Campiranon, *School of Tourism & Leisure Management, The University of Queensland, 11 Salisbury Road, Ipswich, 4305, Queensland, Australia. E-mail: s4085712@student.uq.edu.au*

Conor Carroll, *Department of Management and Marketing, Kemmy Business School, University of Limerick, Limerick, Ireland. Tel: +353 61-202398, Fax: +353 61-223196*

Kaye Chon, *Conference Chairman, School of Hotel and Tourism Management, The Hong Kong Polytechnic University, Hung Hom, Kowloon, Hong Kong. Tel: +852 2766-6382, Fax: +852 2362-6422, E-mail: hmkchon@polyu. edu.hk, www.polyu.edu.hk/htm*

Malcolm Cooper, *Graduate School of Asia Pacific Studies, Ritsumeikan Asia Pacific University, Jumonjibaru, Beppu 874-8477, Japan.*

John C. Crotts, *Professor of Hospitality and Tourism Management, School of Business and Economics, College of Charleston (SC), 66 George Street, Charleston, SC 29424, USA. Tel: +1 843-953-6916, Fax: +1 843-953-5697, E-mail: ns@cofc.edu*

Sara Dolnicar, *School of Management and Marketing, University of Wollongong' Northfields Avenue, Wollongong, 2522 NSW, Australia. Tel: +61 2-4221-3862, Fax: +61 2-4221-4154, E-mail: sarad@uow.edu.au*

Thomas E. Drabek, *John Evans Professor, Emeritus, Department of Sociology and Criminology, University of Denver, Sturm Hall, Room 440, 2000 E. Asbury Ave., Denver, CO 80208. E-mail: tarabek@du.edu*

Axel Dreyer, *Tourism Section, University of Applied Studies and Research, Harz, Wernigerode, Germany. Fax: +49 3943/659-299, E-mail: prof.dreyer@t-online.de*

Patricia Erfurt, *Graduate School of Asia Pacific Studies, Ritsumeikan Asia Pacific University, Jumonjibaru, Beppu 874-8577, Japan. Fax: +81 977-781001, E-mail: Patrer04@apu.ac.jp*

Walter Freyer, *Dresden University of Technology, Dresden, Germany, Fax: +49 351-463-36807, E-mail: tourism@rcs.urz.tu-dresden.de*

Ian Glendon, *School of Applied Psychology-Business, Griffith University, PM 50 Gold Coast Mail Centre, Queensland 9726, Australia. Tel: +61 7-5552-8964, Fax: +61 7-5552-829, E-mail: i.glendon@griffith.edu.au*

Yetta K. Gurtner, *PhD Candidate, Centre for Disaster Studies, School of Tropical Environmental Studies and Geography, Faculty of Science and Engineering, James Cook University, Townsville, Australia. Tel: +61 7-47239318, Fax: +61 7-47814020, E-mail: yetta.gurtner@jcu.edu.au*

Derek Hall, *Visiting Professor, Häme Polytechnic, Mustiala, Finland, and Partner, Seabank Associates, Maidens, Scotland, UK. Fax: +44 1655-331442, E-mail: derekhall.seabank@virgin.net*

Wan Shawaluddin Wan Hassan, *School of Social Science, University Malaysia Sabah, Malaysia. E-mail: wshawal@yahoo.com*

Joan Henderson, *Associate Professor, Division of Marketing and International Business, Nanyang Business School, Nanyang Technological University, Nanyang Avenue, Singapore 639798. Tel: +65 6790-6116, Fax: +65 6791-3697 (overseas) 6692 4217 (local), E-mail: ahenderson@ntu.edu.sg*

Tzung-Cheng Huan, *PhD, Associate Professor, Graduate Institute of Leisure Industry Management, College of Management, National Chia-Yi University, 151 Lin Shen East Road, Chia-Yi, Taiwan, Republic of China. Tel/Fax: +886 5-2751573, E-mail: tchuan@mail.ncyu.edu.tw*

Igoe Josephine, *Department of Management and Marketing, Kemmy Business School, University of Limerick, Limerick, Ireland. Tel: +353 61-202398, Fax: +353 61-223196*

Eric Laws, *School of Business, James Cook University, PO Box 6811, Cairns, 4879, Australia. E-mail: e.laws@runbox.com*

Stephen W. Litvin, *DBA, Associate Professor of Hospitality and Tourism Management, School of Business and Economics, College of Charleston (SC), 66 George Street, Charleston, SC 29424, USA. Tel: +1 843-953-7317, Fax: +1 843-953-5697, E-mail: litvins@cofc.edu*

Andrew Lyon, *Senior Lecturer in Tourism, University of Chester, Parkgate Road, Chester CH1 4BJ, UK. Tel: +44 1244-511808, Fax: +44 1244-392825, E-mail: a.lyon@chester.ac.uk*

Lynette M. McDonald, *Department of Tourism and Hotel Management, Griffith University, PMB 50 Gold Coast Mail Centre, Queensland 9726, Australia. Tel: +61 7-5552-8170, Fax: +61 7-5552-8507, E-mail: l.mcdonald@griffith. edu.au*

Pedro Moreira, *Institute for Tourism Studies, Macau SAR, PR China, University of Strathclyde, Glasgow, Scotland, UK. Fax: +44 853-519058, E-mail: pmoreirasys@netscape.net*

Sinead O'Keefe, *Department of Management and Marketing, Kemmy Business School, University of Limerick, Limerick, Ireland. Tel: +353 61-202398, Fax: +353 61-223196*

Bruce Prideaux, *Professor of Marketing and Tourism Management, James Cook University, PO Box 6811, Cairns, 4879, Australia. Tel: +61 7-40421039, Fax: +61 7-4781-4111. E-mail: Bruce.Prideaux@jcu.edu.au*

Harald Pechlaner, *School of Economics and Business, Free University of Bozen-Bolzano, Italy. Fax: +39 0471-055-499, E-mail: harald.pechlaner@ unibz.it*

Frieda Raich, *Institute for Management and Tourism, Eurac Research, Bozen-Bolzano Italy. Fax: +39 0471-055-499, E-mail: fraich@eurac.edu*

Rosemarie Reynolds, *PhD Assistant Professor, College of Business, Embry-Riddle Aeronautical University, 600 South Clyde Morris Boulevard, Daytona Beach, FL 32114, USA. Tel: +1 386-226-6721, Fax: +1 386-226-6694, E-mail: reyno9bd@erau.edu*

Dawna L. Rhoades, *PhD Associate Professor, College of Business, Embry-Riddle Aeronautical University, 600 South Clyde Morris Boulevard, Daytona Beach, FL 32114, USA. Tel: +1 386/226-7756, Fax: +1 386-226-6694, E-mail: rhoadesd@erau.edu*

Miriam Scaglione, *Institute for Economics & Tourism, University of Applied Sciences Valais, Switzerland. E-mail: miriam.scaglione@hevs.ch*

Peter Schmidt, *James Cook University, Townsville, QLD 4811, Australia, Fax: +61 7-4781-4111, E-mail: peter.schmidt@jcu.edu.au*

Alexander Schröder, *Dresden University of Technology, D-01062, Dresden, Germany. Tel: +49 351-463-2581, Fax: +49 351-463-36807. E-mail: tourism@rcs.urz.tu-dresden.de*

Noel Scott, *School of Tourism & Leisure Management, The University of Queensland, 11 Salisbury Road, Ipswich, 4305, Queensland, Australia. Fax: +61 7-3381-1024, E-mail: noel.scott@uq.edu.au*

Brian W. Sloboda, *US Department of Transport, Research and Innovative Technology Administration, 400 Seventh Street, SW (Room 3430), Washington DC 20590, USA. Voice-mail: +1 202-366-5342, E-mail: brian.sloboda@dot.gov*

Beverley Sparks, *Department of Tourism and Hotel Management, Griffith University, PMB 50 Gold Coast Mail Centre, Queensland 9726, Australia. Tel: +61 7-5552-8766, Fax: +61 7-5552-8978, E-mail: b.sparks@griffith.edu.au*

Siobhan Tiernan, *Department of Management and Marketing, Kemmy Business School, University of Limerick, Limerick, Ireland. Tel: +353 61-202398, Fax: +353 61-223196, E-mail: Siobhan.Tiernan@ul.ie*

Amy Worton, *Research Assistant, University of Chester, Parkgate Road, Chester CH1 4BJ, UK. Tel: +44 1244-511808, Fax: +44 1244-392825, E-mail: a.lyon@chester.ac.uk*

Preface: The Tsunami of 26 December 2005, PATA's Initial Responses

PETER SEMONE, FORMER PRESIDENT OF PATA

Let me begin, on behalf of the entire PATA family, by expressing our sympathies to the families and friends of people who perished on 26 December 2004. Many of them were tourism industry colleagues or tourists. Since that fateful day, we have seen an outpouring of humanitarian compassion around the world. The unprecedented global fundraising response indicates how the plight of the victims and survivors emotionally impacted all of us regardless of our background.

PATA (the Pacific Asia Travel Association) was founded in 1951. Today, it has grown to include over 1000 leading public and private sector members organizations, including National Tourism Organizations, travel and accommodation businesses, travel agents, the media and educators. At the grassroots level, PATA's network includes 50 chapters throughout the Asia Pacific region and in Europe and North America, representing some 4000 individuals with a passion for the business of travel and tourism in Asia Pacific. PATA provides a range of services to its members including publications such as the PATA *Compass Magazine*, and the monthly, *Issues and Trends*. PATA also organizes an annual conference enabling the industry and governments to discuss policy issues, and annual Travel Mart meetings to bring together sellers of Asia Pacific travel with buyers from around the world. In addition to providing superior networking and business development opportunities for its members, PATA produces a continual stream of information on Asia Pacific market intelligence; collating, analysing and reporting on trends in the industry. PATA also acts as a leading advocate by communicating with stakeholders and the media on important regional and sectoral issues such as sustainable tourism and crisis management.

PATA's extended family around the globe was touched by the tsunami, and motivated to help. The PATA Tsunami Recovery Fund (details of which I will outline later in this preface) is just one manifestation. The disaster is foremost a humanitarian one. Tourists and travel industry professionals suffered alongside fishermen, farmers and families on an otherwise peaceful and innocent Sunday morning. The waves tore down the barriers between rich and poor, urban and rural, and united us all. This unprecedented disaster has received an unprecedented response. And rightly so.

PATA's response to the humanitarian tragedy of 26 December was fast. It began when one of our managers saw an early morning TV news report of the tidal wave striking Phuket. Although it was Sunday, he immediately set off for our office in central Bangkok and began to telephone colleagues he thought might still be in town during the Christmas holiday. A small group of staff soon assembled and, as we watched the news broadcasts, we saw that the scale of the tragedy was enormous, affecting many areas around the Indian Ocean. We started to think through what we could best do, and realized that accurate information about the local effects of the tsunami was not yet available. We telephoned our contacts and members throughout the region and asked our staff who were taking holidays away from Bangkok to investigate and report on the local situations.

First Day

- On the day of the disaster, PATA had established a clearly hyperlinked dedicated zone on its website, *PATA.org* online by about 17:30 h. This gave such details as we had been able to verify and was constantly updated during the next few weeks.
- On the same day, PATA also issued a media release entitled, 'PATA Says Search and Rescue Should be Priority'. This message was also sent to a database of about 80 travel industry communicators – public relations and communications directors, for onward circulation to their own network of media and industry contacts.
- PATA sent out messages of condolences to members in affected countries and asked them what support they needed from the Association.

Second Day

- On the morning of Monday, 27 December, PATA sent the Director of Business Development, Mr Stephen Yong, to Phuket. Stephen accompanied representatives of the Tourism Authority of Thailand (TAT) on an inspection of coastal areas of Phuket and Phangnga provinces. He worked alongside the TAT for 4 days.
- There was widespread confusion in the immediate aftermath of the tsunami about the actual effects on the region and its tourism industry. We were receiving phone calls from our members in Europe and America asking whether our office had been damaged, and whether it was still safe to send tourists to the region. On 27 December, PATA put

out its second key message: 'Most of Asia Unaffected by Tsunami.'
Again this went to the communicators' database to secure a multiplier
effect and get the message out to as many people as possible that most
tourist resorts around the Indian Ocean remained undamaged and
fully functional.

The Next Few Days

The leading news organizations, CNN, CNBC, BBC, Bloomberg, *Asian
Wall Street Journal*, *TIME* and *Straits Times*, to name just a few, were now
asking PATA for information and comment. In between collating the
information flowing into our offices from members, staff and the media,
PATA Managing Director-Strategic Intelligence Centre, Mr John
Koldowski, was giving non-stop phone interviews to leading news
organizations.

- John went live on CNBC's *Squawk Box* programmes on 28 December
  and 3 January.
- On 29 December, he was interviewed live on BBC World's *Asia Business
  Report*.
- Also on 29 December, PATA put out the first special edition of
  News@PATA dedicated to the tsunami disaster and how it had
  impacted the travel industry around the Indian Ocean.

From its founding in 1951, one feature of PATA has been its charitable
work, including scholarships for tourism industry staff in the PATA area.
By 30 December, PATA had formalized its charitable initiative and put out
a release announcing the launch of the PATA Tsunami Recovery Fund,
spearheaded by PATA's charitable arm, the PATA Foundation. Through
this Fund, PATA invited PATA members, chapters, governments, tourist
authorities, travel professionals and individual travellers to pledge money.
The funds have been dedicated to a recovery programme for the benefit of
tourism-dependent professionals in Asia Pacific resort destinations affected
by the disaster.

On 30 December, I sent a personal message to all chapter chairpersons
updating them on how PATA had responded with the launch of a fund and
the distribution of key messages. The chapter communiqué encouraged
chapters to donate to the PATA Tsunami Recovery Fund.

Throughout the week, PATA Regional Director-North America,
Mr Jim Ferguson, was working closely with chapters in his region to
coordinate their fundraising efforts. Jim also secured a shipment of
drinking water from Phoenix, Arizona to Sumatra.

Over the New Year's long weekend, PATA worked hard, constantly
updating useful information on PATA.org and giving detailed responses to
media queries.

On 4 January, PATA President and CEO Mr Peter de Jong told BBC
World TV's *Fast Track* consumer travel programme that one of the best

ways to help affected destinations was not to cancel holidays, but to book trips to the main touristic destinations affected by the tsunami. To assist our overseas members in their marketing of the PATA region, we advised them that this interview would appear on *Fast Track* on 8 January and be repeated throughout the week.

Peter de Jong repeated these key messages in an interview with Sandy Dhuyvetter of *TravelTalkRADIO*. Peter said: 'Speed of response was of the essence – as was sensitivity. This was a humanitarian tragedy. Tourism was only one element.' He added: 'PATA's response to date has been proactive with strong input from regional directors in the Pacific, Europe and North America as well as colleagues at PATA head office.'

In summary, the following messages were broadcast by PATA from the onset of our tsunami crisis management activities.

- This is a major humanitarian tragedy; tourism is only one element.
- This is NOT an Asian crisis; it is a crisis confined to SOME PARTS of the Indian Ocean coast.
- Travel and tourism continues uninterrupted across most of Asia and in most parts of many of the affected countries; indeed many travel destinations in Asia are heavily/fully booked.
- Many displaced tourists at affected destinations are choosing to stay in nearby hotels inland or in other resorts rather than go home.
- There is good solidarity among the travel industry, for example competitors are helping each other out.
- Many travel industry operators are asking how/where to pledge money for relief.

I cannot overemphasize the importance of crisis preparedness in the travel and tourism industry. Here in Asia, we have experienced 3 years of extraordinary crisis-related challenges: from terrorism to health crises to natural disaster. In response to these, we have developed a systematic programme of crisis preparedness for our members. This consists of short specialist workshops during our regional meetings, and the commissioning and dissemination, of a 16-page booklet, *Crisis: It Won't Happen to Us* (Pacific Asia Travel Association, Bangkok). This points out that the essence of effective crisis management is to expect the unexpected. The booklet is also available on our website, free of charge. A more detailed crisis management manual has been prepared in conjunction with APEC and the WTO, and is available to members upon request.

It is worth noting the ten steps to a crisis plan as proposed in PATA's *Crisis: It Won't Happen to Us*:

1. Initiate the formation of a crisis management team, comprised of senior officials empowered with the authority to make and implement decisions in the midst of a crisis.

2. Contact all emergency and civil organizations that could be involved in a crisis and insist on high level contact and participation in the planning process.

3. Ensure consistency in the crisis management team and coordinate regular meetings.

4. Recognize that extraordinary times call for extraordinary measures and ensure that the crisis management team is empowered to spend money during a crisis.

5. Determine which risks are important to deal with and continually assess emerging risks.

6. Develop 'What if …' contingency plans to serve as a troubleshooting guide during an actual crisis.

7. Ensure that instructions and assignments are clear, current and rehearsed, and that key stakeholders and emergency services are able to be contacted at short notice and are privy to the crisis plans of the organization.

8. Encourage incorporation of crisis management activities into the plans and priorities of all stakeholders as well as the official job descriptions of all employees and officials of the organization.

9. Train members of the crisis management team in some form of crisis communications and media relations

10. Identify and approach individuals with specialist skills and knowledge in order that they can be quickly brought in to assist the organization in crisis.

I welcome the publication of *Crisis Management in Tourism*, and applaud the initiative of its editors and chapter contributors; the need for more research into appropriate and effective responses to crisis situations is urgent. Each crisis is unique in the way it originates and develops, as the analysis in this book clearly shows, requiring great flexibility in the ways that managers and their teams respond. Managers can only gain in confidence and understanding of the complexity of tasks they will encounter during a crisis by studying the experiences of others.

One thing is certain, there will be another crisis for the tourism industry, and when it rears its ugly head we must respond in a quick, agile and professional fashion. By failing to do so, we run the risk of escalating the consequences of future crises which in the end will cost more jobs, more despair and more bankruptcies; and for an industry that is reliant on small and medium sized enterprises, we can ill afford that risk. In recent decades, tourism has proven its ability to create employment opportunities, provide foreign exchange and enhance human understanding. As more developing economies become reliant on the outcomes of tourism, it is incumbent upon all tourism practitioners to enhance their ability to sustain this very fragile industry, of which one aspect is risk and crisis management.

1 Crisis Management in Tourism: Challenges for Managers and Researchers

ERIC LAWS, BRUCE PRIDEAUX AND KAYE CHON

Introduction

As the editors and contributors were working on this book, one of the most severe natural disasters in recorded history struck and devastated many places and communities around the Indian Ocean on 26 December 2004, after a suboceanic earthquake generated a vast tsunami. Only 3 years previously, the terrorist attack of 11 September 2001 (9/11) caused great damage, suffering and shock in the USA. Both of these events had significant consequences for the operation of tourism businesses. In both of these events, tourists and the tourism industry, although gravely affected, were not the most numerous nor the most seriously affected. In the concluding chapter, we discuss two further crises, the New Orleans hurricane and the strong possibility of a global bird flu pandemic, and draw lessons from them for the future management of tourism crises.

The standard way of assessing the gravity of a tourism crisis is by expressing it as the number (or proportion) of lost arrivals, visitor nights or spending, but this is a far lower order of importance than loss of life, infrastructure damage, loss of homes, and economic or cultural damage. Indeed, the situations, problems and responses discussed in this book are often of a minor order of importance when such devastating events occur. However, it is often the case that long-term recovery for the area is partly dependent on the re-establishment of a viable tourism sector, so it is important that we learn from the experience of the types of events analysed here how to manage the tourism aspects of a crisis, and how and when to begin restoration of tourist activities following the initial recovery, and rehabilitation of areas which have suffered a major crisis.

A crisis can occur at any time, in the most unlikely place and for reasons which may not be apparent until after the event. This book is mainly concerned with reporting and analysing how managers have responded to some of the various crises which have afflicted the tourism industry in recent years. In the 26 chapters of this book, contributors examine international and local events which have disrupted the main sectors of tourism in many countries around the world.

After reading this book, it will be apparent that some crises are largely restricted to the tourism industry, and arose from problematic characteristics in its own operations. The origins of other crises lay completely outside the influence of tourism sector managers, and many of these crises devastated large areas and killed, injured or damaged many sectors of the local population or key infrastructure and industries.

Some of the crises discussed in this book were unexpected and unforecast; in other cases, it was recognized by government or managers that a disaster might occur at some time, but its probability, what the disaster would be, its immediate consequences and the steps necessary to overcome it and to resume normality (even if that was to be different from the previous norms) were seldom well understood.

In the wake of major crises, notably the terrorist attacks on the USA in September 2001, the fears of a widespread epidemic engendered by the outbreak of severe acute respiratory syndrome (SARS) or bird flu, and the tsunami, many academics have turned their attention to better understanding how to analyse crises events.

Taken together, the chapters in this book propose improvements to current theories and provide extensive reviews and bibliographies of recent tourism research in this field, while bringing together a collection of studies of how tourism crisis events have been managed. This chapter now discusses the varied, complex and changing managerial responses needed to deal with a typical crisis, then presents a brief review of current crisis management theory, applying its most salient points to the tourism industry. The chapter concludes with an overview of the structure and contents of the book.

Profile of Management Tasks Following a Tourism Crisis

This book deals with real crisis situations and the efforts of managers (and others) to overcome the resultant difficulties, or to set up systems in anticipation of future problems. Each crisis, and each of the organizations and individuals affected, has individual characteristics, and therefore it is unrealistic to search for a simple crisis management solution. However, there appear to be some common features of crises situations and, to illustrate this, the editors now present a scenario of the evolution of a 'typical' crisis and the range of management skills needed to deal with it.

Imagine a long-established and successful company selling holiday experiences – for this example let us suppose it is a cruise line with a dozen modern ships operating in established cruising locations. A company such as this could be devastated by several possible events such as the unexplained sinking of one of its vessels, a terrorist hijacking, a major engine room problem, the outbreak of food poisoning on board, or the outbreak of war or insurgency in its cruise area. As a simpler example, a departure could be delayed by adverse weather affecting incoming flights carrying many of the passengers (or crew) for its next cruise.

Clearly, these events vary in their seriousness, and the difficulty of overcoming them. What is common to these situations is the need to:

- deal immediately with the crisis itself;
- respond to the concerns and needs of the people directly affected;
- minimize the damage which might result from adverse publicity and consequent loss of custom; and
- resolve difficulties with suppliers and other business partners.

Suddenly, managers are required to develop interim and longer term solutions to the crisis, but often the extent and complexity of the problem (and its underlying causes) are not immediately apparent. To take a minor example of this, an engine room problem might seem to be relatively easy and quick to remedy by replacing a component, but it may take some time to source the right part, and dismantling to enable it to be fitted might reveal other failures in the engine system, further delaying completion of the repair. If the ship is at sea when the problem arises, the difficulty of resolving them is exacerbated.

Not only do managers have to solve the mechanical problems, but they have to respond to and placate passengers who tend to become increasingly upset by extended delays and what appear to them to be erroneous or misleading explanations of how long it will take to fix the problem (see Laws, 2004 for analysis of these twin managerial responsibilities). If the cruise has to be cancelled, or curtailed or to divert, then passengers have to be provided with alternative travel facilities to return them home or to accommodate them in the meantime. Large numbers of them are likely to become increasingly troublesome as they ask for information, or seek alternatives to what the company offers, and many will also demand compensation. Most will also feel the need to contact relatives and friends to reassure them or to arrange for different times or places to be met on their return, and although the ubiquitous ownership of internationally capable mobile phones has somewhat eased the pressure on the organization in this respect, it is still good practice for the company to provide every client with at least one complimentary phone call in such circumstances, but this imposes further demands not only on the available telephone services but also on the staff. Until relatively recently, few companies provided much training for staff in the interpersonal skills needed to deal with these situations, nor did their operational procedures state clearly who should take immediate responsibility, nor specify the discretion and limits set on their use of company resources to the benefit of their clients.

A crisis is therefore likely to change suddenly and expand the range of matters for which a manager is responsible. Often, the normal patterns of communications, expertise and leadership within an organization are severely disrupted in the immediate aftermath of a crisis. Furthermore, the crisis may involve other organizations or government agencies, each having its own ways of operating and its own set of priorities. This increased complexity of the managerial environment puts managers (and staff) under great strain, and it should be realized that this may occur in the context of their own private concerns, as they themselves (or their families) are often amongst the victims of the crisis.

As a crisis unfolds locally, apart from demanding attention from head office staff, it may also trigger the need for them to take proactive steps to deal with clients booked for departures in the immediate future. Some clients may agree to postpone their departure, others may accept alternative dates or destinations, while others may prefer to cancel and accept (or demand) a refund. All are likely to require lengthy discussions with the organization's staff and will probably expect, or may demand, compensation. For those who accept an alternative holiday, the organization is also faced with the additional work of rebooking them or of scheduling new cruises. Even those with departures in the medium future may phone, or ask their travel agents to do so, to obtain information and reassurance about their holiday. Taken together, then, there is a sharp increase in the workload in order to deal with future clients.

In the more serious circumstances where death or serious injury occurs, another set of problems arises. In the first place, the need is for effective rescue and medical resources; fortunately, ship and aircrews are generally well trained for these eventualities. Increasingly, hotel and destination staff are better able to cope and local emergency services better able to liaise, and coordinate the necessary tasks. At the same time, the uninjured have to be shepherded to safety and looked after in terms of their physical and psychological needs. Often, it is a matter of judgement as to what are the appropriate steps to take to ensure the safety of survivors, and in severe weather or other difficult conditions it may not be clear what to do for the best; consequently, further injury or death may occur before the crisis is resolved. As has been found in recent disasters, even where bodies can be retrieved, there are often great difficulties in identifying the dead, storing their bodies, or being certain as to the number of survivors, and the number of injured or missing tourists (and staff). These roles are mainly the responsibility of governmental or international emergency agencies, but it may take a considerable time for them to deploy their specialists and the necessary equipment, so in reality local staff are often immediately involved in these grim tasks. They and head office staff are also likely to be involved in the harrowing business of contacting relatives or at least of responding to their enquiries as news of the crisis is broadcast.

This latter point introduces another layer of responses; those needed to deal with the media. In the very early stages of a crisis, it is often not at all clear what the scale is, what the likely duration will be of solving the crisis, and exactly who has been affected. There may be reporters on the ground, or passengers may phone or e-mail media contacts, sometimes providing verbal or video clips which are inserted into live news broadcasts which may be repeated many times on the 24 h rolling news services. In these ways, misinformation may spread. When asked for comment, the head office is often unable to provide accurate information in the initial period after a crisis, and may be tempted to give anodyne statements which have the effect of further worrying relatives or those soon to depart on similar holidays. In fact, the media may have broadcast more up to date information than the organization has access to because they have a global network of correspondents while their editorial staff are skilled at piecing together, and presenting in dramatic form, the story of complex events as they occur. (Of course, it has to be recognized that media reports are often factually inaccurate and tend anyway to emphasize the more dramatic aspects of a crisis.)

In the longer term, the organization, in managing the aftermath of a crisis when the immediate and short-term problems have been dealt with, will turn to the media with a combination of advertising and public relations to communicate to their client base that the crisis has been resolved. Public relations and marketing campaigns are also deployed to stimulate demand in order to fill some of the business lost through cancellation (or non-booking by concerned holidaymakers who chose to buy from alternative suppliers, or not to take a holiday at all).

There is one further important set of problems to add to the list of tasks outlined above. During and after the crises, the organization also has to manage its ongoing relations with others in its network of partner organizations. The role of retail agents in liaising between clients and the cruise company has been alluded to above – the point to note here is that this role imposes considerable demands on retail staff in terms of their time and their skills in dealing with worried (or annoyed) clients. Other partners include suppliers, for example of bunkering (fuel) and food, the harbours where the ship normally docks, and the coaching and other businesses that supply local excursions for cruise guests. Many of these services will have to be cancelled at very short notice; but, apart from the contractual obligations between partners, there are more fundamental issues of trust and reciprocity. It is often the case that some of the support organizations will make considerable efforts beyond their contractual responsibilities to assist in dealing with the problems that result from a crisis. Indeed, competitors often rally round, providing extra staff, accommodation or other resources to support a fellow member of the tourism industry.

In summary then, a crisis precipitates a complex and changing situation where the normal rules of action for the organization are suspended and other tasks take priority. These other tasks lack the normal clarity of organizational procedures, and at first many appear to be equally urgent, although there may be no consensus about what to do, how to do it and who should be undertaking the work. Crises are chaotic, dynamic and dangerous, and this book provides detailed studies of recent situations to assist in the better understanding of how to manage future tourism crises of whatever nature they may be. This chapter now outlines the current theoretical understanding of crisis management in tourism.

Overview of Crisis Management[1]

A crisis is synonymous with an event which disrupts the pre-existing state of affairs. It is a serious event that can have many causes including natural, political, financial or technical. Whatever the cause, there is a widely held expectation that after appropriate steps have been taken, the situation will return to normality, with the various people and organizations resuming their previous ways of working together. However, increasingly, it is recognized that after a serious crisis, a new set of business relationships and ways of doing things becomes established as the new normality.

Santana (2003) has noted that the word crisis is derived from the Greek 'Krisis' meaning decision or turning point, and observes that the word is widely misused when applied to minor problems. In this book, the term 'crisis' is broadly understood as a shock for the tourism industry, an event of serious magnitude that disrupts its orderly operation and requires immediate but largely unplanned managerial efforts to overcome the resultant problems. One of the key messages of this book is the need for pre-planning to deal with crisis situations.

Crises occur on a scale spectrum that ranges from local through to global. At the local level, the crisis may be triggered by as simple an event as a resort being damaged by fire, resulting in tourists immediately staying away and instead visiting alternative locations. The consequences for operators (and staff and suppliers) in the damaged resort may be serious, but on a national or international scale there is virtually no impact in this case. However, other crises can have a significant impact on the national tourism industry. The 2002 Bali nightclub bombing that killed 202 persons had a significant impact on inbound tourism to Bali; this was exacerbated by another attack in mid-2005, and by late 2005 the destination had not recovered to the level of inbound visitors prior to the bombing.

The earthquake and resultant tsumanis around the Indian Ocean littorals occurred on 26 December 2004 and significantly reduced tourism flows into beach resorts in Sri Lanka, India, Thailand and elsewhere, but the impact on local populations is far more serious than the consequences of this type of disaster for tourists: management responses to deal with tourism issues need to be evaluated in the light of broader crisis responses. For example, within a few hours of the tsunami, the UK media announced that charter flights to some of the destinations affected were going to operate as planned, but they would not be flying new tourists into the damaged areas, instead they were being used to evacuate tourists caught up in the disaster. A few days later, the media reported that emergency supplies were being freighted in on the empty planes.

Globally, some types of crisis can also have significant impacts on tourism flows. The 2003 SARS outbreak in Asia resulted in major disruption of visitor flows within, into and out of parts of Asia. Cooper (2005) observed that the Japanese simply stopped travelling overseas. McKercher and Pine (2005) argued that the result is privation for those unable to travel due to restrictions, and the the magnitude of the rebound effect in the post-crisis period is in direct proportion to the extent of privation felt by affected individuals. It is pertinent to observe that SARS killed only 774 persons in 2003 (http://www.who.int/csr/sars/country/table 2004_04_21/en/), but efforts to manage it by restricting travel had an enormous and immediate economic impact.

The comparison of fatalities and the impact of the disease on the tourism industry highlighted by SARS illustrate another significant but little understood relationship involving perceptions of risk (Prideaux and Master, 2001; Prideaux *et al.*, 2004). The media has a significant positive role to play is alerting the population to crisis situations, but, conversely, the visual and often graphic nature of contemporary reporting on many occasions exaggerates the scale of the crisis and its impact. In this sense, adverse media reporting may have a greater impact on tourism than the crisis (Cooper, 2005).

Prideaux *et al.* (2003) recommended a synthesis between risk specification, identification and management, and forecasting. In such a synthesis, forecasting could be based on revised variables determined by risk analysis or forward-looking scenarios as an alternative to current forecasting techniques. In a discussion on quantitative risk analysis, Haimes *et al.* (2002, p. 383) observed that 'It is clear that the first and most important step in a quantitative risk analysis (QRA) is identifying the set of risk scenarios. If the number of risk scenarios is large, then the second step must be to filter and rank the scenarios according their importance.' Prideaux *et al.* (2003, p. 510) noted that 'Ranking of risk, where the level of probability of occurrence and the degree of impact can be established, provides data that can then be used as a basis for forecasting'. The possible range of scenarios is large, resulting in the need to rank them by the probability of their occurrence on a scale that must start with highly probable through to improbable. Scenario ranking techniques must also include the flexibility to adjust the scale of probability. Prior to the 9/11 terrorist attack on the USA, an incident of this nature could be described as a highly improbable risk, but afterwards the level of risk of further attacks was moved to highly probable, and the US authorities introduced a range of measures to combat future terrorism. Many of these, including greatly increased screening of incoming (and departing) passengers and new technology embedded into passports, are affecting the way that tourism operates, not just to and within the USA, but around the globe.

The preceding discussion, and many of the chapters in this book as well as other published research into tourism crises, concentrates on single crisis events. However, there are cases where several crises afflict an area in quick succession, and often in these very complex situations the effects spread to neighbouring areas, thus amplifying and complicating the management of the crisis. For example, within less than a decade, Indonesia has been subjected to a series of unrelated major problems including the smoke effects of unauthorized forest clearing, the Asian financial meltdown, various insurgencies and religious violence, terrorist attacks targeted at tourist facilities, and the tsunami of 26 December 2004.

The chapters in this volume reinforce the points that a wide range of events can trigger crisis situations, and that many of them are not caused by the tourism industry, nor can the industry directly affect their course of development. The foot and mouth outbreak to which the UK government responded by drastic measures, exemplifies the effects on tourism of an event which was completely beyond its reach and that directly affected a different sector – agriculture. This case also demonstrates the limitations and adverse consequences of government policy based on the needs of a single sector of the economy (farming) and thereby underlines the need for a more systemic understanding of crisis management. Conversely, in areas of potential risk, such as Alpine regions, tourists feel safer when preventive crisis management tools are in place and made obvious by the authorities (Peters and Pikkemaat, 2005).

Although the actual timing, location and severity of earthquakes, hurricanes or avalanches cannot be accurately predicted with current technology, it is certainly possible to learn from past crises, to pre-plan emergency procedures, and to mitigate the severity of such events by adopting appropriate building codes, providing alternative escape routes and information about them, and related measures. Similarly, some sectors of the industry, particularly air transportation, are relatively prone to problems caused by, for example, strikes or bad weather, or serious accidents resulting from technical failures or errors by their crew or ground controllers. While technical expertise can improve crisis avoidance or minimize the disruption resulting from a component failure, good management is also needed to deal both with the needs of those caught up in the situation and with adverse publicity which might result.

Good crisis management is partly about the ability of organizations to learn from experience (that of others as well as their own) and partly about the ability and willingness of a lead organization to undertake the roles of researching and then disseminating the information which is required for effective pre-planning. For example, the Alaskan government has produced a manual for officials who might have to deal with crisis causing injury (http://www.chems.alaska.gov/EMS/Assets/Downloads/mciworkbook.pdf).

Another publication *Crisis: It Won't Happen to Us* (Pacific Asia Travel Association, 2003) is a good example of collecting and disseminating best practice for member organizations. The rapid responses by PATA through its member website and public announcement during the first week of the tsunami was also a very helpful source of professional information and advice to travel industry experts around the world, and is discussed in the Preface to this book.

Overview of Crisis Management Theory[1]

Faulkner (2001) synthesized crisis situations based on research by Fink (1986, p. 20), Keown-McMullan (1997, p. 9) and Weiner and Kahn (1972, p. 21), and identified the following key factors:

- A triggering event, which is so significant that it challenges the existing structure, routine operations or survival of the organization.
- The situation becomes characterized by 'fluid, unstable, dynamic' situations (Fink, 1986, p. 20).
- The managerial environment is high threat, short decision time and an element of surprise and urgency.
- There is a perception of an inability to cope among those directly affected.
- A turning point, when decisive change, which may have both positive and negative connotations, is imminent.

Complexity or chaos theory (Faulkner, 2001) provides an insightful paradigm for the investigation of rapidly changing complex situations where multiple influences impact on non-equilibrium systems. In these conditions of uncertainty, there is a need to incorporate contingencies for the unexpected into policy. Chaos theory demonstrates that there are elements of system behaviour that are intrinsically unstable and not amenable to formal forecasting. If this is the case, a new approach to forecasting is required. Possible ways forward may include political audits and risk analysis to develop a sense of the possible patterns of events allowing these to be factored into projections of future tourism activity using a series of scenarios. The latter may involve the use of a scenario-building approach incorporating elements of van der Heijden's (1997) strategic conversion model, elements of the learning organization approach based on a structured participatory dialogue (Senge, 1990) or elements of risk management described by Haimes *et al.* (2002). Whichever direction is taken, there are a number of factors that must be identified and factored into considerations of the possible course of events in the future. A typical large-scale disruption precipitates complex movements away from the previous relationships which usually tend towards stability and equilibrium. Keown-McMullan (1997, p. 9) noted that organizations will undergo significant change even when they are successful in managing a crisis situation. The previous discussion highlights the inadequacy of traditional Newtonian (linear) thinking with its presumption of stability.

In observing that our environment appears to have become increasingly 'turbulent and crisis prone', Richardson (1994) has suggested this might be so not only because we have become a more complex and crowded world, but also because we now have more powerful technology that has a real capacity to generate disasters, which complicates the process of isolating cause and effect relationships. For this reason, the boundaries between natural disasters and those induced by human action (which comprise two of the three main parts of this book) are becoming increasingly blurred, and this needs to be taken into account in any analysis of such phenomena (Capra, 1996; Keown-McMullan, 1997). However, as well as negative outcomes, crises and disasters also have potentially positive results such as stimulus to innovation, or the recognition of new markets.

Richardson's (1994) analysis of crisis management in organizations provides another perspective on community adjustment capabilities by distinguishing between 'single' and 'double loop' learning approaches. In the former, the response to disasters involves a linear reorientation 'more' or less in keeping with traditional objectives and traditional responses (Richardson, 1994, p. 5). Alternatively, the double loop learning approach challenges traditional beliefs about what society and management is and should do. This approach recognizes that management systems can themselves engender the ingredients of chaos and catastrophe, and that managers must also be more aware and pro-actively concerned about organizations as the creators of crises.

In an organization or tourism destination, potential crises or disasters may be avoided or, at least, their worst effects minimized by active crisis management. On the one hand, anticipative crisis management may identify trigger variables, e.g. by simulating potential crises, by using scenario techniques or by using early warning systems. On the other hand, crisis prevention management must be initiated in case anticipative crisis management does not prevent the upcoming operational crisis (Reinecke, 1997). In the second phase, typical crisis symptoms can already be recognized. Thus, it is of prime urgency to assess the crisis early enough and to adopt existing crisis plans within the enterprise or destination. Later, in the operational crisis management stage, the goal is to manage the ongoing crisis and to limit damage (Dreyer, 2001).

In the field of tourism research, only relatively few studies have applied established crisis models (Dreyer, 2001; Glaeßer, 2001). One of the most extensive disaster management frameworks in tourism was developed by Faulkner (2001, p. 44) who provides a six-phase process:

1. Pre-event phase: disaster contingency plans, scenarios or probability assessments play a major role in the disaster management strategy.
2. Prodromol phase: the disaster is imminent, and warning systems and command centres are established. In this second phase, contingency plan actions are initiated.
3. Emergency phase: disaster effects are felt and actions are necessary to protect people or property in the tourism destination.
4. Intermediate phase: short-term and immediate needs of people have to be addressed by emergency and rescue teams. A clear media communication strategy is crucial in this phase.
5. Long-term (recovery) phase: the damaged infrastructure has to be rebuilt, and environmentally damaged areas have to be reconstructed.
6. Resolution phase: this phase corresponds to Fink's (1986) resolution stage where routine is restored or a new, improved state occurs.

However, the development of effective crisis management tools and future crisis management research require international knowledge exchange platforms as well as systematic and complete documentations about crisis management processes to benchmark or learn from comparable examples in tourism destinations.

Given the complex, interdependent structure of the international tourism industry, it is not surprising that many different crises can impact its operations. This book presents analytical accounts of crises which have afflicted tourism in many parts of the globe, and of many different types including terrorism, epidemics and natural disasters. Overall, it is clear that no tourism sector or location should be complacent; instead, all should plan for the eventuality that a crisis could affect them suddenly and dramatically.

Structure of the Book

One of the challenges for editors of books such as this is how best to organize contents which deal with a wide range of situations and offer a variety of analytical and theoretical approaches. We have elected to present our readers with a simple organizing schema as readers' interests will inevitably differ. After this introductory chapter, Part I contains ten chapters in which the theoretical foundations of crisis management are a primary concern of the contributing authors. These chapters range quite widely both in geographic coverage and in the types of crisis which they analyse.

Part II consists of five chapters which we have somewhat arbitrarily described as Tourism Crises Arising from Natural Causes. Similarly, the seven chapters in Part III are collected under the heading Tourism Crises Resulting from Human Actions. We wish to emphasize that the 12 chapters in Parts II and III are not only highly informed descriptions of recent management responses to natural and human crises, they also contribute to the evolving understanding of crisis management research.

Part IV of this book has two chapters. Chapter 25 is a reprint of a paper by Prideaux, Faulkner and Laws originally published in *Tourism Management*. It is included here for two reasons. It provides a complexity theory-based analysis of how a tourist area can be affected by a series of disasters. We also include it as a tribute to Bill Faulkner, who, sadly, died before it was published.

The concluding chapter of this book presents a preliminary discussion of lessons to be drawn from the New Orleans hurricane, synthesizes crisis management theory, and highlights areas which the editors regard as critical for further research effort.

The editors hope that this volume will contribute to the more effective management of future crises, through enhancing understanding of recent events and by providing a benchmark collection of current tourism research on which new theories, research methods and policy may be built.

Note

[1] The theoretical discussion in this chapter draws on Laws and Prideaux (2005).

References

Capra, F. (1996) *The Web of Life*. Harpers Collins Publishers, London.

Cooper, M.J.M. (2005) Japanese tourism and the SARS epidemic of 2003. *Journal of Travel and Tourism Marketing* 19 (2/3), 117–133.

Dreyer, A. (2001) *Krisenmanagement im Tourismus*. Oldenbourg, Munich.

Faulkner, B. (2001) Towards a framework for disaster management. *Tourism Management* 22, 135–147.

Fink, S. (1986) *Crisis Management*. American Association of Management, New York.

Glaeßer, D. (2003) *Crisis Management in the Tourism Industry*. Butterworth-Heinemann, Oxford.

Haimes, Y., Kaplan, S. and Lambert, J.H. (2002) Risk filtering, ranking, and management framework using hierarchical holographic modelling. *Risk Analysis* 22, 383–397.

Keown-McMullan, C. (1997) Crisis: when does a molehill become a mountain? *Disaster Prevention and Management* 6, 4–10.

Laws, E. (2004) *Improving Tourism and Hospitality Services*. CAB International, Wallingford, UK.

Laws, E. and Prideaux, B. (2005) Crisis management: a suggested typology. *Journal of Travel and Tourism Marketing* 19 (2/3), 1–8.

McKercher, B. and Pine, R. (2005) Privation as a stimulus to travel demand? *Journal of Travel and Tourism Marketing* 19 (2/3), 107–116.

Pacific Asia Travel Association (2003) *Crisis: It Won't Happen to Us*. Pacific Asia Travel Association, Bangkok.

Peters, M. and Pikkemaat, B. (2005) Crisis management in Alpine winter sports resorts – the 1999 avalanche disaster in Tyrol. *Journal of Travel and Tourism Marketing* 19 (2/3), 9–20.

Prideaux, B. and Master, H. (2001) Health and safety issues effecting international tourists in Australia. *Asia Pacific Journal of Tourism* 6 (2), 24–32.

Prideaux, B., Laws, E. and Faulkner, B. (2003) Events in Indonesia: exploring the limits to formal tourism trends forecasting methods in complex crisis situations. *Tourism Management* 24, 475–487.

Prideaux, B., Agrusa, J., Donlon, J. and Curran, C. (2004) Exotic or erotic – contrasting images for defining destinations. *Asia Pacific Journal of Tourism Research* 9 (1), 5–18.

Reinecke, W. (1997) *Krisenmanagement: Richtiger Umgang mit den Medien in Krisensituationen- Ursachen- Verhalten- Strategien- Techniken- Ein Leitfaden*. Stamm, Essen.

Richardson, B. (1994) Crisis management and the management strategy: time to 'loop the loop'. *Disaster Prevention and Management* 3 (3), 59–80.

Santana, G. (2003) Crisis management and tourism: beyond the rhetoric. *Journal of Travel and Tourism Marketing* 15, 299–321.

Senge, P.M. (1990) *The Fifth Principle: the Art and Practice of the Learning Organisation*. Doubleday, New York.

van der Heijden, K. (1997) *Scenarios: the Art of Strategic Conversion*. Wiley, Chichester, UK.

Weiner, A.J. and Kahn, H. (1972) Crisis and arms control. In: Hermann, C.F. (ed.) *International Crises: Insights from Behaviour Research*. The Free Press, New York, p. 21.

2 Post-crisis Forecasting: Better Make Haste Slowly

MIRIAM SCAGLIONE

Introduction

One of the effects of any crisis in tourism is the downturn in the tourism economy indicators, i.e. the number of overnights, the numbers of arrivals, and visitors' expenditure. The basic question after an unpredicted crisis is: 'How bad will the effects be, and how long will they last?' The first part of the question addresses the changes in the rate of growth (acceleration or deceleration) of the relevant variables named above, whereas the second refers to the concerns about how long it will take for indicators to return to the level prevailing before the crisis, if at all.

While research into strategies to prevent possible crises developing is very important, these are beyond the scope of this study. The emphasis here is study of the possible evolution *over time* of the negative effects once the event has happened. Glaesser (2003) classes the phases of a crisis in two major categories: prevention and coping with the crisis. The phase of prevention has the role of anticipating and compensating the negative effects by the preparation of measures which will be applied after the event has happened. The second phase, coping, is also defeatist, in that the crisis could have been foreseen, but it was not the case. The coping phase begins with the identification of the situation, and its main goal, other than to study the causes which brought it about, is to take all the measures necessary to bring the crisis to an end.

After a crisis, it is not only the time needed to take decisions which becomes critical but also the deficit or perhaps the excess of information. In most cases, the high level of complexity makes the decision-making process and post-crisis planning very difficult (Glaesser, 2003). Making predictions about the negative effects of a crisis in such a situation is therefore very difficult, especially as it must be done quickly.

The forecaster can choose between three different, but not mutually exclusive, approaches or strategies. This chapter discusses three of the most commonly used: (i) forecasting by analogies; (ii) forecasting by building scenarios using econometric models; and (iii) forecasting by using intervention variables in univariate times series analysis.

The structure of the discussion is as follows. The first part presents the main elements of the three strategies and explains the first one. The second part explains the statistical methodology for time series analysis and intervention variables. The third part gives an example of the third strategy through an analysis of the local and commercial passenger movements for Geneva International Airport and for Zürich Airport after the events of 11 September 2001 (9/11), and the bankruptcy of the national carrier Swissair on 2 October 2001. Finally, the chapter draws a conclusion from the comparison of the three strategies.

The Forecaster's 'Toolbox'

The three strategies use different types of forecasting methods; nevertheless, some of these are present in more than one. Figure 2.1 shows an overview (adapted from Armstrong, 2001b) of the methods relevant to the present discussion.

There are two main categories of forecasting: judgemental methods and statistical methods. Judgemental forecasting is defined as '[a] subjective integration of information to produce a forecast. Such methods can vary from unstructured to highly structured' (Armstrong, 2001a). Statistical methods rely on the theories of that field (i.e. econometric theory, time series analysis). Judgemental and statistical models are nevertheless connected, in that the subjective integration of the information can feed the statistical methods, hence Armstrong's observation (2001b) that judgemental methods pervade all aspects of

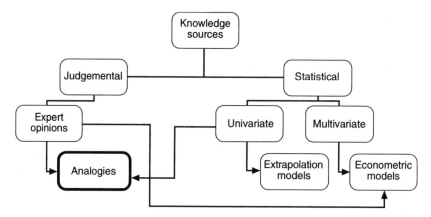

Fig. 2.1. Relationship between forecasting methods relevant for the discussion. Adapted from Armstrong (2001b, p. 9).

forecasting. The method known as 'expert opinions' refers to the knowledge that recruited experts have of the phenomena under study, in this case the tourism industry. Nevertheless, the opinions of experts can sometimes be biased. Certain techniques are available to obtain judgements which are as reliable as possible.

Harvey (2001) and MacGregor (2001) give the main principles for increasing the reliability of opinions given by experts. They recommend decomposing the problem into components which are forecast individually and then combined. Such a decomposition not only allows for an improvement in the accuracy of the forecast by using different methods but also makes it possible to evaluate alternative sources of information for each component. Other important features are feedback from the forecast and the cross-validation of the management solution. The feedback is very useful when every expert making a judgemental forecast need to assess her or his performance and refine the task.

Overconfidence in making a judgemental forecast is another important issue which must be eliminated. Arkes (2001) proposes using cross-validation techniques which involve the consideration of alternatives in the proposed plan, especially when the situation is a new one. Cross-validation of the forecast can make it possible to reduce overconfidence in the author of the forecasting. This may be achieved by using a forecaster external to the team responsible for developing and implementing the plan to estimate its probability of success.

The Delphi method (Parenté and Anderson-Parenté, 1987) is a very extended and highly structured tool for collecting expert opinion. One of its main advantages is that the expert remains anonymous and can, if he wishes, justify his opinion and so influence the other experts in order to reach a consensus. Another advantage of Delphi is that the team of experts does not need to be in the same room, since they can use online questionnaires, as in Armstrong (2003).

Experts usually give their opinion through reasoning by analogy. Analogies are the extrapolation of possible outcomes based on similar situations which occurred before the one under consideration. The underlying idea is that the previous situations have recurring patterns which the expert can grasp. According to Stekler (2003), there are basically two different situations. First, those when the events forecast are more or less predictable because there are enough examples in the past to build generalizations, i.e. a possible turning point in a business cycle, whether a recession or an expansion. McNees (1992) illustrates very clearly how economists analyse past recessions in order to identify analogies in the leading variables which can be useful in predicting the turning point.

Secondly, there are the outcomes of very unpredictable events such as terrorist attacks. In the opinion of the author, the degree of similarity between the most unpredictable events is still an open question. As this kind of event is, fortunately, very infrequent and takes place in different parts of the world, how could one have enough elements to generalize as to where analogies lie?

The right part of the tree in Fig. 2.1 contains a number of quantitative statistical methods. The univariate methods stand for the analysis of one time series, i.e. overnights in a destination or the number of passengers in an airport. They only use the prior values of the time series to make a forecast because it is assumed that all the information necessary is contained in the historical data. They are also called pure extrapolation models. The other kind of extrapolation model is the cross-sectional extrapolation, which assumes that the evidence of one set of data can be generalized to another set, i.e. that the dynamic of the total number of passengers in an airport should be similar to the number of total movements at the same airport. This is the why univariate models are linked to analogies. Armstrong (2001b, p. 215) observed that univariate models are very appealing because they are 'objective, replicable and inexpensive. This makes it a useful approach when you need short-term forecasts.'

The right leaf of the statistical methods covers *econometric* models, which use models of the same designation. Econometric models use one or more regression equations to capture the relationship between the dependent (indigenous) variables with the explanatory (exogenous) ones; these are *multivariate models*. A very important step in the econometric method is the determination of the set of variables to use on the basis of economic theory and previous work; they 'provide an ideal way to integrate judgmental and statistics sources' (Armstrong, 2001b). This kind of model also allows for an answer to questions of the 'what-if …?' type by the use of *ex-post* or *conditional* forecasting (Allen and Fildes, 2001). Conditional forecasting consists of assumptions about the values of the explanatory variables over a forecast horizon, so allowing prediction of the future outcomes of the indigenous variable(s). In this way, the forecaster can establish several scenarios, depending on the assumptions about the explanatory variables.

Predicting Effects of Unusual Events

The first and more straightforward strategy consists of reasoning by *analogies*. The report: *Impact of Terrorism on World Tourism. Likely Scenarios and Future Strategies* (Poon and Adams, 2001) is a very good example of this approach. It appeared in November 2001, approximately a month and a half after 9/11. The report presented an analysis of certain past, similar events such as the Gulf War (Iraqi invasion of Kuwait on 2 August 1990) and mostly based the future scenarios on analogies in the behaviour of different tourist market segments. When policymakers need a very quick and reliable answer, this is often the only possible way. As Armstrong (2001a, p. 57) observes: 'In many situation, the first step is to ask experts. Sometimes this is enough, as experts may make excellent forecasts.'

The second strategy is to *build different scenarios*. This approach consists of the analysis of external or exogenous factors that could have influence on the studied events; eventually this can lead to building an econometric model in order to give quantitative outputs to the different scenarios proposed. In order to carry out this task, and depending on the resources available for the study, one or several groups of experts are requested to give their opinion not only on the selection of the relevant factors (the exogenous variables), but also on the weight and the future evolution of each of them.

One example of this method is a report entitled: 'What if there is a war in Iraq? The potential impact on domestic and select international travel markets to Canada' (Canadian Tourism Research Institute, 2003). While this work addresses the prevention phase of the crisis, it illustrates this strategy quite clearly. The authors had identified five exogenous factors with different degrees of relationship to domestic and international travel: the price of oil; equity markets; military spending; terrorist reprisals; and the confidence level of consumers. They also noted another relevant factor to be taken into account, i.e. whether the economy is going to contract or to expand. In this case, two main scenarios are predicted: a war that is contained and a disruptive war. Both scenarios assume the victory of the USA and its allies, but the contained one supposes that no significant complications will develop; the disruptive scenario, on the other hand, assumes that complications would prolong the uncertainty in the region. The report chose these two scenarios on the basis of the psychological impacts observed after the Gulf War of 1990–1991 and the events of 9/11 (Canadian Tourism Research Institute, 2003). The study goes on to present various econometric models for both scenarios (contained or disruptive war), and gives forecasts of overnights series, by country origin, for each one at a 4-year horizon. This strategy is naturally much more expensive than one based only on analogies, but the advantage is that the outcomes are quantitative as they use econometric models.

The third strategy, based on the interventions analysis of the relevant time series for tourism, requires waiting a few observations ahead before making any prediction. Times series analysis is a formal model, but '[f]ormal models are designed to predict average relationships and not events that lie outside the range of normal experiences' (Stekler, 2003, p. 161) as is the case with unpredictable events. In order to illustrate this fact, Fig. 2.2 shows the monthly number of local passengers at Zürich Airport from January 1999 to May 2003, and the predictions based on a univariate model without any adjustment immediately after September 2001. It is clear from Figs 2.2 and 2.3 that without any adjustment, the result is misleading as the forecast greatly overestimated the observed number of passengers after September 2001.

Coping with such unpredictable events therefore requires some adjustment tools in the formal model. With this in view, Young and Ord (2002) and Ord and Young (2004) apply interventions analysis to univariate transportation time series data modelling. The aim of the following section is to present the framework for the univariate series analysis using the structural times series (STS) model (Harvey, 1990). It first presents the

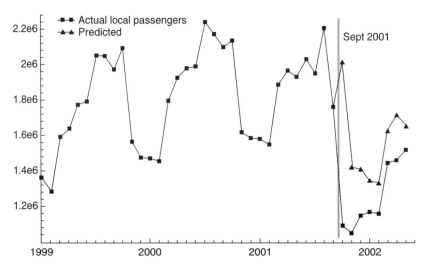

Fig. 2.2. Number of local passengers (monthly) at Zurich Airport, actual and predicted, from September 2001.

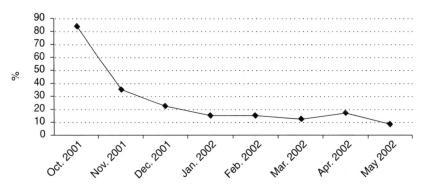

Fig. 2.3. Percentage of overestimation in the monthly prediction from October 2001 to May 2002 for the number of local passengers.

theory and then the implementation of intervention variables as tools to make the adjustment explained above.

There are other statistical methods, i.e. ARIMA (Box *et al.*, 1994), which could be used, but there are basically two reasons why the STS model is preferable. First, STS methods do not need either testing for unit root test or processing of the data in order to achieve stationarity, as is the case in ARIMA modelling. Secondly, STS models decompose time series into unobservable components in such a way that policymakers have a very complete picture of the phenomena at a glance, and in terms which are easily understandable even for the statistical lay-person (Scaglione, 2003).

Structural Time Series

The aim of the STS model is to capture the salient characteristic of stochastic phenomena, usually in the form of trends, seasonal or other irregular components, explanatory variables and intervention variables. This can reveal components of a series, which would otherwise be unobserved, greatly contributing to comprehension of the phenomena. In order to adjust STS models, the software STAMP (Koopman *et al.*, 2000) was used.

An STS multivariate model such as the following

Observed variables = trend + seasonal + explanatory variables +autoreg.
component or cycle + intervention + irregular

may be written respecting the preceding order as:

$$\mathbf{y}_t = \boldsymbol{\mu}_t + \boldsymbol{\gamma}_t + \sum_{\tau=0}^{s} \delta_\tau \mathbf{x}_{t-\tau} + \boldsymbol{\psi}_t + \boldsymbol{\Lambda} \mathbf{I}_t + \boldsymbol{\varepsilon}_t \quad \boldsymbol{\varepsilon}_t \sim NID(0, \Sigma_\varepsilon^2) \quad t = 1, \cdots, \mathrm{T}, \ (1)$$

where $\boldsymbol{\mu}_t$ is the stochastic trend composed of two elements, namely the *level* and the *slope*. It has the following form:

$$\mathbf{I}_{t_{slp}} = \begin{cases} 0 & \text{if } t < t_{Slp} \\ t - t_{slp} & \text{if } t \geq t_{Slp} \end{cases} \quad t = 1, \cdots, T$$

where x_t is a $K \times 1$ vector of explanatory variables and $\mathbf{I}_t$ is a $K^* \times 1$ vector of interventions. Elements in the parameter matrices, δ and Λ may be specified to be zero, thereby excluding certain variables from particular equations. See Appendix I for a definition of cycles and seasonal components.

The trend is intended to capture the long-trend movements in the series. The stochastic trend described below allows the model to handle trends other than linear ones, unlike standard classical regression models (Harvey, 1990).

There is a classification of different kinds of STS forms depending on whether the hyperparameters (variance of each component) are null or not. The most general form is the basic structural model (BSM) whose components, including the level, the slope and the seasonal components, are all stochastic. This is the starting point for the STAMP program which tests in order to eliminate any component not required (herafter 'test down'). The list of possible forms of STS is available in Harvey (1990), Koopman *et al.* (2000) and Ord and Young (2004).

The form required in the examples in the next section are the random walk, plus a drift with a seasonal component. The level is therefore stochastic, the slope is fixed and the irregular component is not required. The seasonal component, depending on the case, could be any of the three possibilities mentioned in Appendix I.

When no exogenous variable is included, the model is referred to as 'no causal'. Causal models are those which include one or more exogenous, namely explanatory, variables. These are used in order to show the influence of one or more exogenous variables on the trend. Finally, the intervention term component is a stochastic process which is intended to represent known events which can modify the pattern of the series. The intervention term can be considered as a special kind of exogenous variable. This variety will be referred to hereafter as exogenous intervention variables.

STAMP has pre-programmed the following exogenous intervention variables; Fig. 2.4. shows a schematic example of each of them:

1. AO: this is a usually large value of the *irregular* disturbance at a particular time. It can be captured by an *impulse* intervention variable which takes the value of the outliers one at the time and zero elsewhere. If t_{ao} is the time of the outlier, then the exogenous intervention variable $\mathbf{I}_{t_{ao}}$ has the following form:

$$\mathbf{I}_{t_{ao}} = \begin{cases} 1 & \text{if } t = t_{ao} \\ 0 & \text{if } t \neq t_{ao} \end{cases} \quad t = 1, \cdots, T$$

2. LS: this kind of intervention handles a *structural break* in which the level of the series shifts up or down. It is modelled by a *step* intervention variable which has a value of zero before the event and of one after it. If t_{LS} is the time of the level shift, then the exogenous intervention variable $\mathbf{I}_{t_{LS}}$ has the following form:

$$\mathbf{I}_{t_{LS}} = \begin{cases} 0 & \text{if } t < t_{LS} \\ 1 & \text{if } t \geq t_{LS} \end{cases} \quad t = 1, \cdots, T$$

3. Slp: a change in the slope of the trend is a transitory shock to the slope equation in the trend at time t_{slp}. Thus Equation 3 must be rewritten as:

$$\beta_t = \beta_{t-1} + I_{t_{slp}}^{Slp} + \varsigma_t$$

where

$$\mathbf{I}_{t_{slp}} = \begin{cases} 0 & \text{if } t < t_{Slp} \\ t - t_{slp} & \text{if } t \geq t_{Slp} \end{cases} \quad t = 1, \cdots, T$$

4. TC: this kind of intervention is used in the presences of transient level change that affects all the values t of the observed series $t \geq t_{TC}$, where t_{TC} is the particular time where affected. However, the effect decays exponentially at a rate δ and an initial impact at t_{TC}. Since $0 < \delta < 1$, the effect eventually disappears. For this reason, this model is referred to as a transient change (TC) model. The exogenous intervention variable $\mathbf{I}_{t_{LTC}}$ has the following form:

$$\mathbf{I}_{t_{TC}} = \begin{cases} 0 & \text{if } t < t_{TC} \\ \delta^{t_{TC}-t} & \text{if } t \geq t_{TC} \end{cases} \quad t = 1, \cdots, T$$

The last feature is not pre-programmed in the STAMP package in the same way as the two former ones, but it is included here as an exogenous variable in the model *by hand*. In each model, several operations were carried out with values for δ from 0.3 to 0.8, and the Student's *t*-statistics were used to identify not only the presence of such TC intervention but also the value of δ.

Ord and Young (2004) pointed out that the choice of 0.7 as a convenient value for δ relies on the well-known text by Chen and Liu (1995) and on the fact that the 'half-life' of TC is about 3 months. The weights of the TC column variable are 1, 0.7 and 0.49, respectively, for the 3 months after the beginning of the intervention effect. A value of 0.8 for δ will have a half-life of 8 months and of 0.9 around 9 months. A δ value greater than 0.9 will be very close to an LS intervention, and less than 0.3 will be represented by one or two period AO.

The following section is an example of the use of the intervention frame in the study of the airports traffic.

The Example of Swiss Airports

The terrorist attacks on the Word Trade Center and the Pentagon in the USA had important effects on the global air transportation industry. In Switzerland, this was compounded by the bankruptcy of the national carrier Swissair on 2 October 2001. In Scaglione and Mungall (2002, 2004, 2005), the authors analysed the combined effects of these two facts by modelling time series indicators (movements and passengers) using STS for Zürich Airport (hereafter ZHR), the Aéroport International de Genève (AIG) and EuroAirport (Basel), Switzerland's three most important airports.

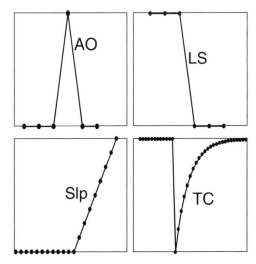

Fig. 2.4. Example of the effects of intervention variables on the trend; the *x*-axis represents time and the *y*-axis the trend of the adjusted time series.

The goal was to forecast the long-term growth of the total number of aircraft and passenger movements over a 4-year period for each of the three airports to verify if and when they would reach 2001 movement levels. Given that the study began in June 2002, and that the data for that year were incomplete, the authors used a two-stage strategy as follows.

First, monthly data variables from January 1999 to May 2002 were used and a univariate model for each variable built, in order to forecast 7 months ahead and to produce the total forecast for 2002. Once the estimate for each variable was obtained, the total number of movements and passengers for each airport for 2002 could be calculated (Scaglione and Mungall, 2002). Table 2.1. shows the forecast and observed values for each airport and for the whole of 2002.

Secondly, three different bivariate models were built, one for each airport, whose variable is the following vector: $\mathbf{y}_t = \begin{pmatrix} m_t \\ p_t \end{pmatrix}$, where m_t denotes the total number of movements for a given airport and p_t denotes the total number of passengers.

Only the results of the second step have been published in Scaglione and Mungall (2002). Two examples of the forecast of the first step are discussed below: the series of local passengers for ZHR airport and of commercial passengers for AIG.

Methodology

The methodology was similar to that suggested by Ord and Young (2004), as follows:

1. Develop a model for the series prior to August 2001, incorporating intervention where necessary, as in July 2001 (level shift, LS). This is probably related to the economic difficulties of Swissair and the foreign carriers in which it was a stakeholder. These carriers were the Belgian airline Sabena and the French airline AOM (Olson, 2001). Hereafter this model will be referred to as the 1LS model.
2. Use the data available as of May 2002, run the same model with LS (July 2001) and TC ($\delta = 0.8$ at October 2001) components, as specified

Table 2.1. Observed and forecast values for 2002 with the percentage of absolute error.

Airport	Total commercial movements			Total local or commercial passengers		
	Forecast 2002	Observed 2002	Error	Forecast 2002	Observed 2002	Error
Zurich	256,388	259,149	1.07	17,590,760	17,902,073	1.74
Geneva	128,421	131,888	2.63	7,676,556	7,581,992	−1.25
Basel	86,570	87,995	1.63	3,069,919	2,997,742	−2.41

Local passengers for ZHR and Basel, and Commercial for Genève.

above, and 'test down' to eliminate insignificant coefficients. Hereafter this model will be referred as the TC model.

3. Use the data available as of May 2002, run a model with only two LS interventions, in July 2001 and October 2001. In Ord and Young (2004), the authors run the model without interventions but in our case that was not possible, owing, on one hand, to a lack of convergence of the STAMP program and, on the other, when convergence was achieved, to the model being unacceptable from the point of view of goodness-of-fit test, particularly the normality test. Hereafter this model will be referred as the 2LS model.

4. Use the data available as of May 2002 to run a model with three LS interventions: July 2001, October 2001 and November 2001. Hereafter this model will be referred as the 3LS model.

5. Use the models developed in steps 2, 3 and 4 (TC, 2LS and 3LS, respectively) to generate successive one-step-ahead forecasts from all observations in order to assess which one of them makes the best prediction for each of the different forecasting origins from October 2001 to April 2002.

The TC intervention has $\delta = 0.8$; therefore, the half-duration of the intervention is 4 months.

In order to show that the series are predicted with an origin value from October 2001 to May 2002, the mean absolute percentage error (MAPE) was used. The MAPE is used in the same way as in Ord and Young (2004) to measure the forecast accuracy of the models: the greater its value, the less accurate are the predictions.

The MAPE is defined as follows:

$$MAPE = \frac{\sum |e_t / y_t|}{n} \tag{4}$$

where e_t is the error at time t; y_t is the observed value at time t, and n is the number of observations predicted. The summations cover the period from the origin of the forecast to the latest observation available, for May 2002.

Discussion

Figure 2.5 shows the values of MAPE (y-axis) for each model against the different forecasting origin (x-axis). When the origin of the forecast is October 2001, the model which performs best, making the best prediction, is the TC model. Tables 2.2, 2.3 and 2.4 show, respectively, the coefficient and the P-value for the Student's t-test for each intervention and the last observation for each model, the hyperparameters, i.e. the standard deviation of the components, and the statistical diagnosis test, all having as their last observation the one referred to in Table 2.2. The description of the diagnosis test is in Appendix II.

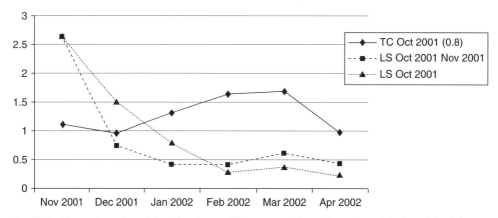

Fig. 2.5. Map values (*y*-axis) of the three different models against the origin (*x*-axis) of the forecast up to May 2002.

Table 2.2. Intervention variables for passengers.

		Level shift		Temporary change		
Airport	Model	Date (coefficient)	t-values	Date (coefficient)	t-values	Last observation
Zurich	1LS	July 2001 (−181,140)	0.016			August 2001
Zurich	TC	July 2001 (243,190)	0.002	November 2001 (593,460)	0.000	December 2001
		October 2001 (−880,000)	0.000			November 2001
Zurich	2LS	July 2001 (−265,400)	0.007			
		October 2001 (−626,580)	0.000			
Zurich	3LS	July 2001(−243,400)	0.002			December 2001
		October 2001 (−892,330)	0.000			
		November 2001 (563,820)	0.000			
Geneva				October 2001 (−241,600)	0.000	May 2003

Table 2.3. Hyperparameter standard deviation and model type classification for passengers.

Airport	Models	Level	Slope	Autoregressive	Irr	Seasonal
Zurich	1LS	35,588	Fixed	No	No	35,523.0
Zurich	TC	22,942	Fixed	No	No	9,341.6
Zurich	2LS	23,126	Fixed	No	No	12,868.0
Zurich	3LS	23,325	Fixed	No	No	8,636.4
Geneva		13,817	Fixed	No	No	2,379.1

Table 2.4. Statistics test diagnostic.

Airport	Passengers	SE	Normality	Heteroskedasticity	DW (T)	Box–Ljung df = 6	R^2
Zurich	1LS	59,480	4.07	3.77 (DF (6,6))	1.75 (32)	4.48	0.35
Zurich	TC	71,932	3.67	4.75 (DF (7,7))	2.28 (36)	9.60	0.77
Zurich	2LS	95,172	4.67	10.51 (DF (7,7))	2.99 (35)	4.61	0.60
Zurich	3LS	32,706	3.90	1.94 (DF (7,7))	1.97 (36)	1.79	0.79
Geneva		24,713	1.57	4.43 (DF (9,9))	2.07 (40)	3.18	0.67

The following paragraph is an attempt to imitate what the interpretation of the model would be once the data for November 2001 and December 2001 became available.

Figure 2.6 shows the plot of the TC model superimposed with the 2LS model. The performance of the TC model is better than that of the LS because the latter cannot prevent the trend from declining, so that it does not recognize the subsequent gradual recovery, almost to the levels of August 2001. Nevertheless, this latest information was not available for the forecaster in November 2001. The latter does know, however, that the Student's t-statistic is very significant for both intervention coefficients in October 2001 and in both models (TC and 2LS). Figure 2.6. and Table 2.2 show the values of both coefficients. On the basis of those results and once the figures for November 2001 became available, the forecaster could conclude that at least a partial recovery, in the 3 next months, could not be ruled out.

When the next observation (December 2001) arrived, a review of the models was carried out with this new origin. The automatic detection model for intervention of STAMP suggested that a new LS intervention, in addition to the LS in October 2001, was necessary at November 2001. This then made it possible to calculate the 3LS model.

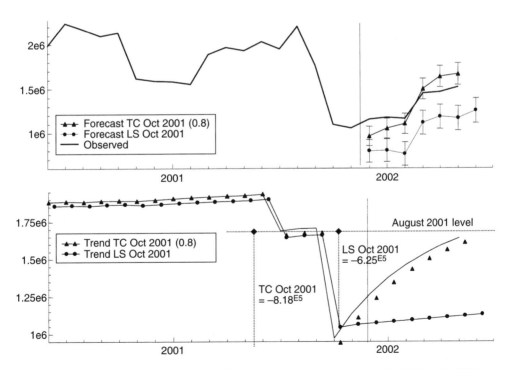

Fig. 2.6. Forecast and observed values for the two models having, beside LS in July 2001, for one TC October 2001 and for the other LS October 2001 with the bands showing 1 SD (subgraph above). Trend of the models (subgraph below). Origin forecast November 2001.

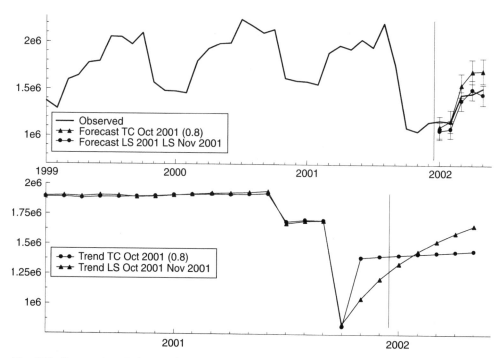

Fig. 2.7. Forecast and observed values for the two models having, beside LS in July 2001, for one TC October 2001 and for the other LS October 2001 with the bands showing 1 SD (subgraph above). Trends of the model (subgraph below). Origin forecast December 2001.

Figure 2.7. shows that the 3LS model has a degree of accuracy similar to the TC model; nevertheless, the 3LS model is slightly better, although at the time the forecast was made this information was not available to the forecaster. The forecaster's decision should be based on Table 2.2 and Fig. 2.7, which shows the plot of both models having December 2001 as the forecast origin. The trend plots (subgraph below) suggest that the recovery will probably be partial, but not gradual, over a period of 1 month. The coefficients for the two LS interventions for the 3LS model are: −8.9E5 in October 2001 and 5.6E5 for November 2001, so the recovery will be partial. In October 2001, the loss was around 890,000 passengers and the recovery in November 2001 would be less than 570,000 passengers.

Finally, Fig. 2.5 shows that as new data values were obtained, the series seemed to be corrected quickly, and hence no improvement in the prediction was shown by the use of intervention variables. Therefore, the intervention analysis was relevant in the few months following the focused event.

Another example is the time series for commercial passengers for AIG. Considerations similar to those in the case of the ZHR passenger analysis also apply here. The forecast is presented in Fig. 2.8, with the trends (with and without intervention) and the actual values for commercial passengers of AIG. In December 2001, the intervention TC with a $\delta = 0.3$ is very significant, as is shown in Table 2.2. Given the value of $\delta = 0.3$, it can therefore be predicted that at that moment the effect will remain for a period of 3 months at the most and that the figures will reach a level similar to that in September 2001, which is the case.

These two examples show, albeit empirically, that the use of intervention variables in the framework of the STS model cannot only handle the adjustments of the trend over two or four periods in the future (i.e. in this case months), but can also answer the question raised at the beginning of this chapter: 'How long will the effect last, and how bad will the figures turn out to be?'

In addition, having to make observations of the future is necessary for this kind of analysis. Other limitations include those outside the forecaster's control and those that relate to the behaviour of the forecaster.

The quality of the data available comes within the first limitation. The forecaster carries out the first prediction and makes revisions as soon as further data become available; for most of the time, therefore, the forecast is made on the strength of provisional data. Stekler (1967) discusses the effects of data revision in forecasting macroeconomic factors, finding that the difference between provisional data and final data can cause errors in the level, the magnitude and the direction of the changes. These are fundamental points when statistical methods are used for coping with a

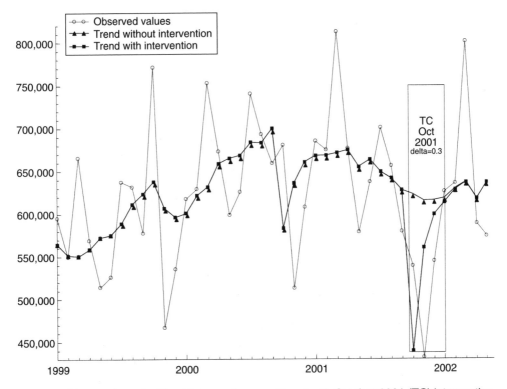

Fig. 2.8. Observed trend without interventions and trend with October 2001 (TC) intervention for commercial passengers of Aéroport International de Genève.

crisis, and the conclusion could change radically if, for example, the direction of the change is wrong.

The second kind of limitation relates to the forecaster's behaviour: the process of interpreting data, forecaster bias and forecaster preferences. 'Forecasters begin with subjective probabilities about the likelihood of an event and revise their prior probabilities as a new information becomes available' (Stekler, 2003, p. 161). Schnader and Stekler (1998) analysed failures in the prediction of economic turning point cycles. They claim that one factor which caused the failure of the prediction of the 1990 recession was the peculiar behaviour of the USA Index of Leading Series (ILS). There is a rule which still stands: a signal of a peak occurs when the ILS declines for three consecutive months; but on that occasion, it did not hold. Consequently, forecasters had particularly low prior probabilities about recession, and whenever this is the case the recession will not be predicted. The authors claim that another source of error was the subjective cost of a wrong prediction. In the opinion of Paul A. Samuelson, this kind of situation has occurred all too often: as he observed in 1996, 'Wall Street indices predicted nine out of the last five recessions!' (Stephenson, 2004). This pressure could be very strong, so that: ' ... even if the data were better and the forecaster did not have extremely low priors they might be reluctant to predict a recession if they felt that the costs of predicting a false turn were very high' (Schnader and Stekler, 1998, p. 520). These observations about macroeconomic forecasting can also be applied to the study of tourism time series. These statistical methods are therefore not exempt from personal bias.

Conclusions

In the preceding sections, it was pointed out that the judgemental methods can prove to be biased because the opinions of experts are equally so. Nevertheless, this fact can also be present in the statistical methods. The advantages of the three strategies outlined are evident. While an analogy reasoning strategy is the quickest method, the validity of analogies based on generalizations of a crisis situation is, in the present writer's view, an open question. The strategy based on building scenarios is the most expensive option; it gives quantitative predictions but takes time to come to fruition.

In comparison, the intervention analysis of tourism time series seems to be not expensive, and if carried out without bias and with good quality provisional data appears to be a very useful tool for short-term forecasting. Its disadvantage is that one has to wait at least 2 months after the crisis in order to be able to grasp the change in the trend. Although policymakers are always very impatient to look into a crystal ball after a crisis, the best advice one can give them is nevertheless to **make haste slowly.**

Acknowledgements

The author gratefully acknowledges the support of colleagues Dr Roland Schegg for his wise comments on the first draft, Mr Merrick Fall for editorial assistance in English, and Mme Sandrine Thalmann for her devoted bibliographical research.

References

Allen, P.G. and Fildes, R. (2001) Econometric forecasting. In: Armstrong, J.S. (ed.) *Principles of Forecasting*. Kluwer Academic Publishers, Boston, Massachusetts, pp. 301–362.

Arkes, H.R. (2001) Overconfidence in judgemental forecast. In: Armstrong, J.S. (ed.) *Principles of Forecasting*. Kluwer Academic Publishers, Boston, Massachusetts, pp. 495–511.

Armstrong, J.S. (2001a) The forecasting dictionary. In: Armstrong, J.S. (ed.) *Principles of Forecasting*. Kluwer Academic Publishers, Boston, Massachusetts, pp. 761–819.

Armstrong, J.S. (ed.) (2001b) *Principles of Forecasting*. Kluwer Academic Publishers, Boston, Massachusetts.

Armstrong, J.S. (2003) Delphi. http://armstrong.wharton.upenn.edu/delphi2/ (accessed 14 March 2004)

Box, G., Jenkins, G.M. and Reinsel, G.C. (1994) *Time Series Analysis. Forecasting and Control*. Prentice Hall, Englewood Cliffs, New Jersey.

Canadian Tourism Research Institute (2003) What if there is a war in Iraq? The potential impact on domestic and select international travel markets to Canada. Canadian Tourism Commission: ftp.canadatourism.com/ctxuploads/en_publications/ WarScenarioSummary.pdf

Chen, C. and Liu, L.-M. (1995) Join estimation of model parameters and outliers effects in time series. *Journal of the American Statistical Association* 88, 284–297.

Glaesser, D. (2003) *Crisis Management in the Tourism Industry*. Butterworth-Heinemann, Oxford.

Harvey, A.C. (1990) *Forecasting, Structural Time Models and Kalman Filter*. Cambridge University Press, Cambridge.

Harvey, N. (2001) Improving judgment in forecasting. In: Armstrong, J.S. (ed.) *Principles of Forecasting*. Kluwer Academic Publishers, Boston, Massachusetts, pp. 59–80.

Koopman, S.J., Harvey, A.C., Doornik, J.A. and Shephard, N. (2000) *Stamp: Structural Time Series Analyser, Modeller and Predictor*. Timberlake Consultant Ltd, London.

MacGregor, D.G. (2001) Decomposition for judgmental forecasting and estimation. In: Armstrong, J.S. (ed.) *Principles of Forecasting*. Kluwer Academic Publishers, Boston, Massachusetts, pp. 107–123.

McNees, S.K. (1992) The 1990–91 recession in historical perspective. *New England Economic Review* (Jan/Feb), 3–22.

Olson, E. (2001) World business briefing Europe: Switzerland: sale by Swissair. *The New York Times* 31 July, p. 1.

Ord, K. and Young, P. (2004) Estimating the impact of recent intervention on transportation indicators. Paper presented at the TRB 83rd Annual Meeting, Washington, DC.

Parenté, F.J. and Anderson-Parenté, J.K. (1987) Delphi inquiry system. In: Wright, G. and Ayton, P. (eds) *Judgmental Forecasting*. John Wiley and Sons Ltd, Hoboken, New Jersey, pp. 129–155.

Poon, A. and Adams, E. (2001) *Impact of Terrorism on World Tourism. Likely Scenarios and Future Strategies*. Tourism Intelligence International, Bielefeld, Germany.

Scaglione, M. (2003) Users views. Stamp as

a tourism research tool [pdf-Newsletter]. Timberlake Consultants Limited. http://www.timberlake.co.uk/software/Oxm etrics/OxNewsletter3.pdf (accessed 2 February 2004)

Scaglione, M. and Mungall, A. (2002) Forecasting Swiss airports: coming back from the future. Paper presented at the AIEST 52nd Congress. Air transportation and tourism, Bahia, Brazil.

Scaglione, M. and Mungall, A. (2004) Combined effects of Swissair bankruptcy and September 11th on Swiss airports. Paper presented at the TRB 83rd Annual Meeting, Washington, DC.

Scaglione, M., and Mungall, A. (2005) Air traffic in three main swiss national airports: application of *STAMP* in forecasting future trends. *Journal of Transportation and Statistics* 8 (1), 13–22.

Schnader, M. and Stekler, H. (1998) Source of turning point in forecast errors. *Applied Economics Letters* 5, 519–521.

Stekler, H.O. (1967) Data revision and economic forecasting. *Journal of the American Statistical Association* 61 (1), 470–483.

Stekler, H.O. (2003) Improving our ability to predict the unusual event. *International Journal of Forecasting* 19, 161–163.

Stephenson, D.B. (2004) Famous forecasting quotes. http://www.met.rdg.ac.uk/cag/fore casting/quotes.html (accessed 10 March 2004)

Young, P. and Ord, K. (2002) Monitoring transportation indicators, and an analysis of the effects of September 11. Paper presented at the 22nd International Symposium on Forecasting, Dublin, Ireland.

Appendix I

From Koopman *et al.* (2000)

Cycle component

For a univariate model, the cycle ψ_t has the following statistical specification:

$$\begin{bmatrix} \psi_t \\ \psi_t^* \end{bmatrix} = \rho \begin{bmatrix} \cos\lambda_c & \sin\lambda_c \\ -\sin\lambda_c & \cos\lambda_c \end{bmatrix} \begin{bmatrix} \psi_{t-1} \\ \psi_{t-1}^* \end{bmatrix} + \begin{bmatrix} \kappa_t \\ \kappa_{t-1} \end{bmatrix}, \qquad t = 1, \cdots T \qquad (5)$$

where λ_c is the frequency, in radians, in the range $0 < \lambda_c < 1$, κ_t and κ_{t-1}^* are two mutually uncorrelated white noise disturbances with zero means and common variance σ_κ^2, and ρ is the damping factor. The period is $2\pi/\lambda_c$.

The stochastic cycle becomes a first-order autoregressive process if λ_c is 0 or π, which has the following form:

$$\psi_t = \Phi\psi_{t-1} + \kappa_t \qquad \kappa_t \sim NID(0, \Sigma_\kappa^2) \qquad t = 1, \cdots, T \qquad (6)$$

in the multivariate form.

Seasonal components

The seasonal pattern is expected to repeat itself more or less regularly. Let γ_{jt} denote the observations of season j at time t and let s be the number of seasons. Although all s seasonal components are continually evolving, it is clear that only one affects the observations at any particular point in time, i.e.

$$\gamma_t = \gamma_{jt}, \qquad t = 1, \dots T$$

when season j is prevailing at time t. The three different possible forms for the seasonal component are the followings forms for univariate models:

1. Fixed seasonality component: $\gamma_t = \sum_{j=1}^{s} \gamma_{jt} = 0$ (7)

2. Dummy seasonality component: $\gamma_t = \sum_{j=1}^{s-1} \gamma_{t-j} + \omega_t$ (8)

where ω_t is a white-noise disturbance term with mean zero and variance σ_ω^2.

3. Trigonometric seasonality component: $\gamma_t = \sum_{j=1}^{[s/2]} \gamma^*_{t,j}$ (9)

where $\gamma^*_{t,j}$ has the form of Equation 6 with $\rho = 1$ and $\lambda_c = \lambda_j = 2\pi j/s$, $j = 1,2, \dots, |s/2|$

Appendix II

The diagnostic and goodness-of-fit are based on the following statistics:

s: the equation standard error

N: Doornik–Hansen normality test statistic, which is the Bowman–Shenton statistics with the correction of Doornik and Hansen, distributed approximately, under the null hypothesis as ch2(2), critical value* 6.
H(df): heteroskedasticity, distributed approximately as F(df,df)
DW: or Durbin–Watson statistics, distributed approximately as $N(0,1/T)$, T being the number of observations.
Q(df): Box–Ljung Q-statistic: test of residual serial correlation, based on the first df residual autocorrelations and distributed as chi2(df).
R2: coefficient of determination.

See Koopman et al. (2000).

3 Policy Response to Rural Dangers: Managing Educational Visits in the Wake of the Foot and Mouth and *E. coli* Crises

DEREK HALL

Introduction

This chapter examines policy responses for the management of educational visits to rural areas in a post-crisis environment and their implications for the sustainability of rural tourism and recreation businesses. The analysis is contextualized in two ways. First, the chapter briefly examines the role of rural areas as an educational environment for young people, and particularly for urban children divorced from the non-urban environment. The literature suggests that encouraging children to appreciate the countryside can stimulate their parents and friends to take a greater interest in rural recreation and tourism, and thereby assist rural economies.

Secondly, the chapter briefly addresses the strategic approach to foot and mouth disease (FMD) crisis management taken by the UK government during 2001–2002 that had a far more devastating effect on the rural tourism industry than it did on farming, with continuing knock-on effects for rural tourism and recreation development. Further, it suggests that with the continued presence of the verocytotoxin-producing bacterium *Escherichia coli* O157 (infection from which can result in acute renal failure), and other potentially transmittable infections such as the gastrointestinal cryptosporidiosis, interaction with animals, often a central feature of farm-based tourism and recreation activities, requires a sensitive but effective and consistent visitor management policy.

The chapter then goes on to examine and critically evaluate the policy context and approaches of 19 Scottish local authorities to the potential and perceived dangers confronting education visits to the countryside in the wake of the FMD and *E. coli* crises, and their implications for rural tourism businesses.

The Rural Area as an Important Educational Environment for Young People

Rural areas provide an important educational environment for young people, and particularly for those raised in cities who may be divorced from many aspects of the non-urban environment and have mis-perceptions about the origins of the food they eat, with consequent health and welfare implications. Partly for such reasons, the UK Policy Commission on the Future of Food and Farming (Curry Commission) argued that a key objective of public policy should be to reconnect consumers with what they eat and how it is produced (Policy Commission on the Future of Food and Farming, 2002, p. 6). The need for schools to develop stronger links with farms was made explicit. The government responded that it recognized the importance of young people experiencing the 'outdoor classroom' and noted that 'children benefit from hands-on experiences of plants and animals' (House of Commons, 2002, p. 47). In fact, the role of farms as a school journey experience has been debated in the UK for more than a century. Almost half a century ago, *Schools and the Countryside* (Ministry of Education, 1958) emphasized the cumulative value of farm studies and the need for children to undertake farm visits at different stages during their school life.

Dillon *et al.* (2003) found that school-age students' rural knowledge and understanding appeared to be poor, and that studies of students' environmental awareness were not integrated into any wider conceptual framework such as the food chain. There was a strong case for improving teaching and learning concerning food, farming and land management, and the inter-relationships between them. There was also a need for a more integrated approach in order for young people to have a well-developed relational view of the environment and its inter-relationships with social issues. Currently they are 'subjected to an education system underpinned by the anthropomorphic values of liberalism and modernity' (Loughland *et al.*, 2003, p. 14), within which animals are organized into hierarchies, both plants and animals are regarded as pets or pests (Marshall, 1992) and nature is constructed as an object of gaze. Myers *et al.* (2003) argue that curriculum change, and implicitly a greater engagement with animal-related environments, can help children of all ages be more aware of, and articulate about values underlying environmental care. The enhanced experiential welfare derived from interacting with both tame and relatively wild creatures can generate a sense of respect, understanding and compassion (Katcher and Beck, 1988). Interaction with animals has the potential to encapsulate all four realms of experience – entertainment, education, escapism and aestheticism (Pine and Gilmore, 1998, p. 102), although animal rights' supporters (Regan, 1988) might argue that the use of animals as objects of human recreation is outdated and often barbaric.

Several studies have indicated that children can be a catalyst in generating a family visit to a particular attraction or destination (e.g.

Swinyard and Sim, 1987; Seaton and Tagg, 1995; Thornton *et al.*, 1997), and that they can enrich the nature of the adult experience (Ryan, 1992). Older children appear to play a greater role in tourist group holiday decisions (Madrigal, 1993; Pasumarty *et al.*, 1996); younger children exert more influence on actual tourist behaviour while on holiday. In the UK, under-16s account for almost one-third of all trips to visitor attractions (British Tourism Authority/English Tourist Board, 1998), with figures of up to 39% for leisure parks and 47% for farm-based attractions. The latter would suggest at least that the presence of a child, if not its articulated wishes, encourages adults to visit such attractions and environments. Although Turley (2001) suggests that the influence of children on the demand for tourism and recreation experiences is under-researched and undervalued (Howard and Madrigal, 1990; Cullingford, 1995; Thornton *et al.*, 1997), in her own study of zoo visits, she was able to highlight the important part children play in influencing demand for day-visit destinations and recreational activities.

Research would therefore suggest that encouraging children to appreciate relational environmental values, and especially those relating to animals and the environmental context of rural areas, can act as a stimulus to greater use of rural recreation and tourism attractions there. This has implications beyond the education of pupils, for education policy towards school visits to rural areas and for the providers of farm-based and other rural attractions (e.g. Hall *et al.*, 2002). In a context where many of the UK's rural businesses may still see themselves as being in crisis, this catalytic role of children may be critical in helping to re-invigorate rural attractions and the businesses depending upon them.

Crisis in the UK Countryside

Actual crisis: foot and mouth disease (FMD)

The total annual output of the agricultural industry in Britain is worth about £15 billion (US$22 billion) a year. Of that, livestock farming generates about £5 billion (US$7.5 billion), or less than 1% of the total national income. In contrast, tourism generates £64 billion (US$96 billion) – accounting for 4% of gross domestic product and employing 2 million people – four times greater than the entire agricultural sector.

Although the government was initially slow to react when the highly infectious FMD was first detected in cattle early in 2001, a subsequent draconian response aimed to stop the spread of FMD by closing most footpaths and other rights-of-way across Britain. Together with the closure of tourist destinations and attractions including forests and some sporting events, the direct impact of these measures was, in effect, 'to place the entire British countryside under quarantine' (Sharpley, 2003, p. 45). The highly fragmented nature of the tourism industry is exposed in a crisis: small enterprises cannot offset their losses like larger ones, and 80% of the

UK's tourism businesses employ fewer than ten people. Specialist rural businesses were particularly adversely affected by these acts, such as the 22-bed hotel in Pitlochry in the Scottish Highlands providing walking holidays, which was forced to close early in the crisis because of cancelled bookings, despite being located over 100 miles away from the nearest FMD outbreak (Hall, 2001). Further, the policy of 'contiguous culling' – the slaughter of animals on farms within a 3 km radius of confirmed cases – acted to remove the key recreational attraction of a living and working countryside. Media images of pyres of slaughtered animals reinforced a sense of crisis in, and repulsion from the British countryside.

Such was the alarm at the damage caused to tourism as a whole in Scotland, that immediately the proscriptions were lifted, 23 major rural interest groups collaborated on the production, promotion and distribution of *The Comeback Code* (Scottish Natural Heritage/Scottish Executive Rural Affairs Department, 2001). This encouraged rural recreation users to return to and sensitively use the post-FMD countryside. Its domestic emphasis was particularly necessary as most government effort was being put into restoring confidence in international markets.

The House of Commons Committee of Public Accounts, UK Parliament (2003), echoing and reinforcing findings of the National Audit Office investigation of the previous year (National Audit Office, 2002), found that tourism businesses across Britain lost up to £5.4 billion (US$8 billion) as a result of the 2001 FMD outbreak and responses to it, a figure nine times greater than the losses incurred by agriculture. While the tourism industry collapsed, farmers received compensation worth almost £1.4 billion (US$2 billion) and were able to take advantage of crisis management shortcomings by inflating compensation claims. In contrast, the tourism industry was offered £40 million (US$60 million) (Hetherington, 2002), although bureaucratic hurdles constrained access to this, particularly for small tourism businesses. The Committee condemned the government's contingency plans for focusing only on the needs of agriculture and neglecting the difficulties of tourism and other non-farming sectors. As a result, rural tourism businesses throughout Britain have been left in a continuing fragile economic position. Yet, the experience of rural crisis needs to be viewed within the wider context of a relatively rapid growth in the importance of animals as rural tourism and recreation attractions (Hall *et al.*, 2002), with 'nature-based' tourism growing by 30% per year (Young, 1998). This raises a second area of risk.

Potential crisis: *E. coli* O157 and cryptosporidiosis

Although FMD was a costly and distressing actual crisis for the UK countryside and rural tourism, there persists the potential for a crisis resulting from other health issues: those relating to the interaction between animals and humans. Working and interacting with animals exposes humans to zoonoses (diseases transmitted from vertebrate animals) such as *E. coli*

O157 and cryptosporidiosis, which can be harmful if basic hygiene measures are not followed. The UK Health and Safety Executive (Health and Safety Executive, (HSE) 2002a, b, c) advises all farmers and owners of animal attractions to assume that all their ruminants (cattle, sheep, deer and goats) carry these. However, this does not normally cause an animal any harm or illness. Indeed, a difficulty in identifying animals which carry the organism is that they usually exhibit no signs of disease (Scottish Office Education and Industry Department, 1996). If contracted by humans, however, the toxins that *E. coli* produces can cause illness ranging from diarrhoea to kidney failure, with possible fatal consequences. Young children and the elderly are at greatest risk. Infection can occur through a number of routes including direct contact with animals, contact with animal faeces, and the consumption of contaminated foods, as well as person-to-person contagion.

A number of outbreaks involving children have been associated with educational and recreational visits to open farms (Health and Safety Executive, 2001), although individual cases are reckoned to be substantially under-reported (Payne, 2003). This bacterium can also be carried by pets and wild birds: rabbits were blamed for an outbreak at a wildlife park in England in 2001 (Meikle, 2001). It is a particular risk for children visiting lambing farms in spring. As a physical threat to rural visitors themselves, therefore, *E. coli* is much more damaging: FMD, although able to be spread by human activity and vehicles, does not affect humans. Controlling the risks from *E. coli* O157 helps to control risks from most other zoonoses such as cryptosporidiosis, which can cause diarrhoea and abdominal pain with flu-like symptoms for up to 6 weeks (Health and Safety Executive, 2002a, c). Clearly, if *E. coli* O157 in particular was to develop into a major threat to rural visitors such as school children, this would have profound implications for policy relating to educational visits, for the nature of children's learning and understanding of rural environments, and for many rural tourism and recreation-related businesses.

The Policy Context

In addition to the research, publication and inspection roles of the HSE, in Scotland central government advice on school visits in the face of *E. coli* O157 (Scotish Office Education and Industry Deparment, 1996; Scottish Exective Department of Health, 2000) and regional health board (RHB) advisory notes on *E. coli* and *Cryptosporidium* have been key reference sources for local education authorities (LEAs) charged with administering school visits. As such, the policy context for educational visits to rural attractions overlaps the boundaries of education, health, recreation and agriculture policy domains. Within such a context, in the wake of FMD, all of Scotland's LEAs were formally contacted in late summer 2002, to request information on their 'policy' towards school visits to farms and other animal-related attractions in rural areas. Of the total sample of 32, 19 responded with documents and/or in written detail.

Five major components emerged as influencing policy towards education visits in the face of continuing potential risk: (i) direct and indirect central government legislative and advisory prescriptions; (ii) the local authority political and administrative structure and culture, and its interpretation of central government advice; (iii) the role of partnerships and collaboration; (iv) the short- to medium-term impact of changing cultures, fashions and crises; and, finally, (v) the rural environment in which such visits take place.

Advice and prescription from the Scottish Executive and its predecessor the Scottish Office, the HSE and RHBs acted as key reference points for LEAs. Table 3.1 indicates the range of policy documents variously mentioned in the survey. Analysis of these suggests a critical need for revising, updating, consolidating and integrating policy guidelines in the face of the growth of animal attractions and the stated need for children's rural and animal experiences. Although most documents referred to by LEAs dated from 1996 onwards, others were issued in 1980, 1987, 1988 and 1989. Notably, more than a year after the FMD outbreaks, no specific reference was made to the disease or its likely impact on the nature of visiting animal-related attractions.

In terms of the qualitative comments made on the authorities' own position and performance, only one LEA (Q) explicitly stated that it recognized the need to update material, in this case the appropriate section in its health and safety policy document, claiming that the authority

Table 3.1. Key Scottish policy documents featured in the survey.

	Date	Source	Title/significance
1	10/80	Strathclyde Regional Council	*Animals in Primary and Nursery Schools*
2	10/88	Strathclyde Regional Council	*Excursions by Children to Livestock Markets*
3	12/96	Scottish Office Education and Industry Department	*Visits to Farms (Following a Fatal Outbreak of* E. coli*)*
4	5/98	Greater Glasgow Health Board	*Upsurge in Cryptosporidium*
5	1/99	Glasgow City	*Community Education Excursions and Education Visits*
6	2/99	Argyle & Clyde Health Board	*Health Risks From Farm Visits – Focusing on Cryptosporidium*
7	2/99	Health & Safety Executive	*Avoiding Ill Health at Open Farms: AIS23 and Supplement*
8	?/99	Greater Glasgow Health Board	*Tips for Visits to Farms, Zoos and Wildlife Parks*
9	5/00	Scottish Executive Department of Health	*CMO Issues Advice on Farm Visits*
10	6/00	Health & Safety Executive	*Avoiding Ill Health at Open Farms and Supplement, second revision*
11	3/01	Health & Safety Executive	*Children's poster competition to improve farm safety*
12	5/01	Grampian Health Board	E. coli O157 updated
13	2/02	Health & Safety Executive	*Common Zoonoses in Agriculture: AIS2 revised*
14	3/02	Scottish Executive Public Health Division	*Recreational Use of Animal Pasture*

was about to adopt and adapt the code of practice from another Scottish LEA.

The role of the HSE appeared crucial, some of its source material (notably Health and Safety Executive, 2002a, b) being almost uniformly acknowledged by all LEAs responding. However, an HSE children's poster campaign in 2001 to improve farm safety was referred to by only one LEA (respondent T). In another case, reference was made to a 1995 HSE video on farm safety as part of a pack of teaching materials which was felt to be 'potentially disturbing for many young children'. Following 'concerns expressed by a number of parents', the education officer (M) strongly recommended that school heads consider carefully the contents of the video before using it with their pupils.

LEA officials sometimes appeared unsure and inconsistent in their attitude towards whether they were facilitating policy or advice. The head of schools within one LEA's department of educational and social services (D) emphasized that since the issue of school visits to rural attractions with animals had not been considered by a council committee, 'we do not have a policy. Rather, these documents have the status of advice being developed at officer level.' Similarly, the health and safety officer of a department of education, culture and lifelong learning (E) stated that his council did 'not have an actual policy as such', but issued guidelines to schools. On the other hand, one support services manager (R) explicity referred to a section of his authority's *Communicable Diseases: Guidance on Infection Control and Exclusion Periods in Schools* document as being the 'council's policy on farm visits for schools'. In response to the circulation of the Scottish Office Education and Industry Department (1996), a head of resource management (C) asserted that 'the letter is written in the form of guidance to head teachers. I feel, however, that the "health tips" listed should be an essential feature of any visit to a farm.'

Indeed, the role of facilitators or gatekeepers within LEAs appeared important in diffusing or filtering policy guidelines and action requirements to schools. One authority's (Q) coordinator for outdoor learning, for example, acted as the recipient for school visits permission forms and in turn referred schools to the Royal Highland Education Trust (RHET) website (see below), provided HSE (2002a, b) written guidelines and risk assessment forms, and reminded schools of the Scottish Executive Department of Health Circular on farms visits (2000) (which also reissued the *Health Tips for Teachers Leading School Visits to Farms* first circulated with Scottish Office Education and Industry Department, 1996). An education safety office (L) stressed that good examples of an activity or an excursion were made available to all its schools through the authority's education website.

LEAs' expressed views on the role of visits were usually positive. Typical was a head of schools and community education (C) who stated that his 'council's view (was) that properly managed contact with animals constitutes a valid and worthwhile educational experience for pupils'. The 1999 pamphlet *Health Tips for Visits to Farms, Zoos and Wildlife Parks*, a joint collaboration between six local authorities and the Greater Glasgow Health Board, suggests that, despite the potential health risks, 'visits to these places should not be discouraged' but points to the need for strictly observing basic guidelines, in themselves largely derived from a central government source (Scottish Office Education and Industry Department, 1996). However, in a May 2000 circular to all schools in his area, one deputy director of education (D) indicated that following representations from a local farm park, he had consulted the Head of Protective Services regarding pre-5 visits and, in view of the perceived risk, indicated to appropriate heads that pre-5 children should not go on excursions to farm parks or working farms. Further, a May 1998 letter from a livestock auctioneers and valuers to their LEA (P) pointed to recent cases of cryptosporidium linked to the handling of lambs, and requested schools not to allow their children to touch animals on visits to their cattle market.

There has evolved a complex structure and set of inter-relationships between a range of public, private and voluntary associations involved in governing the UK countryside. For Sharpley (2003, pp. 40–41) this indicates a shift in emphasis from 'government' to 'governance', and is exemplified in partnerships for educational recreation in rural areas which represent a bewildering variety of institutions. The most important of these in Scotland is the RHET, an educational charity, established in 1999 (superseding the Scottish Farm and Countryside Educational Trust). The Royal Highland Education Trust (2003) aims to create the opportunity for each child in Scotland to learn about the countryside and to ensure a wider understanding of its 'environmental, economic and social realities'. This remit includes providing opportunities through its farm links scheme for schoolchildren to visit a farm or the countryside. RHET supplies schools with resource materials, provides risk assessment processes, makes initial contacts with farmers on behalf of the school, and debriefs teachers and farmers following visits. This emphasis on farms and its role in promoting agriculture appeared largely to ignore the wider rural recreation and tourism context, to the potential detriment of the sector's businesses.

A number of LEAs surveyed highlighted the role of the RHET, although some still referred by name to its predecessor. Respondent F, for example, emphasized that 'most' of the LEA's primary schools had farm links under the RHET scheme and detailed risk assessments were discussed with RHET representatives, although it was also assumed that any open farm or animal attraction would have its own detailed risk assessments and operating procedures in place for visiting school groups, which is a self-limiting assumption.

Summary and Conclusions

This chapter has highlighted, first, the importance of interactional visits to rural areas as an important educational experience for school age children. Secondly, it has suggested that such children, in their role as influencers of adults' recreational choice, can act as a catalyst – particularly important after a crisis such as FMD – in the rejuvenation and sustainability of rural attractions. Thirdly, despite the common use or summarizing of key advisory documents by most LEAs surveyed, there is a critical need for updating and integrating policy guidelines in the face of the growth of animal attractions and the stated need for children's rural and animal experiences. Fourthly, differences in apparent levels of awareness, response and departmental responsibility between local authorities raise issues of policy consistency and clarity. Fifthly, there is a range of stakeholders involved in visit management and policy influence, leading to variations in interpretations of risk and proscription. Finally, such a range of stakeholders does underline the important need for developing networks and partnerships at a number of levels in overcoming actual and perceived constraints on rural recreation and tourism activity.

The significance of this area of recreational activity being on or crossing the boundaries between education, health, recreation and agricultural policy domains is illustrated both in the range of departments and organizations referred to in the course of this short examination, and in the frequent lack of consistency and integration in approach. Rural visits need to be viewed within the wider context of education visit policy. At the time of writing (Autumn 2003), the Scottish Executive's Education Department was reviewing the safety guidelines for educational visits following a series of high profile fatal accidents involving Scottish school children (e.g. Macleod, 2003), but more especially in the wake of new guidelines for England and Wales.

The evidence would suggest a requirement for closer collaboration between education administrators and those involved in the management of recreational resources to assist the latter's market positioning. This reinforces one of Ritchie's (2003) key arguments that without adequate research and management the potential impacts and benefits of educational tourism will not be maximized. However, although agencies such as RHET are meant to act in such a mediating role, they tend to reinforce a bias towards the role of agriculture and farm-based activity at the expense of other rural attraction businesses and their sustainability, perhaps perpetuating the narrow policy focus evident in government response to FMD.

References

British Tourism Authority/English Tourist Board (1998) *Sightseeing in the UK in 1997.* BTA/ETB Research Services, London.

Cullingford, C. (1995) Children's attitudes to holidays overseas. *Tourism Management* 16, 121–127.

Dillon, J., Rickinson, M., Sanders, D., Tearney, K. and Benefield, P. (2003) *Improving the Understanding of Food, Farming and Land Management Amongst School-age Children: a Literature Review.* National Foundation for Educational Research and King's College London, London.

Hall, D. (2001) FMD – view from Scotland. *Tourism* Autumn, p. 14.

Hall, D.R., Roberts, L.A., Wemelsfelder, F.

and Farish, M. (2002) A critical evaluation of animal-related rural recreation and tourism attractions. In: Anon (ed.) *Development, Community and Conservation: Conference Papers*, Vol. 1. Bhundelkand University, Jhansi and Centre for Tourism Research & Development, Lucknow, pp. 150–164.

Health and Safety Executive (2001) *E. coli O157*. HSE Books, London.

Health and Safety Executive (2002a) *Avoiding Ill Health at Open Farms – Advice to Farmers.* Agriculture Information Sheet No. 23 (revised). HSE Books, London.

Health and Safety Executive (2002b) *Avoiding Ill Health at Open Farms – Advice to Teachers.* AIS23 Supplement (revised). HSE Books, London.

Health and Safety Executive (2002c) *Common Zoonoses in Agriculture.* Agriculture Information Sheet No. 2 (revised). HSE Books, London.

Hetherington, P. (2002) Tourism receives £40m boost. *The Guardian* 25 February.

House of Commons (2002) *Response to the Report of the Policy Commission on the Future of Farming and Food by HM Government (Cm. 5709).* The Stationery Office, London.

House of Commons Committee of Public Accounts, UK Parliament (2003) *The 2001 Outbreak of Foot and Mouth Disease. Fifth Report of Session 2002–03 (HC487)*. The Stationery Office, London.

Howard, D.R. and Madrigal, R. (1990) Who makes the decision: the parent or the child? The perceived influence of parents and children on the purchase of recreational services. *Journal of Leisure Research* 22, 244–258.

Katcher, A.H. and Beck, A.M. (1988) Health and caring for living things. In: Rowan, A. (ed.) *Animals and People Sharing the World.* University Press of New England, Hanover, New Hampshire, pp. 53–73.

Loughland, T., Reid, A., Walker, K. and Petocz, P. (2003) Factors influencing young people's conceptions of environment. *Environmental Education Research* 9, 3–20.

Macleod, M. (2003) School trips safety crackdown. *Scotland on Sunday* 3 August.

Madrigal, R. (1993) Parents' perceptions of family members' relative influence in vacation decision making. *Journal of Travel and Tourism Marketing* 2 (4), 39–57.

Marshall, P. (1992) *Nature's Web.* M.E. Sharpe, London.

Meikle, J. (2001) Rabbits blamed as *E. coli* infects 10 children. *The Guardian* 9 November.

Ministry of Education (1958) *Schools and the Countryside.* HMSO, London.

Myers, O.E., Saunders, C.D. and Garrett, E. (2003) What do children think animals need? Aesthetic and psycho-social conceptions. *Environmental Education Research* 9, 305–325.

National Audit Office (2002) *The 2001 Outbreak of Foot and Mouth Disease (Parts 1 and 2) (HC939 2001–2002)*. National Audit Office, London.

Pasumarty, K., Dolinsky, A., Stinerock, R. and Korol, T. (1996) Consumer behaviour and marketing strategy: a multinational study of children's involvement in the purchase of hospitality services. *Hospitality Research Journal* 19 (4), 87–112.

Payne, C.J.I. (2003) Vero cytoxin-producing *Escherichia coli* O157 gastroenteritis in farm visitors, North Wales. *Emerging Infectious Diseases*, 9 (5) <http://www.cdc.gov/ncidod/EID/vol9no5/02–0237.htm > (accessed 4 June 2003).

Pine, B.J. and Gilmore, J.H. (1998) Welcome to the experience economy. *Harvard Business Review* July–August, 97–105.

Policy Commission on the Future of Food and Farming (2002) *Farming and Food: a Sustainable Future.* The Stationery Office, London.

Regan, T. (1988) *The Case for Animal Rights.* Routledge, London.

Ritchie, B.W. (2003) *Managing Educational Tourism.* Channel View, Clevedon, UK.

Roberts, L. and Hall, D. (2001) *Rural Tourism: Principles to Practice.* CAB International, Wallingford, UK.

The Royal Highland Education Trust (2003) The Royal Highland Education Trust. Ingliston: RHET <http://www.rhet.rhass.org.uk> (accessed 13 June 2003).

Ryan, C. (1992) The child as a visitor. In: Brent Ritchie, J.R., Hawkins, D.E., Go, F. and Frechtling, D. (eds) *World Travel and Tourism Review: Indicators, Trends and Issues*, Vol. 2. CAB International, Wallingford, UK, pp. 135–139.

Scottish Executive Department of Health (2000) *CMO Issues Advice on Farm Visits*. Scottish Executive, Edinburgh.

Scottish Natural Heritage/Scottish Executive Rural Affairs Department (2001) *The Comeback Code*. Scottish Natural Heritage/Scottish Executive, Edinburgh.

Scottish Office Education and Industry Department (1996) *Visits to Farms/Health Tips for Teachers Leading School Visits to Farms*. Letter and Appendix to Directors of Education in Scotland, 16 December. SOEID, Edinburgh.

Seaton, A.V. and Tagg, S. (1995) The family vacation in Europe: paedonomic aspects of choices and satisfactions. *Journal of Travel and Tourism Marketing* 4 (1), 1–21.

Sharpley, R. (2003) Rural tourism and sustainability – a critique. In: Hall, D., Roberts, L. and Mitchell, M. (eds) *New Directions in Rural Tourism*. Ashgate, Aldershot, UK, pp. 38–53.

Swinyard, W.R. and Sim, C.P. (1987) Perception of children's influence on family decision processes. *Journal of Consumer Marketing* 4 (1), 25–38.

Thornton, P.R., Shaw, G. and Williams, A.M. (1997) Tourist group holiday decision-making and behaviour: the influence of children. *Tourism Management* 18, 287–297.

Turley, S.K. (2001) Children and the demand for recreational experiences: the case of zoos. *Leisure Studies* 20, 1–18.

Young, K. (1998) *Seal Watching in the UK and Republic of Ireland*. International Fund for Animal Welfare UK, London.

4 The Evolution of an Emergency Management Tourism Faculty Resource

THOMAS E. DRABEK

Introduction

When most people are away from home, their thoughts are focused on the excitement of experiencing new places, people and cultures, not personal safety. However, sometimes the tranquility of a vacation or even a business trip is interrupted by disaster! Imagine waking up to the sounds of sirens, alerting citizens of an imminent hurricane evacuation. Or worse, pieces of ceiling falling into your bed grimly announcing the earthquake damage to your hotel. When confronting an unfamiliar event in a place at which you have just arrived, feelings of uncertainty are exacerbated. Questions require answers – the quicker the better.

Behavioural research on human responses to disaster has a long history and significant intellectual content (e.g. Barton, 1969; Dynes, 1970; Drabek, 1986). For a variety of reasons, however, tourists and other types of transients, e.g. business travellers, were seldom captured within the study samples of researchers examining responses to hurricanes (e.g. Moore *et al.*, 1963), tornadoes (e.g. Taylor *et al.*, 1970), earthquakes (Geipel, 1991) or other forms of disaster.

There were a few exceptions, of course, like the work of Baker (1979, 1991) who completed a series of 'behavioural evacuation surveys' for the US Army Corps of Engineers. Similarly, Murphy and Bayley (1989) highlighted the unique vulnerabilities of tourists caught in disaster, namely lack of familiarity with both place and event. Too often, many tourist destinations are high-risk areas, e.g. hurricane-prone coastal beaches, avalanche-prone ski resorts, etc.

Overall, however, tourist behaviour during large-scale disasters, like that of the managers and employees to whom they might turn for answers, remained a void in the research literature. This gap was highlighted by a research team from the Oak Ridge National Laboratory in Tennessee in

1987 (i.e. Sorensen *et al.*, 1987). After reviewing 336 studies of evacuation behaviour, they drew several relevant conclusions that became the basis of a series of research studies. Two examples tell the story.

1. 'Tourists are another special population which may require special planning. In the 1982 Hurricane Iwa in the Hawaiian Islands, local officials had problems deciding how to warn the tourists (Chiu *et al.*, 1983). There has been very little research on evacuating tourist areas such as beach communities, resorts, or cities with large seasonal tourist populations' (Sorensen *et al.*, 1987, p. 118).
2. 'Transient populations do present difficulties in disseminating evacuation warnings. Anecdotal information suggests that there have been problems with warning vacationers of impending hurricanes and with warning campers in recreational areas to evacuate because of flash floods. Little systematic data exist on the receipt of warnings and the evacuation behavior of transient populations. Research on this topic could be valuable in developing evacuation plans in areas where large transient populations might be exposed to threats' (Sorensen *et al.*, 1987, p. 133).

A Research History

In an effort to fill this void, a series of studies were initiated (Drabek, 1994, 1996a, 1999). First, 185 tourist business managers were interviewed about their approaches to disaster preparedness and experiences following major disasters (Drabek, 1994). The first phase of this study focused on tourist locations where local governments had implemented evacuation planning initiatives. Three field sites were selected: (i) Pinellas County, Florida; (ii) the city of Galveston, Texas; and (iii) Sevier County, Tennessee. Samples of firms selected ($n = 65$) reflected the geographic distribution throughout the jurisdiction and variation in mission (i.e. 39% accommodation, 28% entertainment–retail, 25% restaurant only and 8%, travel). The second phase documented managerial responses following extensive flooding in Washington state during 1990 (Whatcom and Snohomish Counties (33 firms)) and Hurricane Bob the following year (Carteret and Dare County, North Carolina (45 firms); York County, Maine (23 firms); and Cape Cod/Martha's Vineyard, Massachusetts (20 firms)).

The major conclusion of this study was that *the tourist industry is a ticking time bomb; it represented a vulnerability of enormous catastrophic potential* (Drabek, 1994, p. 1). While some disaster planning had been completed, it was patchy at best. Less than a quarter (22%) of the executives indicated that they revised their plans annually; few (5%) conducted annual exercises. Multivariate analyses documented six key social constraints that predicted the extent of disaster planning within these 185 firms: (i) intraorganizational factors (e.g. a written plan being mandated by the parent company or federal regulation); (ii) local emergency manager contact; (iii) size of firm; (iv) managerial risk perception; (v) manager's participation in professional organizations; and (vi) community disaster subculture (Drabek, 1994, p. 3).

Given these and other observations, an action agenda was proposed, including the recommendation '... that officials with the Federal Emergency Management Agency, probably the Emergency Management Institute, initiate a partnership with professional tourism associations, so that appropriate faculty might attend a summer educational workshop on disaster awareness, preparedness, response, and recovery ... this workshop should challenge all attendees to create new course materials and to devise a peer exchange system to maintain its vitality and diffusion' (Drabek, 1994, p. 255).

Tourists and other types of transients, e.g. business travellers, migrant workers and homeless persons, were the focus of the next study (Drabek, 1996a). Five disasters were selected and 18 specific field sites were visited so that transient populations could be identified (n = 682): (i) Hurricane Bob (August 1991) (n = 191); (ii) the Big Bear Lake region (California) (28 June 1991) (n = 33); (iii) Hurricane Andrew (August 1992) (n = 163); (iv) Hurricane Iniki (September 1992) (n = 240); and (v) Northridge earthquake (Los Angeles area, California) (17 January 1994). Additionally, accommodation executives (n = 69) and community emergency officials (n = 76) were interviewed to provide event context and liaison with transients. Most, but not all transients were interviewed on the telephone after responding to a written request letter. Some of these were in response to a letter sent by an accommodation executive. Others were initiated by the author who explained that their name was recorded in a tourist destination log book a few days before disaster struck, e.g. Chamber of Commerce office, museum or other such venue. A mail back questionnaire was used to gather background information and reactions to a variety of policy options pertaining to specific evacuation procedures and disaster preparedness generally (return rate = 87%).

These data documented dozens of significant response patterns and policy preferences. Similar to residential populations, for example, transients initially respond to disaster warnings with threat denial. Warning sources differ significantly, however, with tourists often reporting receipt of threat information from accommodation staff, other tourists and employees of nearby businesses. Frequently these sources neutralize emergent threat perceptions. resulting in delay and argument.

A substantial gap was documented in the expectations of customers and managers regarding emergency preparedness (see Drabek, 2000). For example, one questionnaire item was as follows: 'Local governments should require all firms providing lodging, including RV parks and campgrounds, to have written disaster-evacuation plans.' The results? Almost all tourists (91%) agreed, whereas only half (50%) of the managers did.

These perceptual gaps regarding policy were reflected further in responses to a closing interview item, i.e. 'What is the one most important thing about this experience that you would like to say to people in the tourist industry?' Nine key themes were gleaned from content analysis: (i) 'Be pro-active with your warnings, don't deny the threat' (20%); (ii) 'Keep people informed with periodic updates' (12%); (iii) 'Have a disaster plan in place' (11%); (iv) 'Have a hazard brochure or post your disaster evacuation plans and procedures in the room' (8%); (v) 'Be visible and available so guests will know you are in charge' (8%); (vi) 'Train your employees' (8%); (vii) 'Be prepared to help guests find emergency shelter' (6%); (viii) 'Recognize that transients are not familiar with either the area or the threat' (5%); and (ix) 'Be prepared to provide food and other emergency supplies' (5%) (adapted from Drabek, 1996a, pp. 294–297).

The final study focused on the employee perspective (Drabek, 1999). Interviews were completed with 406 employees of 118 firms following seven disasters: (i) Hurricane Felix (August 1995); (ii) Hurricane Fran (September 1996); (iii) flooding in Washoe County, Nevada (January 1997); (iv) flooding in Stanislaus County, California (January 1997); (v) flooding in Yuba and Sutter Counties, California (January 1997); (vi) flooding in Larimer County, Colorado (July 1997); and (vii) flooding in Logan County, Colorado (July 1997).

During their evacuation, some employees experienced acute work–family tensions. Multivariate analysis documented nine key social constraints, including having children living at home, being a racial or ethnic minority, having a history of prior evacuations and being employed by a disaster-relevant firm, such as a hotel that remained open to accommodate media personnel (see Drabek, 1999, pp. 168–171). Upon reflection, some (21%) perceived an improvement in morale because of the disaster experience, most (65%) reported 'no change', but a significant minority (15%) described severe adverse impacts (see Drabek, 1999, pp. 174–178). *Those employed by firms that had done little or no disaster preparedness were the ones who most commonly said that morale had deteriorated.* Similarly, multivariate analysis documented that those most dissatisfied with the responses of their management during the evacuation reflected eight key social constraints, including the absence of offers of assistance from their bosses, having a larger number of children and/or pets at home and never receiving any on-the-job disaster training (see Drabek, 1999, pp. 178–180).

What advice would employees offer? Questionnaire responses to an open-ended question revealed seven types of recommendations: (i) 'better communication' (34%); (ii) 'close earlier' (26%); (iii) 'provide employee assistance' (11%); (iv) 'do more preparednesss' (11%); (v) 'retain more staff to implement protective actions' (7%); (vi) 'establish return procedures' (7%); and (vii) 'provide pay for employee time off during such evacuations' (5%). (See Drabek, 1999, pp. 196–197.)

How could these ideas ever reach tourist managers or be implemented into their firms and communities? As these studies were being completed, the author found himself at a unique strategic implementation site.

The FEMA Higher Education Project

During the autumn of 1995, the author and a small group of other disaster researchers were invited to a workshop at the Emergency Management Institute located at the National Emergency Training Center in Emmitsburg, Maryland. The broad contours of a new initiative entitled 'The Higher Education Project' were outlined and numerous implementation strategies were discussed, including potential emergency management programme needs within colleges and universities, specific courses currently being offered, graduate education needs, and so forth. Under the guidance of the project director, Dr B. Wayne Blanchard, a series of small personal services contracts were designed and awarded for the preparation of 'Instructor Guides' that hopefully would facilitate the recruitment of a new faculty and implementation of new course offerings in emergency management. Exactly what would define such an 'Instructor Guide' (IG) remained unclear, but the process was viewed as a necessary first step. The group also recommended that FEMA should sponsor an annual conference to which all persons teaching emergency management courses, broadly defined, should be invited.

By the time of the first conference, June 1996, two IGs had been completed (Drabek, 1996b, c) and others were nearing completion, e.g. *Political and Policy Basis of Emergency Management* (Sylves, 1998). By 2003, the annual conference had grown in size and reflected the expanded scope of 'homeland security' programmes precipitated in part by terrorist attacks, e.g. the World Trade Center, the Pentagon and the related airplane crash near Shanksville, Pennsylvania (11 September 2001). In contrast to the five collegiate emergency management programmes that existed in 1995 when this project began, 96 were identified at the 2003 conference. Additionally about 100 more institutions were in the process of exploring related curricular expansions (Blanchard, 2003).

Each IG provides an example course syllabus and detailed notations for each class session (semester length). All class session units comprise a list of student objectives, recommended student readings and exercises, suggested professional background readings, and detailed lecture notes that include relevant examples, case studies, research studies, etc. These documents have been placed on the Internet (accessed 23 September 2003: www.training.fema.gov/emiweb/edu/completeCourses.asp). They may be *downloaded without cost*. Thirteen IGs are available, and additional courses are under development. Completed courses include: *The Social Dimensions of Disaster* (Drabek, 1996b); *Sociology of Disaster* (Drabek, 1996c); *The Political and Policy Basis of Emergency Management* (Sylves, 1998); *Research and Analysis Methods in Emergency Management* (Kincaid, 1998); *Business and Industry Crisis Management, Disaster Recovery, and Organizational Continuity* (Shaw, 1999); *Technology and Emergency Management* (Pine, 1999); *Public Administration and Emergency Management* (Waugh, 2000a); *Individual and Community Disaster Education* (Rottman, 2000); *Principles and Practice of Hazards Mitigation* (Brower and Bohl, 2000); *Terrorism and Emergency*

Management (Waugh, 2000b); *Emergency Management Principles and Application for Tourism, Hospitality, and Travel Management Industries* (Drabek and Gee, 2000); *Building Disaster Resilient Communities* (Burby, 2002); and *A Social Vulnerability Approach to Disasters* (Enarson *et al.*, 2003).

Within this context, discussions regarding the research recommendation that FEMA should build additional partnerships with tourism associations, including a relevant faculty, became focused on the IG series. These culminated with the eventual completion of a new faculty resource (Drabek and Gee, 2000).

A Faculty Resource

While conducting fieldwork on Hurricane Iniki, the author sought liaison assistance from a former University of Denver classmate, Dean Chuck Y. Gee, School of Travel Industry Management, University of Hawaii at Manoa. As discussions continued regarding an IG on tourism for a faculty in both emergency management programmes *and* schools of tourism, hospitality and travel management, the author proposed a collaborative venture. During 1998 and 1999, assisted by staff at our respective institutions, we designed a syllabus, selected student and faculty readings, and prepared the lecture notes. Finally, after an elaborate review process, reflecting input from academics, emergency managers, emergency officials and private sector tourism executives, the IG was posted on the Internet, i.e. *Emergency Management Principles and Application for Tourism, Hospitality, and Travel Management Industries* (Drabek and Gee, 2000).

The tourism IG (622 pages) is comprised of 42 units and an extensive bibliography. Following a 'course orientation' session, students are introduced to 'the big picture' through such modules as these: 'Overview of Disasters and Hazards in the USA Today', 'Overview of Disasters and Threats to Tourists' and 'Understanding All-hazards Emergency Management'. Behavioural research on disaster preparedness within tourist-related firms is then explored through units entitled: 'Behavioral Study of Managerial Responses to Disasters' and 'Customer Responses and Expectations During Disaster'. Aspects of an organizational crisis plan are then dissected through a focus on such topics as: 'Organizational Roles and Responsibilities', 'Operational Communications', 'Public Communications', 'Human Safety', 'Property Security' and 'Testing and Exercising'. Post-event activities are surveyed through units entitled: 'Innkeepers' Liability and Other Insurance Issues', 'Disaster Recovery and Restoring Operations' and 'Rebuilding the Destination Image'. Also included are a disaster simulation exercise and numerous specialized topics such as: 'The International Dimension: Issues Relating to Foreign Tourists', 'The Nature and Types of Political Threats' and 'Special Considerations for Transportation Disasters'.

Conclusion

Within the USA, there are approximately 300 university or college departments or programmes in tourism, hospitality or travel management. While certain topics, such as 'loss prevention', 'risk management' and 'security', are included in many of these curricula, emergency management principles, including the theoretical and research-based foundations, are not. Hopefully this faculty resource will challenge some to change. Hopefully it will facilitate their implementation of change. Unfortunately, the rapidly changing levels of risk for tourism managers and their customers may accelerate such change, as recent terrorist-based attacks on so-called 'soft targets' have demonstrated. The vulnerability has been exposed; the challenge is clear; the issue is not whether such curricular transformation will occur, but only *when*.

Acknowledgements

I wish to thank Ruth Ann Drabek for her work on this chapter.

References

Baker, E.J. (1979) Predicting response to hurricane warnings: a reanalysis of data from four studies. *Mass Emergencies* 4, 9–24.

Baker, E.J. (1991) Hurricane evacuation behaviour. *International Journal of Mass Emergencies and Disasters* 9, 287–310.

Barton, A.H. (1969) *Communities in Disaster: a Sociological Analysis of Collective Stress Situations.* Doubleday and Company, Inc., Garden City, New York.

Blanchard, B.W. (2003) *June 9–13 FEMA EM HiEd Project Activity Report.* Emergency Management Institute, Federal Emergency Management Agency, Emmitsburg, Maryland.

Brower, D.J. and Bohl, C.C. (2000) *Principles and Practice of Hazards Mitigation: Instructor Guide.* Emergency Management Institute, Federal Emergency Management Agency, Emmitsburg, Maryland.

Burby, R.J. (2002) *Building Disaster Resilient Communities: Instructor Guide.* Emergency Management Institute, Federal Emergency Management Agency, Emmitsburg, Maryland.

Chiu, A.N.L., Escalante, L.J., Mitchell, K.,

Perry, D.C., Schroeder, T.A. and Walton, T. (1983) *Hurricane Iwa, Hawaii, November 23, 1982.* National Academy of Sciences, Washington, DC.

Drabek, T.E. (1986) *Human System Responses to Disaster: an Inventory of Sociological Findings.* Springer-Verlag, New York.

Drabek, T.E. (1994) *Disaster Evacuation and the Tourist Industry.* Institute of Behavioral Science, University of Colorado, Boulder, Colorado.

Drabek, T.E. (1996a) *Disaster Evacuation Behavior: Tourists and Other Transients.* Institute of Behavioral Science, University of Colorado, Boulder, Colorado.

Drabek, T.E. (1996b) *The Social Dimensions of Disaster: Instructor Guide.* Emergency Management Institute, Federal Emergency Management Agency, Emmitsburg, Maryland.

Drabek, T.E. (1996c) *Sociology of Disaster: Instructor Guide.* Emergency Management Institute, Federal Emergency Management Agency, Emmitsburg, Maryland.

Drabek, T.E. (1999) *Disaster-induced Employee Evacuation.* Institute of

Behavioral Science, University of Colorado, Boulder, Colorado.

Drabek, T.E. (2000) Disaster evacuations: tourist-business managers rarely act as customers expect. *Cornell Hotel and Restaurant Administration Quarterly* 41 (4), 48–57.

Drabek, T.E. and Gee, C.Y. (2000) *Emergency Management Principles and Application for Tourism, Hospitality, and Travel Management Industries: Instructor Guide*. Emergency Management Institute, Federal Emergency Management Agency, Emmitsburg, Maryland.

Dynes, R.R. (1970) *Organized Behavior in Disaster*. Heath Lexington Books, Lexington, Massachusetts.

Enarson, E., Childers, C., Morrow, B.H., Thomas, D. and Wisner, B. (2003) *A Social Vulnerability Approach to Disasters: Instructor Guide*. Emergency Management Institute, Federal Emergency Management Agency, Emmitsburg, Maryland.

Geipel, R. (1991) *Long-term Consequences of Disasters: the Reconstruction of Friuli, Italy, in its International Context, 1976–1988*. Springer-Verlag, New York.

Kincaid, J.P. (1998) *Research and Analysis Methods in Emergency Management: Instructor Guide*. Emergency Management Institute, Federal Emergency Management Agency, Emmitsburg, Maryland.

Moore, H.E., Bates, F.L., Layman, M.V. and Parenton, V.J. (1963) *Before the Wind: a Study of Response to Hurricane Carla*. National Academy of Sciences, Washington, DC.

Murphy, P.E. and Bayley, R. (1989) Tourism and disaster planning. *Geographical Review* 79, 36–46.

Pine, J.C. (1999) *Technology and Emergency Management: Instructor Guide*. Emergency Management Institute, Federal Emergency Management Agency, Emmitsburg, Maryland.

Rottman, S.J. (2000) *Individual and Community Disaster Education Course: Instructor Guide*. Emergency Management Institute, Federal Emergency Management Agency, Emmitsburg, Maryland.

Shaw, G. (1999) *Business and Industry Crisis Management, Disaster Recovery, and Organizational Continuity: Instructor Guide*. Emergency Management Institute, Federal Emergency Management Agency, Emmitsburg, Maryland.

Sorensen, J.H., Vogt, B.M. and Mileti, D.S. (1987) *Evacuation: an Assessment of Planning and Research*. Oak Ridge National Laboratory, Oak Ridge, Tennessee.

Sylves, R.T. (1998) *Political and Policy Basis of Emergency Management: Instructor Guide*. Emergency Management Institute, Federal Emergency Management Agency, Emmitsburg, Maryland.

Taylor, J.B., Zurcher, L.A. and Key, W.H. (1970) *Tornado: a Community Responds to Disaster*. University of Washington Press, Seattle, Washington.

Waugh, W.L., Jr (2000a) *Public Administration and Emergency Management: Instructor Guide*. Emergency Management Institute, Federal Emergency Management Agency, Emmitsburg, Maryland.

Waugh, W.L., Jr (2000b) *Terrorism and Emergency Management: Instructor Guide*. Emergency Management Institute, Federal Emergency Management Agency, Emmitsburg, Maryland.

5 Aftermath of Crises and Disasters: Notes for an Impact Assessment Approach

PEDRO MOREIRA

Introduction

The beginning of the millennium was marked by a series of events that strongly affected the expectations of development of the tourism industry. With the increase of uncertainty, an intense search for answers began, and crisis management recently became a very important area of tourism research.

Tourism involves elements of uncertainty and unpredictability that have always been in a way part of its attraction. Distance travelling has always involved risks, but the difference now is that these risks are progressively more evident. The terrorist attacks in New York, USA on 11 September 2001 (9/11) and Bali, Indonesia 12 October 2002, and the severe acute respiratory syndrome (SARS) crisis in 2002–2003 are just some of the events that created this psychological link, driving the perception of the risks associated with travelling to a new dimension. These events changed the tourism industry worldwide and harmed the international image of specific destinations, leading to decreases in the flux of flights and tourist arrivals and, in domino effect, to crisis in tourism-related business operations.

Although crisis and disaster are, as will be discussed, different concepts, these share characteristics that allow the creation of a general model based on one of the most extreme forms of disaster to highlight key aspects of damage assessment applicable to crisis management and to more theory-oriented comparison studies.

The first part of this chapter presents a discussion of the definitions of crisis and disaster, introducing some of the criteria that allow the differentiation and the integration of both concepts. It is also proposed that earthquakes, being one of the most extreme forms of disaster, might be used to structure a general model of crisis and disaster assessment, and that definitions of that field, such as magnitude and intensity, might be important in the understanding of low probability and high consequence scenarios, and can be applied both to prevention and to crisis and disaster management. The second part of the chapter includes a model of crisis and disaster assessment and the original scales of the intensity and magnitude of earthquakes that inspired it. Like these scales, the model integrates a quantitative and a qualitative approach, preserving the value of the complementarity of tangible and intangible information. Finally, the last part discusses the potential of the model in the face of recent contributions in this field and its implications for crisis management and future research.

Crises and Disasters

Crises are periods of great uncertainty in which predictability and control are lost or severely diminished. These low probability and high impact situations (Weick, 1988; Pearson and Clair, 1998) are associated with critical changes and threats of destruction (Glaesser, 2003). A crisis is a situation in which there is a dominance of the internal origin of the initial events, while a disaster is defined as a situation where an external and unpredictable catastrophic change is associated with a low degree of control over the evolution of events (Faulkner, 2001). In both cases, the final consequences depend on the pre-crisis or pre-disaster vulnerabilities.

As Faulkner (2001) notes, although disasters are by definition low probability events, that does not mean that tourism destinations are immune to them. However, it is also understandable that the low probability or the inexistence in the recent past of specific disasters results in the underestimation of risk. Our knowledge about crises and disasters and our perceptions of risk emerge substantially from the analysis of past events, and the probability of occurrence attributed to events that are considered highly unlikely is in principle only expected to rise with the real occurrence of similar events. However, the past does not reveal all the possible sources of destruction. For example, a large-scale terrorist attack is now considered more likely than before the events of 9/11 (Prideaux, 2003; Prideaux *et al.*, 2003). The occurrence of the event itself altered the risk perception and transformed a highly improbable risk into a highly probable one. When an important crisis or disaster occurs, the risk perception changes and it becomes unviable to consider that specific event as an impossible or highly unlikely risk any more.

Now terrorism and epidemics are perceived to be more plausible, more real threats than before, a direct consequence of the recent events in the change of the risk mindframe. Emergency plans for crisis or disasters are designed under the same mindframe and therefore mostly directed to problems that are known and expected. To react to new threats, the development of the understanding of the nature of crises and disasters seems critical, as plans generally offer a script of response to past threats, but not to new, never faced ones (Mitroff and Alpaslan, 2003).

Justifying the resources involved in an emergency or contingency plan to deal with an event that has not yet occurred or that is considered highly unlikely to occur is, however, very difficult and even more so the more specific those plans are. One alternative approach is to create emergency plans that are applicable to a broader range of contingencies and designed to respond to common characteristics of different crises or disasters. After discussing the differences between the concepts, we will present some of these general characteristics and suggest that there are several aspects that can be measured to evaluate the extension of the immediate and delayed damage that is expected as a consequence of crisis and disaster situations.

Table 5.1 presents seven criteria that differentiate crises from disasters. The first criterion is the dominant origin of the initial events. Crises usually have an internal origin, related to the progressive development of vulnerabilities or to inadequate reactions to external changes. Among several typologies of crisis initiators in organizations, Mitroff and Alpaslan (2003) distinguish: (i) natural accidents, originated by non-human causes; (ii) normal accidents, originated by systems complexity (initially termed by Perrow, 1999); and (iii) abnormal accidents, originated by deliberate human action. Earthquakes, typhoons, storms and floods are included in the first category. The term 'normal accidents' is generally associated with highly sophisticated technology (e.g. power-generating systems such as nuclear or thermoelectric plants, dams, chemical factories, airplanes and air traffic control systems), in which the complexity of the interactions between the extraordinarily high number of factors increases the likelihood of occurrence of problems. The third category includes sabotage, terrorism and war. This typology supports two important aspects of crises and disasters: first, that there is a continuum between the internal or external dominant origin of a crisis, and, secondly, that there is the possibility of a sequential pattern of crises and disasters, i.e. crisis–disaster or disaster–crisis, also suggested by the Pearson and Clair (1998) array of organizational crises.

The second criterion, the frequency of occurrence, concerns the objective number of times that the event took place and influences the subjective perception of risk, since the more frequent and more recent and

Table 5.1. Crises versus disasters: differentiating criteria.

Differentiating criteria	Crises	Disasters
Dominant origin of the initial events	Internal	External
Frequency of occurrence	Higher	Lower
Events timeline	Prolonged	Brief
Forecast potential	Higher	Lower
Degree of control over the evolution of the events	Higher	Lower
Reaction time frame	Preceded by a period that allows decision and action	Immediately before or only after the initial events
Impacts and consequences	Lower	Higher

serious the previous occurrences, the higher will be the risk perception associated with that specific risk. Comparing the two concepts, disasters are generally considered less frequent than crises, although the risk perception should be higher for the former due to the severity of the consequences.

The third criterion is the timeline associated with the initial events. The time interval is often longer for crises than for disasters. Crises are extended in time, whilst disasters can generate extreme losses in moments.

A fourth difference between crises and disasters is the forecast potential, the possibility to anticipate or predict the events. One of the reasons why disasters produce such high losses is the low predictability, and the fact that some occurrences cannot even be anticipated. Even considering that there is order in the apparent chaos of disasters and admitting the regularity of catastrophic events, it is extraordinarily difficult to predict accurately the time and the place where they will occur. As crises develop over a longer period, there are generally more indicators of the evolution of the conditions, allowing a better anticipation and a more accurate prediction of the possible consequences.

The fifth criterion is the degree of control over the situation, the ability to react and reduce the losses. In the case of disasters, this degree of control is very restricted, low enough to justify an expression such as 'acts of God' that clearly reflects the human vulnerability to these events and the inability to neutralize its consequences. Crises, on the other hand, are situations in which there is a higher control and in which the final consequences are determined in a higher degree by decisions and actions. Furthermore, the effects of disasters are sometimes severe enough to restrict countermeasures since the existing resources that could make the difference have been destroyed or are inaccessible, debilitating the response capacity when it is most needed.

The sixth distinction between a crisis and a disaster is the reaction timeframe, less demanding in a crisis than in a disaster due to a longer events timeline and to the slower pace of the changes.

The final criterion of distinction between crises and disasters is the impact and the consequences of the events. The dimension of the consequences is higher in disasters than in crises and, in situations where a crisis degenerates into a disaster, this could be the only criterion supporting the recategorization of a given situation. While in a crisis the losses can be very high, a disaster presents, comparatively, catastrophic figures of destruction.

An emerging notion from these seven criteria is that each is defined by a continuum and not by the presence or the absence of a differentiating characteristic. The differentiation therefore relies on the proximity of the limits of the continuum, making it difficult to distinguish situations where the values of the criteria are positioned closer to the centre than to the limits of the range.

However, the fact that this set of criteria can be applicable both to crises and to disasters introduces the possibility of the integration of the concepts in a broader frame. Crises and disasters share a common nature:

both are characterized by sudden and unpredictable changes that challenge the ability to cope (Faulkner, 2001), and in both cases the intensity of the effects depends on the existing vulnerabilities to specific shocks. The term shock designates disrupting events or pre-crisis conditions (Prideaux *et al.*, 2003). Shocks can be defined as specific events, changes or developments of the current conditions to a turning point that creates or severely increases the response demands from the tourism industry and that are clear indicators of a future degradation of the status quo.

Shocks can initiate either crisis or disasters, depending on the specific combination of the characteristics of the events and of the position these assume over each criterion continuum. Moreover, the two situations might be sequential, as the deterioration of a crisis situation might produce a disaster, and an initial event characterized as a disaster can generate the conditions for the future emergence of a crisis. Finally, both crises and disasters are associated with conditions that support the integrated study of this area. Figure 5.1 presents these conditions or integrating elements.

Faulkner (2001) suggests the possibility of this integration, presenting a synthesis of the essential characteristics of crises and disasters, based on the works of Weiner and Kahn (1972), Fink (1986) and Keown-McMullan (1997). That synthesis included the following characteristics: (i) a triggering event, with an impact strong enough to challenge the survival of the present status quo; (ii) high threat, unpredictability, urgency and reduced time for decision making; (iii) a perception of inability to cope with the situation; (iv) a critical turning point, when decisive change is

Fig. 5.1. Crises and disasters: integrating elements. Disequilibrium between the demands of the situation and the response capacity. Impacts and consequences depend on the previous existence of vulnerability.

imminent; and (v) an evolution of the situation that is both dynamic and dominated by instability. These similarities between crises and disasters allow an integrated assessment model, capable of evaluating very different disruptive events that pose threats to the tourism industry. The possibility of designing a scale to evaluate and rank these events complements the shocks taxonomy presented by Prideaux *et al.* (2003), focusing on the impacts and consequences of these events rather than on their origin and predictability.

A general model based on the most extreme disasters can provide a means of assessing, comparing and ranking impacts on and consequences of different levels of severity. In the field of crisis and disaster management, such a model might support the development of general emergency plans applicable to a wider range of situations, leading to a higher efficiency in the allocation of resources. These plans might also be organized in a modular concept to offer a gradual increase in the level of response to increasingly demanding scenarios, preserving the effectiveness of the solutions. The model can also be applicable to research. The scale systematizes and synthesizes information to produce a final classification that can serve as a basis for comparative studies of different disruptive events and types of effects, in terms of both the objective and the subjective impacts of crises and disasters.

Earthquakes are among the most extreme disasters. The knowledge transference from this field opens up the possibility for the structuring of a framework of general application to low probability–high impact crises and disasters. In the following section, some concepts from earthquake assessment theory are presented, introducing the proposed general scale for crisis and disaster impact assessment.

Earthquakes: Concepts and Inputs to Crisis and Disaster Management

One of the characteristics of disruptive events is their power to disorganize, to initialize uncertainty from the moment they occur. The first impact is capable of creating the status of disorganization that Weick named 'cosmology episodes' (Weick, 1985) or *vù jadé* (Weick, 1993), as the opposite of the French expression *dejá vù*, leading individuals and organizations to a completely new setting in which their previous references are irrelevant or useless, to an edge of collapse or structural change that severely constrains their ability to make the correct decisions needed to face the events.

It is our argument that the first impact of severe crises and disasters is strong enough to create this type of status of disorganization. Following the first wave of information about casualties and material losses, it will first affect the apprehension and analysis of reality, then disrupt all the patterns of behaviour, and finally blur the foresight of future scenarios, disturbing the capability to generate plans or scripts for future action.

While surely important and dramatic, the first impacts are only the most visible part of the crisis. Frequently, the initial events do not allow time for reaction, and nothing much can be done to minimize the first damage on the most vulnerable points if these were beyond the reach of forecasting and prevention. The secondary effects, although less visible immediately, as they are obscured by the initial losses, should not be neglected from the first moments due to their crucial influence in the recovery from the crisis.

Crisis secondary effects are comparable with earthquake shock waves, with a time delay after the original events and long-range impacts, extending their influence to distant sites. As in the case of earthquakes, the most intense and immediate damage is located in the epicentre, but the total extension of the impacts spreads to a much wider area.

Navendra Aggarwal, an economics correspondent for *The Straits Times* writing on 14 October, the Monday after the Bali nightclub explosions, immediately stated that according to businessmen and analysts the attack would increase the downward pressure on the economy, not referring then to the Balinese or Indonesian economies, but to that of Singapore. In these analysts' opinion, the possibility of additional attacks in the region would affect the foreign investment in all of South East Asia.

The problem of studying crises and disasters is not so much to identify the epicentre, often sadly clear, but to identify the total range of consequences both in time and in space. The delayed effect of crises and disasters can be as powerful as the effect of a tsunami, a giant earthquake-generated ocean wave. In 1960, one of these waves caused by the Chile earthquake (9.6 on the Richter Scale) travelled 17,000 km across the Pacific Ocean and, 22 h after leaving Chile, arrived at Japan's coastline with 10-foot waves causing 200 deaths.[1] More recently, in December 2004, an undersea earthquake (Richter magnitude 9.0) off the northwestern coast of Sumatra and the tsunami that followed it affected several countries in Asia and Africa, causing catastrophic destruction and over 280,000 deaths.[2] This tsunami later crossed the Pacific and the Atlantic and was recorded as far as New Zealand and the east and west coasts of North and South America.[3] It can be argued that, like tsunamis, in the present global economy in which the media provide a fast means to transport information (New York's 9/11 was broadcast live; right after the Bali attacks there were images and a full coverage of the blasts site on international TV channels; the SARS crisis received TV attention for months), events that take place in any part of the world can and do influence business and specifically tourism-related business worldwide, even in destinations that are extremely distant from the site where the original events occurred.

Besides the direct and immediate effects of disruptive events, the delayed and indirect effects perhaps have a stronger economic impact on tourism. The events of 9/11 struck an already vulnerable sector, generating an airlines' crisis by generally decreasing air travelling, and the Bali explosions and the SARS crisis caused a fall in arrivals to East Asian destinations, when the economies were looking at tourism as a way to recover from the Asian financial crisis.

By establishing a parallel with the Richter and Mercalli earthquake scales, we will try to suggest some possible ways of assessing the severity of crises and disasters, considering both the immediate–direct and the delayed–indirect effects of disrupting events or shocks. The concepts of magnitude and intensity, comprising, respectively, the quantitative and more objective measures in the case of the Richter Scale, and the qualitative and more subjective evaluation in the case of the Mercalli Scale, are the basis of the evaluation of the severity of an earthquake. The severity of a crisis or of a disaster can be evaluated in a similar way, combining the analysis of the magnitude and intensity of the phenomenon. Shedlock and Pakiser (1994) distinguished magnitude (usually assessed by the Richter Scale), defined as a measure of amplitude of the seismic waves, from intensity (expressed on the modified Mercalli Scale), defined as a subjective measure describing the strength of the shock felt at a specific location.

In the case of earthquakes, the magnitude is calculated from the instrument readings during the event, while the intensity is evaluated afterwards based on the analysis of witness reports and site inspections. The tragic numbers affected by the Kobe earthquake of 1995 (7.2 on the Richter Scale) in Japan offer supporting evidence for the important weight of the vulnerabilities in the final consequences of a crisis or disaster. Over 50% of the more than 6000 fatalities were elderly citizens who lived in the districts with antiquated urban infrastructures and high population density (Nakamura, 2000). Another major earthquake of comparable magnitude (7.5 on the Richter Scale) in the same year killed two-thirds of the residents of the Sakhalin Island in Russia (nearly 2000 dead), but the low population density of the most affected areas resulted in a much lower number of casualties, although evident vulnerabilities, such as the age of the buildings, the outdated or inadequate construction technology and the low quality of the construction materials, existed (Porfiriev, 1996). A similar magnitude (7.6 on the Richter Scale) was registered in the 1999 earthquake in Taiwan. However, in this case, the population density was higher and the final numbers of the disaster indicate 2400 dead and 100,000 homeless, showing the large extension of the devastating effects of the earthquake (Huan *et al.*, 2004). A lower magnitude earthquake (6.7 on the Ritcher Scale), occurred in 1994 in Northridge, USA, causing 57 fatalities. However, the material damage due to the localization of the epicentre in a heavily urbanized area made it, at that time, the most costly disaster in the history of the USA (Tierney, 1997).

As in the case of earthquakes, in a crisis or disaster situation, a large magnitude does not necessarily determine a large intensity, as the intensity depends essentially on the vulnerability of the site. Thus, the evaluation of the severity of crises and disasters should be dual, relying on both indicators. The magnitude of a crisis or disaster can be extracted from the first effects of destruction (type of original event, casualties, and first evaluations of material damage and estimations of economic losses) shortly after the initial events, while the intensity evaluation depends on a deeper analysis that, understandably, requires more time but provides more extensive and complete information.

Aftermath of Crises and Disasters: an Impact Assessment Model

The aftermath of a crisis or disaster is determined by the initial catastrophic events and by the conditions of vulnerability which exist in the affected site. The initial events start a process or sequence that, fostered or stalled by the target site's own vulnerabilities, will finally produce the consequences of the crisis or disaster. The site vulnerabilities therefore play a moderating role in the intensity of the effects. In a crisis or disaster, as happens specifically with earthquakes, the outcomes for the same type or magnitude of the initial events can be very different in the end; better or worse depending on if the site is vulnerable or if it is strong enough to cope with the demanding scenario.

The assessment of the severity of crisis and disaster impacts combines the magnitude, expressing the force of the initial events, and the intensity, which captures the total extension of the damage, including the delayed effects and the long-range impacts.

Richter's idea of naming the concept of magnitude came from his amateur interest in astronomy (Spall, 1980). In astronomy, the term magnitude is used to measure the brightness of a star. In seismology, the magnitude of an earthquake is given by the amplitude of the seismic waves (Shedlock and Pakiser, 1994) recorded by the seismographs, therefore focusing on the initializing cause of the intensity effects that are evaluated by the Mercalli Scale. The modified Mercalli Scale (the original scale was created in 1902 and then modified in 1931) is the generally accepted intensity measure for earthquakes, and consists of 12 progressive levels assigned a Roman numeral from I to XII, from low intensity to high intensity. According to Bolt (1993), the methodology to assess the intensity of an earthquake is simple, consisting of: (i) assigning a numeral at each location according to the descriptions of the effects; (ii) contouring the zones of similar effect; (iii) assuming the location to occur near the region of maximum intensity; and (iv) characterizing the earthquake by the largest Roman numeral found.

The advantage of this scale is that it can be used even if magnitude data from seismographs are not available. On the other hand, one disadvantage of the method is that, because the scale focuses essentially on the effects, the vulnerability variation of the local conditions may bias the understanding of the strength of the earthquake if it is only inferred from the effects and not from the causes, which are associated with the Richter Scale of magnitude. However, in the case of crises and disasters, the first events generally have a high visibility, so the magnitude and intensity can be analysed together, providing a way to double-check the information available and to extract better conclusions from it.

As a reference, Table 5.2 presents the earthquakes' severity magnitude and intensity scales.

Table 5.2. Earthquake severity: magnitude and intensity scales.

Magnitude level		Intensity level	
Richter Scale	Expected damage	Mercalli Scale	Description of effects
		I	Not felt except by a very few under especially favourable conditions. Machines can record it.
		II	Felt only by a few persons at rest, especially on the upper floors of buildings. Suspended objects may swing.
		III	Felt quite noticeably by persons indoors. Vibrations similar to the passing of a truck. Many people do not recognize it as an earthquake.
4	This magnitude earthquake is widely felt and is strong enough to crack plaster.	IV	Felt indoors by many, outdoors by a few during the day. Dishes, windows, doors disturbed. Standing cars rock noticeably.
		V	Felt by nearly everyone. Small objects will fall over and doors will swing. Pendulum clocks may stop.
5	A strong vibration shakes the earth, damaging chimneys and weak buildings.	VI	Felt by everyone, many frightened, some people run outside in fright. Some heavy furniture moves, fallen plaster. Damage slight.
6	Strong enough to badly damage average buildings.	VII	People find it difficult to stand. Furniture breaks, bricks fall, plaster cracks. Damage slight in specially designed structures, slight to moderate in well-built ordinary structures, considerable in poorly built or badly designed structures.
7	Strong enough to destroy even well-built structures.	VIII	Difficult to drive. Buildings, walls chimneys and monuments collapse. Damage slight in specially designed structures, considerable in ordinary substantial buildings, great in poorly built structures.
8	Even special, earthquake-resistant buildings will be badly damaged.	IX	General panic, people and animals running in confusion. Building foundations are damaged and underground pipes crack. Damage considerable in specially designed structures, great in substantial buildings, with partial collapse.
		X	Brick, wooden and frame buildings will collapse. Rails are bent.
		XI	The ground shifts so much that railroad lines are distorted. Underground pipes are destroyed and highways cut. Fissures appear on the ground. Few, if any structures remain standing. Bridges destroyed.
9	There is widespread destruction.	XII	Damage total. Lines of sight and level are distorted. Objects are made airborne, rivers are altered, and large fissures appear.

Adapted from US Geological Survey http://gldsss7.cr.usgs.gov/neis/general/handouts/mag_vs_int.htmal, retrieved 22 November 2002; and ThinkQuest 2000 http://library.thinkquest.org/C003603/english/ earthquakes/earthquakestrength.shtml, retrieved 14 November 2002.

There is not a true correspondence between the scales once the intensity varies according to the vulnerability of the affected area. An earthquake can then have several intensity values, which will be higher as the design and quality of the construction structures decrease, or lower as the distance to the epicentre decreases. The correspondence is therefore presented only for the readers' reference of the possible results according to the earthquake machine-recorded magnitude.

The Richter Scale of magnitude is a logarithmic progression with no top limit, capable of evaluating any earthquake, an objective value calculated from the readings of machine-recorded variations. The Mercalli Scale of intensity is based on human observation, and therefore is subjective, but produces more complete information, with a higher sensitivity to the vulnerability variations, providing an immediate map of the critical zones where the higher risk is expected and immediate response is required.

Applying the analogy, the following quantitative indicators are considered relevant to the evaluation of the magnitude of crises and disasters affecting tourism: the number and seriousness of casualties; material losses; impact on major infrastructures; evolution of the number of arrivals and occupancy rates; general economic effects; and specific effects on the tourism industry. The qualitative indicators measuring the intensity analyse the more subjective aspects of the destination's response capacity, image evolution and perception of the risk. Table 5.3 shows the suggested magnitude and intensity general scale of crises and disasters.

The proposed framework to assess the severity of crises and disasters can serve at least three major functions: (i) rapidly to evaluate the situation and therefore assist decision makers in the preparation of effective responses to it; (ii) to highlight general aspects of crisis and disaster scenarios that should be considered in emergency plans; and (iii) to offer an initial theoretical model able to support future empirical research, allowing comparisons between different types of crises and disasters and their impacts on tourism. A rapid diagnostic assessment of the situation increases the response power and reduces further losses. Regarding the Sakhalin earthquake, Porfiriev (1996, p. 226) concluded the following: 'the substantial delay in estimating casualties and losses and in conducting active rescue operations decreased their efficiency, leading to additional casualties.' In the field of prevention, the model points to the advantages of general emergency plans that, whilst not fully adapted to any specific crisis or disaster, provide a basis for an effective response to the shared effects of very different scenarios. This implies a modular design of the crisis and disaster emergency plans, combining a general platform capable of responding to a wide range of events with additional modules directed to specific crises or disasters. Finally, the model can eventually offer some insights into crisis and disaster general theory from the application of concepts from a specific field of knowledge. Such insights might stimulate further research and extend the research focus from the short-term to the long-term consequences and from the local to the long-range effects, thus contributing to a wider comprehension of the implications of crises and disasters on the evolution of tourism.

Conclusions

Even in a phenomenon so difficult to predict as an earthquake, improvements have been made in estimating the locations and

Table 5.3. Impact of crises and disasters: a general scale of magnitude and intensity.

Magnitude level	Quantitative data	Intensity level	Qualitative data
Level 1	Restricted number of death casualties, general pattern of minor injuries. Reduced material losses. No major infrastructure affected. Arrivals and occupancy figures remain unchanged or slightly decrease. Economy is not significantly affected. Tourism related-prices unaltered or slightly decreased.	Level I	Some local discomfort and apprehension concerning the future but normal activities are resumed almost immediately after the crisis or disaster. Infrastructures and public services have capacity to deal with the situation. Reduced national and international media interest in the following days. Risk of similar events or replicas is considered low by the population and the travellers.
Level 2	Large number of death casualties and injuries, both minor and severe. Significant material losses. Major infrastructures affected. Arrivals and occupancy figures drop. Economic effects are felt but still considered to be restricted to the short term. Tourism-related prices suffer a strong decrease, and promotion packages. proliferate.	Level II	Strong local apprehension concerning the future and delay in resuming normal activities after the crisis or disaster. Infrastructures and public services face episodic response capacity overloads but are still able to respond to the situation after some adaptations. Extensive national and international media interest in the following days. Risk of further replicas is considered high by the population and the travellers. Negative effects in the destination image. Some travelling warnings are issued to the specific destination.
Level 3	Massive number of death casualties, general pattern of severe injuries. Extensive material losses. Critical infrastructures affected. Arrivals and occupancy figures fall to record levels. Economic effects are undeniable and expected to endure in the long term. Tourism is submersed in a deep crisis.	Level III	Generalized fear concerning the future, panic episodes, radical change of behaviour patterns and daily activities. Infrastructures and public services are not prepared to answer to the magnitude of the crisis, facing a constant overload. Extensive national and international media interest in the following weeks. Risk is considered very high and even stronger replicas are considered to be imminent by the population and the travellers. Embassies and foreign companies under special security measures or repatriating personnel. Travelling warnings generalize worldwide issued by several countries and international organizations.

probabilities of occurrence of damaging earthquakes, identifying sites of great hazard and designing stronger structures that could offer a better response to the worse effects (Sheldlock and Pakiser, 1994). Charles Richter, the creator of the Richter Scale for evaluating the magnitude of earthquakes, said in an interview given to Henri Spall of the US Geological

Survey (Spall, 1980, p. 3), that 'most loss of life and property has been due to the collapse of antiquated and unsafe structures'. In the field of tourism, as in the case of earthquakes, the destinations or organizations that are not prepared to resist or react to a crisis or disaster may not survive the first impact. However, in the same way that structures can be built with characteristics that present higher resistance to earthquakes, organizations can also be designed and managed to enhance their capacity to face and cope with disruptive events.

In a way, crises and disasters are by definition unpredictable, and our limited forecasting capability does not allow the design of too specific response plans. The reaction to crises and disasters cannot be totally planned, and a stronger alternative to a multiplicity of specific emergency plans may be the development of general plans that can be combined with modules that are more specific.

The possibility of measuring and classifying crises and disasters offers an instrument to organize and synthesize the information available and suggests the design of progressive plans targeting different levels of crises and disasters, not specifically directed to the nature of the initial events but organized in terms of the present and future impacts. Such an approach rationalizes the allocation of resources and provides a powerful advantage because, due to its focus on the common characteristics of different crises and disasters, more than preparing destinations or organizations to face known or expected events, can enhance the promptness of response to unknown or unexpected scenarios.

Tourism is a demand-driven industry (McKercher, 1999). Crises and disasters determine strong fluctuations in the tourism demand, and it seems important to understand better how. Tierney (1997) called attention to the small number of studies analysing disaster impacts on business sectors, and Faulkner and Vikulov (2001) noted that the study of crises and disasters lacks systematic analysis of information, producing fragmented research, whilst a reliable understanding of these phenomena is still missing. It was our initial purpose to gather some notes on crises and disasters and to organize these into a general model applicable to very different scenarios, contributing to that understanding.

A model inspired by extreme natural disasters can be applicable to the fields of crisis and disaster management and research. The measurement and categorization possibilities of the model can add value to comparative studies of the tourism impacts of crises and disasters originating from very different events, and general reaction plans can be designed based on the common effects expected.

This perspective might also open up the possibility for the confluence of knowledge from different fields. Further research is still needed to extract value from this initial framework. Empirical studies comparing the overall severity of crises and disasters with the influence of each one of the parameters of the magnitude and intensity scales would contribute to improving the internal consistency of the model. Pizam and Fleisher (2002) found that the frequency of terrorist attacks had a stronger influence on the decline in tourism demand than did the severity of those attacks. It is possible to extend this line of research to other types of crises and disasters, comparing the level of severity of the impacts (ranked by the levels of magnitude or intensity) and the frequency of the disrupting events, as determinants of the fluctuation of objective tourism indicators such as the arrivals or the occupancy rates.

The impacts of crises and disasters can be severe enough to introduce a radical change in the tourism equation of a city, a country or even worldwide. The effects can extend to large geographic zones and persist over long periods. The importance of this area is undeniable, and further research is crucial to enhance the comprehension of the implications of these phenomena.

Notes

[1] Gerard Fryer, Hawaii Institute of Geophysics and Planetology, University of Hawaii, http://www.soest.hawaii.edu/GG/ASK/chile-tsunami.html (retrieved 27 December 2002). University of Washington, Geophysics Department, http://www.ess.washington.edu/tsunami/general/physics/characteristics.html (retrieved 22 November 2002).

[2] USA Geological Survey, http://earthquake.usgs.gov/regional/world/byyear.php (retrieved 4 July 2006).

[3] USA Geological Survey, http://earthquake.usgs.gov/eqcenter/eqnews/2004/usslav/#summary (retrieved 4 July 2006).

References

Bolt, B. (1993) Earthquakes – Newly Revised and Expanded. Freeman. http://www. eas.slu.edu/Earthquake_Center/mercalli.html (accessed 22 October 2002)

Faulkner, B. (2001) Towards a framework for tourism disaster management. *Tourism Management* 22, 135–147.

Faulkner, B. and Vikulov, S. (2001) Katherine, washed out one day, back on track on the next: a post-mortem of a tourism disaster. *Tourism Management* 22, 331–344.

Fink, S. (1986) *Crisis Management.* American Association of Management, New York.

Glaesser, D. (2003) *Crisis Management in the Tourism Industry.* Butterworth-Heinemann, Oxford.

Huan, T., Beaman, J. and Shelby, L. (2004) No-escape natural disaster: mitigating impacts on tourism. *Annals of Tourism Research* 31, 255–273.

Keown-McMullan, C. (1997) Crisis: when does a molehill become a mountain? *Disaster Prevention and Management* 4 (2), 20–37.

McKercher, B. (1999) A chaos approach to tourism. *Tourism Management* 20, 425–434.

Mitroff, I. and Alpasan, M. (2003) Preparing for evil. *Harvard Business Review* April, pp. 109–115.

Nakamura, A. (2000) The need and development of crisis management in Japan's public administration: lessons from the Kobe earthquake. *Journal of Contingencies and Crisis Management* 8, 23–29.

Pearson, C. and Clair, J. (1998) Reframing crisis management. *Academy of Management Review* 23, 59–76.

Perrow, C. (1999) *Normal Accidents: Living with High-risk Technologies.* Princeton University Press, Princeton, New Jersey.

Pizam, A. and Fleischer, A. (2002) Severity

versus frequency of acts of terrorism: which has a larger impact on tourism demand? *Journal of Travel Research* 40, 337–339.

Porfiriev, B. (1996) Social aftermath and organizational response to a major disaster: the case of the 1999 Sakhalin earthquake in Russia. *Journal of Contingencies and Crisis Management* 4, 218–227.

Prideaux, B. (2003) The need to use disaster planning frameworks to respond to major tourism disasters: analysis of Australia's response to tourism disasters in 2001. *Journal of Travel and Tourism Marketing* 15, 281–298.

Prideaux, B., Laws, E. and Faulkner, B. (2003) Events in Indonesia: exploring the limits to formal tourism trends forecasting methods in complex crisis situations. *Tourism Management* 24, 475–487.

Sheldlock, K. and Pakiser, L. (1994) *Earthquakes* (Electronic version). US Geological Survey, Denver, Colorado.

Spall, H. (1980) Charles F. Richter – an interview. *Earthquake Information Bulletin*, 12 (1). Retrieved 15 November 2002, from http://neics.usgs.gov/neis/seismology/people/int_richter.html

Tierney, K. (1997) Business impacts of the Northridge earthquake. *Journal of Contingencies and Crisis Management* 5 (2), 87–97.

Weick, K. (1985) Cosmos vs. chaos: sense and nonsense in electronic contexts. *Organizational Dynamics* 14 (Autumn), 50–64.

Weick, K. (1988) Enacted sensemaking in crisis situations. *Journal of Management Studies* 25, 305–317.

Weick, K. (1993) The collapse of sensemaking in organizations: the Mann Gulch disaster. *Administrative Science Quarterly* 38, 628–652.

Weiner, A. and Kahn, H. (1972) Crisis and arms control. In: Hermann, C.F. (ed.) *International Crises: Insights from Behaviour Research*. Free Press, New York, p. 21.

6 Western and Eastern Approaches to Crisis Management for Global Tourism: Some Differences

PETER SCHMIDT AND MIKE BERRELL

Introduction

Thinking critically beyond conventional notions of crisis management (CM) was an idea to emerge from a meeting of an expert focus group to discuss issues in CM generally. The focus group was convened during the mid-1990s to uncover the main currents of thought in CM (Schmidt, 1995). Developing new ideas about CM has significant implications for the global tourism industry. Today, an assessment of events such as the terrorist attack on New York's World Trade Center on 11 September 2001 (9/11), the South East Asia tsunami of 26 December 2004, and the 2001 Interlaken canyoning disaster in Austria reinforce the need for effective CM in the tourism industry. Today, the stakeholders of global tourism must be fully cognizant of best practice in the management of risk in their industry (cf. Smits and Ezzat, 2003). The potential social, economic and political impact of natural as well as human-made disasters on global tourism planning suggests that the pursuit of cutting-edge CM strategies may be a source of competitive advantage for organizations involved in the tourism industry.

The notion of global tourism necessarily involves thinking about national cultures. Today, the principles and practices associated with determining the influence of national culture on human behaviour are now at a post-theory stage, i.e. as a field of study, this area is so well developed, albeit from a late start, that its principles and practices hardly need in-depth defence (cf. Kluckhohn and Strodtbeck, 1961; Hall, 1976; Adler, 1983; Trompenaars, 1993; Deresky, 2000; Lane et al., 2000; Gannon and Newman, 2002; Trompenaars and Hampden-Turner, 2004). Some 40 years of scholarship in the field has produced a number of definitive works, which describe the multitude of cultural influences on the behaviour of people. Subsequently, this literature allows us to offer conjectures about how different groups in global tourism might react in difficult circumstances. For the sake of brevity, the generic influences of national culture on behaviour are set out below. However, this abbreviated overview should not lessen the significant intellectual complexity of this field of study. The literature cited above suggests that national cultures outwardly vary across several dimensions and, furthermore, such differences result in unique forms of behaviour. While some behaviour arises from conscious motivation, other behaviour has more deeply embedded motivation.

For example, while a Western country such as Australia is a low context society, a country such as Malaysia is a high context one. Differences in thinking by each cultural group about CM in global tourism can be considerable. The wider external environment influences the behaviour of members of high context cultures, where the value of long-term relationships and dealing with insiders as well as the specifics of a situation and implicit forms of knowledge all cast their influence. In contrast, behaviour in low context cultures is motivated more by universal principles, short-term relationships, people external to the in-group and explicit forms of knowledge (Hall, 1976; Adler, 2002). Kluckhohn and Strodtbeck (1961) also identify differences in people's basic orientation to interpersonal and environmental relationships, their modes of activity, and understanding of temporal matters. In addition, members of low and high context cultures think differently about causality, space and cosmology (Adler, 2002). Geert Hofstede (1994) also describes a framework that accounts for the influence of national culture on how people might react and respond to crises in global tourism. The subtitle of this popular text, 'software of the mind', indicates the deep-seated nature of culture's influence and its capacity unconsciously to programme behaviour. In particular, his ideas that some cultures accept quite large differentials in the distribution of power within organizations, that some groups have a low tolerance for uncertainty and that others are status-bound in their social interactions help explain the responses of people to stressful situations in global tourism.

There is a myriad of examples in the literature on how one's national culture influences and shapes responses to circumstance, from attitudes to law (Berrell and Wrathall, 2003) to behaviour in the workplace (Berrell *et al.*, 2001). In the context of global tourism and CM, the literature suggests that typical Western responses to a crisis would be rooted in rational approaches underpinned by universal ideas (cf. Turner and Pigeon, 1997; Adler, 2002). The idea that discontinuity can be avoided, or at least taken into account by rational practices, is a principal driver of best-practice CM in the West. However, in some Eastern countries, the literature suggests that the responses of people to a crisis will be subtly affected by differences in the prevailing cultural architecture. In this light, the influence of Western CM practices on Eastern approaches to managing a crisis remains problematic. For example, the cultural architecture supporting some nations may predispose their particularistic practitioners of CM to adopt more abrogating stances compared with those adopted by their counterparts in the West when faced with a crisis. Against this background, this chapter briefly sketches the evolution of approaches to CM in the West and mounts a discussion of the extent to which responses to a crisis are determined or at least substantially shaped by one's national culture. In the context of the expanding global tourism industry, the issue of the cultural architecture of CM cannot be ignored.

Crisis Management in the West

Several spectacular blunders as well as some notable achievements influenced the development of CM as a discrete management practice in the West, especially since the early 1980s. For example, the Tylenol drug crisis of 1983 was a significant influence (Murray and Shohen, 1992). The success achieved by Johnson and Johnson in handling the crisis legitimized the notion that CM was synonymous with public relations damage control. In recent times, however, the public relations function of CM is viewed as only one component in a holistic process (Jeynes, 2002). The public relations component is now appropriately referred to as crisis communication (CC). Nevertheless, even this seemingly neutral view of CC runs the risk of being interpreted as just another after-the-fact spin-doctoring of an event – consequently, it is partially discredited by Mitroff and Anagnos (2001). Communication in CM is far more than managers dealing with a sometimes hostile media. More generally, CM in global tourism now encompasses all stakeholders as well as members of the global society (Fearn-Banks, 1996; Burnett, 1998; Sapriel, 2003). Tourists, operators, governments and the wider society all have a stake in CM in global tourism. The considerable fallout from events such as 9/11 or the South East Asian tsunami of 2004 reinforces this view. In recognition of the diversity of stakeholders, even the definition of CC – the specialist communication component of CM – has been broadened to encompass all stakeholders (Jeynes, 2002).

Pearson and Clair's (1998) definition of a crisis is useful not only because it has wide acceptance but also because it emphasizes the need for timely action. Expanding Pearson and Clair's definition, a crisis in global tourism is a 'low probability, high impact event' that threatens the viability of tourism and its stakeholders, either directly or indirectly. While determining the cause of a crisis may be problematic and time consuming, resolution must be swift and decisive. Accordingly, taxonomies of crisis types were developed to handle high impact events. These taxonomies have been expanded from the nine described by Meyers (1986) now to include Pearson and Clair's (1998) 27 and Rike's (2003) 35 categories. Classification of a particular crisis within a taxonomy is necessary in order to prescribe the actions required to reduce the impact of an event (Meyers, 1986; cf. Meyers and Holusha, 1986). Such prescribed actions, however, need to be well documented. Traditionally, such documentation has been paper bound.

In 2002, Peter Schmidt (2002a) advanced the field of CM by suggesting that a fuzzy logic classification scheme might now be appropriate given that a particular crisis can exhibit features common to several categories. The conventional approach to CM has been to identify the type of crisis and build a crisis classification scheme or taxonomy. Using the particular classification, the appropriate section of the most up-to-date version of the crisis manual is consulted. This manual sets out the pre-defined actions necessary for responding to the crisis. However, what if an event fits several crisis categories? Furthermore, what is the result when a crisis team fails to recognize these shared elements and responds only to a single aspect of the crisis? Recent events in Thailand at Surat Thani, the nearest mainland city to the international global tourist destination of Koh Samui, saw emergency response teams cope with the complexities of several crises. A plane crash in the 1990s triggered the conventional (pre-determined) emergency response for dealing with accidents of this type. In this CM scenario, the baggage collection area in the airport's arrival hall provided the most convenient air-conditioned storage for the bodies of the victims of the accident. The crisis response team unfortunately failed to recognize that the crisis also had within it the seeds of a tourism crisis, even a health crisis that equally needed to be addressed. The aftermath of a recent boating accident at Koh Samui also saw a parade of body bags pass directly by recently arrived tourists queuing to board another vessel. The global tourism aspect of these disasters seems to have been either forgotten or ignored.

The fuzzy classification taxonomy proposed by Schmidt (2002a) categorizes 'low probability, high impact events' based on an event's membership of the various classes of crises. In this system, the Thailand plane crash would have been interpreted as a multicategory crisis. Fuzzy logic classifications are useful in such circumstances because, as dynamic, computer-generated processes, they can be guided by a question and answer approach. Responses depend on the dynamic fuzzy logic classification in which the crisis is placed. The response takes the form of a heuristic, which suggests the appropriate actions based on the input of relevant and contingent information. As such, the heuristic, which is effectively a sophisticated *e*-check list, does not require a pre-defined plan of action. Consequently, the problem of updating hard copy manuals is significantly reduced and, in many cases, abolished. The heuristic itself becomes the essential component of CM; it is a 'living document'.

The seeds of CM are located in emergency response planning, which is appropriate to predicting events that include fires, storms and floods. In the business world, business continuity planning is used to ensure continuity through periods of crisis such as computer downtime. Nevertheless, the distinction between CM and contingency planning per se is clearly drawn by Loosemore (1998), who suggests that crises are unexpected events for which no contingency plans are readily available. Temple (2003) also highlights the impossibility of predicting all crises and subsequently points to the difficulty of having suitable contingency plans at hand for low probability events. Rather than directing resources toward developing a contingency plan for each conceivable crisis, the focus has now shifted towards developing a general capability to cope with whatever crisis may arise. This can include actions such as developing 'crisis preparedness' (Mitroff, 1988; Mitroff et al., 1989; Pearson and Mitroff, 1993) or ensuring stakeholders have the potential to respond appropriately to a crisis through 'behavioural readiness' (Smits and Ezzat, 2003). Abandoning the task of developing specific contingency plans for each possible crisis does not exclude the need to carry out specific 'vulnerability audits' or 'risk mapping' exercises (Sapriel, 2003) as part of building crisis preparedness. Nevertheless, that fact that Thailand did not have a tsunami warning system in place in December 2004, even though this strategy in risk management had been mooted previously, suggests that vulnerability audits and the like must be adequately resourced after risks are identified.

Reflecting on the attributes of a learning organization (Senge, 1994) suggests that CM would also benefit from a post-crisis review period. Mitroff and Anagnos (2001) advocate this position and suggest that any review be undertaken on a 'no fault basis'. However, Vaughan (1990) cautions against the clarity with which mistakes are seen in hindsight. He cites the first Challenger disaster as an example of this clarity. In hindsight, it was relatively easy to ask why the mistakes were not detected in a timely fashion. Thinking of this type can result in apportioning blame, which interferes with organizational learning. Mindful of this, the report of the Columbia Accident Investigation Board (2003) highlighted the organizational causes of the accident. These faults, which had remained undetected within the organization, include problems with gaps in organizational learning and the role of corporate culture. These aspects of the organization needed to be rectified if future accidents are to be avoided. The findings of the 9/11 Commission also acknowledge the role of hindsight in CM (National Commission on Terrorist Attacks upon the USA, 2004). Unfortunately, although hindsight revealed that intelligence existed in 1995 about the possibility of attacks of this type, this intelligence was not communicated effectively (cf. Monk, 2001).

The tenets of modern approaches to CM have also been forged into a process model informed by the principles of strategic management (Nunamaker et al., 1989; Preble, 1997; Pearson and Clair, 1998; Jeynes, 2002; Schmidt, 2002a, b). The shift in approach to CM outlined above constitutes one aspect of the basic story of CM in the West. However, to what extent are the principles and practices of CM in the West applicable to an emerging economy in South East Asia such as Malaysia? Moreover, given that Malaysia relies on global tourism as a significant export earner, the answer to this question is of some consequence. The strategic nature of CM in Malaysia prompted the recent investigation of CM reported here.

The Crisis Management Approach In Malaysia

The discussion of CM in Malaysia below, which provides an example of approaches to CM in a non-Western context, was derived from data gathered using an adaptation of a 2002 questionnaire of the American

Management Association (AMA). The opinions of a variety of Malaysian managers were tapped using the reworked AMA questionnaire in an Internet-administered survey focusing on 1000 public companies listed on the Kuala Lumpur Stock Exchange (KLSE) (Schmidt, 2003). Given that global tourism contributes significantly to Malaysia's economic success, the opinions of Malaysia's business leaders concerning CM and risk management are important.

According to PriceWaterhouseCoopers (2005), tourism numbers are on the move again in Malaysia following the negative impact of severe acute respiratory syndrome (SARS) and 9/11 on global tourism. Spending by tourists was set to rise by 43% and arrivals were expected to accelerate between July and September of 2004 to monthly averages of 1.5 million tourists. Tourism Malaysia indicates that specific tourist initiatives can add some 300,000 tourists each month during certain nationwide campaigns. The Tourism Ministry also expected that the economy would rake in RM30 billion in foreign exchange in 2004. In 2002, tourists in Malaysia spent RM22.29 billion (PriceWaterhouseCoopers, 2005). UNPAN's Economic Management and Outlook (Malaysia) estimates that 30% of all retail sales in Malaysia is generated by tourist-related activities (UNPAN, 2005). With estimates of tourism contributing up to 10% to the nation's GDP, one would expect that the captains of Malaysian industry would be acutely attuned to CM issues in not only their own domain in particular but also in global tourism in general.

The publicly listed companies on the KLSE were targeted because these organizations have significant and wide-ranging obligations to the investing public. Moreover, corporate governance is a duty of all senior managers of corporations, and one can assume that in Malaysia, where global tourism is so strategically important to the national economy, senior managers across the board would be cognizant of risk factors in CM for global tourism. Subsequently, this group would be predisposed to view CM as either a direct or an indirect form of competitive advantage. In addition to the survey data, a case study methodology was applied to companies that had responded to the survey with a willingness to participate in this subsequent activity. A structured interview protocol was devised, but the process allowed for general comments at the conclusion of each interview.

For the survey reported here, the value of a comparison between current practices in Malaysia and a notional Western standard was achieved by the negotiated arrangement with the AMA. Questions from the 2002 AMA CM Survey formed the basis of the adaptation in Malaysia in 2003. In this context, the AMA results provide a loose benchmark by which to compare the responses of the Malaysian managers. The AMA survey (2002) consisted of ten questions, most of which required 'yes'/'no' or 'low'/'medium'/'high' responses to a specific question related to CM. In particular, the extracted questions required managers to nominate risks that concerned them from a pick-list of eight or more categories. In addition, respondents were asked to indicate whether these risks were included in the organization's CM plan and the level of back-up communication systems in place to reduce the impact of a crisis.

The interview data were analysed using a qualitative research method commonly applied in semiotics and structural anthropology (Fiske and Hartley, 1979; Kronenfeld and Decker, 1979; Bogden and Biklen, 1992). Repeated words and phrases become the key for unlocking deeper meanings within the various responses. Placing words and phrases within a set of structural oppositions and comparing their fit in the context of CM derives such meaning. Oppositions included those of manager/employees, responsibility/delegation or reactive/pro-active. This placement in turn is compared with motivations characteristic of either a low context or high context culture and interpreted accordingly (cf. Gloet and Berrell, 2003).

The invitation letter and survey instrument was sent to the e-mail addresses of publicly listed companies on the KLSE. Furthermore, the potential of a North American benchmark was disseminated via a press release and in the communication that accompanied the distribution process. It was anticipated that Malaysian managers would be motivated to participate in the survey given this benchmarking function. However, comparisons between the two sets of data were always going to be problematic for several reasons. The AMA survey was not an open survey to all members of the KLSE's equivalent organization, the New York Stock Exchange, but was conducted only among members of the AMA. While these limitations are clearly acknowledged, the 2003 Malaysian data are best thought of as a CM health check. In this context, they raised the CM consciousness of Malaysian managers and emphasized the need for developing CM planning as a responsibility of all senior managers.

Results

Response rates from Internet-administered surveys can be as high as 10%. However, the response rate for the 2003 CM survey was 8%. In total, about 80 companies responded. While this number is small compared with response rates achieved through traditional survey methods, ultimately the opinions of a fair number of senior managers in KLSE-listed companies were tapped regarding CM. The KLSE-listed companies that responded to the survey represented the following industry sectors: multinational manufacturing, finance, airlines, transportation, hospitals and health, and local manufacturing. All have a strong interest in global tourism. No responses were received from companies in the primary industry sector.

The choice of using a case study method in the 2003 CM survey was based on the expected low return rate from the Internet-based survey. Issues of cost and expediency also influenced the decision. While Internet-based surveys have low response rates, in Malaysia personal communication is important in a cultural context. Consequently, even traditional survey methods run the risk of low returns. In this environment, the case study approach proved auspicious because evidence emerged during the interviews that despite a low response rate, discussion about CM had been triggered in Malaysia's management network. For instance, one of several comments emerging from the interviews suggested that in 'certain places', the CM survey had 'kicked up quite a storm'. Of the 80 companies surveyed, 15 indicated a willingness to engage in a case study. The interview protocol in particular was constructed to derive information concerning the possibility of using a fuzzy logic classification in CM. Interviews were conducted, recorded and transcribed in English.

Closer investigation of the case study data revealed that while some of managers were initially reluctant to respond to the survey, the same group had also been motivated to engage consultants to assist them in formulating a CM plan for their organization. In this sense, there was a contingent action research element in the project, which emerged during the investigation. In the context of CM, it is not always possible, or even advisable, to adopt the stance of a neutral observer (cf. Shrivastava, 1993). Thus, one implicit outcome of the survey was to alert Malaysian managers of the need to adopt credible CM approaches in circumstances where such approaches were judged by the researchers to be lacking.

Aspects of the 2003 survey are highlighted because these responses have particular relevance and implications for global tourism. Responses to these questions provide a snapshot of the crisis preparedness and behavioural readiness of some Malaysian companies. Three questions from the 2003 survey are extracted here. One question asked Malaysian managers to estimate the level of concern their organization had with risks associated with specific activities. The AMA results are presented in each table as a benchmark. These responses are particularly relevant to vulnerability audits or risk mapping activities. Respondents rated the level of concern with specific activities as being low, medium or high. Activities ranged from employee screening and selection, planning for business regeneration, and evacuation planning for disasters, to the threats posed by the *e*-business environment, inappropriate workplace behaviour, handling hazardous substances, company travel and employee safety around common areas such as the car park. The results are set out in Table 6.1.

Table 6.1. Level of concern with specific risks.

Activity or event	AMA			Malaysia[a]		
	Low	Moderate	High	Low	Moderate	High
Employee screening/selection	17	45	38	23	54	23
Business resumption planning	20	45	37	13	26	58
Evacuation planning for disasters	27	40	33	19	26	52
Cyber threats	28	41	31	26	39	32
Workplace violence	26	44	30	23	45	26
Hazardous materials	38	35	27	35	36	26
Travel safety	34	45	21	48	23	26
Car park safety	42	41	17	45	42	10

[a] *n* = 80 KLSE companies; all responses are expressed as a percentage.

While acknowledging the limitations in comparing the AMA and Malaysian data, the level of concern among Malaysian managers with employee screening and selection may be a worry in an age of heightened risk of international terrorism. This risk could be added to future vulnerability audits.

Another question sought to determine whether certain risks had been taken seriously enough by the organization to be incorporated into the organization's CM planning (see Table 6.2). These risks included events associated with the failure of technology and subsequent loss of data, criminal activity, and disturbances from terrorism or political unrest. Being a victim of fraud, natural disasters, industrial accidents, workplace violence or the unethical behaviour of employees was also included.

The data below suggest that the Malaysian managers differ from the AMA respondents in sufficiently planning for CM in three areas: risks associated with natural disasters, workplace behaviour and disturbances such as acts of terrorism or political unrest. However, CM planning for acts of terrorism could be improved in both Malaysia and the USA.

A further question focused on the CC element of CM. Managers were asked whether their organization had back-up communication plans in the following areas: senior management team, contractors, employees, family members, key stakeholders, the media, emergency organizations such as fire and ambulance services, insurance carriers, regulatory bodies and legal entities. The level of CC in current CM planning is set out in Table 6.3.

In these areas of CC, differences in back-up communication plans are noted between Malaysian and AMA respondents in the areas of employees, media, emergency services and legal entities. The relative lack of CC in the emergency service area in Malaysia also emerges as an area for concern. It is worth noting, however, that the need for communication plans for dealing with legal entities among AMA respondents might reflect a more litigious business community in the USA.

On the evidence above, it cannot be concluded that Malaysian corporations are not as 'crisis prepared' as their counterparts in the USA. Nevertheless, a number of the issues have implications for CM in Malaysia given global tourism's significant contribution to Malaysia's gross domestic

Table 6.2. Issues included in an organization's CM plan.

Potential event	AMA	Malaysia[a]
Technology system failures or loss of data	83	71
Crime	39	29
Disturbances (terrorism, political unrest)	33	32
Major fraud	31	35
Natural disasters	71	45
Industrial accidents/fatalities	66	58
Workplace violence or unethical behaviour of employees	57	35
Major business problems with potentially negative impact across the company	47	42

[a] $n = 80$ KLSE companies; all responses are expressed as a percentage.

Table 6.3. Level of back-up communication management in crisis management plans.

Type of communication back-up	AMA	Malaysia[a]
Senior management team	80	77
Contractors	34	29
Employees	77	55
Family members	30	32
Key stakeholders	44	35
Media	40	23
Emergency services	61	45
Insurance carriers	51	42
Regulatory bodies	40	45
Legal entities	53	26

[a] $n = 80$ KLSE companies; all responses expressed as a percentage.

product (GDP) in general and retail sales in particular. Furthermore, the extent to which national culture intrudes into decision making in CM in Malaysia is yet to be fully determined. Some conjectures about culture's influence on Malaysian CM are offered below. The aftermath of the recent South East Asian tsunami disaster and heightened threats of global terrorism both provide a sobering backdrop to this discussion.

Discussion

Culture is embedded in one's consciousness to the extent that most people in CM situations would be habitually unsuspecting of its influence on either their behaviour or the behaviour of others (see Triandis, 1983; Adler, 2002). As such, culture's influence can be interpreted as an 'invisible jet stream' – a form of unconscious motivation (Hall, 1976). However, Malaysia is a pluralistic and secular society. It is composed of quite distinctive cultural groups that include indigenous Malays (55%), Chinese (30%) and Indians (10%). The Malays, followers of Islam, constitute the largest single cultural entity. While Schmidt's (2003) survey did not deliberately set out to be representative of the Malaysian population, there was a balance of Malays and Chinese Malaysians in the interview stage. Both belong to high context cultural groups. Based on previous work in a similar setting (Berrell and Gloet, 1999), some conjectures are offered below about the influence of culture on CM and the potential of a fuzzy logic approach to CM in Malaysia.

The exercise of power in Malaysian organizations often depends on a rigid adherence to legitimate authority conveyed through well-defined management positions and aided by particularistic and patronage relationships. In the context of CM, this would mean that the implementation of a fuzzy logic approach to CM might face cultural barriers. In addition, a complex system of formal and informal communication channels and a highly regulated environment are characteristic of high context organizations. In Malaysia, substantive decision making in CM would normally remain the province of the most senior people, often at the level of a Chief Executive Officer (CEO). In CM environments where status and administrative power are commensurate, 'who' makes a decision becomes more important than the actual outcome. The cultural architecture also influences the speed of responses in CM. For instance, the status-bound nature of decision making in many Asian countries requires the presence of the most senior people in emergencies to assume responsibility for major decisions. This necessity may impede expeditious responses to a crisis.

Anecdotal evidence suggests that Malaysia, a predominantly Muslim country, had until quite recently exhibited a strong attitude of 'it couldn't happen here' with regard to terrorism and related crises in distant lands. The Malaysian government has always actively promoted Malaysia as a safe destination among the stakeholders of global tourism. With Islamic terrorism now on their doorstep in southern Thailand, Malaysians have been forced to take this issue more seriously, at least at the rhetorical level. As indicated above in Table 6.1, only 32% of Malaysian organizations have terrorist and related disturbances factored into their CM plan, about half see evacuation planning for disasters as a high priority, and only 45% have back-up plans for CC in emergency services. How many global tourists would feel entirely comfortable visiting the most northern states of Malaysia in the context of Malaysia's disaster preparedness?

Decision making in CM within organizations braced by not only hierarchical structures but also formal and personal relationship networks can reduce pro-active engagement and participation in CM. This reduces the potential of Schmidt's (2002a) fuzzy logic approach in CM as a means of achieving best practice in Malaysia, among other high context societies. Accordingly, the communication process of CM may not add value to decision making in such settings. Malaysian managers remain accustomed to systems and processes outwardly based on seniority. One the one hand, the interview data suggested that the need to use a fuzzy logic approach to classifying any particular crisis was seen by respondents as a legitimate proposition. On the other hand, it was also evident that this proposition moved managers outside their comfort zone. Some respondents were 'unsure of how it would work'; others 'would need to get advice on the system'. In other words, the fuzzy logic proposition placed CM in an uncertain setting, beyond 'black and white' thinking to encompass 'shades of grey'.

Based on the interview data, there is scope to explore in depth the extent to which hierarchical decision-making structures and top-down status-bound management processes might constitute a barrier to the adoption of fuzzy logic classification schemes in CM in high context societies. In addition, the notion that a computer-generated heuristic could guide managerial decision making in CM was not well received by Malaysian managers. In general, this group prefers unambiguous settings with a degree of certainty in their CM activity (cf. Hofstede, 1994).

Unfortunately, as the recent tsunami disaster demonstrates, as a response to a 'low probability, high impact event', CM demands immediate and decisive action, often from people on the ground. Anecdotal evidence from the tsunami disaster in Aceh in Indonesia, Sri Lanka and Thailand suggests that while people at the immediate site reacted swiftly, subsequent coordinated efforts in CM were lacking. The potential number of global tourists that can be affected by disasters of this type clearly demonstrates that tourism operators should be concerned with the CM capabilities of the destinations they choose.

The Malays are also predisposed to a worldview characterized by the pre-determined nature of events. While this specific aspect of CM was not explored in the survey, other studies indicate the significant impact of this worldview in similar settings and processes (Berrell and Gloet, 1999). In high context societies, approaches to CM are often characterized by an orientation toward *allowing things to happen*, compared with the low context orientation toward *making things happen* (see Adler, 2002). In the realm of causality, Malay managers tend to let a sequence of events run its course. Low context decision making, in contrast, intervenes in events in order to make things happen through critical inquiry accompanied by problem-solving approaches. In comparison, the Malays, for example, are inclined to seek deterministic explanations, which may result in fewer systematic explorations of causality. The effect here is a barrier to building best practice CM. This orientation reflects the nexus between religious and secular life among Malays. The extent to which this orientation impinges on CM remains to be fully explicated.

On the evidence, it seems that Malaysia would benefit from a review of its approach to vulnerability audits and the risk mapping component of crisis preparedness in general. While a fuzzy logic classification is well suited to a matrix approach to CM, now emerging as best practice in the West, the large power–distance relationships and hierarchical management structures that characterize Malaysian organizations may thwart this approach. Certainly, factors other than culture determine organizational behaviour in CM and, therefore, more research is needed in general (Markoczy, 1995; Adler, 2002). Other research is also necessary in CM in the area of infrastructure, especially in emerging economies. For example, a recent natural landslide on the major North–South toll road in Malaysia created a disruption of logistics with devastating effects. It required an extended period of diverting all trucks using the road. Imagine this occurring simultaneously with a significant act of terrorism or a natural disaster on a larger scale?

Conclusion

The value of the comparisons between the two sets of data seems primarily to be in raising the CM consciousness of Malaysian managers. The need for CM to become an essential element of a Malaysian manager's best practice repertoire is evident. In the aftermath of the recent unpredicted tsunami and the more predictable boating disaster in Koh Samui in south Thailand in early 2005, there has never been a more opportune time to address CM in South East Asian tourism planning generally.

Although two approaches in CM are identified and discussed in this chapter in the context of best practice, i.e. a fuzzy logic classification of a crisis and a heuristic-guided response to a crisis, the implementation of either approach faces barriers given the cultural architecture of some non-Western cultures. Notwithstanding these obstacles, Malaysian managers may now be disposed to revamp CM for global tourism. It is anticipated that the fuzzy logic classification and its heuristic, the dynamic e-learning tool, can play a part of the renovation of CM in global tourism, in both Western and non-Western contexts.

References

Adler, N. (1983) Cross-cultural management research: the ostrich and the trend. *Academy of Management Review* 8, 226–232.

Adler, N. (2002) *International Dimensions of Organizational Behaviour*, 4th edn. South-Western College Publishing, Cincinnati, Ohio.

Berrell, M. and Gloet, M. (1999) Reflections on the cultural dimensions of educational administration. *Journal of Educational Administration and Foundations* 14, 10–32.

Berrell, M. and Wrathall, J. (2003) Changing attitudes to intellectual property in China, the nexus between culture and the rule of law. In: Coate, B., Brooks, R., Fraser, I. and Xu, L. (eds) *China in the New Era, Proceedings: 15th Annual Conference of the Association for Chinese Economic Studies Australia (ACESA).* RMIT Development Unit, Melbourne, Australia.

Berrell, M., Wrathall, J. and Gloet, M. (2001) Managing international employment relations: when national culture and organizational culture take different roads on the same journey. In: Spooner, K. and Innes, C. (eds) *Employment Relations in the New Economy: Proceedings of the Ninth Annual Conference of the International of the International Employment Relations Association.* IERA, UWS, Sydney, pp. 107–120.

Bogden, R. and Biklen, S. (1992) *Quantitative Research for Education.* Allyn and Bacon, Boston, Massachusetts.

Burnett, J. (1998) A strategic approach to managing crisis. *Public Relations Review* 22 December.

Columbia Accident Investigation Board (2003) *Report.* Government Printing Office, Washington, DC.

Deresky, H. (2000) *International Management, Managing Across Borders and Cultures*, 3rd edn. Prentice-Hall, Upper Saddle River, New Jersey.

Fearn-Banks, K. (1996) *Crisis Communications: a Casebook Approach.* Lawrence Erlbaum Associates, Mahwah, New Jersey.

Fiske, J. and Hartley, J. (1978) *Reading Television.* Methuen, London.

Gannon, M. and Newman, K. (eds) (2002) *The Blackwell Handbook of Cross-cultural Management.* Blackwell, Oxford.

Gloet, M. and Berrell, M. (2003) A model for examining the changing role of HRM in Chinese organizations: a knowledge perspective, In: Coate, B., Brooks, R., Fraser, I. and Xu, L. (eds) *China in the new Era, Proceedings: 15th Annual Conference of the Association for Chinese Economic Studies Australia (ACESA).* RMIT Development Unit, Melbourne, Australia.

Hall, E. (1976) *Beyond Culture.* Anchor-Doubleday, New York.

Hofstede, G. (1994) *Cultures and Organizat-*

ions: *Software of the Mind – Intercultural Cooperation and its Importance for Survival.* Harper Collins, London.

Jeynes, J. (2002) *Risk Management: 10 Principles.* Butterworth-Heinemann, Oxford.

Kluckhohn, F. and Strodtbeck, F. (1961) *Variations in Value Orientations.* Row Peterson, Evanston, Illinois.

Kronenfeld, J. and Decker, H. (1979) Structural anthropology. *Annual Review of Anthropology* 8, 503–541.

Lane, H., Di Steffano, J. and Maznevski, M. (eds) (2000) *International Management Behaviour*, 4th edn. Blackwell, Oxford.

Loosemore, M. (1998) The influence of communication structure upon crisis management efficiency. *Construction Management and Economics* 16, 661–671.

Markoczy, L. (1995) States and belief states. *International Journal of Human Resource Management* 6, 249–269.

Meyers, G. (1986) *When it Hits the Fan: Managing the Nine Crises of Business.* Houghton Mifflin, Boston, Massachusetts.

Meyers, G. and Holusha, J. (1986) *Managing a Crisis, a Positive Approach.* Unwin Hyman, London.

Mitroff, I. (1988) Crisis management: cutting through the confusion. *Sloan Management Review* 29, 15–20.

Mitroff, I. and Anagnos, G. (2001) *Managing Crises Before They Happen.* AMACOM, New York.

Mitroff, I., Pauchant, T., Finney, M. and Pearson, C. (1989) Do some organizations cause their own crises? The cultural profiles of crisis-prone vs. crisis-prepared organizations. *Industrial Crisis Quarterly* 3, 269–283.

Monk, P. (2001) Why didn't we think of that? *Australian Financial Review.* 2 November.

Murray, E. and Shohen, S. (1992) Lessons from the Tylenol tragedy on surviving a corporate crisis. *Medical Marketing and Media* 27 (2), February.

National Commission on Terrorist Attacks upon the USA (2004) *The 9/11 Commission Report: Final Report of the National Commission on Terrorist Attacks upon the USA.* Norton, New York.

Nunamaker, J., Weber, E. and Chen, M. (1989) Organizational crisis management systems: planning for intelligent action. *Journal of Management Information Systems* 5 (4), 7–32.

Pearson, C. and Clair, J. (1998) Reframing crisis management. *Academy of Management Review* 23, 59–76.

Pearson, C. and Mitroff, I. (1993) From crisis prone to crisis prepared: a framework for crisis management. *Academy of Management Executive* 7 (1), 48–59.

Preble, J. (1997) Integrating the crisis management perspective into the strategic management process. *Journal of Management Studies* 34, 769–791.

PriceWaterhouseCoopers (2005) Country Index, www.pwc.com/extweb/frmclp11. nsf/DocID/9588CAC8AAA36FFC85256EDF00 632814, (accessed 21 January 2005).

Rike, B. (2003) Prepared or not … that is the vital question. *Information Management Journal* 37 (3), 25–33.

Sapriel, C. (2003) Effective crisis management: tools and best practice for the new millennium. *Journal of Communication Management* 7, 348–355.

Senge, P. (1994) *The Fifth Discipline Fieldbook: Strategies and Tools for Building a Learning Organization*, Doubleday/ Currency, New York.

Schmidt, P. (1995) *Report on Electronic Brainstorming Session of Crisis Management Experts at Griffith University, July 1995.* Defense Restricted Publication.

Schmidt, P. (2002a) Crisis Management. Doctor of Business Administration dissertation, Southern Cross University, Lismore, Australia.

Schmidt, P. (2002b) Crisis management in Malaysia. *Proceedings: 2002 Hawaii International Conference on Business*, Hawaaii.

Schmidt, P. (2003) *Preliminary Analysis of the Crisis Management Survey of Managers in Malaysia.* Draft Research Report, JCU Melbourne Campus, Melbourne.

Shrivastava, P. (1993) Crisis theory and practice: towards a sustainable future. *Industrial and Environmental Crisis Quarterly* 7, 23–42.

Smits, S. and Ezzat, N. (2003) Thinking the unthinkable – leadership's role in creating behavioural readiness for crisis management. *Competitiveness Review* 13 (1).

Temple, R. (2003) Responding to a crisis requires overcoming barriers to effective advance planning. *Public Relations Quarterly* 48 (1).

Triandis, H. (1983) Dimensions of cultural variations as parameters of organizational theories. *International Studies of Management and Organization* 12, 139–169.

Trompenaars, F. (1993) *Riding the Waves of Culture: Understanding Cultural Diversity in Business*. Economist Books, London.

Trompenaars, F. and Hampden-Turner, C. (2004) *Managing People Across Cultures*. Capstone, Chichester, UK.

Turner, B. and Pigeon N. (1997) *Man-made Disasters*, 2nd edn. Butterworth-Heinemann, Oxford.

UNPAN (2005) Economic Management and Outlook (Malaysia), http://www.unpan.org/autoretrieve/regional.asp?region=asia+and+pacific&content=country+profiles, (accessed 29 January 2005).

Vaughan, D. (1990) Autonomy, independence, and social control: NASA and the Space Shuttle Challenger. *Administrative Science Quarterly* 35, 225–257.

7 Crisis in Bali: Lessons in Tourism Recovery

Yetta K. Gurtner

Introduction

Despite recent threats and significant disruptions, tourism has perhaps become the world's largest growth industry (World Tourism Organizaton, 2004). It generates hundreds of billions of dollars annually through income, revenues, employment, investment and infrastructure development, with seemingly limitless potential. Based on a complex inter-relationship between supply and demand, it is also highly sensitive to change. To maintain productivity, governments and relevant stakeholders must endeavour to insulate the tourism sector from sudden and sustained adverse conditions. The implementation of effective preparation and management procedures has the potential to determine the difference between industry resilience and recession. Destinations lacking an adequate capacity to respond to negative events remain particularly vulnerable and susceptible to crises.

Since the late 1960s, the tropical island of Bali had developed a growing reputation as a popular international tourist destination with an ethos of harmonious balance, tranquillity and safety. Rich in natural assets and cultural heritage, it had seemed isolated from the turmoil and political instability that had affected other areas of Indonesia and greater South East Asia. While tourism revenues and direct arrival figures continued to increase, few had considered the possibility of a single event with the potential to undermine the fortune of the entire region.

The terrorist attacks of 12 October 2002 caused extensive structural and human devastation, secured international media attention and revealed the weaknesses of an unsuspecting and ill-prepared destination. Bereft of its image of stability, Bali was effectively plunged into tourism crisis. Strongly reliant on the income generated through tourist expenditure, most residents have experienced some degree of socio-economic difficulty. As short-, medium- and long-term impacts have become apparent, the government and responding agencies have had to develop a series of reactive strategies to restore safety, facilitate community recovery and mitigate any future contingencies. Although not all initiatives have been successful, the lessons and experience of Bali demonstrate the value of developing a pro-active relationship between the tourism sector and crisis management planning.

Tourism and Crisis Management – A Theoretical Perspective

Tourism crisis

As an industry reliant on an atmosphere of safety, security and positive perceptions, the tourism sector and popular destinations are inherently vulnerable to disaster and crisis conditions (Pizam and Mansfield, 1996; Somnez *et al.*, 1999). Adverse situations associated with distress, fear, anxiety, trauma and panic are the antithesis to the enjoyment, pleasure, relaxation and stability often sought in the tourist experience (Santana, 2003). If a prospective destination is associated with any negative images or sentiments, consumers can simply choose to cancel, defer or substitute for alternative locations – such actions may precipitate a tourism crisis.

The World Tourism Organization (2004) defines tourism crisis 'as any unexpected event that affects a travellers confidence in a destination and interferes with the ability to continue operating normally'. Based on extensive research of afflicted destinations, Somnez *et al.* (1994, p. 2:2 cited in Somnez *et al.*, 1999) use the term 'tourism crisis' to describe circumstances:

> which can threaten the normal operation and conduct of tourism related businesses: damage a tourist destination's overall reputation for safety, attractiveness, and comfort by negatively affecting visitor's perceptions of that destination; and, in turn, cause a downturn in the local travel and tourism economy and interrupt the continuity of business operations for the local travel and tourism industry, by the reduction in tourist arrivals and expenditures.

While the scope and magnitude of a 'triggering' event may vary, history and experience have demonstrated that no destination is immune from crisis (Bierman, 2003; Glaesser, 2003). Given the complex inter-relationship of industry, community and destination, subsequent impacts are highly unpredictable and highly differential. The prospect for significant negative effects is greater in areas with poor infrastructure, limited social security and a strong economic reliance on the tourism sector (conditions commonly found in developing nations) (Matsny, 2001). For decades, multinational organizations, industry professionals and scholars have recommended that popular tourist destinations implement some form of crisis management planning to minimize the threat and impact of any potential hazard (Gee and Gain, 1986; Faulkner, 2001; World Travel and Tourism Council, 2003; World Tourism Organization, 2004).

Integrated crisis management and tourism

As a science or applied approach, crisis management is still considered a juvenile yet rapidly emerging field of investigation. There is still no universally accepted definition or model of integrated crisis management; however, it has been described as 'an ongoing integrated and comprehensive effort that organizations effectively put into place in an attempt to first and foremost understand and prevent crisis, and to effectively manage those that occur, taking into account in each and every step of their planning and training activities, the interest of their stakeholders' (Santana, 1999 cited in Santana, 2003, p. 308). Based on a continuum of phases incorporating reduction, readiness, response, recovery and mitigation, it is ideally a self-appreciating system where experiences and lessons learnt are considered in the development of improved strategies.

Traditionally, in the event of disaster at a popular destination, various sectors of the community respond while tourism industry representatives instigate independent and reactive strategies of promotion and recovery marketing. Integrated planning and crisis management is about adopting a more unified, coordinated and pro-active approach – governments, business, residents and tourism stakeholders working in conjunction with other agencies and emergency service providers to reduce the risk and influence of serious adversity (Asian Disaster Preparedness Center, 2001; Matsny, 2001). As an industry reliant on image and positive perceptions, research indicates that effective strategies for tourist destinations should specifically address communication, safety and security, market research and promotion (Asian Disaster Preparedness Center, 2001; Faulkner, 2001; World Tourism Organization, 2003).

The reality of destination crisis planning

Whether as a consequence of ignorance, internal resistance, community-based conflict and/or cost (Quarantelli, 1998), the majority of tourist destinations have failed to establish an adequate level of disaster and crisis planning. Most authorities and relevant stakeholders continue to lack the management capabilities, flexibility and confidence to deal effectively with unexpected, complex and critical situations (Faulkner, 1999; Santana, 2003). While some organizations may have a formal crisis management plan, these are generally reactive and designed to address limited professional objectives rather than incorporating the priorities of the wider community. Experience suggests that publicized images of incompetence, negligence, instability and inefficiency in times of adversity can exacerbate and/or prolong crisis conditions (Asian Disaster Preparedness Center, 2001).

In an era where war, acts of terrorism and substantial natural disasters seem to be a daily occurrence, unprepared tourist destinations and reliant populations continue to remain particularly vulnerable and susceptible. Conceptually, integrated crisis management planning provides a promising solution to enhance overall operational capabilities and industry fortitude. While it may not be possible to prevent or avoid a crisis, it is important for relevant stakeholders to be aware of strategies that may facilitate resilience. Beyond the proclamations of theoretical rhetoric, industry representatives and crisis managers understand tangible actions, lessons and practical solutions. The authentic experience of recent tourism crises reveals some fundamental concepts and challenges which should be deliberated in resisting and responding to detrimental circumstances.

The Bali Experience

The plunge into crisis

At approximately 11.20 p.m., 12 October 2002, the island of Bali, in the Indonesian archipelago, was rocked by a series of terrorist bombings. The most devastating of these explosions occurred at the site of Paddys and the Sari Club, two popular night spots in the renowned tourist entertainment strip of Legian Street, Kuta. On a Saturday night during the peak tourist season, both venues were crowded. Without apparent provocation or forewarning, unsuspecting staff, patrons, tourists and bystanders became victims of a heinous crime. While the direct physical and structural damage was significant, the individual, emotional and psychological affliction was devastating.

Although emergency response efforts were admirable, the community of Bali was obviously ill prepared and ill equipped to deal effectively with any large-scale disaster. Official figures placed the final death toll from this incident at 202, while hundreds more suffered injuries with varying degrees of severity (ABC Online, 2004). Distraught tourists abandoned the island as most hotel occupancy rates dropped to single figures (BPS Statistics Indonesia, 2003). Amidst the disbelief, grief and confusion, residents of Kuta and Bali were faced with the daunting reality of a tourism crisis. As commerce lagged and socio-economic pressures increased, reactive strategies were developed to improve regional stability and relieve the immediate suffering. For tourism stakeholders, the restoration of consumer confidence and a positive destination image was a recovery priority.

In an effort to support the struggling tourism industry of Bali, the Pacific Asia Travel Association (PATA) quickly deployed representatives to assist with management issues and conduct an objective assessment of initial response strategies. Based on local knowledge and cumulative industry experience, the Bali Recovery Task Force (Pacific Asia Travel Association, 2003) developed a comprehensive report and series of associated recommendations. As the adverse impacts and repercussions of this incident have persisted however, it is imperative to consistently review and reassess the appropriateness of operational management methodology. The challenge to overcome crisis conditions effectively and achieve greater community resilience has become a sobering experience for both the tourism industry and the community of Bali.

Communication and media management

Consistent with the findings of the PATA Recovery Task Force (2003), Bali lost significant international integrity in the immediate aftermath of the terrorist attacks due to the absence of sufficient media control and a designated spokesperson. While emergency relief efforts prioritize the protection of life and property, activities undertaken by destination authorities and the tourism sector in the first 24 h of a crisis are crucial (World Tourism Organization, 2003; World Travel and Tourism Council, 2003). Regardless of circumstances, responsible management requires the maintenance of credibility. Honesty, transparency, professionalism and good communications with the public and media can improve chances of a faster recovery. Despite the genuine concerted effort of volunteers, local public relations firms and relevant authorities, Bali obviously lacked familiarity with effective crisis communication procedures.

While the scale and magnitude of these terrorist bombings would have been sufficient to attract considerable media attention, the international composition of the victims ensured a captive and global audience. The abundance of eyewitness video recordings and photographs meant that copious images of devastation and adversity quickly became publicly available. Raw, unedited footage of the fiery inferno, twisted metal, car bodies, debris and human carnage soon dominated newspapers, television and the Internet (ABC Online, 2004). Subsequent pictures of seemingly chaotic administration, inadequate medical facilities and the emotional descriptions from both victims and volunteers enhanced the mounting negative perceptions.

A practical approach to effective crisis management does not recommend censorship of such descriptions and images; rather they need to be presented factually without exaggeration, speculation or sensationalism (Pizam and Mansfield, 1996; World Tourism Organization, 2003). Sensitivity and compassion for victims and their relatives should be a major concern of both the media and relevant authorities. To avoid possible misconceptions, tourism stakeholders in Bali should have ensured that such pictures of the incident were placed in the right context. Direct damage from the attacks was limited to a specific locality, as the rest of the island and its tourism infrastructure remained physically intact. Similarly, the images of adversity needed to be balanced by the positive features such as the courageous and tireless efforts of the rescue workers, medical staff and volunteers, unreserved altruism and community solidarity.

A temporary media centre was established the day after the attack to assist the endeavours of government representatives, officials and journalists; however, the conduct of subsequent press conferences and public statements remained uncoordinated (Pacific Asia Travel Association, 2003). Unofficial venues ranged from the Hard Rock Hotel, 'Ground Zero', Sanglah Hospital, Police Headquarters to the Governor's Office in Denpasar. As various individuals were presented as authoritative speakers, a failure to cross-reference and communicate between the various organizations and institutions meant that the information used in many of these briefings seemed inconsistent. Without a centralized authority or source of accurate data, it was difficult for anyone to ascertain the facts. Language differences and the proficiency of available translators created further complications. Numerous web sites were established by government agencies and independent groups; however, reliable information and updates remained sporadic.

While the Governor of Bali issued several public statements and the President of the Republic of Indonesia visited the afflicted region, many international observers felt that the government failed to demonstrate adequate leadership and authority (Bali Discovery Tours, 2004). In adverse conditions, the community often expects the ruling body to provide guidance, instil confidence and return conditions of regional stability (United Nations Development Programme, 1992). Without a consistent identifiable spokesperson or dependable messages of safety and security, the public remained apprehensive about official statements and initiatives (World Tourism Organization, 2003). Even attempts to establish accurate records and clarify victims and family information were limited by available resources and a culture of suspicion towards authority (BaliSOS, 2003).

Although initial media management and communication was far from ideal, Bali has strived to surmount these shortcomings. As associations and relationships between governments, media, businesses, responding organizations and the community were increased post-crisis, they have provided an unprecedented opportunity to create informal networks. Established dialogue and interaction, at any level, enhances communication capabilities (Quarantelli, 1998). The immediacy of the crisis situation also forced the confrontation and resolution of many inter- and intraorganizational disputes and jurisdictional issues. The shared adversity of this situation demonstrated how the many disparate elements of society can work well together if sufficiently motivated.

During the resultant investigations and trials of alleged perpetrators, the Governor's Office has conscientiously adopted a more prominent, authoritative role in the provision of accurate information for public dissemination (Bali Discovery Tours, 2004). The local Minister for Tourism has also increased the influence and profile of his department by consistently and publicly highlighting emergent issues and counterstrategies. The difficultly has been in ensuring such messages reach a wider audience both locally and internationally. Unfortunately, Indonesia's well-established reputation for government dishonesty, corruption and unreliable statistics undermines the tenacity of many official statements.

A number of independent initiatives to help restore destination integrity have been developed and funded by elements of the business community, hospitality industry and/or various non-government organizations (NGOs) with differing degrees of success. While the conduct of familiarization trips for foreign journalists can be an effective strategy to promote balanced media reporting, such efforts can backfire in the absence of careful planning and organization. Similarly, the advent of numerous recovery slogans, events and inspired messages of reassurances from an eclectic range of sources can be counterproductive. Bali still lacks the single unified voice that could be achieved through a collaborative partnership of stakeholders.

The successful portrayal of the Ritual Cleansing Ceremony and conduct of the Memorial Anniversary Service and concurrent Kuta Karnival of Life are evidence of better local media management skills; however, some improvements can still be made. While it is important to respect and remain sensitive to the victims of the Bali bombings tragedy, greater emphasis should now be given to both positive and unrelated new stories. Recent events have established the foundations for a more reliable network of information and improved media handling capabilities; the challenge is to continue to develop and utilize these qualities.

Recommended pro-active strategies for future crisis communication and preparedness planning include the development of a dedicated public relations office, establishing a specific media response protocol, the formation of a representative consultative body and basic resource allocation (World Tourism Organization, 2003).

Safety and security

The moment the terrorist bombs exploded in Kuta, issues of safety and security became an imperative for both the tourists and residents of Bali. Beyond the intensity of search and rescue efforts, an atmosphere of fear and uncertainty prevailed. Even as subsequent days procured numerous governmental assurances and an influx of official security forces, it was impossible for anyone to provide absolute personal guarantees. Experience from similarly afflicted destinations suggests that such perceptions of danger may only be reduced by highly visible and tangible political, economic and military actions (Beirman, 2003). The public must also be confident of their efficacy.

As a consequence of the choices and actions made by tourists in a host destination, they are generally considered a more vulnerable component of the population (Ritcher and Waugh, 1986). Travellers relaxing or enjoying a holiday have a tendency to be less aware of direct risks than they are in familiar home surroundings. Similarly, such tourists are often ignorant of local hazards, appropriate response procedures and the location of medical and/or emergency centres. Confusion can be amplified where language and cultural differences exist. For those in Bali during the bombings, risk, loss and danger became the pervasive impulses.

Such concerns were strengthened by early speculation that characterized Western tourists as the primary targets of this terrorist attack (later confirmed by the perpetrators). Uncertain whether the assault was designed to be an isolated incident or simply the first in a reign of terror, most tourists chose to abandon Bali. While such rumours also suggested that the incident was committed by Muslims, many residents with an Islamic background chose to flee the island fearing possible reprisals by an angry Hindu majority (Consultative Group of Indonesia, 2003). While professionals, relatives and volunteers from every sector of society worked to assist the victims, social cohesion was in a precarious state.

Having cordoned off the blast site, Indonesian police and military personnel made the search for evidence and pursuit of justice an immediate priority (Consultative Group of Indonesia, 2003; Bali Discovery Tours, 2004). These efforts were assisted by the involvement of international forensic experts and associated specialists. With the increase in national security forces, local community groups also activated their own traditional police to patrol the streets and help promote an atmosphere of social stability. Despite dwindling patron numbers, the majority of establishments introduced greater security precautions including increased guards, formal check-points, body searches and vehicle inspections.

At the national level, the Indonesian government strove to contend with growing international concerns regarding existing safety conditions. Additional police were assigned to the island of Bali, while new, strict anti-terrorism legislation was passed (Bali Discovery Tours, 2004). An intelligence-sharing arrangement was developed with numerous international agencies to enhance future threat detection and prevention capabilities. Similarly, the government agreed to a review and upgrade of security procedures at ports, airports and other major transport facilities around the nation. Regardless of such measures, the majority of foreign countries implemented comprehensive travel advisories recommending citizens 'defer all non-essential travel to Indonesia'.

Nervous and anxious travellers opted to cancel arrangements, defer holidays or travel to alternative destinations. As many insurers have been reluctant to cover travel in regions under government advisory or 'acts of terrorism', a large number of tourists have felt that the perils of visiting Bali are too high. Although some people have a morbid fascination with death and destruction (dark tourism), or are attracted by dangerous situations, the majority of travellers are deterred by high risk perceptions. While negative impressions and images lingered, Bali remained in crisis.

Sensitive to the possibility of further terrorist attacks, the international travelling public soon became aware of wider impacting health and safety issues. Severe acute respiratory syndrome (SARS) and the avian (bird) flu affected travelling confidence worldwide. Although no cases of SARS were ever officially reported in Bali, authorities appeared reluctant to implement any of the mitigation strategies recommended by the World

Health Organization (WHO) (BaliSOS, 2003). Coinciding global events including the Iraq War and the martial campaign against a vaguely delineated 'axis of evil' caused further international uncertainty.

Indonesia's political decision not to support actively the conduct of the 'Coalition of the Willing' at the time increased foreign scrutiny of existing military and security measures. Continued regional instability in provinces such as Aceh and Ambon, and the suspected operation of numerous Islamic militant groups has received much adverse media attention. Similarly, the terrorist bombings of the J.W. Mariott Hotel in Jakarta, August 2003 and the Australian Embassy in September 2004 undermined the credibility of consistent assertions of enhanced safety for tourist and Westerners. While local conditions appear to have stabilized, economic pressures for the community of Bali seem to have affected an increase in small-scale crime including drugs, prostitution, paedophilia and gambling. Tourists also continue to be the victims of isolated incidents of theft, kidnapping and blackmail schemes (crimes consequently blamed on 'outside criminal elements').

Although authorities have pursued numerous strategies to enhance safety and security throughout Indonesia, concerns continue to remain regarding their adequacy. Within Bali, emergency responders, medical facilities and associated staff have been the beneficiaries of significant resource and training upgrades (most notably the improvements financed at Sanglah Hospital). The majority of the original bombing suspects were identified and convicted. Environmental health and hygiene issues have also been the subject of greater community awareness and action. In addition to the independent initiatives of most establishments, increases in security personnel have been aligned with the designation of more Tourist Police and improved security procedures at transport terminals and public facilities. Reality reveals Bali as a more vigilant and better prepared destination.

In terms of fear and risk perceptions, however, logic has a limited influence on a fastidious and sensitive travelling public (Pizam and Mansfield, 1996). While tourism is returning to Bali, the stigma of terrorism continues to affect yields. Authorities need to be more pro-active in demonstrating and communicating about the island's enhanced security measures. As many countries seem reluctant to revoke government travel warnings, the message needs to be taken direct to the generating market. Unfortunately, maintaining pro-active measures requires significant resources which are difficult to sustain in an environment of reduced profits.

Promotion and market research

Prior to the Kuta nightclub bombings, Bali had attained an enviable reputation as a safe, peaceful and enjoyable destination. Accommodation, services and facilities existed to cater for every class and budget of traveller.

While advertising campaigns and literature existed, such promotion rarely necessitated excessive investment or expenditure. As the island seemed impervious to the unfavourable conditions and perceptions that had affected other nearby destinations, selling the 'Bali experience' to potential consumers was considered relatively easy.

With awareness and knowledge of the tragic terrorist attacks on Bali, the international public openly expressed feelings of outrage, remorse and apprehension. The imagery and emotions associated with the incident heightened risk perceptions and created an enhanced sense of intimidation. Consequent to such sentiment, there was an immediate downturn in the desirability of Bali as a destination. As transport carriers assisted the mass exodus of tourists, a large number of scheduled flights were cancelled or rerouted. From this position of disruption, an already shocked and devastated local tourism industry had to develop reactive strategies to counter negative perceptions and restore consumer confidence.

Extensive research and case studies as presented in the book by Pizam and Mansfield (1996), *Tourism, Crime and International Security Issues*, demonstrate that a positive destination image is integral to a subjective belief in personal safety and security. While early statements and reassurances issued by Indonesian authorities generally seemed to lack conviction and credibility, international governments were quick to impose comprehensive travel advisories. As business became increasingly competitive and desperate, heavy discounting and promotional incentives were introduced to entice travellers to the island. Many organizations and agencies chose to broaden their prospects through the active pursuit of a less sensitive domestic and regional market. Although this has proven to be a successful strategy, the length of stay and expenditure of such travellers is often considerably less than realized in pre-crisis conditions (Beirman, 2003; Bali Discovery Tours, 2004).

In an effort to facilitate recovery, the Indonesian government contracted the services of a reputable international tourism agency; however, similarly to the outcome of the PATA suggestions, few initiatives were allocated adequate time, budget or resources. Lacking the unified marketing approach of an integrated partnership, various elements of the tourism and hospitality industry have devised their own independent strategies to ascertain the resumption of profitable commerce. Initial campaigns and slogans such as 'Bali for the World' and 'Unified in Diversity: United We Stand' were designed to demonstrate the strength of both industry and community, while broadening the Bali brand to encompass culture and heritage. Other ventures have included hosting numerous international events, conventions and promotional travel shows, and active participation in overseas trade exhibitions (Bali Discovery Tours, 2004).

Significant investment has been committed to the development of dedicated web sites, brochures and promotional material; however, the eclectic nature of such efforts has generated much confusion and encouraged market fragmentation. Even with the enlisted support of famous tourists, media personalities and substantial prize offerings, most of the international events hosted in Bali have failed to attract considered media attention or interest (Karyadi, 2003). Negative images and fear of further terrorism remain influential. Continued financial pressures and constraints have forced many to re-evaluate traditional institutional attitudes and marketing strategies. In combining available resources and balancing competing interests, it becomes possible to raise the standard and intrinsic value of promotions.

The fundamental principle of effective promotion in any context is knowledge and understanding of the market. Beyond simple statistics and demographics, the tourism industry relies on catering to the ever-changing needs, wants and expectations of visitors. Advertising agencies need consistently to analyse the social and cultural aspects of generating markets, monitor trends and generate dynamic, innovative and appropriate campaigns (World Tourism Organization, 2003). The administrative and recording processes of travel agents, transport carriers, tourism plant and associated elements of the public and private sector already collect the majority of such data. Through collaborative information sharing and investment, it would become possible to profile and address the ultimate consumer while developing new niche markets and products to attract special interest travellers.

Although such a consensus has yet to be realized for Bali, existing promotional, marketing and recovery strategies appear to have achieved a substantial measure of success. In spite of regional instability and foreign advisories, tourist numbers have been increasing, business is improving and numerous surveys report visitor satisfaction at a considerably high level. Perceptions of safety and security remain an issue; however, capabilities and facilities on the island have improved as a result of this situation. While a lower spending market segment has been efficiently cultivated, greater allocation of funds is required to attain more comprehensive international market coverage. Rather than fostering competition between stakeholders, further financial assistance and investment should be committed to mutual monitoring and mitigating future threats to destination image.

Holistic recovery

While tourism recovery is generally focused on strategies for government, business and tourism agents, the cooperation and participation of a host community is central to achieving greater destination resilience and an enhanced operational experience (Matsny, 2001). Integrated crisis management is about being holistic, pro-active, appropriate and durable. To be able to support and maintain such resolve, the following principles should be considered at all phases and levels of crisis management (Natural Hazards Research and Applications Information Center, 2001, pp. 9–2):

1. Maintain and, if possible, enhance its residents' quality of life.
2. Enhance local economic vitality.
3. Ensure social and intergenerational equity.
4. Maintain and, if possible, enhance environmental quality.
5. Incorporate disaster resilience and mitigation.
6. Use a consensus-building, participatory process when making decisions.

A crisis can be a catalyst to implementing a more sustainable approach to recovery strategies and continued tourist development.

In the midst of crisis conditions, it is often the residents and businesses of a host community that experience financial and emotional hardship. While damaged infrastructure and utilities may be fixed or replaced, indirect victims generally receive limited assistance. For the population of Bali, the trauma and disbelief created by the terrorist attacks was amplified by direct socio-economic concerns. While community solidarity, religious ritual and ceremony were able to alleviate some of the short-term pressures, most remained anxious about their future. Depression, desperation, heightened social tension, vexatious touting, verbal aggression and overt illegal activities were all increasingly evident post-bombing. With salary cut-backs, reduced working hours, bankruptcy and unemployment as common practice, many have simply tried to retain a sense of normalcy in their lives.

As recovery strategies endeavour to accomplish improved communication, safety and promotion – continued negative impressions and reactions at the host community level have the potential to spoil both the satisfaction and enjoyment of the tourist experience. International sympathy and concern immediately following the Bali bombings elicited substantial financial contributions and material resources to help assist the families and direct victims of the attacks. Numerous NGOs, international aid agencies, humanitarians and volunteers dedicated additional time and effort to develop wider ranging social support programmes to assist the vulnerable, increase public access to health and education, and promote a more diversified economy (Bali Recovery Group, 2003; Parum Samigita Group Forum, 2004).

In the absence of official funding for a social safety net, the residents of Bali have also had to develop many of their own coping mechanisms. Such strategies have included access to limited personal savings, selling assets, return migration to villages and sharing facilities (Consultative Group of Indonesia, 2003; Kalla, 2003; Karyadi, 2003). Closer affiliations and shared adversity seem to have facilitated greater public interest and community awareness. Since the start of the tourism crisis, a variety of pro-active, self-initiated programmes have been introduced to address growing environmental, social and economic concerns. Using networks and contacts established after the tragedy, prominent local groups have managed to stimulate public forums, web sites and media coverage to promote open participation and discussion of relevant community issues (BaliSOS, 2003; Parum Samigita Group Forum, 2004).

Ideally, maintenance, development and restoration of a destination's tourism sector should be planned with the full awareness and support of the local community (Mitchell, 2003). By maximizing public consultation and input, it becomes possible to address local aspirations, respect traditions, ensure cultural sensitivity and incorporate indigenous knowledge. Through improved education and understanding, tourism and development practices may also be aligned to facilitate conservation and environmental protection.

Unfortunately for Bali, the community has yet to become so completely empowered. In spite of attempts to increase media access and publicity, many residents still remain ignorant of political decisions and official actions. Numerous developments have been considered and initiated since the bombings, with limited public consultation or discourse. Even the multimillion dollar Kuta pavement and drainage works financed primarily by the World Bank have demonstrated inappropriate design and construction – which may have been avoided through local knowledge (Parum Samigita Group Forum, 2004). As more department stores, resorts and entertainment venues are built for tourists, pollution, sewage, communal access to water and environmental destruction become greater regional issues. Rather than focus on direct economic returns, sustainable recovery and development needs to be compatible with long-term goals that pro-actively enhance community vitality (Natural Hazards Research and Applications Information Center, 2001).

In militating against crisis, officials and relevant industry stakeholders must also remain cognizant of their approach to other issues related to tourism, such as the behaviour and level of resentment generated by tourists within a host community. Identified as one of the key motives for the Bali bombings, Westerners in Kuta were generally seen as insensitive, inconsiderate, amoral and elitist (Bali Discovery Tours, 2004). Cultural tourism encourages understanding, appreciation and celebration of both the similarities and differences between races. With such a rich and vibrant heritage, Bali has much to offer the informed traveller. Wider dissemination and education of local customs and appropriate social norms has the potential to reduce inadvertent disrespect or tension created by ignorance. Similarly, greater consideration and tolerance fosters improved personal relationships and interaction.

By actively engaging and involving the host community in crisis planning, it is possible to reduce the socio-economic vulnerability of a destination. Beyond risk and adversity, management strategies should embrace the opportunity to create a stronger more resilient society. With increased local awareness, participation and control of developments, greater social, economic and environmental stability can be achieved. The development and maintenance of improved positive tourist–host interactions should enhance a destination's reputation. While the residents of Bali are optimistic about recent returns in visitor numbers, it is essential to ensure that such gains are not undermined by lack of social support and dissention.

Continuing challenges for Bali

In an effort to develop effective crisis management strategies, Bali has been consistently constrained by limited resources and an inability successfully to unite the disparate elements of the tourism sector, government and community. While many approaches and circumstances have improved post-crisis, the complexities of the island's economic and unique socio-political structure continue to be an impediment. An integrated and holistic recovery framework is designed to help all stakeholders work toward fully coordinating available assistance and funding, while seeking ways to accomplish other community goals and priorities (Natural Hazards Research and Applications Information Center, 2001).

With an active policy of deliberate and relatively unrestricted tourism investment over the past few decades, many residents and businesses in Bali have developed an over-reliance on tourism receipts. In such circumstances, destabilization of the tourism sector has direct, indirect and flow-on effects for all members of the community. While the island continues to have a strong agricultural base and social support network, sustainability advocates a shift in education, training and development priorities towards greater economic diversification and the generation of alternative employment prospects (Consultative Group of Indonesia, 2003). In the absence of an externally funded social safety net or cooperative, socio-economic security at the individual and local level requires greater commitment to personal savings and investment. Businesses and industry representatives must also invest adequate human, material and financial capital to develop resilience and mitigation.

Given that the viability of the tourism sector relies on the maintenance of social stability and positive perceptions, official government strategies should ideally compliment such local and regional objectives. As a Hindu enclave in a predominantly Muslim nation, the efforts of Bali have been plagued by social, cultural and ideological differences. The central government of Indonesia and the National Tourism Authority are located on the densely populated island of Java. Recent initiatives to decentralize power and responsibility have resulted in poorly defined jurisdictional responsibilities and resource allocation. Local authorities and departments around the country have essentially become self-supporting. While tax and revenues continue to flow to Jakarta, the people of Bali have had very little input or influence in subsequent spending. The Indonesian government rarely offers financial accountability and transparency to the general public.

Acutely sensitive and aware of regional issues, Bali's regional government continues to operate in an environment of limited authority and few resources. While many national efforts to increase security and promotion for Bali have complimented local plans, specific priorities and preferred methods of implementation have varied. Industry, humanitarian and stakeholder cooperation has been similarly undermined by a failure to relinquish independent aims and objectives in favour of a broader consensus (Parum Samigita Group Forum, 2004). Communication and marketing strategies have been beset by lack of familiarity, trust and conviction. Successful social initiatives have generally been too poorly funded and/or localized to have universal consequence. The efficacy and vitality of many recovery strategies have been compromised by lack of wholesale endorsement.

While Bali has almost recovered to former conditions, the experience and hardships of significant tourism crises should be sufficient to motivate all stakeholders actively to commit to a better comprehension of risk, prevention and improved operational capacities. It is the actual process of crisis management planning that creates the opportunity to surmount many of the existing constraints to effective communication and collaboration (Quarantelli, 1998). Meaningful participation and an inclusive approach allow for the development of informal linkages and communication between stakeholders from all levels of society. By openly sharing information, knowledge, skills and educational/training practice, it becomes possible to generate greater consideration and respect. Although the creation of a unified, independently funded partnership of shareholders is not necessarily an automatic outcome, greater understanding and familiarity facilitate objective risk assessment and the flexibility to respond appropriately to uncertainty.

Conclusion

As Bali's revitalization demonstrates, comprehensive integration of crisis recovery strategies is not essential to ensure resumption of tourism commerce and productivity following a significant adverse incident. Development, hazards, emergency response and reconstruction will occur irrespective of existing plans and management capabilities. Effective crisis management, however, is about minimizing the extent and duration of any negative impacts. A holistic and sustainable management framework can enhance community and destination resilience to tourism crisis.

While every destination, triggering event and subsequent crisis situation is unique, the experience of an afflicted destination can assist in the analysis and deliberation of appropriate management strategies (Pizam and Mansfield, 1996; Somnez *et al.*, 1999; Beirman, 2003). The concept of integrated crisis management is about the coordinated and collaborative efforts of all levels of government, society and relevant stakeholders. The lessons of Bali demonstrate how reactive communication, safety, marketing and community recovery strategies may have benefited from foresight, planning and a more comprehensive, unified approach to tourism management.

In an unpredictable and volatile world, the tourism industry continues to be highly sensitive and vulnerable to crises. Popular destinations and host communities cannot afford to remain complacent about adversity. While no destination is immune from crisis, appropriate levels of vigilance, preparation and resilience will minimize impacts and improve the rate of tourism recovery.

References

ABC Online (2004) ABC News Online – Bali Archive Homepage, http://abc.net.au/news/indepth/bali/archive/default.htm (accessed 14 September 2004).

Asian Disaster Preparedness Center (2001) Tourism disaster management strategies: prerequisites and ingredients. *Asian Disaster Management News*, 7, Vol. 7 nos 2 and 3 April–September 2001. Available at: http://www.adpc.ait. ac.th/infores/news letter/2001/theme-2.html (accessed 18 March 2003).

Bali Recovery Group (2003) Bali Recovery Group Homepage, http://www.balirecoverygroup.org/ (accessed 20 November 2002).

Bali Discovery Tours (2004) Bali Update Archive, http://www.balidiscovery.com/update/archive.htm (accessed 30 September 2004).

BaliSOS (2003) BaliSOS Bali Emergency Network Homepage, http://www.balisos. com (accessed 21 September 2004).

Beirman, D. (2003) *Restoring Tourism Destinations in Crisis: a Strategic Marketing Approach*. Allen and Unwin, Sydney.

BPS Statistics Indonesia (2003) Tourism Statistics, http://www.bps.go.id/sector/tourism/index.html (accessed 5 October 2004).

Consultative Group of Indonesia (2003) *Bali Beyond the Tradegy. Impact and Challenges for Tourism-led Development in Indonesia*. Consultative Group of Indonesia.

Faulkner, B. (2001) Towards a framework for tourism disaster management. *Tourism Management* 22, 135–147.

Gee, C. and Gain, C. (1986) Coping with crisis. *Travel and Tourism Analyst* June, pp. 3–12.

Glaesser, D. (2003) *Crisis Management in the Tourism Industry*. Butterworth-Heinemann, Oxford.

Kalla, J. (2003) *Mitigating Against the Social and Economic Costs of the Terrorist Attack on Bali*. Promoting Equitable Growth, Investment and Poverty Reduction, Bali. The Consultative Group of Indonesia.

Karyadi, N. (2003) *Restoring Faith: Social and Economic Mitigation in Post-bomb Bali*. Promoting Equitable Growth, Investment and Poverty Reduction, Bali. Consultative Group of Indonesia.

Matsny, L. (2001) Travel light: new paths for international tourism. *World Watch Paper* December, p. 159.

Mitchell, R. (2003) Community-based tourism: moving from rhetoric to practice. E-Review of Tourism Research (ERTR) Vol. 1, No. 1, 2003 (online) http://ertr. tamu.edu (accessed 9 February 2004).

Natural Hazards Research and Applications Information Center (2001) *Holistic Disaster Recovery: Ideas for Building Local Sustainability after a Natural Disaster*. Natural Hazards Research and Applications Information Center, University of Colorado, Boulder, Colorado.

Pacific Asia Travel Association (2003) *The PATA Bali Recovery Task Force: Report and Recommendations*. Pacific Asia Travel Association, Bangkok.

Parum Samigita Group Forum (2004) Samigita – the Bali forum, http://groups.yahoo.com/groups/samigita (accessed 12 June 2005).

Pizam, A. and Mansfield, Y. (eds) (1996) *Tourism, Crime and International Security Issues*. John Wiley and Sons, Chichester, UK.

Quarantelli, E. (1998) *Major Criteria for Judging Disaster Planning and their Applicability in Developing Societies*. Disaster Research Centre, University of Delaware, Newark, Delaware.

Richter, L. and Waugh, W. (1986) Terrorism and tourism as logical companions. *Tourism Management* 7, 230–239

Santana, G. (2003) Crisis management and tourism: beyond the rhetoric. *Journal of Travel and Tourism Marketing* 15, 299–231.

Somnez, S., Apostopoulos, Y. and Tarlow, P. (1999) Tourism in crisis: managing the effects of terrorism. *Journal of Travel Research* 38, 13–18.

United Nations Development Programme (1992) An Overview of Disaster Management, http://www.undmtp.org/english/ Overview/overview.pdf (accessed 22 April 2003).

World Bank (2003) *Confronting Crisis: Impacts and Response to the Bali Tragedy.* Promoting Equitable Growth, Investment and Poverty Reduction, Bali. Consultative Group of Indonesia.

World Tourism Organization (2003) Crisis Guidelines for the Tourism Industry, http://www.world-tourism.org/ market_research/Crisis%20and%20Disas ter%20Management%20Guidelines.pdf. (accessed 3 July 2003).

World Tourism Organization (2004) World Tourism Organisation Homepage, http://www.world-tourism.org/ (accessed 10 September 2004).

World Travel and Tourism Council (2003) Travel and Tourism Security Action Plan, http://www.wttc.org/publications/pdf/ SecurityActionPlanFINAL%2004apr03mth 2.pdf. (accessed 3 August 2004).

8 'Crises' that Scare Tourists: Investigating Tourists' Travel-related Concerns

SARA DOLNICAR

Introduction

The importance of perceived risk by tourists – while first studied in the broader context of general consumer behaviour (Bauer, 1960) – has been of ongoing interest to the tourism industry and research. The topic is of interest to tourism even in times when no major actual risks need to be feared given that the intangible nature of the tourism product brings uncertainty in the destination or vacation choice process. However, global political events such as terrorism attacks and the emergence of global epidemics have reignited awareness of the importance of risk perceptions, adding a new dimension to the potential consequences of not understanding what scares tourists. The relevance of the topic to the tourism industry is essentially driven by the fear of demand fluctuations due to unpredictable events that are beyond the control of tourism authorities and the industry. Consequently, it is important to gain in-depth understanding of concerns tourists have and the way they might react to different kinds of events in the course of a travel or destination choice process. Being aware of such aspects empowers tourism authorities and the industry to develop the right products, send the optimal communication messages and possibly target the most suitable market segments to ensure continuing demand in future times of crisis.

Prior work

Prior work in this area can broadly be grouped into specific investigations of particular concerns, fears or perceived risks of tourists on the one hand, and more general investigations into the patterns of tourism consumer behaviour in response to perceived risks. Among the specific investigations into particular aspects of tourist concerns, two categories of perceived risks have attracted most attention: diseases and terrorism.

In the area of health-related studies, Cossens and Gin (1994) studied how tourist decision making is affected by the knowledge of high human immunodeficiency virus (HIV) rates at destinations, a topic first discussed by Cohen (1988). Investigating how strongly certain risks are perceived to be present in different regions of the world as well as the seriousness of the risk, the confidence tourists had in the local health system and their factual knowledge about HIV/AIDS, Cossens and Gin came to the conclusion that tourists assigned higher risk evaluations to countries with high HIV rates, and that about 15% were actually influenced in their travel decision by such information.

In the context of safety concerns and their influence on tourist's travel decisions, Demos (1992) reported a negative association of the crime rate and inbound tourism in Washington, DC. While this association is based on aggregate data and no causal conclusions can be drawn, the survey conducted in Washington, DC by the author does indicate high levels of safety-related perceived risk among visitors. From a tourism management point of view, this is relevant information in itself (independent of the actual association with crime rate levels) due to the possible negative effects of such high levels of perceived risk on tourism demand. Pinhey and Iverson (1994) find support for Demos's conclusions in a study of Japanese travellers and reveal a number of socio-demographic factors which are associated with the strength of negative safety concerns. A number of articles were published on the inter-relationship of terrorism and crime, and tourism (Chesney-Lind and Lind, 1986; Richter and Waugh, 1986; Wahab, 1996; Sonmez *et al.*, 1999; Mawby *et al.*, 2000; Crotts, 2003). These were, however, not investigating the influence of perceived risk on tourist behaviour.

A number of larger scale empirical studies have investigated the role of perceived risks as a broader construct in tourism decision making. Roehl and Fesenmaier (1992) used findings from the area of consumer behaviour as their starting point, selecting six broad risk category items for the survey: equipment risk; financial risk; physical risk; psychological risk; satisfaction risk; and time risk. They derived underlying factors of the items and use the factor scores to construct a posteriori (Mazanec, 2000) or data-driven (Dolnicar, 2004) segments of tourists with specific reaction patterns to the listed risk items. These resulting groups of tourists are referred to as place risk group, functional risk group and risk neutral group. Group membership is shown to be associated with significantly different patterns of travel behaviour. Similar segmentation studies conducted by Dolnicar (2005a, b) support the validity of Roehl and Fesenmaier's findings a decade later using both an a priori (Mazanec, 2000) and a data-driven segmentation approach. In both cases, distinctly different segments with regard to concerns tourists have in relation to travel are identified. These segments demonstrate significant differences regarding additional characteristics, for instance media behaviour, which makes target marketing of such 'fear segments' viable. Sonmez and Graefe (1998) conducted an empirical study including the Roehl and Fesenmaier items and adding terrorism, health and political instability. They found that perceived risks and perceived safety are associated with expressed intentions to travel by respondents.

The present chapter reports on the results of two empirical studies that aimed at eliciting currently perceived risks from the tourist marketplace and investigates the differences in statements of concerns with respect to different tourism settings.

Methodology

Data were collected from two sources capturing different subsegments of the tourism market. One study was conducted at an Australian University with undergraduate students across all faculties. Both open-ended questions and lists of risks were included in the questionnaire given to the students. The lists of risks were derived from student focus groups which were held prior to developing the survey instrument. A total of 373 completed questionnaires form the basis of the data set.

The second study was conducted in cooperation with a leading Australian tour operator specializing in adventure travel. Data were collected at the tour operator's outlets across Australia during the exploratory phase; and online by e-mailing all the members of a newsletter mailing list during the quantitative phase. In the qualitative phase, questionnaires including one single question were handed out to tourists entering the premises. They were offered a well-targeted incentive to complete the questionnaire: the opportunity to win a vacation for two people worth approximately AUS$4000. The statements resulting from the exploratory study were analyzed using descriptive statistics and used subsequently to develop the survey tool for the quantitative phase. The following items were included in the list: an act of terrorism; war/military conflict; political instability; travel warning issued before travel; natural disasters (landslides, earthquakes); life-threatening diseases, e.g. severe acute respiratory syndrome (SARS); general health concerns; lack of access to Western medical facilities; lack of access to clean food and water; high personal mental and physical challenge; theft; unreliable airline; lack of suitable pre-trip training and preparation; and fear of travelling in a small group. Respondents were asked whether these concerns would prevent them from booking a trip. A total of 649 respondents completed the questionnaire online.

Descriptive statistics were computed on the basis of the available data sets using SPSS in its 12.1.0 version. The limitation of the data sets is that both capture particular subsegments of the tourist population: students and adventure travellers, respectively. While this does not weaken the results derived in the context of these subsegments, it should be noted that the results cannot be generalized to the general tourist population.

Results

As described above, the student questionnaire contained both open-ended questions and a list of risks for evaluation. The open-ended questions were worded as follows: 'When deciding on how to spend the next vacation, which aspects of this decision do you perceive as risky? What are you concerned about?', 'When going on vacation in Australia, which are the risks you perceive? What are you worried about?', 'When going on vacation overseas, which are the risks you perceive? What are you worried about?'

Safety-related factors were mentioned by 42% of the respondents. Responses to the open-ended questions were more frequently given in the context of overseas travel than was the case for domestic travel, where only 9% shared the safety concern. Similarly, a fifth of the respondents stated health concerns regarding an overseas trip; only 6% were concerned about health-related aspects of their trip when staying in Australia. Details of the aspects stated are provided in Table 8.1. As can be seen, terrorism and war dominate the list of safety-related perceived risks; diseases cause most worries among health-related statements.

Table 8.1 also illustrates how clearly respondents discriminate between the overseas and the domestic context. This is particularly visible in the areas of war, terrorism, diseases and theft, all of which are hardly mentioned in the Australian context. The reverse is the case regarding the fear of being attacked by animals, as well as concerns about roads and transportation: Australia as a tourism destination appears to trigger much more concern with respect to these aspects than do overseas destinations. These differences suggest the existence of a destination-specific risk image which is present in tourists' minds in a similar way to classic destination images focused on travel benefits. Such destination risk images would be likely to influence the tourist decision-making process in a very similar way, limiting inclusion in the evoked set and consequent development of preferences (Woodside and Lysonski, 1989) for destinations with the lowest perceived destination risk attributes.

In addition to the open-ended question, students were presented with a list of risks and were first asked to state whether the occurrence of this risk would increase or decrease their booking probability and then requested to do the following: 'Please indicate the strength of this influence by writing a percentage value. 1% means that the influence on the booking decision is very low, 100% means it is highest.' The average values assigned by all the respondents are provided in Table 8.2. The first two items – characterized by the highest assigned influence levels – are the two positive items, for which respondents indicated that it would increase rather than decrease their booking probability. A 50% influence on the booking decision is expressed by respondents. Almost as strong is the effect of bad weather. The tourists concerns raised most frequently in the open-ended questions (terrorism and diseases) are seen to have the highest influence on the booking decision, excluding the two positive items and bad weather,

Table 8.1. Open-ended statements within fear categories (in absolute numbers of respondents).

		General	Domestic	Overseas
Safety	Terrorism	47	2	73
	War	21	1	20
	Violence	8		3
	Attacks	4	1	
	Bombings	4		3
	Kidnapping/being held hostage	4		4
	Crime	2	2	8
	Attacked/bitten by animal		16	1
Health	Disease	12	1	19
	Injury	4	3	2
	Accident	2	8	2
	Hygiene	1		6
	Food supply	1		3
Money	Not enough money	4	3	3
	Money access	1		2
	Wasting money	1	4	
Air travel	Plane crash	2	5	2
	Plane safety	1		2
Cultural risk	Culture clash	5		1
	Social	4	2	3
	Language	3		17
	Discrimination	2	1	3
Loss of property	Theft	7	3	19
	Luggage	2	5	7
	Robbery	2		6
	Valuables/passport	1	1	11
Other tourists	Crowded	2	6	
Other	Transportation/roads	1	24	9
	Getting lost	5	10	8
	Environment	3	4	2
	Natural disasters	3	2	1

with influence values of 44 and 40%, respectively. Social risk, the dimension omitted by Roehl and Fesenmaier (1992) due to the detrimental effect on the scale reliability (probably indicating a different dimension of perceived risk altogether), was consistently rated lowest among students: the three respective items were assigned influence values between 13 and 22%.

Finally, the probability of occurrence of the listed concerns was investigated by asking respondents: 'Please indicate for the kinds of trips stated in the first row, how strongly you think each of the risks applies to this particular kind of travel on a percentage scale, where 0% indicates that the risk does not exist in that particular kind of travel and 100% indicates that the risk is extremely high.'

Table 8.3 shows the average percentages across all respondents for each context and averaged across all four contexts. The event perceived as

Table 8.2. Average strength of event influence on booking decision on a scale from low (1%) to high (100%).

	n	Mean (%)	SD
I might undertake thrilling activities[a]	333	51	32
I might travel to exotic and unusual places[a]	340	51	32
The weather might be bad	333	48	38
I might be a victim of terrorism	334	44	45
I might be exposed to the risk of contagious diseases	336	40	42
I might get bad value for money	346	32	38
There might be a lot of insecurity involved	331	29	31
I might get sick	331	28	33
I might injure myself	332	28	32
The natural environment might be hostile	331	28	34
It might be a waste of time	329	26	34
The vacation might not be satisfying	332	25	29
My trip might cause environmental damage	327	24	82
I might not have a great time	326	23	27
I might feel socially uncomfortable	337	22	24
The vacation might not reflect my personality	332	18	24
People might have a bad opinion of me	331	13	21

[a] These two items were positively worded; consequently they increase rather than decrease booking probability.

most likely varies across contexts: contagious diseases are assigned the highest probability of all perceived risks in the overseas travel context, bad weather leads the list of perceived risks for domestic and adventure travel, and not getting good value for money is stated to be the most likely risk in the culture tourism trip. For a further discussion of the destination- and context-specific differences, see Dolnicar (2005a). By computing the sum over all assigned probabilities for the four contexts, a risk occurrence indicator can be computed. The resulting values are shown in the bottom row of Table 8.3.

It becomes evident from these values that overseas trips are perceived as most risky in sum, followed by culture trips and adventure trips. However, from a managerial point of view, the nature of the risks associated with specific destinations or travel contexts are of higher practical value than such a composite index, as it enables destination management to communicate with their target markets more efficiently either by emphasizing that they are a low-risk destination or by actively providing information that reduces the levels of certain risks associated with that particular destination or travel context.

A final conclusion that can be drawn from the risk probability analysis is that – across all contexts – respondents assign higher probabilities to more commonly occurring events, such as bad value for money or bad weather. This is not surprising. It is, however, surprising that concerns such as contagious diseases and terrorism are assigned higher probabilities than all social risk items and items such as not having a great time or the

Table 8.3. Average estimated occurrence of events at different destinations and in different travel contexts (in average assigned percentages).

	Overseas	SD	Domestic	SD	Adventure	SD	Culture	SD	Total average
I might get bad value for money	55	28	33	26	41	29	42	28	43
The weather might be bad	45	30	40	29	46	31	34	30	41
I might undertake thrilling activities	44	32	39	79	53	37	28	29	41
I might injure myself	41	31	31	29	55	37	27	28	38
I might get sick	50	31	28	28	37	30	33	29	37
I might travel to exotic and unusual places	46	36	29	29	37	34	36	33	37
I might be exposed to the risk of contagious diseases	56	31	23	29	28	29	37	31	36
I might be a victim of terrorism	54	34	25	29	26	30	38	33	36
The natural environment might be hostile	46	30	27	25	35	30	34	32	35
The vacation might not be satisfying	35	31	33	26	33	28	37	29	34
There might be a lot of insecurity involved	44	31	23	23	38	31	31	28	34
I might feel socially uncomfortable	40	29	18	21	26	26	37	30	30
I might not have a great time	29	29	28	27	29	29	31	28	29
It might be a waste of time	23	28	25	27	27	29	32	31	27
My trip might cause environmental damage	24	28	23	28	30	31	24	29	25
The vacation might not reflect my personality	23	25	19	22	25	29	25	28	23
People might have a bad opinion of me	26	28	17	22	19	23	24	27	22
Average negative risk evaluation across contexts	39		26		32		33		

vacation being a waste of time. While follow-up research would be required to gain more insight into the reasons for this paradox (which contradicts the absolute probability of the occurrence of the respective events), a possible hypothesis could be the increased awareness of tourists of major global events due to higher levels of media reporting on global epidemics and terrorism activity.

The first phase of the investigation of adventure tourists' concerns consisted of collecting their perceived risks. The exact wording of the question was as follows: 'When deciding on how to spend the next holiday, which aspects of this decision do you perceive as risky? What are you concerned about? Please write down all the concerns/worries/fears that come to your mind.' The aim was to collect unaided statements of tourists in order to capture the broadest possible list of concerns that are on tourists' minds during the process of vacation planning. Given that the collaborating tour operator was very careful not to burden the respondents too much, personal characteristics were not collected at this point. The fieldwork resulted in a wide variety of statements which led to the selection of the items used in the quantitative stage of the survey and can be roughly classified into the following groups: political risk (examples of statements include 'real danger of being caught in military conflict', 'unsafe to travel to chosen location because of war'), environmental risk (e.g. 'landslides'), health risk (e.g. 'sudden illness needing immediate treatment', 'medical advice not to take the trip', 'life-threatening diseases'), planning risk (e.g. 'my travel arrangements could not be confirmed', 'assured flight home') and property risk (e.g. 'security of luggage etc. on travel, e.g. buses and trains'). A detailed statistic of the responses is provided in Table 8.4.

The adventure tourists' views on perceived risks which would prevent them from booking were explored in the following question: 'Which of the following risks that can occur prior to or during your trip would prevent you from booking the trip on your side? (Please tick all appropriate boxes in both columns.)' The result is provided in Table 8.5. Note that respondents were only able to answer by ticking or not ticking each listed perceived risk. The percentages thus indicate the proportion of the sample who stated that each respective concern from the list would prevent them from booking.

As can be seen, war and miliary conflict is the most powerful concern: it would prevent about 80% of tourists from booking. The next risk factor likely to prevent 60% of the adventure travellers from booking is found to be the occurrence of life-threatening diseases, followed closely by acts of terrorism.

General health concerns and the lack of access to Western medical facilities would only prevent 19 and 14%, respectively, of adventure travellers from booking, and risk of theft is almost negligible, with only one in ten respondents stating that they would not book for that reason.

Of particular interest in Table 8.5 is the fairly high reaction to travel warnings. Almost half of the adventure tourists would consider not booking a trip if a travel warning were issued by the Australian government. This indicates a high reactivity and a potential danger for tour operators specializing in countries which have high probabilities of being mentioned on the government's warning list.

Conclusions, Limitations and Future Work

Tourists' concerns were investigated among two subsegments of tourists: adventure tourists and student tourists. For each of the subsegments, both unaided open questions and closed questions with a number of perceived risk items listed in the questionnaire were used. The unaided questions aimed at deriving statements not influenced by options to choose from. The closed questions aimed at deriving valid proportions of subsegments regarding the concerns that most influenced their tourist's behaviour or travel planning behaviour.

The results indicate that – no matter which subsegment and no matter which approach to questioning – the fear of terrorism and contagious

Table 8.4. Perceived fears of adventure tourists (in numbers of respondents).

	General	Domestic	Overseas		General	Domestic	Overseas
Safety	157	34	177	Of which:			
				Terrorism	47	2	73
				War	21	1	20
				Violence	8		3
				Attacks	4	1	
				Bombings	4		3
				Kidnapping	4		4
				Crime	2	2	8
				Animal attack		16	1
Health	48	21	76	Of which:			
				Disease	12	1	19
				Injury	4	3	2
				Accident	2	8	2
				Hygiene	1		6
				Food supply	1		3
Political stability	30		18				
Value for money	30	20	25				
Money	25	19	25	Of which:			
				Not enough money	4	3	3
				Money access	1		2
				Wasting money	1	4	
Destination	26	4	5				
Air travel	23	10	25	Of which:			
				Plane crash	2	5	2
				Plane safety	1		2
Cultural risk	20	6	37	Of which:			
				Culture clash	5		1
				Social	4	2	3
				Language	3		17
				Discrimination	2	1	3
Weather	18	28	2				
Loss of property	13	9	45	Of which:			
				Theft	7	3	19
				Luggage	2	5	7
				Robbery	2		6
				Valuables/passport	1	1	11
Accommodation	6	7	2				
Other tourists	4	7		Of which:			
				Crowded	2	6	
Other	60	80	39	Of which:			
				Transportation/roads	1	24	9
				Getting lost	5	10	8
				Environment	3	4	2
				Natural disasters	3	2	1

Source: Dolnicar (2005b).

Table 8.5. Concerns that would prevent tourists from booking.

	Respondents	Percentage
War/military conflict	510	79
Life-threatening diseases, e.g. SARS	386	59
An act of terrorism	361	56
Lack of access to clean food and water	298	46
Political instability	297	46
Travel warning issued before travel	297	46
Unreliable airline	292	45
Natural disasters (landslides, earthquakes)	222	34
Lack of suitable pre-trip training and preparation	208	32
General health concerns	121	19
High personal mental and physical challenge	92	14
Lack of access to Western medical facilities	88	14
Theft	60	9
Fear of travelling in a small group	15	2

diseases is present in today's tourist's mind and has the power of dramatically modifying tourist behaviour. For instance, 80% of adventure tourists state that a war or military conflict would prevent them from booking. The managerial implications of this finding are significant and numerous. First, the tourism industry needs to learn as much as possible about what can potentially scare the market segment catered for from booking. Secondly, ways of delivering information should be investigated to ease the concerns of travellers. For instance, a military conflict may well be happening in parts of a country, while other parts could be totally unaffected. Such information would have to be communicated effectively and quickly to customers in a situation where, for instance, travel warnings are issued and tourists are tempted to react instantly by cancelling (or not booking) a trip. Finally, market segments could exist that are less affected in their travel behaviour by potential risks they might encounter. If this is the case, such segments should be identified and profiled. They could represent a stable customer base that can consistently be harvested independently of global events, thus providing the tourism industry with the security of stable demand patterns.

Another interesting insight from the investigation of perceived fears among tourists is the distinct nature of differences of expressed concerns across both destinations and travel contexts. Again, this has important consequences for the tourism industry. Destination management, for instance, could develop destination risk image profiles in the same way they are presently analyzing and optimizing the general images of destinations as perceived by tourists. The destination risk image profile could then be managed either to match particular segments of tourists or generally to minimize any negative risk perceptions. Furthermore, tourism operators specializing in certain areas of tourism, for instance cultural tourism or adventure tourism, should be aware of the main concerns tourists have that are specific to their product, in order to be able to communicate optimally with their target market.

While this investigation has led to some significant insights and allowed a number of recommendations to be deduced for tourism industry practise, the study naturally has it limitations. First, all findings are valid only for the samples under study and cannot be generalized to the total tourist population. Secondly, all the presented analyses are based on behavioural intentions; the extension to the study of actual tourist behaviour would be desirable in future. Thirdly, the results presented were based on sample totals, not investigating the possible existence of segments among tourists who systematically differ in their risk perceptions and/or reactivity to risk. Future work in this direction should therefore be conducted. For instance, are there market segments who have systematically different perceptions of how likely certain risks are to occur in different tourism contexts? Are there segments who are affected to a different extent in their booking behaviour if they are concerned about certain issues? Furthermore, and on a more theoretical note, the asymmetry of positive and negative perceived risks which became evident from the question on how strongly the occurrence of certain events would influence the booking probability should be studied in more detail. Another open issue is the question of whether the effect of tourist concerns on booking or cancelling behaviour is compensatory or not: are there certain concerns which can under no circumstances be compensated? Which concerns can be successfully compensated and in which way can tourists be prevented from not booking or cancelling trips?

Acknowledgements

This research was funded through the New Partnership Grant Scheme at the University of Wollongong. I thank all the students of the Applied Marketing Research Class in 2003 involved in the fieldwork of the student survey as well as their tutors Kye Ling Gan, Geoffrey Chard and Andrew Smith for supporting them. I also thank management of the collaborating tour operator for their genuine research enthusiasm, and Tracey Dickson and Katie Lazarevski who were involved in this project as research assistants.

References

Bauer, R.A. (1960) Consumer behaviour as risk taking. In: Hancock, R.S. (ed.) *Dynamic Marketing for a Changing World.* American Marketing Association, Chicago, Illinois, pp. 389–398.

Chesney-Lind, M. and Lind, I.Y. (1986) Visitors as victims – crimes against tourists in Hawaii. *Annals of Tourism Research* 13, 167–191.

Cohen, B. (1988) Tourism and AIDS in Thailand. *Annals of Tourism Research* 15, 467–495.

Cossens, J. and Gin, S. (1994) Tourism and AIDS: the perceived risk of HIV infection on destination choice. *Journal of Travel and Tourism Marketing* 3 (4), 1–20.

Crotts, J.C. (2003) Theoretical perspectives on tourist criminal victimisation. *Journal of Tourism Studies* 14, 92–98.

Demos, E. (1992) Concern for safety: a potential problem in the tourist industry. *Journal of Travel and Tourism Marketing* 1, 81–88.

Dolnicar, S. (2004) Beyond 'commonsense segmentation' – a systematics of segmentation approaches in tourism. *Journal of Travel Research* 42, 244–250.

Dolnicar, S. (2005a) Understanding barriers to leisure travel – using tourist fears as marketing basis. *Journal of Vacation Marketing* 11, 197–208.

Dolnicar, S. (2005b) Fear segments in tourism. CD Proceedings of the 14th International Research Conference of the Council for Australian University Tourism and Hospitality Education (CAUTHE), Alice Springs.

Mawby, R.I., Brunt, P. and Hambly, Z. (2000) Fear of crime among British holiday-makers. *British Journal of Criminology* 40, 468–480.

Mazanec, J. (2000) Market segmentation. In: Jafari, J. (ed.) *Encyclopedia of Tourism.* Routledge, London, pp. 374–375.

Pinhey, T.K. and Iverson, T.J. (1994) Safety concerns of Japanese visitors to Guam. *Journal of Travel and Tourism Marketing* 3 (2), 87–94.

Richter, L.K. and Waugh, W.L.J. (1986) Terrorism and tourism as logical companions. *Tourism Management* 7, 230–238.

Roehl, W.S. and Fesenmaier, D.R. (1992) Risk perceptions and pleasure travel: an exploratory analysis. *Journal of Travel Research* 30 (4), 17–26.

Sonmez, S.F. and Graefe, A.R. (1998) Determining future travel behaviour from past travel experience and perceptions of risk and safety. *Journal of Travel Research*, 37 (2), 171–177.

Sonmez, S.F., Apostolopoulos, Y. and Tarlow, P. (1999) Tourism in crisis: managing the effects of terrorism. *Journal of Travel Research* 38, 3–8.

Wahab, S. (1996) Tourism and terrorism: synthesis of the problem with emphasis on Egypt. In: Pizam, A. and Mansfield, Y. (eds) *Tourism, Crime and International Security Issues.* John Wiley, New York, pp. 175–186.

Woodside, A. and Lysonski, S. (1989) A general model of traveller destination choice. *Journal of Travel Research* 27 (4) 8–14.

9

For Better or Worse: Consumer Perceptions of Factors Impacting Company Crisis Outcome

LYNETTE M. MCDONALD, BEVERLEY SPARKS AND IAN GLENDON

Tourism crises can be triggered by natural or human-caused disasters (Sönmez et al., 1999). Crises that have dramatically impacted travel and tourism operators include the 2003 severe acute respiratory syndrome (SARS) virus outbreak, the 2003 Iraq War and terrorist attacks such as the 2002 Bali bombings and that of 11 September 2001 (9/11) on the World Trade Center in New York. The New York terrorist attack constituted an extreme example of the many crises that a business operation might face (Stafford et al., 2002). These crises have the potential to threaten the viability of tourism destinations, and the enterprises associated with them, at regional or world level. While recent focus has been on major events impacting the travel and tourism sector, this chapter investigates crises that originate at the organization or enterprise level and impact travel and tourism operators. In particular, it focuses upon the perspectives provided by consumers of tourism services.

Fink (1986) defined organizational crises as events that run the risk of escalating in intensity, falling under close media or government scrutiny, interfering with normal business operations, jeopardizing a company's public image and damaging the bottom line. It may be no longer a question of whether a major crisis will strike an organization, but only a matter of when, which type and how (Mitroff and Pearson, 1993). Crises may generate substantial negative publicity and ill-feeling towards companies, costing tourism and travel operators millions of dollars in lost sales, eroded market share and reputation damage.

Three crises that involved or affected tourism industry operators in Australia include the Ansett Airlines safety crisis, the *Legionella* outbreak at the Melbourne Aquarium and the Esso gas crisis which saw large numbers of room cancellations at Melbourne hotels. The next section elaborates on the background of these company crises.

In 2001, Ansett, one of Australia's oldest domestic airline carriers, had its fleet of ten Boeing 767s grounded following safety checks that revealed wing cracks. The grounding cost Ansett AUS$4.24 million, mostly in purchase of alternative seats and leasing, and AUS$20 million for an advertising campaign (AAP, 2001), while the company lost an estimated 20% of its market share to alternative carriers (Goodsir, 2001). Ansett ceased operations later that year. Australia's largest *Legionella* outbreak occurred in April 2000 at the newly opened tourist attraction, the Melbourne Aquarium, killing two people, infecting 111 others and resulting in trading losses of more than AUS$3 million (*The Age*, 2000). The outbreak had its source in the Aquarium's air-conditioning cooling towers (*The Age*, 2000). The legal claim resulting from the class action against the Aquarium was estimated to be more than AUS$35 million (Minter Ellison Lawyers, 2003). The gas crisis started with an explosion, and subsequent fire, at the Esso gas plant in rural Victoria in September 1998, killing two employees and injuring eight others (*Courier Mail*, 2003). The crisis left Melbourne, Australia's second largest city, and its resident population of 3 million without gas for cooking and showers for 2 weeks (Hannan, 1999). The crisis also had flow-on effects to businesses dependent on tourism. For example, because many Melbourne hotels were dependent on gas for cooking and hot water, scores of interstate and overseas visitors cancelled or changed hotel reservations (Mallinson, 1999). Businesses and consumers were estimated to have lost AUS$1.4 billion during that time (*Courier Mail*, 2003).

As a crisis can seriously impact on the viability of a tourism business, it seems timely to consider the factors that affect the crisis outcome in order to help organizations best manage crisis situations to minimize negative ramifications, i.e. within a crisis context, how does the action or inaction of an organization affect consumer sentiment, and especially emotional response processes that may later affect actions such as word of mouth or purchase intent?

Literature Review

Since research on company crises is a relatively new field, there is no clear consensus as to what might be the most important features to study. Factors investigated in crisis studies include the company's message or 'account' of its role in the crisis (Griffin *et al.*, 1991; Jorgensen, 1994, 1996), the message source (Griffin *et al.*, 1991; Weinberger *et al.*, 1991), the amount and intensity of media attention (Weinberger and Romeo, 1989), type of media coverage (Weinberger *et al.*, 1991), crisis responsibility (Jorgensen, 1996), attitudes to the company (Griffin *et al.*, 1991; Jorgensen, 1994, 1996) and attributions about the cause of the crisis (Jorgensen, 1994, 1996). Researchers in the fields of service failure and product recall have established that certain factors impact outcomes such as consumers' likely buying behaviour. These factors include company reputation (Siomkos and

Shrivastava, 1993), familiarity of the company name (Mowen and Ellis, 1981), and the number and degree of injuries (Mowen, 1979; Mowen and Ellis, 1981).

The focus in crisis studies and those for service failure and product recall has been on factors impacting purchase intent, rather than on understanding the consumer processes that act as its antecedents, or on identifying other factors that consumers themselves consider important in a crisis situation. While a small number of crisis studies provided important insight into attitudes and attributions which precede purchase intent, there are also clear pointers to the importance of emotions. Although the study of emotions has attracted much research interest in many fields, the role of consumer emotions in company crises has largely been ignored. Apart from anger and sympathy, the emotions that crises elicit in consumers has rarely been explored, although a study by Frederickson *et al.* (2003) on resilience following the 9/11 terrorist attacks found that people recalled 20 different emotions.

Weiner's (1986, 1995) attributional theory (WAT) has been applied to the examination of consumer reactions to company crises and service failures. WAT predicts that following an unexpected negative event, observers appraise the cause of the event, determining whether the event had an internal or external cause and how controllable that cause was. These causal beliefs give rise to inferences of responsibility. Feelings of anger and sympathy follow which, in turn, direct social behaviour. Mitigating factors, such as a company's account of its role in the crisis, can reduce the responsibility judgement. Three studies (Folkes *et al.*, 1987; Jorgensen, 1994, 1996) directly examined attributions, anger and purchase intentions, finding that anger preceded negative purchase intentions, highlighting the potential significance of emotions in a crisis. Yet the range of emotions that company crises elicit in consumers, other than anger and sympathy, has not been explored, nor has likely crisis behaviour apart from purchase intent and investment intent. Thus, the first objective of our study was to examine the range of emotions and behaviours that various crises may evoke from consumers.

Additionally, although previous research in service failure and product recall indicated that factors such as company reputation and injury levels helped determine consumer outcomes, no research has investigated what factors consumers themselves considered important in company crises. Thus, the second main objective of the study was to investigate whether any unexpected variables impacted crisis outcome, apart from those already identified in the literature on crises, product recall and service failures.

As this study was exploratory, the following research questions were formulated:

- What emotions and what behaviour do various crisis types evoke?
- What other crisis factors influence consumer reactions?

To fill in these knowledge gaps, we conducted a series of focus groups investigating consumers' thoughts, emotions, behaviours and other factors considered important regarding recalled organizational crises. As the literature indicated that demographic characteristics of gender, age, culture, income and education influence an individual's reactions, participants were allocated into groups based on high or low dimensions of these characteristics. Specifically, gender affects emotional expression, with men more likely to express their anger (Timmers *et al.*, 1998), while the tendency to respond with anger to frustrating situations generally steadily declines with age for both men and women (Knight *et al.*, 1985). There are also cultural differences regarding whether we are more likely to blame others for a negative event. Those from collectivist cultures (e.g. Asian, Latin American and Islamic) are more likely to consider external or situational factors surrounding the person or the company, while those from individualist cultures (e.g. Western European, North American) are more likely to attribute it to the personal dispositions of those involved (e.g. Fletcher and Ward, 1988). Additionally, following a crisis, Weinberger and Romeo (1989) found that the negative impact on product sales was stronger, in both the short and long term, for individuals with lower incomes and lower education, than for those in higher groups.

The results from the first research question have been reported elsewhere by McDonald and Härtel (2002) and revealed that consumers experience a large variety of both positive and negative emotions and behaviours, with these appearing dependent upon the attributions made about the cause of the crisis.

The results of the second research question are reported here using examples given from three crises participants discussed which involved or impacted tourism industry operators: the Ansett Airlines safety crisis, the Melbourne Aquarium *Legionella* outbreak and the Esso gas crisis. We discuss new variables that emerged, which have not previously been identified in the literature on crisis, product recall and service failure. These consisted of a broad range of attitudes towards companies' management, crisis management, crisis advertising, government and the media, and negative inferences about the company management. Other factors that emerged were company reputation, the company's account of its role in the crisis, the credibility of both the company message and the message source, crisis responsibility and severity of harm. Possible implications for crisis management are proposed and recommendations made.

Data Collection

Focus groups were the chosen research method as they promote group interaction and prompt recall. They also facilitate open and spontaneous responses from participants, while providing rich, detailed information and insights (Morgan, 1998). Focus group research provides data on how people say they behaved and may provide an information-sharing context similar to that experienced in normal conversation (Morgan, 1998).

The 53 participants were allocated to eight groups matched on high and low dimensions of age, income, education and cultural orientation (individualism/collectivism). Each group contained a gender mix. Focus Group 1 (FG1) was of higher age, FG2 had a higher level of education, FG3 had higher income, FG4 had lower income, FG5 was of lower age, FG6 had a lower level of education, FG7 was individualist and FG8 was collectivist.

Congruent with Lunt's (1996) recommendations that focus groups ideally should be sized between six and ten individuals to ensure adequate member participation, the focus groups averaged seven participants. Recruitment techniques included public notification of the study through print, radio and TV stories that resulted from a media campaign targeting metropolitan media. The focus groups were videotaped and transcribed.

Rather than force discussion of particular crises that participants may not have found relevant, a professional moderator provided a crisis definition, then asked participants to recall important crises and their memorable aspects, with a strong focus on feelings, thoughts and actions taken.

While participants across the eight groups recalled 12 crises that fitted Fink's (1986) crisis definition, seven proved more salient to participants and, as a result, were more heavily discussed. These had occurred in Australia and had impacted most focus group participants either directly or indirectly. Of the seven, three crises involved tourism industry operators, the Ansett Airlines safety crisis, the *Legionella* outbreak at the Melbourne Aquarium and the Esso gas plant explosion, and had personally impacted participants. Several focus group participants had experienced flight cancellations due to the Ansett Airlines groundings, and all knew of the safety crisis. With the Melbourne Aquarium *Legionella* outbreak, one focus group participant was a member of the class action against the Aquarium, while many others in the groups had visited the Aquarium during the infection period or had close family members who had visited during that time. All focus group participants had been personally impacted by the gas crisis, except one who had lived interstate at the time.

Analysis

While a theoretical model was developed prior to the study, an inductive method was used to allow patterns, themes and categories to emerge (Patton, 1990). The videotape transcriptions and the white-board discussion summaries were content analysed following the recommendations of Miles and Huberman (1984). Pattern coding was used to sort those summaries into a smaller number of overarching themes or constructs (Miles and Huberman, 1984). This involved an iterative approach, cycling back and forth between the transcripts, considering the constructs already defined in the literature, and the more abstract determination of what codes should exist. The results were re-analysed based on revised themes and coding categories, looking for connections and divergence among the themes identified, and among the responses of different groups. The results were interpreted within a positivist paradigm, with word counts used and thematic associations explored.

Issues of reliability were handled by leaving an audit trail regarding data collection and analysis. As validity in qualitative research is best demonstrated by careful documentation of the analytical procedure (Miles and Huberman, 1984), our full analysis made extensive use of tabulated data, giving percentages where possible to provide evidence backing up the validity of findings and conclusions.

Results

In this section, results from the discussions are summarized, with typical quotes selected from the three tourism crises. Participants are referred to by the number of their focus group, gender and place in the group (e.g. FG7M3 refers to Focus Group 7, male participant 3).

Themes previously identified in the crisis research literature which emerged were crisis responsibility, company accounts, message and source credibility, and attitudes, while those from the product recall literature were company reputation and severity of harm. New codes identified were dispositional attributions towards the company, and a range of attitudes to company management, crisis management, advertising, and government and the media.

Severity of harm and responsibility

Severity of harm in a crisis refers to the number and severity of injuries or deaths of people and animals, and harm to the environment. Companies in a high injury condition are perceived less favourably and as less consumeristic than those in a low injury situation (Mowen and Ellis, 1981). Severity of injury also affects the placement of blame (Tedeschi and Nesler, 1993) and responsibility (Kelly and Campbell, 1997). Although little research has focused on company responsibility in a crisis, Jorgensen (1996) found that consumer anger and reduced purchase intentions followed a judgement of company responsibility. This led us to expect that companies would be deemed responsible for high injury crises, with flow-on effects for consumer anger and purchase intent. However, the findings were inconsistent.

While the Ansett crisis involved no injuries, both the Esso gas crisis and the *Legionella* outbreak at the Melbourne Aquarium were high injury, each causing two deaths. Additionally, the *Legionella* outbreak infected 111 people (*The Age*, 2001), with many hospitalized.

Participants considered that the Melbourne Aquarium crisis resulted from a combination of factors. As Melbourne had experienced a number of *Legionella* outbreaks, the outbreak source was believed to be pervasive bacteria in the environment. However, participants also held the Aquarium and the building owners responsible, attributing the cause to a lack of water tower maintenance, resulting from cost-cutting combined with a lack of regular testing. This, in turn, was viewed as caused by the government's move to company self-regulation of safety procedures. The dominant emotion generated by the Melbourne Aquarium crisis was fear, constituting 35% of all emotion words used in discussion of this crisis, as many had visited the Aquarium during the infection period, or had family who had. Substantial anger was also reported (31% of emotion words). Those who had visited the Melbourne Aquarium during the *Legionella* outbreak, reporting fear over contracting *Legionella*, were most vehement in their plans never to visit the Aquarium again, while some less directly affected participants had visited this popular tourist attraction after the crisis or stated an intention to visit.

While the Ansett situation incurred no injuries (although it had the potential to be high injury), participants were most likely to hold the Ansett company responsible for the crisis. However, there were two main judgements of responsibility: the first and most common one saw Ansett at fault for the groundings due to inadequate aircraft maintenance; the second saw the government agency, the Civil Aviation Safety Authority (CASA) and, in part, the media, to blame for 'scapegoating' Ansett and creating a 'witch hunt', blaming Ansett for CASA's own inadequacies in enforcing safety regulations. As FG2M1 said:

> Ansett was a scapegoat ... Ansett at least had the guts to come up and to say, 'listen, our quality control procedures, our maintenance procedures here are not good enough. Could we have CASA look into it, please?' And if it weren't for them, CASA wouldn't have known anything about it.

The perceived Ansett-responsible crisis generated high levels of anger towards the company, with anger words constituting 55% of all emotion words used in discussion of this crisis, followed by fear at 20%. As FG1M4 said referring to Ansett, 'Now when lives are at stake and nothing is done about it, that's when the anger comes up'. As a result, several participants stated that they intended to avoid flying Ansett in future. While the CASA-responsible crisis also generated a high number of anger words (50%), these feelings were directed instead at CASA and the government. One participant (FG2F2), who believed that Ansett was honest and that CASA was at fault, stated her intention to continue flying with Ansett.

With the Esso gas crisis, most participants recalled that the government's Royal Commission had held the company responsible and exonerated the workers that Esso had blamed for the crisis. As a result, company-directed anger was the dominant emotion reported, constituting 57% of all emotion words used in discussion of this crisis. The next main emotion was sympathy (24% of emotion words) expressed towards the families of the killed workers as well as businesses affected by the crisis.

Towards Esso, most participants cited inaction following the gas crisis as Esso holds the monopoly on piped gas in Victoria. However, one participant disconnected their gas supply and another was considering self-sufficiency, while one participant boycotted Esso vehicle fuel.

In sum, in the high injury *Legionella* outbreak, the Melbourne Aquarium was held partly responsible; many participants reported strong fear and avoidance of the tourist outlet. In the no injury Ansett safety crisis, Ansett was mostly judged strongly responsible, with participants voicing much anger and some negative purchase intent. In the high injury Esso crisis, Esso was held highly responsible, with much company-directed anger and some negative purchase intent. Degree of responsibility may provide a stronger key to consumer reactions than severity of injury. Therefore, following a judgement of responsibility for a crisis, while consumer anger and reduced purchase intentions were expected, in this study, fear may have had a stronger impact on behavioural intentions. Congruent with Jorgensen (1996), these crises generated negative emotions such as anger and dislike towards the companies, and impacted behaviour.

The implication is that, in a crisis where the company is viewed as responsible, tourism organizations can expect customer anger and exit behaviour. Where there is high consumer fear, as seen both in this study and in the 2003 SARS outbreak, consumer avoidance will result.

Accounts

During a crisis, company spokespersons usually deliver statements about the crisis during media conferences, interviews or via media releases. These statements frequently contain an account of the company's role in the crisis, designed to minimize responsibility. Five main account types have been identified: silence ('no comment'); denial of responsibility; excuse (which includes shifting blame or 'scapegoating'); justification of the company's actions; and confession (including apology) (Scott and Lyman, 1968; Schlenker, 1980; Hill *et al.*, 1992).

Participants noted that Ansett, Esso and the Melbourne Aquarium used the excuse strategy of blame shifting. Regarding Ansett, FG3M2 said, 'I think the Ansett one stands out that nobody would accept their responsibility. It was easy to work out who it was – it was somebody else.'

Three focus groups mentioned Esso's blame shifting. For example, in FG4, there was the following exchange: FG4M3, 'The company was blaming the workers and they decided to target the ones that were dead.' FG4F3: 'And the unions. They were …' FG4M4, 'Scapegoats. Scapegoats'. FG4M3. 'Blame everywhere. They were really going shooting up blame everywhere.'

Regarding the Melbourne Aquarium, FG1M2 said:

> They were blaming subcontractors … the builder, he wiped his hands of it. I've subcontracted … to this gentleman here. And when I subcontract that, I wipe my hands because he's the subcontractor. It's his job.

As Jorgensen (1996) found that company accounts influence consumer purchase intentions via anger, inappropriate company responses may generate anger, while reducing purchase intentions. Congruent with this, focus group participants regarded company use of these excuses with some hostility and much scepticism, and voiced negative attitudes. In fact, there appeared to be an expectation that 'scapegoating' was normal company strategy, as Fitzpatrick and Rubon (1995) found in their analysis of media stories. The implication is that tourism organizations need to be aware that strategies such as trying to shift blame by scapegoating may backfire and generate consumer hostility and reduced purchase intentions.

Credibility of company message and spokesperson

Assessment of the credibility of a message involves both the content of the message and the credibility of the message source – the crisis spokesperson. Message credibility refers to whether the message is perceived as truthful. Credibility of the message source includes an evaluation of trustworthinessness (Weiner and Mowen, 1986).

In the focus group discussions, a recurring theme was the credibility of the company spokesperson, often the Chief Executive Officer (CEO), as well as message credibility. These appeared to be linked not only to emotions, but also to consumer attitudes and behaviour, particularly in the Ansett and Melbourne Aquarium crises.

Some focus group participants perceived the Melbourne Aquarium message as credible and the spokesperson as honest. As FG7F1 said:

> ... the general manager of the Aquarium or whoever the primary spokesperson was, in terms of their absolute honesty ... the impression I had ... was the genuineness with which they were concerned, distraught about what had occurred, (leaving) absolutely no stone unturned to ensure that they could do everything reasonable within their capacity to mitigate against that in the future. And it comes back to this whole credibility and perception thing ... I think that was outstanding ...

In contrast, Ansett was perceived negatively. FG2M5 commented:

> I heard one interview with the general manager ... he lied through his teeth. Well, if he's the sort of person to manage Ansett, I wouldn't fly with them. He certainly wasn't honest. He said all the planes would be back in the air in two days time and yet another eight went out. He must have known another eight were going to go out.

People may become angry because someone lied to them (Susskind and Field, 1996). As anger results in negative purchase and investment intentions (Jorgensen, 1996), the implication for tourism operators is that when consumers judge the company message to be a lie, this may elicit anger and exit behaviour.

Negative dispositional attributions

When a message is judged to be a lie, Weiner *et al.* (1991) found that people may make negative dispositional attributions about the message source's moral character, e.g. their honesty, sincerity and trustworthiness. People may also make these negative character inferences when those involved in wrongdoing show no penitence (Weiner *et al.*, 1991). These dispositional attributions have not previously been investigated in relation to company crises.

After judging the spokesperson's statement to be a lie, focus group participants made negative dispositional attributions about both Esso and Ansett management. The 1999 Royal Commission investigation into the Esso explosion had exonerated the dead workers that Esso had blamed for the crisis and instead held the company at fault (Hannan, 1999). As FG4M2 angrily said, referring to Esso management, 'They're a bunch of liars'. Focus group participants also made dispositional attributions about Ansett management. FG3 had the following interchange. FG3F1: 'Bastards!' FG3M1: 'Bastards! It's very Australian.' FG3M4: 'Bastards! Illegitimate. They're illegitimate offspring.' Such dispositional attributions reveal strong negative attitudes towards these companies caught lying, and contribute to the public's lack of trust in the integrity of organizations.

Company reputation

It is commonly assumed that a good reputation plays a protective role in a crisis. In fact, results of product recall studies (e.g. Siomkos, 1989; Siomkos and Kurzbard, 1992; Siomkos and Shrivastava, 1993) found that a familiar and highly respected company is regarded more favourably in a recall and has a more favourable outcome than a less familiar company. There was, therefore, an expectation that reputable companies would have more favourable crisis outcomes.

Yet for Ansett, one of Australia's oldest and most respected airlines, this did not occur. Instead, focus group participants were hostile towards Ansett, which collapsed soon after the groundings of its 767s. This highlights how little is known about the role of company reputation in a crisis. The implication is that, even with a strong reputation, a company may be severely damaged by a crisis – when it is considered to be at fault.

Attitudes

Early work on attitudes assumed that they were causally related to behaviour, and common sense also suggests a relationship (Robbins *et al.*, 1994). However, a small number of crisis studies (Griffin *et al.*, 1991; Jorgensen, 1996) indicated that attitudes were unreliable predictors of consumer purchase intentions. Our study also found no strong reported links between attitude and behaviour. However, we did identify an array of negative attitudes not previously identified in the literature: attitudes to government and regulatory authorities; attitudes to media; attitudes to advertising; and attitudes to management and crisis management. These attitudes and how they may impact tourism organizations will now be discussed.

Attitudes to companies and managers

Participants revealed some negative pre-existing consumer attitudes towards business which may have affected their reactions to the crises. Negative attitudes to companies may be traced to the consumer movement of the 1960s, which resulted from businesses caught cheating customers or providing inferior products (Wilcox *et al.*, 1998).

Negative attitudes about companies were evident in comments made about Esso and may have impacted judgements of responsibility about the crisis cause. Regarding Esso, FG1M2 rhetorically asked why the crisis occurred. 'You know why? They cut corners. And they kept on cutting corners. Because you know what they were interested in? The enormous profits. They weren't interested in you, me or anyone else sitting in this room or anyone outside.' In FG2, there was the following exchange, FG2M1: '... their standards, quality control procedures were probably pretty lax.' FG2F3: 'So, profits before care or standards.' FG2M4: 'The problem you're describing there ... the companies not being concerned, I mean every company is the same way.'

In general, participants had very poor opinions of company management, believing (except for the younger age cohort) that management was largely to blame for company crises. As FG3M1 said of Ansett, 'You don't blame an airline for having a plane hijacked. But if it's a safety regulation, that's a different story. That's a management problem.'

A number of participants considered that managers should be held personally accountable, to the extent of being jailed, for the results of their decisions. As FG3M4 said:

> I'm very cynical. I believe that in Nuremburg the defence was, 'we were following orders'. But now it's 'we were following shareholders' orders'. And I actually see very little moral difference because they actually don't see people being bayoneted or dying or unemployed or taken out on the wire for all that stuff. They are totally insulated from the impacts of their decisions or relative competence.

For tourism operators, this means that there is an increasing demand for greater company accountability, including personal responsibility for crisis outcomes. It is becoming less likely that consumers will write off a crisis as an unfortunate 'accident'. This was evident following the 1999 white water rafting tragedy at Interlaken, Switzerland, which killed 21 young adventurers, when five managers of the now-defunct Adventure World company and three tour guides stood trial for manslaughter (Gower, 2001).

Attitudes to crisis management

A number of participants had views on whether the crisis handling was appropriate. The Ansett crisis was considered badly handled, while views diverged on the Aquarium.

Regarding Ansett, FG7M3 said: 'Well they could have handled it much better than they did ... the sloppiness of the procedures to deal with the lack of planes, the way that the people basically were just left hanging about not knowing what's going on.'

Different views emerged about the Melbourne Aquarium. As FG1F3 said: '... the spokesman from the Aquarium was quite upfront and was trying to be honest with the public and I was quite impressed with that. So as far as PR went, it was the right way to handle it.' Yet a legionnaire sufferer, FG1F2, believed post-crisis handling could have been improved. She said:

> I think that what's hit me most of all is the fact that ... nine months after. I went into hospital, I was very very sick ... at one time I thought I was dying ... but what really has annoyed me since is the fact that they opened the Aquarium to a big reception, welcoming people back into it ... and I sort of thought at the time well, wouldn't it have been nice had they sent all those people that contracted Legionella's disease from the Aquarium an invitation?

Stakeholders believe that companies are still not satisfactorily planning for, or managing, crises. In fact, González-Herrero and Pratt's (1998) survey of almost 400 tourist organizations (airlines, hotels, cruise lines, holiday resorts, car rental, bus companies and amusement parks) in the USA and Spain found that many had no crisis plans.

Attitudes to advertising

Seven participants spoke with strong annoyance of Ansett's AUS$20 million advertising campaign (AAP, 2001), designed to claw back market share. While this may be because the crisis was seen as the company's fault, one likely reason is that participants saw this as inappropriately spent funds in a crisis caused by lack of maintenance through cost cutting. A typical comment by one participant, FG7F3, was, 'they are actually in this advertising campaign when they could be using the money for safer systems'.

However, in other crises (the remaining four crises which participants discussed) where the company was not perceived to be at fault, advertising campaigns were liked and found reassuring. This may indicate that costly advertising campaigns may be best avoided when participants view the crisis as the fault of the company, particularly where it is primarily caused by cost cutting.

Attitudes to government/regulatory authorities regarding consumer safety

A striking factor emerging from these discussions was consumers' perception of the importance of government's role in maintaining community safety standards. The State government was widely perceived as either not enforcing safety regulations or as abrogating responsibility for public safety to private companies. In the Esso gas crisis and the Melbourne Aquarium crisis, the common perception was that private companies' drive for profit causes cost cutting, which reduces safety procedures.

The *Legionella* outbreak at the Melbourne Aquarium was perceived as resulting from government deregulation, with subsequent reliance upon private enterprise to self-regulate safety procedures. One comment by FG1F3 sums up general feelings:

> I felt angry. I felt that the government needs to do more inspections and regulations. And I just felt that it's all just become laissez-faire and it's up to private companies. And I felt that if the government had done more inspections across the board, these sort of things wouldn't happen. I was annoyed more at the government.

In the Esso gas crisis, although Esso was considered responsible, the crisis was also viewed by a number of participants as being linked to the Government's privatization of a public utility.

As the common theme was that private companies' drive for profit comes at the expense of safety procedures, tourist organizations in crisis need to highlight good safety records and adherence to safety procedures. For example, when the Arthurs Seat Chairlift (Victoria, Australia) collapsed in January 2003, injuring 18 people, the chairlift owner quickly pointed out in media releases and an advertisement the company's long-term safety record, while also apologizing and extending sympathy to those injured (AAP, 2003).

Attitudes to media

Participants' attitudes to the media appeared dichotomous: the media were perceived as either manipulating public opinion by 'beating up' a crisis from nothing; or else they had a guardian-like role, informing the public on crisis eruption, progress and resolution.

The 'beat-up' role was particularly obvious in discussions about the Ansett crisis. A number of participants believed that the media helped to manufacture the crisis, e.g. FG7M4: 'it made wonderful news copy, all these stories', and magnify the crisis, e.g. FG2M4: 'I think sometimes the media did give the impression, beating it up a bit, that the damn things would fall out of the sky if they don't tighten these nuts. Well I don't think they've got to that stage.'

Tourism operators experiencing a crisis therefore need to monitor closely and analyse all media stories about their crisis, while maintaining a good working relationship with the media to ensure that their side of the crisis story is accurately portrayed. Use of media monitoring companies during a crisis is a necessary expense.

Demographic factors

In the focus groups, no marked differences in responses were found between the focus groups due to culture, education and income factors. However, the older age group held company managers more accountable for their actions than participants in the younger age group (McDonald and Härtel, 2002). The younger cohort, predominantly university students, was the only group to raise ethical concerns, which may indicate that they are more concerned with ethical implications (McDonald and Härtel, 2002). Additionally, while the younger age group reported multiple boycotts or avoidance behaviour, the older age group did not (McDonald and Härtel, 2002).

Limitations

This study had a number of limitations. Due to the small sample size, data are context-bound and not generalizable across the wider community. Another limitation is that participants' recalled thoughts and feelings might not have accurately reflected those experienced at the time of the crisis, but instead were reconstructed at the time of the discussion in accordance with group norms.

Conclusion

Despite the fact that organizational crises can cost millions of dollars in reputation damage, lost sales and eroded market share, crisis research is still a new field of investigation. This study was the first of its kind to investigate the range of feelings that crises elicit in consumers and the behaviours that result (reported by McDonald and Härtel, 2002) as well as the factors consumers themselves considered important in a crisis, which was the focus of this chapter. Results from eight focus groups indicated a number of factors that may influence crisis outcome for companies, some never before identified in this context.

All three companies reported here attempted to shift blame for the crisis to other companies or other people. While this is a common company strategy, it generated hostility towards the companies. When accounts were primarily seen as blame shifting, they were also greeted with some scepticism. When other crisis messages, such as that delivered by the Ansett CEO, were perceived as lies, anger resulted and negative character attributions were made about company management. Some exit behaviour was reported. Crises were considered to be better handled when the spokespersons were regarded as open and honest. However, in a high harm crisis when the company was perceived as partly at fault (as in the Melbourne Aquarium crisis), when the company spokesperson were seen to be distraught about the crisis impact, they were perceived as credible.

Degree of injury may not be key to predicting consumer reactions, but instead the degree of responsibility that results. While responsibility is linked with consumer anger and reduced purchase intentions, fear may potentially have a stronger impact on consumer behaviour, resulting in avoidance behaviour.

Reputation may not completely provide a protective effect in a crisis, especially when the company is considered to be at fault. Consumers had pre-existing negative attitudes to 'big business', which were exacerbated by the crisis. Participants (except for the younger demographic) held management primarily accountable for the crises, especially when the crisis cause was considered as resulting from safety problems due to cost cutting. In this type of crisis, advertising is best kept to reporting procedures used to safeguard consumers. Governments also received some share of the blame due to their policy of deregulation that placed responsibility for safety on companies. Additionally, media were sometimes considered to play a role in 'beating up' a company crisis.

Recommendations

The results of this study have made evident a number of recommendations that tourism operators may implement in order to minimize negative crisis outcomes.

Develop a crisis plan

Companies need to ensure they have a crisis plan in place, both as a preventative measure, and to ensure best practice in crisis management. While the crisis plan is best handled professionally (e.g. by a public relations firm specializing in this area), the organization needs to make a commitment to recommendations for action that emerge. Crisis planning starts with a determination of factors (internal and external) that could impact the organization, landing them under harsh media scrutiny.

During the crisis, monitor stakeholder perceptions of the company

As was seen in the Ansett crisis, two different sets of views about the responsibility and blame for the crisis emerged, each of which generated different consumer reactions. When Ansett was perceived to be at fault, the credibility of the company message and spokesperson was called into question. Therefore, companies need to monitor closely all crisis media stories and, especially where there are divergent stories appearing, ensure that their role in the crisis is made clear to consumers. It may also be advisable to use research tools such as focus groups to discover the direction of stakeholder opinion and possibly correct faulty perceptions through use of media conferences and media releases.

Avoid self-serving advertising

For crises where cost cutting is perceived as the root cause of the crisis, expensive advertising campaigns may result in consumer hostility. Money is best spent when companies are not perceived to be at fault for the crisis, such as when an external agent was clearly responsible. In this situation (as was made evident in non-tourist crises discussed), advertising campaigns were perceived as reassuring. Thus, a critical issue for any tourist firm involved in a crisis is to consider the locus of the crisis problem and then decide on a strategy regarding the use of advertising as a communication medium.

Publicize procedures to safeguard consumers

In order to engender positive feelings towards the company, companies need to publicize the procedures they are taking to safeguard consumers. This is vital in high injury conditions, as these evoke consumer anger and fear towards the company, which in turn influence product purchase and use of services. In all situations, communication should focus on the importance of consumer safety.

Show care and concern in all statements – especially in injury situations

Companies, such as the Melbourne Aquarium, who are perceived as being genuinely concerned about the crisis impact and trying to mitigate its negative consequences, may be perceived as honest and better at crisis management by stakeholders. For tourism operators, the company communication stance must show genuine care and concern for those affected by the crisis. This is consistent with other researchers' (see Cropanzano *et al.*, 2004) findings that when the cause of a problem is largely internal to the organization, acknowledging the harm done, accepting responsibility and trying to atone the consumer base is an effective form of management. When the company is perceived to manage the crisis badly and shows little consumer concern, durable negative attitudes may be created, affecting consumers' future purchase intentions.

Give credible messages about the crisis

Consumer anger results when a company spokesperson is perceived to be lying. Companies must give credible messages about their role in the crisis and about the ongoing situation. While the public relations stance of 'Tell it all, tell it fast, tell it truthfully', is in direct conflict with the traditional legal stance of 'Say nothing, do nothing, admit nothing' (Regester and Larkin, 1997), the legal stance may serve to aggravate and alienate a sophisticated customer base. Companies perceived to be lying by denying responsibility or else attempting to minimize crisis responsibility by shifting blame to others may find that irate customers take their business elsewhere.

Expect that the bigger the business, the more negative the reaction

Pre-existing negative attitudes to corporations, evident as stereotypes about 'profits at all costs', ensured that participants were prepared to believe the worst about 'big business'. This may translate into difficulty convincing consumers of the company's innocence, even when the company was not at fault. A good reputation may also not fully protect a company, especially when the company is at fault.

References

AAP (2001) Ansett to launch $20m advertising blitz. wysiwyg://10/http://news.com.au/common...y_page/0,4057,1938822%255E1702,00.html (accessed 27 May 2001).

AAP (2003) Chairlift firm to publish apology, www.optusnet.com.au/news/story/aap/20030116/12/domestic/chairlift-vic.inp (accessed 16 January 2003).

Courier Mail (2003) Esso class action lost. www.couriermail.news.com.au/common/story_page/0,5936,6012829%255E421,00.html (accessed 10 June 2004).

Cropanzano, R., Chrobot-Mason, D., Rupp, D.E. and Prehar, C.A. (2004) Accountability for corporate injustice. *Human Resource Management Review* 14, 107–133.

Fink, S. (1986) *Crisis Management: Planning for the Inevitable.* American Management Association, New York.

Fitzpatrick, K.R. and Rubon, M.S. (1995) Public relations vs legal strategies in organizational crisis decisions. *Public Relations Review* 21 (1), 21–34.

Fletcher, G. and Ward, C. (1988) Attribution theory and process: a cross-cultural perspective. In: Bond, I.M. (ed.) *A Cross-cultural Challenge to Social Psychology.* Sage, Newbury Park, California, pp. 230–244.

Folkes, V.S., Koletsky, S. and Graham, J.L. (1987) A field study of causal inferences and consumer reaction: the view from the airport. *Journal of Consumer Research* 13, 534–539.

Frederickson, B.L., Tugade, M.M., Waugh, C.E. and Larkin, G.R. (2003) What good are positive emotions in crises? A prospective study of resilience and emotions following the terrorist attacks on the USA on September 11th, 2001. *Journal of Personality and Social Psychology* 84, 365–376.

Gonzalez-Herrero, A. and Pratt, C.B. (1998) Marketing crises in tourism: communication strategies in the United States and Spain. *Public Relations Review* 24, 83–97.

Goodsir, D. (2001) Ansett sales fall after safety crisis. *The Age.* wysiwyg://8/http://theage.com.au/news/2001/05/09/FFXYQIHJGMC.html (accessed 27 May 2001).

Gower, P. (2001) Canyon tragedy trial waste of time says victim's father. www.nzherald.co.nz/storydisplay.cfm?thesection=news&thesubsection=&storyID=231297 New Zealand Herald, 3 December 2001 (accessed 8 February 2003).

Griffin, M., Babin, B.J. and Attaway, J.S. (1991) An empirical investigation of the impact of negative public publicity on consumer attitudes and intentions. *Advances in Consumer Research* 18, 334–341.

Hannan, E. (1999) Esso should apologise, not run for cover. *The Age.* wysiwyg://12/

http:www.theage.com.au/daily/990629/ne ws3.html (accessed 27 May 2001).

Hill, D.J., Baer, R. and Kosenko, R. (1992) Organizational characteristics and employee excuse making: passing the buck for failed service encounters. *Advances in Consumer Research* 19, 673–677.

Jorgensen, B.K. (1994) Consumer reaction to company-related disasters: the effect of multiple versus single explanations. *Advances in Consumer Research* 21, 348–352.

Jorgensen, B.K. (1996) Components of con-sumer reaction to company-related mishaps: a structural equation model approach. *Advances in Consumer Research* 23, 346–351.

Kelly, K.T. and Campbell, J.L. (1997) Attribution of responsibility for alcohol-related offences. *Psychological Reports* 80, 1159–1165.

Knight, R.G., Ross, R.A., Collins, J.I. and Parmenter, S.A. (1985) Some norms, reli-ability and preliminary validity for an S-R inventory of anger: the Subjective Anger Scale (SAS). *Personality, Individual Differences* 6, 331–339.

Lunt, P. (1996) Rethinking the focus group in media and communications research. *Journal of Communication* 46 (2), 79–99.

Mallinson, H. (1999) Gasless but still opera-tional in Melbourne – an exercise in crisis management. *Australian Journal of Hospitality Management* 6 (2), 45–50.

McDonald, L. and Härtel, C.E.J. (2002) Consumer emotions may run high during crises. Emonet conference electronic pro-ceedings, Gold Coast, July.

Miles, M.B. and Huberman, A.M. (1984) *Qualitative Dataanalysis: a Sourcebook of New Methods.* Sage Publications, Newbury Park, California.

Minter Ellison Lawyers (2003) Track records, Melbourne Aquarium Legionella litigation. www.minterellison.com/ajpe/connect/web/ navigation/AboutUs/TrackRecords/TR+-+Construction+Engineering+%28QBE+In surance%29+Melbourne+Aquarium+Legi onella+litigation (accessed 3 October 2003).

Mitroff, I.I. and Pearson, C.M. (1993) *Crisis Management: A Diagnostic Guide for Improving Your Organization's Crisis-pre-paredness.* Jossey-Bass, San Francisco, California.

Morgan, D.L. (1998) *The Focus Group Guidebook: Focus Group Kit 1.* Sage Publications, Thousand Oaks, California.

Mowen, J.C. (1979) Further information on consumer perceptions of product recalls. *Advances in Consumer Research* 7, 519–523.

Mowen, J.C. and Ellis, H.W. (1981) The product defect: managerial considerations and consumer implications. In: Enis, B. and Roaring, K. (eds) *The Annual Review of Marketing.* American Marketing Association, Chicago, Illinois, pp. 158–172.

Patton, M.Q. (1990) *Qualitative Evaluation and Research Methods,* 2nd edn. Sage Publications, Newbury Park, California.

Regester, M. and Larkin, J. (1997) *Risk Issues and Crisis Management: a Casebook of Best Practice.* Kogan Page, Institute of Public Relations, London.

Robbins, S.P., Waters-Marsh, T., Cacioppe, R. and Millet, B. (1994) *Organizational Behaviour.* Prentice Hall, New York.

Schlenker, B.R. (1980) *Impression Manage-ment.* Brooks/Cole, Monterey, California.

Scott, M.R., and Lyman, S.M. (1968) Accounts. *American Sociological Review* 33, 46–62.

Siomkos, G.J. (1989) Managing product-harm crises. *Industrial Crisis Quarterly* 3, 41–60.

Siomkos, G.J. and Kurzbard, G. (1992) Product harm crisis at the crossroads: monitoring recovery of replacement prod-ucts. *Industrial Crisis Quarterly* 6, 279–294.

Siomkos, G.J. and Shrivastava, P. (1993) Responding to product liability crises. *Long Range Planning* 26 (5), 72–79.

Sönmez, S.F., Apostolopoulos, Y. and Tarlow, P. (1999) Tourism in crisis: managing the effects of terrorism. *Journal of Travel Research* 38, 13–18.

Stafford, G., Yu, L. and Armoo, K. (2002) Crisis management and recovery: how Washington, D.C. hotels responded to terrorism. *Cornell Hotel and Restaurant Administration Quarterly* October, 27–40.

Susskind, L. and Field, P. (1996) *Dealing with an Angry Public: the Mutual Gains Approach to Resolving Disputes.* The Free Press, Simon and Schuster Inc., New York.

Tedeschi, J.T. and Nesler, M.S. (1993) Grievances: development and reactions. In: Felson, R.B. (ed.) *Aggression and Violence: Social Interactionist Perspectives.* American Psychological Association, Washington, DC, pp. 13–46.

The Age (2000) Aquarium head warns business. 7 July, p. 7.

Timmers, M., Fischer, A.H. and Manstead, A.S.R. (1998) Gender differences in motives for regulating emotions. *Personality and Social Psychology Bulletin* 24, 974–986.

Weinberger, M.G. and Romeo, J.B. (1989) The impact of negative product news. *Business Horizons* 32, 44–50.

Weinberger, M.G., Romeo, J.B. and Piracha, A. (1991) Negative product safety news: coverage, responses, and effects. *Business Horizons* 34, 23–31.

Weiner, B. (1986) *An Attributional Theory of Motivation and Emotion.* Springer-Verlag, New York.

Weiner, B. (1995) *Judgments of Responsibility.* The Guilford Press, New York.

Weiner, B. and Mowen, J. (1986) Source credibility: on the independent effects of trust and expertise. *Advances in Consumer Research* 13, 306–310.

Weiner, B., Graham, S., Orli, P. and Zmuidinas, M. (1991) Public confession and forgiveness. *Journal of Personality* 59, 281–312.

Wilcox, D., Ault, P.H. and Agee, W.K. (1998) *Public Relations: Strategies and Tactics,* 5th edn. Harper Collins, New York.

10 Tourism and Terrorism: an Analytical Framework with Special Focus on the Media

WALTER FREYER AND ALEXANDER SCHRÖDER

Introduction

For many years the tourism industry has been affected by terror, war and political crisis. Again and again the peaceful picture of travelling has shown signs of faltering in the face of unexpected events such as terrorist attacks. In the affected regions, events of this nature often have enormous impacts on the economy and social life of residents. In some cases, tourism flows are interrupted as tourists look for other seemingly safe destinations. However, up to now, terrorist attacks at Luxor, Cairo and Bali, the PKK attack in Turkey or the ETA attacks in Spain have not stopped the long-term growth of international tourism. The destinations subjected to terrorist attacks have generally regained lost visitors as holiday-makers quickly forget such incidents and return relatively soon after the occurrences of devastating attacks (Freyer and Schröder, 2005b).

The peak of this development was undoubtedly the attacks of 11 September 2001 (9/11) in the USA, which far surpassed any previous terror attack in its dimension. Not only were there an enormous number of victims, but the method of the assault was different from previous events and the resulting media attention eclipsed that of any previous terrorist incident. In fact, while the attack was not primarily aimed at tourism, its effect on the international tourism economy, the touristic product and tourists themselves was considerable (Nacos, 2002; Schicha and Brosda, 2002).

The media plays an important role during the planning and execution of terrorist activities from the viewpoint of terrorists. The media transmits the events and also the ideological aims of the terrorists to a broad audience by means of far-reaching and extensive reporting. The intensive, sometimes exaggerated and superficial reporting results in an image of unsafe destinations and leads to negative effects not only on the target destinations, but also on those countries that benefit from tourism. This chapter explores elements of the relationship between terrorism and tourism from a media perspective.

The Tourism System

Tourism is an international phenomenon, thus travellers go to holiday destinations all over the world. Because of globalization and modern transport technology, it is easier, faster and cheaper for tourists to travel to distant countries than spending their holidays closer to home (Freyer, 2002). Many of these countries are economically dependent upon tourism for employment, foreign investment and, indirectly, the taxation revenue collected by the public sector. Some authors have described the relationship between tourism and the national economy from a systems perspective. Kaspar (1996) describes tourism as an open system that has economic, political and social elements that are influenced by and in turn influence a range of environmental systems.

The description of tourism as an open system underlines the importance of the environment in understanding the structure and development of tourism. In a similar approach, Freyer (2006) understands tourism as a multidisciplinary system, with travel as a defined object which is influenced by different systems or modules. Primarily six separate systems and/or modules describe, in their entirety, tourism in all its forms (see Fig. 10.1). This approach can be used to explain the impact that terrorism can have on tourism.

The impacts of terrorism can be broken down into six main areas using this multidisciplinary tourism approach. The tourism-related reasons for terrorism come mainly from those six areas (Freyer, 2004, pp. 7–9):

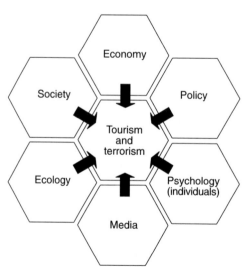

Fig. 10.1. The impact that terrorism can have on tourism. Based on Freyer (2000).

- Economy: differences in the economic condition between states, particularly the allocation of resources due to tourism, which could be found unjust.
- Society: social problems, in matters of social levels, classes as well as values, norms, cultures, traditions or religions, are exacerbated by tourism.
- Ecology/environment: destruction and pollution of environment due to the use of natural resources by tourism.
- Psychological: individual, psychological factors (attitude, behaviour), as inner motivation for terrorist activities.
- Policy: political backgrounds are certainly one of the more central reasons for terrorists, for instance the various forms of participation and non-participation in the source of political power. Thus, political minorities are often agents of terroristic activities.
- Media: they have become an instrument or mouthpiece for terrorists.

Media influences can be positive, for instance assisting in the stimulation of demand by positive reporting, as well as negative. During political crises, the tourism industry may suffer from the results of negative reporting. Similarly, natural and man-made catastrophes also generate negative media images, causing intending visitors to reconsider their travel plans. Where terrorist activity is the centre of media attention, the fear of personal harm that is generated may be sufficient to have a sustained dampening effect on tourism demand.

Terrorism

As a result of the multifaceted nature of terrorism, usually including very complex political aspects, terrorism defies exact and permanent definition (Herzog, 1991; Hoffman, 1999; Laqueur, 2001). The meaning of the term terrorism in contemporary terms is clearly negative and is used to label political enemies and to ostracize their methods. The aim of terrorist activity is primarily political or social in nature. It is meant to influence the behaviour of governments, society, individual social groups or the system of values of any of these groups. The use of particularly violent, inhumane and tyrannical methods against soft targets generates shock, fear and fright. Most attacks are attempted using few resources while causing the most possible damage. Terrorist goals often include reaching a broad audience to publicize their specific cause and undermining government authority.

It is equally difficult to find consensus for defining the forms of terrorism. The various ideological motives serve as a starting point in creating distinctions. The most important ideological orientations of terrorist violence, according to Drake (1998, p. 54) are '... separatism, religion, liberalism, anarchism, communism, conservatism, fascism, single-issues, and organised crime'. Based on this, Laqueur (2001, pp. 100–105) differentiates among the following forms of terrorism:

- national-separatist terrorism (e.g. Basque ETA or the Kurdish PKK);
- religious terrorism (e.g. the Islamic Al Qaeda or Japanese Aum sects);
- political terrorism (e.g. the leftist RAF in Germany or the right-oriented, racist Ku Klux Klan in the USA);
- state terrorism (e.g. the Third Reich or Libya);
- other forms of terrorism (e.g. eco- or cyber-terrorism).

The boundaries between the individual forms are, however, fluid, and therefore cannot be considered independently. For instance, some religious groups have separatist-oriented aims. Other religious terrorist organizations exert a strong influence on leftist-oriented violence. Finally, the terrorism phenomenon is marked by many different variations, with some similarities in patterns. Any attempts to achieve strict demarcation and distinction disappear in the light of the many variations. Because some groups still feel discriminated against or strive for change, terrorist violence is not just a risk of the past, but also a political threat of the present and the future.

The Relationship Between Tourism and Terrorism

Along with methods of distinguishing among terroristic activities according to ideological motivations, the types of targets can also be categorized. Some researchers categorize targets as tactical or short-range, strategic or mid-range and ideological or long-range (Richter and Waugh, 1995). The tactical level is necessary to keep the organization alive and give it capacity to act successfully for the long term. To obtain resources, criminal offences are often carried out in the form of theft or robbery. As a consequence, tourism is used to obtain resources to fund further activities. On the strategic level, attacks on touristic targets are the most frequently used means to achieve ideological aims. An attack on tourism at the strategic level is an attack on the economy or the political elite of a country. Media coverage of an incident in a specific country may intimidate potential visitors who may then substitute safer destinations, thus destabilizing the target countries' economy (Sönmez *et al.*, 1999). Attacks on tourism may also be used by terrorist organizations as a form of 'punishment' for the business community, political system and elements of society for their support of unpopular economic and social policies. In this way, an attack results in a decline in tourism followed by a decline in business, endangering profits and perhaps causing social and political unrest that can be exploited by the terrorist organization.

When tourists are victims of an attack, international media attention is focused on the terrorists. Because tourism is the target, terrorists are able to weaken the economy as well as the power and authority of their political opponents. In destinations where the economy is highly dependent on tourism, a terrorist attack can cause significant economic damage. As a strategic target, tourism is a surrogate; first attack the economy and achieve ideological aims later. If touristic facilities are a target at the ideological level, there is often a direct connection between both. Violence is frequently aimed at the economic and political ruling classes which also own the facilities that are targeted.

In a sense, terrorism may also represent a clash of civilizations, particularly when hosts and tourists have different cultural origins. In some Islamic countries, locals critically observe the behaviour of tourists, who consume alcohol, eat pork, gamble, appear Western and have lower moral standards. These differences can manifest themselves in the eyes of the local population as a growing threat to their own system of values, traditions, norms and religion until a fear of neo-colonialism emerges (Sönmez, 1998). In the most extreme cases, the local population will seek to preserve its cultural and religious identify through acts of terror against tourism. This has been demonstrated in parts of Egypt. The well resourced tourism industry exists alongside a neglected rural infrastructure. This blatant contrast between luxury-oriented tourists and Egyptians who were often living at the subsistence level, even in the 1990s, results in terrorist actions against tourists (Aziz, 1995). In this respect, tourism can be regarded as representing the ideological values, class differences or political cultures of tourists and especially their governments and, therefore, can themselves become targets of terroristic actions.

The impact of terrorists' attacks, depending on the method, can have direct or indirect effects on the tourism system. The actual targets are usually not the victims, the unfortunate tourists, but rather the general social system, the government or the political order. The relationships between crime, violence terrorism and tourism can be classified into different types. These range from tourists as incidental victims to the extreme case of terror attacks against tourists and tourist facilities (Ryan, 1993). Therefore, the violence can be understood as a message, which finds a strong degree of resonance through reports of the incident by mass media, thereby reaching its intended target (Waldmann, 1998). According to Gerrits (1992, p. 46): 'The more people are killed in a bomb attack, or passengers caught in a hijacked plane, the stronger the attention of the media and the interest of the public'.

A triangle of the relationship between terrorism, actual targets and the symbolic tourism is illustrated in Fig. 10.2. In this triangle, the focus of the terrorist violence is their ideological motives.

The depiction in Fig. 10.2 demonstrates that the tourism system is generally used as a means to an end, to reach ideological aims. Between 1985 and 1998, Pizam and Smith counted about 70 important terrorist incidents at destinations in which 71% of the victims were tourists (Pizam and Smith, 2000).

Terrorism and the Media

The aims and motivations of terrorists can be considerably different, but undoubtedly they always aim to attract the attention of a certain audience

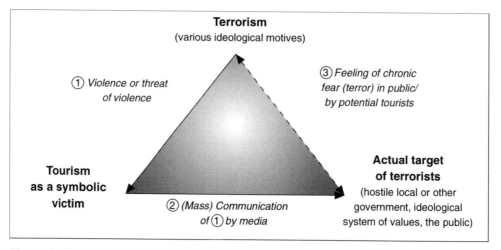

Fig. 10.2. The triangle of the relationship between terrorism and tourism. Based on Schmid (1992).

to convey their particular message. As an important medium in broadcasting information about such acts, the modern news media plays a decisive role in dealing with terrorists. Without this mouthpiece their activities would fade away and the perception of the events would be limited to the immediate victims. To attract the attention of the local as well as international media, their actions are often carefully arranged. The news content is of great importance to the media, which in turn reaches a broad, interested audience (Freyer and Schröder, 2004).

This symbiotic relationship between terrorism and the media first became possible with the development of the international media. Their development occurred in several stages. In 1830, the first steam printing press was developed, and 3 years later the first newspaper with a large circulation was published in the USA. In 1968, the first TV satellite images were broadcast worldwide, followed later by live reporting. Terrorist organizations quickly recognized the possibilities of this new means of mass communication to promote their aims, and it is perhaps no coincidence that the 1968 hijacking of a commercial jet by Palestinian terrorists announced the birth of international terrorism (Hoffman, 1999).

The Effect of the Media

Empirical communication research classifies the effects of mass communication as: dissemination of information (information effect); strengthening of opinion (influence effect); changing of attitude (conviction effect); and components of benefit (benefit effect) (Kroeber-Riel and Weinberg, 2003). If news about terror attacks is published, the amount of news coverage increases significantly because the public has a high demand for information. The media can influence its audience by amplifying or influencing opinions through a process referred to as agenda-setting. Journalists have access to a range of reports, and select information according to the particular criteria they have for publishing. Through emphasis and repetition, this news is ranked by importance by the recipients. The stronger the media message given, the higher the individual dismay, and the more intensive and multidimensional its perception (Apitz, 1987; Bofadelli, 1999). For this reason, there often exist differences between a perceived and real environment, with the effect of arbitrary social behaviour. This can be evident, for example, in travelling. The result is defined in changes to or reinforcement of an attitude, e.g. toward the image of a destination and the security problems associated with it.

The manner of portraying societal risks and selecting topics of interest such as coverage of terrorist activities in mass media is termed risk communication. These reports should enable the public to make competent and responsible decisions about risks. However, journalistic selection of information and topic selection of special themes for broad public interest may distort the actual situation and create a false perception of public risk (Meier and Schanne, 1996). Under these conditions, such things as trip cancellations and a fall in demand at destinations and regions that are actually safe and unaffected by terror attacks can be understood. This is how German media coverage of Egypt created the impression that the entire country was affected by the fundamentalist terror attacks. A statement from the head of the Egyptian tourist office, Bakier, declared that only the area around Assiut was considered dangerous (Schreier, 1994). Another example is Cuba. After social turmoil in Havana in August 1994, about 10,000 people demonstrated and counterdemonstrated in a peaceful event. Some media reports were completely exaggerated, leading to a considerable number of cancellations of trips to Cuba (Chierek, 1995).

Along with the negative effects of the media coverage, positive effects must not be forgotten. In critical situations, the media is the only medium that can quickly inform the public and strongly influence the outcome. Due to its large reach, the media has the ability to forewarn on a large scale, to warn or to alarm.

The Media as an Instrument of Terrorists

The media is mandatory for terrorists. Ted Koppel, anchorman of ABC, made a fitting comparison:

> Without television, terrorism becomes rather like the philosopher's hypothetical tree falling in a forest: no one hears it fall and therefore it has no reason for being. And television without terrorism, while not deprived of all interesting things in the world, is nonetheless deprived of one of the most interesting (www.terrorism.com, 2002).

The media offers a suitable stage for promulgation and detailed portrayal of terror propaganda. This leads to intense media coverage, the aforementioned topic selection, countless background reports and expert analyses, underlining the symbiosis between terrorism and the media. Terrorists use the media to achieve their ideological aims. However, the coverage is mostly of a negative nature and does not leave a positive impression of the terrorists or their goals. Thus, intense coverage can even lead to more terror attacks than normally would have been expected (Brosius and Weimann, 1991; Kuschel and Schröder, 2002).

There are two areas that exhibit a causal relationship between terrorism and media attention that have an adverse effect on social behaviour. First, the media can create time pressure under which those decision makers, such as governments, suffer. Secondly, there is an effect on the influence of the public's attitude regarding personal risks and the associated willingness to travel (Hoffman, 1999). As a result of intense coverage of terrorist activities that may be linked to tourism, there may be a substantial short-term fall in demand for tourism in the affected destination. Above all, frivolous coverage can lead to mid- and long-term negative public attitudes regarding the risk factor of a destination as well as its associated image, thereby further jeopardizing tourism demand.

Changes to Risk Perception and Travel Decisions

The fast-growing event-orientation nature of tourism has created the demand for international travel destinations. In the past, there were residual risks such as 'salt in the soup', but Schmieder (1998) noticed an increase in the demand for safety while on holiday. Risk perception is therefore a decisive factor in travel decisions. When (potential) tourists receive information about risks of terrorism at the destination or with the transportation they intend to use, news of terrorism attacks has a decisive influence on the decision to travel (Sönmez and Graefe, 1998; Freyer and Schröder, 2005a). That is why consumers decide to substitute perceived destinations with a risk of terror attack with a safer alternative. Even after booking a trip, negative information may still alter a decision, leading to a cancelled trip. The feelings of insecurity and fear increase in proportion to the lack of information available about the objective potential for danger. If the fear threshold has been crossed, however, neither information nor emotional messages will prevent a decision either to cancel or to substitute an alternative destination.

If fellow countrymen are victims of terror attacks, the individual's sense of vulnerability increases. Through publicity in the media, the perception of risk is stimulated multidimensionally. This action influences the subjective opinion and with it the subjective risk perception of the consumer. Additionally, individual perceptions of security risks are also associated with regional risks. As an example, a high terrorist risk is connected with the Near East. While there was a decline in visitors to Egypt in 1993 (Schreier,

1994), the evidence is that those holiday-makers who did not cancel their trip had been to the country before. This behaviour reveals the factor of objective risk. The traveller relies upon a competent knowledge or aspect of safety and cultural reality, thereby strengthening the trust in the destination. Large discrepancies between objective risks and the subjective perception of the consumer can arise, the difference in which depends upon the travel experience. On the other hand, Sönmez and Graefe (1998) point out the reverse relationship in which a negative experience with terrorist risks may limit the desire for future travel.

Experience with extreme situations generates fear of more of the same, which in turn can limit long-term travel behaviour. This reaction causes a steep drop in the demand for tourism in the country attacked (see Fig. 10.3). The results of terrorism research confirm that the initial effects of terror attacks are severe, but that the incidents are forgotten and the negative influence on the public diminishes only after a few months. However, if further such negative events occur, the population's attitude will drastically change once again.

Israel

Research reports from the Institute Medien Tenor make clear how coverage can negatively affect demand for tourism. In a time period of 1 year beginning in January 1998, German television reported on hotspots in Israel in every second story. Eighty per cent of them dealt with international crises and terrorism. In the time period from September 2000 to August 2001, there were a similar number of stories in the German media and every fourth story was of a negative nature. Eighty-eight per cent of stories about Isreal in the US media were about terrorist incidents, and two-thirds were negatively portrayed (Medien Tenor, 2001).

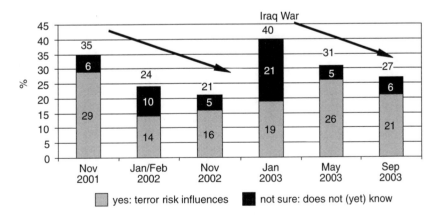

Fig. 10.3. Influence of fear of terror on travel decisions. Source: Forschungsgemeinschaft Urlaub und Reisen (2003).

As Fig. 10.4 shows, the number of German holiday-makers dropped sharply when coverage of terrorist violence in the Near East increased. The graph makes clear to what extent the media influences the risk perception of potential tourists, although in this time period no tourists or touristic targets were affected by violence. This relationship implies that the influence upon the individual's destination image through coverage of terrorist activity has increased.

Israel's tourist industry must deal with these precarious situations. Tourism might not be the target of the attacks, but the effects are identical. The Intifada still in effect in early 2005 resulted in the laying off of 18,000 hotel employees and damage to tourism totalling US$2 billion in 2002 alone (*Financial Times Deutschland*, 2002).

Turkey

Turkey, an important international holiday spot, has also suffered from a number of terrorist attacks. In 1993, a marina in Antalya was the scene of an explosion in which 26 tourists, among them nine Germans, were severely injured. In the time period from 1993 to 1994, a multitude of terrorist attacks were launched by PKK followers and were mostly directed at tourists or tourism infrastructure. The German media conducted an exhaustive coverage of these occurrences and was accused of an anti-Turkey campaign which did not allow objective reporting of the terrorist attacks. Tscharnke researched the coverage of the German Press Agency (dpa), to which practically all large media firms refer. In the time period from April to June 1994, a time period when tourists were making travel plans or could still re-book without great difficulty (no cancellation fees),

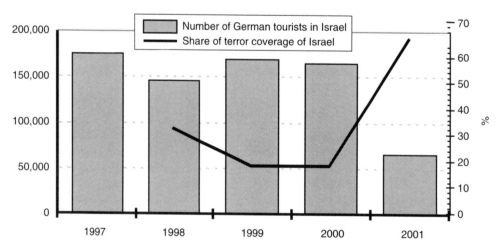

Fig. 10.4. Comparison of number of German tourists in Israel with the share of coverage in the German media. Source: Medien Tenor (2001). Basis: 1621 programmes on seven TV stations.

there were a total of 25 reports about attacks in comparable holiday spots such as Spain, Corsica/France, Greece and Turkey. These reports contained 24 attacks with four dead and 39 injured, and were mostly explosions or attacks with heavy weapons. Most of the attacks – ten attacks and seven reports – were registered in Corsica, followed by Greece with six attacks and four reports. In Turkey, five attacks were registered, precipitating 11 reports and two background stories (see Table 10.1).

Upon closer consideration of the background, there is an explanation for the various intensities of coverage. The attacks were for different reasons but all were directed towards achieving the terrorist's goals. In Greece, the attacks were directed above all against industrial businesses and diplomatic facilities. The Turkish PKK directed its threat at tourism. Four of the five attacks were on tourist facilities, where 23 of the 39 tourists were injured. From a journalistic perspective, and from the perspective of the media consumer, reports of such attacks arouse greater interest than attacks on the police or other state authorities (Tscharnke, 1995).

It should be noted, then, that terrorists consciously select the tourism system as a victim for attacks to gain a higher profile with the media. Selection of touristic targets is stronger in those countries that are dependent upon tourism and, therefore, where the state is more likely to be susceptible to blackmail from the terrorists' perspective.

Conclusion

In tourism, security counts as one of the important element of the tourism industry's ability to deliver a memorable and safe holiday experience. The threat potential of international terrorism must now be taken seriously in every country. Even in apparently safe destinations, it is necessary to consider that all possible events leading to loss of life, injuries or property damage, including a terrorist attack, will have a negative impact on tourism (Pizam and Mansfeld, 1996; World Tourism Organization, 1997; Mansfeld, 1999).

State support of regional security personnel in tourism centres is indispensable. Where dangers from organized crime or terrorism exist, the World Tourism Organization places priority on passing the information

Table 10.1. Number of terrorist attacks in a selected destination and number of reports in the German media.

	Total	Corsica	Greece	Turkey
Number of terrorist attacks (proportion)	24 (100%)	10 (42%)	6 (25%)	5 (21%)
Number of reports (proportion)	25 (100%)	7 (28%)	4 (16%)	13[a] (52%)

[a] Includes two background reports.
Source: Tscharnke, 1995, p. 181.

about the type of threat to the transportation and accommodation industries. It is also necessary to instruct international tour operators and travel agents about these dangers. Furthermore, government officials need to establish harmonious relations with the domestic and international media. Possible travel warnings or, preferably, advisories, about likely risks for holiday-makers should be passed along an information chain to all potential tourists, thereby reducing the room for media speculation. To avoid erroneous information at home and abroad, an open information channel to the media should be maintained. The goal is to provide the clearest possible portrayal of danger and also the measure of security and protection surrounding this destination, which is beneficial for its image. For this, it is necessary to develop a media plan within an active crisis management element. The content could contain, for example, press kits or reports and guides for behaviour at press conferences or toward journalists.

References

Apitz, K. (1987) *Konflikte, Krisen, Katastrophen: Präventivmaßnahmen gegen Imageverlust.* Frankfurter Allgemeine, Frankfurt/Main.

Aziz, H. (1995) Understanding attacks on tourists in Egypt. *Tourism Management* 16, 91–95.

Bofadelli, H. (1999) *Medienforschung I: Grundlagen und theoretische Perspektiven.* WUV-Univ.-Verlag, Konstanz.

Brosius, H.B. and Weimann, G. (1991) The contagiousness of mass-mediated terrorism. *European Journal of Communication* 6, 63–75.

Chierek, M. (1995) Nur ein Medieneffekt oder bedrohliche Tendenzen? *FVW-International* 5, 182.

Drake, C.J.M. (1998) The role of ideology in terrorists' target selection. *Terrorism and Political Violence* 10 (2), 53–85.

Financial Times Deutschland (2002) Gewalt schwächt Konjunktur in Nahost. *Financial Times Deutschland* 16 February, p. 14.

Forschungsgemeinschaft Urlaub und Reisen (2003) *Reiseanalyse 2003.* FUR, Kiel.

Freyer, W. (2000) *Ganzheitlicher Tourismus – Beiträge aus 20 Jahren Tourismusforschung.* FIT-Verlag, Dresden.

Freyer, W. (2002) *Globalisierung und Tourismus,* 2nd edn. FIT-Verlag, Dresden.

Freyer, W. (2004) Von 'Schutz und Sicherheit' zu 'Risiko und Krisen' in der Tourismusforschung. In: Freyer, W. and Groß, S. (eds) *Sicherheit in Tourismus und Verkehr.* FIT-Verlag, Dresden, pp. 1–13.

Freyer, W. (2006) *Tourismus: Einführung in die Fremdenverkehrsökonomie,* 8th edn. Oldenbourg, Munich/Vienna.

Freyer, W. and Schröder, A. (2004) Tourismus und Terrorismus. In: Freyer, W. and Groß, S. (eds) *Sicherheit in Tourismus und Verkehr.* FIT-Verlag, Dresden, pp. 53–83.

Freyer, W. and Schröder, A. (2005a) *Sicheres Reisen angesichts von Risiken und Krisen – Anforderungen an Tourismuswirtschaft und (internationale) Tourismuspolitik.* Berlin.

Freyer, W. and Schröder, A. (2005b) Terrorismus und Tourismus – Strukturen und Interaktionen als Grundlage des Krisenmanagements. In: Pechlaner, H. and Glaeßer, D (eds) *Risiko und Gefahr im Tourismus – Erfolgreicher Umgang mit Krisen und Strukturbrüchen.* Erich Schmidt Verlag, Berlin, pp. 101–113.

Gerrits, R.P. (1992) Terrorists' perspective: memoirs. In: Paletz, D.L. and Schmid, A.P. (eds) *Terrorism and the Media.* Sage, Newbury Park, California, pp. 29–61.

Herzog, T. (1991) *Terrorismus: Versuch einer Definition und Analyse internationaler Übereinkommen zu seiner Bekämpfung.* Lang, Frankfurt am Main/New York.

Hoffman, B. (1999) *Terrorismus – der unerklärte Krieg: Neue Gefahren politischer Gewalt.* Fischer Verlag, Frankfurt/Main.

Kaspar, C. (1996) *Die Tourismuslehre im Grundriss*, 5th edn. Haupt, Bern/Stuttgart.

Kroeber-Riel, W. and Weinberg, P. (2003) *Konsumentenverhalten*, 8th edn. Vahlen, Munich.

Kuschel, R. and Schröder, A. (2002) *Terrorismus und Tourismus – Interaktionen, Auswirkungen und Handlungsstrategien.* FIT-Verlag, Dresden.

Laqueur, W. (2001) *Die globale Bedrohung: Neue Gefahren des Terrorismus.* Propyläen, Berlin.

Mansfeld, Y. (1999) Cycles of war, terror and peace: determinants and management of crisis and recovery of the Israeli tourism industry. *Journal of Travel Research* 38, 32–36.

Medien Tenor (2001) Terror und sonst fast nichts. *Medien Tenor Forschungsbericht* No. 115, pp. 54–56.

Meier, W. and Schanne, M. (1996) *Gesellschaftliche Risiken in den Medien: Zur Rolle des Journalismus bei der Wahrnehmung und Bewältigung gesellschaftlicher Risiken.* Seismo, Zürich.

Nacos, B.L. (2002) *Mass-mediated Terrorism: the Central Role of the Media in Terrorism and Counterterrorism.* Rowman & Littlefield, Lanham, Maryland.

Pizam, A. and Mansfeld, Y. (1996) *Tourism, Crime and International Security Issue.* Haworth Hospitality Press, New York/Toronto/Singapore.

Pizam, A. and Smith, G. (2000) Tourism and terrorism: a quantitative analysis of major terrorist acts and their impact on tourism destination. *Tourism Economics* 6, 123–138.

Richter, L.K. and Waugh, W.L. (1995) Terrorism and tourism as logical companions. In: Medlik, S. (ed.) *Managing Tourism.* Butterworth-Heinemann, Oxford, pp. 318–326.

Ryan, C. (1993) Crime, violence, terrorism and tourism: an accidental or intrinsic relationship. *Tourism Management* 14, 173–183

Schicha, C. and Brosda, C. (2002) *Medien und Terrorismus: Reaktionen auf den 11. September 2001.* Lit, Münster/Hamburg.

Schmieder, F. (1998) Krisenmanagement: Reiseverhalten der Urlauber: Das Grundbedürfnis nach Sicherheit steigt. *FVW-International* No. 6, 76.

Schreier, G. (1994) Krisenmanagement: Wenn Reiseziele in die Schlagzeilen geraten: Ist der Ruf erst ruiniert. *Touristik Management* 15 (4), 26–28.

Sönmez, S.F. (1998) Tourism, terrorism and political instability. *Annals of Tourism Research* 25, 416–456.

Sönmez, S.F. and Graefe, A.R. (1998) Influence of terrorism risk on foreign tourism decisions. *Annals of Tourism Research* 25, 171–177.

Sönmez, S.F., Apostolopoulos, Y. and Tarlow, P. (1999) Tourism in crisis: managing the effects of terrorism. *Journal of Travel Research* 38, 13–19.

Tscharnke, K. (1995) Der tägliche Terror aus dem Nachrichten-Ticker. *FVW-International* No. 5, 181.

Waldmann, P. (1998) *Terrorismus: Provokation der Macht.* Gerling-Akademie-Verlag, Munich.

World Tourism Organization (1997) *Tourist Safety and Security: Practical Measures for Destinations*, 2nd edn. WTO, Madrid.

www.terrorism.com/modules.php?op=modload&name=News&file=article&sid=5657 (accessed 14 July 2003).

11 Factors Influencing Crisis Management in Tourism Destinations

KOM CAMPIRANON AND NOEL SCOTT

Introduction

Managing tourism crises involves organizing a diverse group of people. Step one for managing crises from the Pacific Asia Travel Association (PATA) crisis management report states: 'Initiate the formation of a crisis management team, comprised of senior officials empowered with the authority to make and implement decisions in the midst of a crisis' (Pacific Asia Travel Association, 2003, p. 15). While theoretically a good idea, the notion of organizing diverse groups of people in a crisis situation is very problematic. Of course this is why the importance of pre-planning is stressed in many crisis management books and articles (Faulkner, 2001; Boisclair, 2002; Fleming, 2002; North-Puma, 2003; Pacific Asia Travel Association, 2003).

However, unlike organizations, tourism destinations are much less cohesive and involve many different and diverse groups of stakeholders; the community, individual business operators, sectoral organizations, regional tourism organizations, local, state and national government representatives (and indeed anti-government factions) and many others. In a crisis management situation, these stakeholder groups may have different objectives and priorities. Furthermore, these stakeholder groups may not perceive a crisis in the same way. While in an organizational setting, it may be expected that the culture of the organization is somewhat homogeneous, in a regional setting it may be that different regional or national cultures are found, each of which may view a crisis in a different manner.

Just as the complexity of the organization of tourism destinations affects crisis management, so the scale of recent crises requires consideration of different concepts. Recent crises and their adverse impacts at a regional and national scale require crisis management leadership and planning across tourism destinations (World Tourism Organization, 2005a). Further, the multicountry impacts of recent crises such as severe acute respiratory syndrome (SARS) and the Indian Ocean tsunami highlight the importance of considering cultural differences in order to prepare better for and manage crises. Recent research (e.g. Hofstede, 2001; Liu and Mackinnon, 2002; Schneider and Littrell, 2003) indicates that people from different national cultures tend to have different styles of management.

This chapter is concerned with how socio-cultural and organizational concepts may help us better understand the crisis management process in tourism destinations. It is envisaged that this understanding will be beneficial to governments and organizations by broadening their perspective about the issues involved in tourism destination crisis management. In an effort to respond to such an issue, this chapter addresses the background to the current tsunami crisis situation and examines the relationship between crisis management and three specific concepts: national or regional culture; leadership and resources; and how these concepts may influence the way the crisis management process could be executed.

Cultural Differences

This chapter adopts a definition of culture as the collective programming of the mind which differentiates members of one group or society from those of another (Litvin and Kar, 2003). Although it has been studied in different ways, culture is mostly referred to at either the national or organizational level. Thus, it is crucial explicitly to employ the terms 'national culture' and 'organizational culture' here in this chapter to avoid confusion.

Recent research has suggested that cross-cultural literacy is essential for an international business manager (Fan and Zigang, 2004). Interestingly, the ability to deal with cultural differences ranked first in all eight items of this survey of the essential skills of managers (including law, price competition, information, language, delivery, foreign currency, time differences and cultural differences). It is therefore important for organizations to recognize cross-cultural differences in an international business setting in order to develop a successful international management team (Chang, 2002), as knowledge of national cultural dimensions provides a necessary starting point for understanding co-workers, partners and competitors (Ross, 1999).

Cultural misunderstanding within organizations that operate in different cultural environments (Schneider and Barsoux, 1997) has been found in research studies in a number of areas. The growth of international business highlights the need for universal ethical standards as national cultures embody differing codes of conduct (Beyer and Nino, 1999). Furthermore, managing a cross-cultural team has also created a unique set of problems and issues relating to the effective management of partnerships with different national cultures (Fan and Zigang, 2004). Whilst it could be argued that it is becoming more difficult to draw a distinction between the Eastern and Western style of management (Floyd, 1999), West and East are still different cultures. Transference of Eastern management styles to the West and vice versa is not necessarily successful (Liu and Mackinnon, 2002).

Clearly, management of cultural differences is a major challenge. To cope with this challenge, it is vital to understand the dimensions of national culture differences in order to implement a suitable business strategy in the international environment. This is discussed in the next part of this chapter.

Dimensions of Cultural Differences

The importance of understanding national culture is recognized by Liu and Mackinnon (2002) who note that interest in studying and researching the effects of cross-cultural differences in international management is greater than ever (Chang, 2002). Multinational business strategy research has long acknowledged the significance of national cultural characteristics as determinants of management behaviour (Ross, 1999). Interestingly, studies over the past several decades in the area of national culture continue to support the conclusion that national differences in national culture and values exist (Jones and Davis, 2000).

One of the most widely accepted thinkers in the area of cultural differences is Hofstede, and it is not possible to use the term 'culture' in a field of business without referring to his work (Litvin and Kar, 2003). Hofstede's (2001) dimensions of national culture differences have been used to identify the influence of national culture on management style (e.g. Mwaura *et al.*, 1998; Christie *et al.*, 2003; Kolman *et al.*, 2003). This is endorsed by Mwaura *et al.* (1998) who note that a conceptual framework based on Hofstede's dimensions of national culture allows identification of where and to what extent Western theories of management can be implemented successfully elsewhere. While a number of authors have expressed disagreement with the implication of Hofstede's theory (e.g. Fang, 2003; Abdou and Kliche, 2004; Corbitt *et al.*, 2004; Dolan *et al.*, 2004; Litvin *et al.*, 2004; Mueller, 2004; Reber *et al.*, 2004; Venezia, 2005), we have adopted Hofstede's (2001) dimensions of national culture differences here because of its cited reliability and validity. In fact, Hofstede's theory is the most often cited cross-cultural literature source (e.g. Mwaura *et al.*, 1998; Ross, 1999; Jones and Davis, 2000; Chong and Park, 2003; Christie *et al.*, 2003; Kolman *et al.*, 2003; Litvin and Kar, 2003; Fan and Zigang, 2004) and has been repeatedly validated over time (Christie *et al.*, 2003).

According to Hofstede (2001), dimensions of national culture differences consist of five independent dimensions of national culture differences: power distance; uncertainty avoidance; individualism versus collectivism; masculinity versus femininity; and long-term versus short-term orientation. Each of these is discussed below.

Power distance

Power distance refers to the preferred type of decision making and is a society's way of dealing with power (Pressey and Selassie, 2003). It is defined as the extent to which the less powerful members of organizations within a country expect and accept that power is distributed unequally. Moreover, the concept of power distance also aims to explain a relationship between a manager and a subordinate in a hierarchy, including its value component. Examples include the finding that flat organizational structures are preferable in a low power distance culture, whereas tall organizational structures are preferred in a high power distance culture (Hofstede, 2001).

Uncertainty avoidance

Uncertainty avoidance is the extent to which the members of a culture feel threatened by uncertain or unknown situations. It comprises the values individuals place on the uncertainty of time, leading in some cases to unwillingness to take risks and a greater degree of planning to reduce uncertainty. For instance, senior managers in a low uncertainty avoidance culture tend to engage at a strategy level, whilst those in a high uncertainty avoidance culture tend to become involved at the operational level (Hofstede, 2001).

Individualism versus collectivism

According to Hofstede (2001), individualism stands for a society in which the ties between individuals are loose, and as a result individuals are only expected to look after him/herself and her/his immediate family. Conversely, collectivism stands for a society in which people from birth onwards are integrated into strong, cohesive in-groups, which throughout people's lifetime continue to protect them in exchange for unquestioning loyalty. In management decision making, a collective decision is preferable in a collectivism culture, whilst an individual decision is more likely to be seen in an individualism culture.

Masculinity versus femininity

Masculinity versus femininity is related to the division of emotional roles between men and women. In addition, the duality of the genders is an essential fact that different societies cope with in different ways. Masculinity is found in a society in which social gender roles are clearly distinct; thus men are encouraged to be assertive, tough and focused on material success. Women are expected to be more modest, tender and concerned with the quality of life. Unlike masculinity, femininity stands for a society in which social gender roles overlap, and both men and women are encouraged to be modest, tender and concerned with the quality of life (Hofstede, 2001).

Long-term versus short-term orientation

A long-term orientation stands for the fostering of virtues oriented towards future rewards, perseverance and thrift. Conversely, a short-term orientation stands for the fostering of virtues related to the past and present, based on respect for tradition, preservation of 'face' and fulfilling social obligations. In the business environment, a short-term orientation culture tends to look for short-term results, ending with the strength of the bottom line. On the other hand, a long-term orientation culture builds a strong relationship and market position (Hofstede, 2001).

Australia and Thailand provide good examples of the Western and Eastern cultures that differ on certain cultural dimensions. Australian culture is characterized by a low power distance, weak uncertainty avoidance, and tends to be individualistic. Thai culture has a large power distance, strong uncertainty avoidance, and tends to be collectivistic (Hofstede, 2001).

As a result of this discussion, it is apparent that culture is a useful concept to investigate crisis management style in a variety of national settings.

Relationship of Culture, Decision Making and Leadership

A second concept related to culture is the nature of leadership. Numerous studies have confirmed the influence of national culture on the decision-making process resulting in a diverse range of management styles among countries (Liu and Mackinnon, 2002; Schneider and Littrell, 2003). In other words, people from different nationalities who work together will have different perceptions of their jobs (Chang, 2002). In addition, people from different national cultures may draw different conclusions from the same encounter, leading to cultural misunderstandings (Prentice and Miller, 1999).

Decision making

The impact of national culture on decision making has attracted growing interest (Heales *et al.*, 2004) as decision making is clearly one of the most important tasks in management. People from different cultures tend to have different ways of making decisions, based on the emphasis they place on different phases of the decision-making process (Schramm-Nielsen, 2001). Studies have also suggested that people from divergent national cultures use different negotiation approaches, and they do so because their perceptions of the decision-making situation are conditioned by the characteristics of the national culture from which they come. National culture not only has a great influence on how managers and employees make decisions, but also affects the manner in which they interpret their roles (Chang, 2002). As a result, a number of authors have highlighted that decision making is influenced by national culture (e.g. Fan and Zigang, 2004; Heales *et al.*, 2004).

In some traditional theories, decision making is interpreted as a universalist phenomenon, meaning that the principles of decision-making processes and practices are universal. Managers are presumed to take action in the same way in comparable situations in all countries (Schramm-Nielsen, 2001). Hofstede's (2001) cultural theory suggests otherwise. First, power distance is directly involved with decision making. In the high power distance culture, decision structure is centralized, whilst a decentralized decision is preferred in the low power distance culture. Secondly, individualism versus collectivism is also associated with a decision-making process. As discussed previously, individual decisions are favoured in an individualist culture, and group decisions are favoured in a collectivism culture (Hofstede, 2001).

Thirdly, Hofstede's (2001) cultural dimension of uncertainty avoidance may also be related to risk taking versus risk avoiding in management decisions. According to Fan and Zigang (2004), one of these extreme examples is found between the cultural differences of China and the USA. Chinese and American managers differ greatly in their attitudes toward risks when they make decisions. Having a high uncertainty avoidance culture, Chinese managers normally lack an adventurous spirit and the sense of risk. They tend not to make immediate decisions if they feel the circumstance is uncertain, which in turn could diminish their competitive advantage. On the other hand, low uncertainty avoidance American managers are more likely to accept risks as natural and volunteer to take them, especially when developing new products, exploring a new market and applying new technology. Due to these clear cultural contrasts among countries, Liu and Mackinnon (2002) suggested that cross-cultural training in the task of decision making is required for managers who work in the international environment.

Leadership

Cultural impacts on some aspects of management decision making have already been discussed. In general, leadership is influenced by national culture (Heales *et al.*, 2004; Zagorsek *et al.*, 2004). As propensity to innovate and personal values vary across national cultures, we can expect the description and behaviour of leaders also to vary across national cultures (Schneider and Littrell, 2003). Interestingly, leadership processes are influenced by the national culture in which they takes place (Meng *et al.*, 2003). Thus the perception of leadership reflects the dominant national culture of a country. Asking people to describe the qualities of a good leader is another way of asking them to describe their national culture (Hofstede, 2001).

As a consequence, a particular style of leadership, shaped by national culture, is likely to be considered favourable and to be accepted in that national culture (D'Annunzio-Green, 2002). By adopting Hofstede's (2001) cultural dimension to explain this phenomenon, it is evident that power distance is directly involved with leadership. In the high power distance culture, for example, authoritative leadership and close supervision lead to satisfaction, performance and productivity. On the other hand, consultative leadership is preferred in the low power distance culture. Additionally, Hofstede's masculinity versus femininity theory could also strengthen the influence of national culture, as managers in a femininity culture are expected to use intuition, deal with feelings and seek consensus. On the other hand, managers in a masculinity culture are supposed to be decisive, firm, assertive, aggressive and competitive. Again, masculinity versus femininity reflects the relationship between national culture and a decision-making process (Hofstede, 2001).

As a result of this discussion, we conclude that national culture has a significant impact on organizational decision making and leadership. In the next section, we extend this finding to the management of tourism destinations.

Crisis Management

There are numerous different definitions of a crisis. Faulkner (2001) and Prideaux *et al.* (2003) emphasize the managerial responsibility for a crisis, while Pearson and Claire (1998) are more focused on the characteristics of the event (low probability and ambiguous). Pauchant and Douville (1993) and Reilly (1993) note the novelty and urgency of decision making required in a crisis. Selbst (1978), discussed in Faulkner (2001), examined the internal and external effects of a crisis. From these perspectives, crisis management involves dealing with a novel and urgent problem which has serious and far-reaching implications.

Crisis management, on the other hand, has been studied as a systematic effort by organizational members to avert crises or effectively to manage those that do occur (King, 2002). It involves a set of factors which specifically aim to cope with crises and lessen the actual damage inflicted by the crisis. Basically, crisis management seeks to prevent or lessen the negative outcomes of a crisis and thereby protect the organization, stakeholders and industry from damage (Coombs, 1999). As an extension of risk management, crisis management is also perceived as an established management decision-making aid. It is also used for pro-active decision making that continuously assesses potential risks, prioritizes the risks and implements strategies to cope with those risks (Pacific Asia Travel Association, 2003).

The staged approaches to crisis management provide the mechanism for constructing a framework for organizing the vast and varied crisis management writings (Coombs, 1999). Having said that, Wilks and Moore (2004) noted that there are many frameworks and approaches to crisis management (e.g. Campbell, 1999; Coombs, 1999; Augustine, 2000; Schwartz, 2000; Pacific Asia Travel Association, 2003; Ruff and Aziz, 2003; World Tourism Organization, 2005a). This chapter has, however, adopted a crisis management model proposed by the World Tourism Organization (2005a), as the World Tourism Organization (WTO) is unarguably recognized as the key authority in tourism. The model proposed by the WTO consists of three stages: before the crisis (crisis preparation), during a crisis (crisis response) and following a crisis (crisis recovery). This model will be illustrated later in Fig. 11.1.

Crisis Management for Tourism Destinations – Resources

The characteristics of crisis management for a tourism destination are somewhat different from those involved in managing a crisis in an individual organization. As has been discussed above, tourism destinations involve many different stakeholders who work cooperatively as well as in competition. While the management responsibility for a tourism destination in terms of publicity or marketing may reside with a regional or national tourism organization, responsibility for planning and infrastructure may reside with the government or individual businesses. This fragmentation of control or responsibility may lead to a lack of planning and the availability of resources to address tourism destination crises. The availability of integrated management responsibility across a tourism destination as well as necessary resources, including money, human resources and material, available to respond to crises is also expected to differ across countries and regions.

Managing crises in tourism destinations requires adequate resources. From the review of literature, it is crucial for managers to choose an adequate level of resources useful in a time of crisis (Bland, 1998). This can be seen in a number of crisis situations that have an adverse impact on tourism, such as the SARS outbreak (Henderson, 2003) and 11 September 2001 (9/11) (Rosenthal, 2003). In a terrorism event, for example, it is crucial for organizations to have sufficient resources to manage a crisis effectively through coordination of human and financial resources (Stafford *et al.*, 2002).

Moreover, sophisticated crisis management procedures cannot be implemented at the organizational level if the resources are not available.

In some countries, the emergency services and the military make an enormous contribution preparing for emergencies. In the private sector, it is only some multinational companies such as oil majors and airlines that are able to devote millions of dollars and scores of people to preparing for and handling a crisis (Bland, 1998). The level of resources available to be devoted to crisis management preparation therefore differs across regions and countries.

Culture and Leadership in Crisis Management

The concepts described in the earlier sections of this chapter have been related to crisis management. National culture has a significant impact on crisis management. There are major cultural differences between individual countries and the way that they view a crisis (Bland, 1998). A crisis rips away the commonly homogeneous global culture to reveal different regional values. Johnson and Peppas (2003) agree and point out that crisis intensity varies from country to country and culture to culture, which means that it is very important that crisis response plans are developed for a specific location and also involve input from local management and public officials.

Leadership and crisis management are also closely related (Boin and Hart, 2003). Crisis management, in the sense of prevention and damage control, is an essential responsibility of leadership. Before a crisis occurs, the crisis management process begins with the leadership's perception of risk and a conscious decision to seek ways to prevent or reduce it (Smits and Ezzat, 2003). In times of crisis, leaders must demonstrate strong interpersonal skills (King, 2002; Ucelli, 2002) by implementing the most effective plan of action, sticking with it and continually monitoring the organization's performance (Brenneman, 2000).

National culture and leadership also appear inter-related in management of crises and the crisis response process (e.g. Pinsdorf, 1991; Chandler, 2005). In some developing countries, the national culture is often unsympathetic to the active management of crisis (Elsubbaugh *et al.*, 2004). Normally, people will use locally available ideas and practices to guide their interactions, to coordinate their responses and ultimately to live in culture-specific ways (Prentice and Miller, 1999). As a result, people tend to manage crisis differently among diverse national cultures. This crisis response issue has been acknowledged by several authors (e.g. Elsubbaugh *et al.*, 2004; Chandler, 2005). For instance, senior managers in some countries perceived the need to eradicate the individualistic culture, mostly found in developing countries, and encourage a cooperative culture both horizontally among managers as well as between workers in times of crisis (Elsubbaugh *et al.*, 2004). As a result, it is evident that national culture has an indirect influence over both crisis planning and crisis response processes. To test the relationships among culture, leadership and resources in crisis management, the recent literature of the tsunami crisis is discussed.

The Tsunami Crisis

A tsunami disaster struck countries bordering the Indian Ocean on 26 December 2004. The tourism industry in eight countries was affected, some severely. In a number of those countries, the Maldives, Sri Lanka and Thailand in particular, tourism is an important source of income and employment (World Tourism Organization, 2005b). Interestingly, some linkages between national culture, leadership and aspects of crisis management were found in the reports concerning the crisis in the countries of Thailand, Indonesia, Malaysia and India, as outlined in Table 11.1.

These findings support the conclusion that crisis management is influenced by national culture, leadership style and level of resources available, as is illustrated in Fig. 11.1.

Figure 11.1 outlines a crisis management model for tourism destinations. Adapted from the World Tourism Organization (2005a), this model consists of three stages: crisis preparation, crisis response and crisis recovery. The proposed model also incorporates culture, leadership and resources as factors that influence those stages. From the literature, it could be seen that a crisis outcome and the speed of crisis management have also been directly and indirectly influenced by the three factors.

Conclusion and Managerial Implication

At the heart of every crisis lies tremendous opportunity, and perhaps this is why the Chinese word for crisis is surprisingly composed of two symbols meaning 'danger' and 'opportunity' (Holmes, 2003). In the terrible tragedy of a recent multicountry disaster, this chapter has found some evidence for the proposal that difference in leadership, culture and resources available may influence crisis management in tourism destinations.

Four major implication of this chapter may be identified. First, the different sets of stakeholders necessitate modification of the crisis

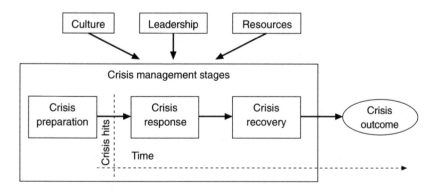

Fig. 11.1. Factors influencing crisis management in tourism destinations.

Table 11.1. Crisis management analysis.

Culture	Leadership	Resource
• The Indonesian President Yudhoyono adopted a 'Javanese' approach by handling the relief disaster programme from behind the scenes and delegating actual management to Vice President Yusuf Kalla and other ministers (*Japan Times*, 2005). • The quiet and indirect qualities of Indonesian national culture, all of which stress social harmony, tend to regard American-style verbal evangelism as rude and arrogant, regardless of a person's intentions. In this culture, silent aid really does speak volumes (Jones, 2005). • The bureaucratic (high power distance culture) system in India caused a slow speed of decision and recovery (Indiresan, 2005). • Although the tsunami damage to Malaysia was far less serious than that in Thailand and Indonesia, while all victims were Malaysian, the cumbersome bureaucratic red tape (high power distance culture) involved in ensuring that aid is disbursed honestly has been heavily criticized by the public (*Japan Times*, 2005).	• The different leadership styles of Thai Prime Minister Thaksin Shinawatra, Indonesian President Susilo Bambang Yudhoyono and Malaysian Prime Minister Abdullah Badawi in organizing relief and reconstruction after the 26 December tsunami hold important lessons for managing peace, politics and stability in the region (*Japan Times*, 2005). • In many of the tsunami-struck locations, there is a tangled web of authority: federal government officials, local officials, police, army, US and other military personnel, local aid agencies, community groups, non-governmental organizations, international relief organizations, the UN. Each of these has some basis for discretion and authority, and each is likely to be wary of instructions issued by others. Together, they form a tangled web of chains of command, with ample opportunity for confusion, resentment, and conflict (Leonard, 2005). • Firm political leadership has enabled Thailand to begin its recovery without delay (Lopez and Larkin, 2005).	• The delay in India joining the advance tsunami warning system and setting up its own national capability due to financial reasons underlines once again the difficulties faced by national security and disaster managers due to the short-sighted approach of financial experts, who reject such proposals on the grounds that they are based on the likelihood of vulnerabilities and not on the possibility or certainty of actual threats (Raman, 2005). • A combination of factors – from more advanced medical, communications and transportation networks to less extensive damage than elsewhere – have enabled Thailand to begin its recovery without delay (Lopez and Larkin, 2005). • Resources of crisis recovery, including the infrastructure, medical, communications and transportation networks, well-equipped military and political stability, vary among these tsunami-struck countries (Lopez and Larkin, 2005). • The speed of destination recovery depends not only on the extent of the damage caused by the disaster or crisis but also, first, on the efficiency with which tourism facilities are reinstated (Sausmarez, 2005).

Source: various authors.

management model as they may perceive crises differently. Secondly, managing crises in tourism destinations and organizations requires translation of concepts previously discussed to a different level of analysis. Part of the reason is because the crisis management model, which has been largely developed for the organizational context, requires adjustment to maximize its effectiveness prior to an implementation in tourism destinations. Thirdly, whilst earlier research has recognized that leadership and resources play a significant part in the crisis management models, this chapter extends those models by taking account of cultural influences (as seen in Fig. 11.1). This statement supports findings from previous studies (e.g. Hofstede, 2001; Liu and Mackinnon, 2002; Schneider and Littrell, 2003) that indicate that people from different national cultures tend to have different styles of management. It is therefore important for governments and organizations to understand the impact of national culture on crisis management. Fourthly, the ability of tourism destinations to address the impact of crises will vary due to differences in the resources available. As emphasized by Bland (1998), it is crucial for a government to assess its resource availability and deployability prior to developing a crisis management plan for specific tourism destinations.

This chapter suggests further research focusing on a relationship between national culture and crisis management. This area would benefit from further explorations in the future. Use of case studies based on Hofstede-like analytical frameworks to investigate the impact of different cultures would appear useful. While Hofstede's theory has been challenged, his work is widely adopted across different fields. It is recommended to other researchers as useful in understanding differences in crisis management across tourism destinations.

References

Abdou, K. and Kliche, S. (2004) The strategic alliances between the Americans and German companies: a cultural perspective. *European Business Review* 16 (1), 8–27.

Augustine, N. (2000) Managing the crisis you tried to prevent. In: Harvest Business School (ed.) *Harvard Business Review on Crisis Management.* Harvard Business School Press, Boston, Massachusetts, pp. 1–31.

Beyer, J. and Nino, D. (1999) Ethics and cultures in international business. *Journal of Management Inquiry* 8, 287–298.

Bland, M. (1998) *Communicating out of a Crisis.* Macmillan Press, London.

Boin, A. and Hart, P. (2003) Public leadership in times of crisis: mission impossible? *Public Administration Review* 63, 544–553.

Boisclair, M. (2002) Reality check. *Successful Meetings* pp. 10–13.

Brenneman, G. (2000) Right away and all at once: how we saved Continental. In: Harvest Business School (ed.) *Harvard*

Business Review on Crisis Management. Harvard Business School Press, Boston, Massachusetts, pp. 87–118.

Campbell, R. (1999) *Crisis Control: Preventing and Managing Corporate Crises.* Prentice Hall, Australia.

Chandler, C. (2005) A wave of corporate charity. *Fortune – European Edition* 151, 15–16.

Chang, L. (2002) Cross-cultural differences in international management using Kluckhohn–Strodtbeck framework. *Journal of the American Academy of Business* 2, 20–28.

Chong, J. and Park, J. (2003) National culture and classical principles of planning. *Cross Cultural Management* 10, 29–40.

Christie, P., Kwon, I., Stoeberl, P. and Baumhart, R. (2003) A cross-cultural comparison of ethical attitudes of business managers: India, Korea and the USA. *Journal of Business Ethics* 46, 263–287.

Coombs, W. (1999) *Ongoing Crisis Communication: Planning, Managing, and Responding.* Sage Publications, London.

Corbitt, B., Peszynski, K., Inthanond, S., Hill, B. and Thanasankit, T. (2004) Cultural differences, information and code systems. *Journal of Global Information Management* 12 (3), 65–86.

D'Annunzio-Green, N. (2002) An examination of the organizational and cross-cultural challenges facing international hotel managers in Russia. *International Journal of Contemporary Hospitality Management* 14, 266–274.

Dolan, S., Diez-Pinol, M., Fernandez-Alles, M., Martin-Prius, A. and Martinez-Fierro, S. (2004) Exploratory study of within-country differences in work and life values: the case of Spanish business students. *International Journal of Cross Cultural Management: CCM* 4, 157–181.

Elsubbaugh, S., Fildes, R. and Rose, M. (2004) Preparation for crisis management: a proposed model and empirical evidence. *Journal of Contingencies and Crisis Management* 12 (3), 112–128.

Fan, P. and Zigang, Z. (2004) Cross-cultural challenges when doing business in China. *Singapore Management Review* 26, 81–90.

Fang, T. (2003) A critique of Hofstede's fifth national culture dimension. *International Journal of Cross Cultural Management: CCM* 3, 347–369.

Faulkner, B. (2001) Towards a framework for tourism disaster management. *Tourism Management* 22, 135–147.

Fleming, J. (2002) Six critical security recommendations for buyers. *Business Travel News* 19, 10–12.

Floyd, D. (1999) Eastern and Western management practices: myth or reality? *Management Decision* 37, 628–632.

Heales, J., Cockcroft, S. and Raduescu, C. (2004) The influence of national culture on the level and outcome of IS development decisions. *Journal of Global Information Technology Management* 7 (4), 3–29.

Henderson, J. (2003) Managing a health-related crisis: SARS in Singapore. *Journal of Vacation Marketing* 10, 67–78.

Hofstede, G. (2001) *Culture's Consequences*, 2nd edn. Sage Publications, Thousand Oaks, California.

Holmes, J. (2003) Asia Pacific Business Opportunities, International Congress and Convention Association, <http:// www.icca world.com/> (accessed 27 May 2005).

Indiresan, P. (2005) Real Crisis Management, The Hindu Business Line, <http:// www.thehindubusinessline.com/2005/01/1 0/stories/2005011000080800.htm> (accessed 23 May 2005).

Japan Times (2005) Three leadership styles in crisis management, The Korea Herald, <http://www.koreaherald.co.kr/SITE/data/ html_dir/2005/03/24/200503240008.asp> (accessed 23 May 2005).

Johnson, V. and Peppas, S. (2003) Crisis management in Belgium: the case of Coca-Cola. *Corporate Communications* 8, 18–23.

Jones, G. and Davis, H. (2000) National culture and innovation: implications for locating global R&D operations. *Management International Review* 40, 11–40.

Jones, N. (2005) A Big Wave or a Sea Change? Indonesia After the Tsunami, The Institute for Global Engagement, <http://www.globalengage.org/issues/200 5/01/tsunami.htm> (accessed 24 May 2005).

King, G., III (2002) Crisis management and team effectiveness: a closer examination. *Journal of Business Ethics* 41, 235–250.

Kolman, L., Noorderhaven, N., Hofstede, G. and Dienes, E. (2003) Cross-cultural differences in central Europe. *Journal of Managerial Psychology* 18, 76–89.

Leonard, H. (2005) 2004 Tsunami Management Challenges, Harvard Business School, <http://www.library.hbs.edu/ tsunami/tsunamichallenges.html> (accessed 25 May 2005).

Litvin, S. and Kar, G. (2003) Individualism/collectivism as a moderating factor to the self-image congruity concept. *Journal of Vacation Marketing* 10, 23–33.

Litvin, S., Crotts, J. and Hefner, F. (2004) Cross-cultural tourist behaviour: a replication and extension involving Hofstede's uncertainty avoidance dimension. *International Journal of Tourism Research* 6, 29–38.

Liu, J. and Mackinnon, A. (2002) Comparative management practices and training: China and Europe. *Journal of Management Development* 21, 118–133.

Lopez, L. and Larkin, J. (2005) Thailand's relief effort stands out; Asian nation moves fast to give aid after tsunami with minimal foreign help. *Wall Street Journal* p. A.7.

Meng, Y., Ashkanasy, N. and Hartel, C. (2003) The effects of Australian tall poppy attitudes on American value based leadership theory. *International Journal of Value-Based Management* 16, 53–65.

Mueller, S. (2004) Gender gaps in potential for entrepreneurship across countries and cultures. *Journal of Developmental Entrepreneurship* 9, 199–221.

Mwaura, G., Sutton, J. and Roberts, D. (1998) Corporate and national culture – an irreconcilable dilemma for the hospitality manager? *International Journal of Contemporary Hospitality Management* 10, 212–220.

North-Puma, L. (2003) What 9/11 taught us. *Tradeshow Week* 33, 10–12.

Pacific Asia Travel Association (2003) *Crisis: It Won't Happen to Us.* Pacific Asia Travel Association, Bangkok.

Pauchant, T. and Douville, R. (1993) Recent research in crisis management: a study of 24 authors' publications from 1986 to 1991. *Industrial and Environmental Crisis Quarterly* 7, 43–63.

Pearson, C.M. and Clair, J.A. (1998) Reframing crisis management. *Academy of Management Review* 23, 59–76.

Pinsdorf, M. (1991) Crashes bare values affecting response success. *Public Relations Journal* 47 (7), 32–34.

Prentice, D. and Miller, D. (1999) *Cultural Divides: Understanding and Overcoming Group Conflict.* Russell Sage Foundation, New York.

Pressey, A. and Selassie, H. (2003) Are cultural differences overrated? Examining the influence of national culture on international buyer–seller relationships. *Journal of Consumer Behaviour* 2, 354–368.

Prideaux, B., Laws, E. and Faulkner, B. (2003) Events in Indonesia: exploring the limits to formal tourism trends forecasting methods in complex crisis situations. *Tourism Management* 24, 475–487.

Raman, B. (2005) The Tsunami and After, South Asia Analysis Group, <http://www.saag.org/papers13/paper1209.html> (accessed 23 May 2005).

Reber, G., Auer-Rizzi, W. and Maly, M. (2004) The behaviour of managers in Austria and the Czech Republic: an intercultural comparison based on the Vroom/Yetton model of leadership and decision-making. *Journal for East European Management Studies* 9, 411–430.

Reilly, A. (1993) Preparing for the worst: the process of effective crisis management. *Industrial and Environmental Crisis Quarterly* 7, 115–143.

Rosenthal, U. (2003) September 11: public administration and the study of crises and crisis management. *Administration and Society* 35, 129–143.

Ross, D. (1999) Culture as a context for multinational business: a framework for assessing the strategy–culture fit. *Multinational Business Review* 17, 13–20.

Ruff, P. and Aziz, K. (2003) *Managing Communications in a Crisis.* Gower Publishing Limited, Aldershot, UK.

Sausmarez, N. (2005) The Indian Ocean tsunami. *Tourism and Hospitality: Planning and Development* 2, 55–59.

Schneider, J. and Littrell, R. (2003) Leadership preferences of German and English managers. *Journal of Management Development* 22, 130–149.

Schneider, S. and Barsoux, J. (1997) *Managing across Cultures.* Prentice-Hall Europe, London.

Schramm-Nielsen, J. (2001) Cultural dimensions of decision-making: Denmark and France compared. *Journal of Managerial Psychology* 16, 404–424.

Schwartz, P. (2000) When good companies do bad things. *Strategy and Leadership* 28 (3), 4–11.

Selbst, P. (1978), in Booth, S. (1993) *Crisis Management Strategy: Competition and Change in Modern Enterprises.* Routledge, New York.

Smits, S. and Ezzat, N. (2003) Thinking the

unthinkable – leadership's role in creating behavioural readiness for crisis management. *Competitiveness Review* 13, 1–23.

Stafford, G., Yu, L. and Armoo, A. (2002) Crisis management and recovery: how Washington, D.C., hotels responded to terrorism. *Cornell Hotel and Restaurant Administration Quarterly* 43 (5), 27–41.

Ucelli, L. (2002) The CEO's 'how to' guide to crisis communications. *Strategy and Leadership* 30 (2), 21–25.

Venezia, G. (2005) Impact of globalization of public administration practices on Hofstede's cultural indices. *Journal of American Academy of Business, Cambridge* 6, 344–350.

Wilks, J. and Moore, S. (2004) Tourism Risk Management for the Asia-Pacific Region, World Tourism Organization, <http:// www.world-tourism.org/tsunami/eng.html> (accessed 23 May 2005).

World Tourism Organization (2005a) Crisis Guidelines for the Tourism Industry, World Tourism Organization, <http://www.world-tourism.org/ tsunami/eng.html> (accessed 23 May 2005).

World Tourism Organization (2005b) Tourism Sector Hopeful about Tsunami Recovery, World Tourism Organization, <http://www. worldtourism.org/newsroom/Releases/20 05/january/tsunami.htm> (accessed 23 May 2005).

Zagorsek, H., Jaklic, M. and Stough, S. (2004) Comparing leadership practices between the USA, Nigeria, and Slovenia: does culture matter? *Cross Cultural Management* 11 (2), 16–35.

12 Crisis Management and Tourism Organizations: a Comparative Study in the European Alps

HARALD PECHLANER, DAGMAR ABFALTER, FRIEDA RAICH AND AXEL DREYER

Introduction

In light of recent extraordinary events, tourism discussions increasingly focus on the topics of 'crisis' and 'disaster'. Having recognized that the tourism and leisure industries are highly vulnerable to exceptional events such as 11 September 2001 (9/11) or severe acute respiratory syndrome (SARS), scientific discussion has focused on the issue of crises and disasters and the development of strategies to assist the tourism industry in recovering from events that are usually not forecastable (Faulkner, 2001). In order to meet the new challenges of the political, economic and societal environments that have arisen from the recent crises, tourism science has to formulate goals, recommendations and solutions for the effective and efficient management of crises. Several tourism researchers have tried to build a framework for tourism crisis management (e.g. Drabek, 1995; Pizam and Mansfield, 1995; Santana, 1999; Sönmez et al., 1999; Steene, 1999; Faulkner, 2001; Dreyer et al., 2004). It has been pointed out that comprehensive crisis management strategies can help mitigate the full impacts of tourism crises or in some cases even prevent a crisis occurring. Although tourism is highly vulnerable to crises and catastrophes, many destinations still seem not to have fully recognized the need for crisis planning.

Nevertheless, peace, safety and security are necessary conditions for tourism destination development and for successful competition. Tourists demand that destinations offer quality services, and assume that their safety and security are guaranteed. However, tourists are often more vulnerable than locals in crisis or disaster situations, as they are less familiar with local hazards and they are more dependent on community support than local residents during a period of crisis (Faulkner, 2001). Whereas most individuals tend to avoid a risky environment, tourists may sometimes be bored by too much familiarity and lack of novelty and seek new experiences, some of which may contain an element of danger. For these reasons, destinations need to establish the balance between perceptions of high risk and of the need for safety when they target specific visitor markets.

Crises and Disasters in the Alpine Tourism Industry

'Crises' and 'disasters' are related but different events. While disasters or catastrophes imply a clearly unpredictable event that can normally only be responded to after the event (Glaesser, 2003), crises have been described as 'the possible but unexpected result of management failures that are concerned with the future course of events set in motion by human action or inaction precipitating the event' (Prideaux *et al.*, 2003, p. 477). They have also been identified as having 'detrimental or negative effects on the organization as a whole, or individuals within it' (Faulkner, 2001, p. 136). Disasters, on the other hand, refer to situations where an enterprise or destination is confronted with sudden unpredictable catastrophic changes over which it has little control (Faulkner, 2001). Crises can range from small-scale internal events such as diverse problems concerning staff (illness, breakdowns, etc.) to external incidents such as terrorist attacks (Coombs, 1999). In the European Alps, events including accidents with cable cars or in tunnels and avalanches, as well as the latent fear of terrorist attacks have led to increased risk awareness and to the development of crisis management plans. When the tourism industry experiences negative events caused by natural disasters, greater public and industry understanding and tolerance are invoked than in the case of human-caused incidents such as terrorist attacks (Sönmez *et al.*, 1999). Still, in the alpine regions, the risk of natural disasters is presumably higher than the risk of crises caused through terrorism.

As a consequence, the alpine tourism industry has to face the problem that global tourism groups increasingly take account of crisis management, which implies concrete effects to ensure that crisis situations can be managed effectively. Tour operators play an essential role as they are considered liable not only for the performance of their services, but also for physical injuries caused to their clients by negligence. As a consequence, tour operators attempt to minimize safety and security risks that their customers may encounter. Issues considered by tour operators include the type of the crisis (whether human-caused or natural), the dimensions of a crisis (limited to a specific region, nation or global), the predicted duration of the crisis, the consequences of the crisis (damage to tourism facilities), the tour operator's own business interests in the destination, and government-generated travel advisory information and warnings. The cancellation or omission of a particular destination from a tour operator's programme is a signal to tourists that a destination is not considered safe (Cavlek, 2002). Because tourists are free to choose from a wide range of destinations and tour offers, they are unlikely to consider travelling near a place where they feel exposed to high risk. On the other hand, tour operators are more likely to support destinations that have a demonstrated ability to cope effectively with crisis situations.

New Requirements for the Management of Potential Crises and Disasters

The requirements for management of potential crises directly affect the management and marketing of alpine destinations. While many large organizations are able to develop permanent crisis management teams, small and micro businesses, which characterize the tourism industry, are not able to devote resources in a similar manner. Leadership is required to provide direction and guidance when dealing with incidents, and nomination of a spokesman responsible for communication with the media is desirable. The complexity of the subject requires a pro-active role and a high degree of coordination from all tourism officials in the public and private management of marketing activities (Cavlek, 2002). Tourism organizations need to plan for the 'unthinkable' in order to achieve their goals and objectives effectively (Santana, 1999). Still, crises are not only considered negatively; on the contrary, some researchers suggest positive effects of crises such as stimuli to innovation or the recognition of new markets (Faulkner and Vikulov, 2001). As a consequence, the focus of attention is shifted from reacting to a specific crisis to the long-term strategic management of potential and latent crises. Crisis management is clearly a task of destination management and an important tool to enhance destination competitiveness. Tourism development within destinations has to be sustainable, not just economically or ecologically, but also socially, culturally and politically. The most competitive destination is one that most effectively creates sustainable well-being for its residents, safety and security being considered qualifying determinants (Ritchie and Crouch, 2003). Faulkner (2001) argues that all organizations have to deal with change at some stage and that all destinations will have to deal with a disaster or crises at some point.

While many disasters are attributable to random natural events beyond the control of the most advanced technology, their impacts can be moderated by planning and management practices. One step proposed by Faulkner (2001) is to assess the risks that an individual destination is exposed to and develop management plans for coping with disaster situations in advance.

Crisis situations usually force managers to make decisions rapidly and with incomplete information, which makes responding to chaotic situations difficult. In his recent article, Ritchie (2004) proposes a strategic, holistic and pro-active crisis management approach in the tourism industry through the development of pro-active scanning and planning, the implantation of strategies for crisis or disaster situations and an evaluation of the effectiveness of these strategies in order to ensure constant refinement.

A team of researchers from Austria, Italy and Germany has performed a research project as an attempt to find answers to these questions. Managers of local and regional tourism organizations and communities in the three alpine regions of the Tyrol in Austria, Alto Adige in Italy and Bavaria in Germany were questioned on their risk and crisis management. The survey asked specific questions concerning risk and crisis management with special consideration of organizational and leadership aspects in alpine tourism destinations.

Method

The research design utilized a mail back self-administered questionnaire sent to a total of 427 tourism organizations in the Tyrol and Alto Adige regions and the alpine part of Bavaria. A total of 121 completed questionnaires were returned, giving an acceptable response rate of 28.3%. Respondents were asked to indicate their agreement or disagreement with statements describing their evaluation of impacts, risks and various trends using 5-point Likert scales. Analysis of specific patterns of reaction of tourism organizations to anticipated crises and disasters could not be tested using analysis of variance (ANOVA), as the assumptions of normal distribution were not met. Therefore, non-parametrical procedures have been applied. The questionnaire was designed to: review actual experiences of respondents to crises; assess the impact on the destination; identify respondents' awareness and personal evaluation of risk and potential crises or disasters; and identify how crisis management activities were undertaken in their organizations. Data were processed using the SPSS statistical package.

Results were then assessed through the use of an expert interview with the head of the tourism office in Galtuer, Austria. Galtuer, a tourism resort situated in the Paznaun Valley in Western Tyrol, was selected because it was the site of an avalanche on 23 February 1999. The village, which up until then claimed to be safe from avalanches, was hit by a fatal avalanche after having been isolated for nearly 2 weeks because of heavy ongoing snow falls. At the time of the avalanche, the village contained about 8000 residents and 20,000 tourists. The avalanche destroyed several houses, buried 60 people and caused 31 deaths and 18 injuries. Eight thousand tourists and locals had to be evacuated from Galtuer and Valzur, a neighbouring village hit by an avalanche the following day. Damage to property has been estimated to more than €5 million (Heumader, 2000). Although no other avalanche has hit the village since that time, the Galtuer avalanche still receives media attention.

Results of the Study

Description of the sample

The survey responses were almost equally divided between regions (Alto Adige 37.2%, Bavaria and Tyrol each 31.4%). Most of the organizations responding to the survey were tourist offices (63.9%), followed by tourist agencies/tourism information offices (19.8%), and communities and municipal offices (15.1%) (see Table 12.1). As a consequence, the majority of the persons responsible for completing the surveys were directors or managers; other positions of responsibility included office managers (8.8%), secretaries (7.9%) or community mayors (5.3%).

Table 12.1. Respondents' profile.

Region	
Alto Adige/South Tyrol	37.2%
Bavaria	31.4%
Tyrol	31.4%
Respondent's position	
Director/manager	57.0%
Office manager	8.8%
Secretary	7.3%
Mayor	5.3%
Organization	
Tourist offices	63.9%
Tourist agencies/tourism information	19.8%
Community/municipal offices	15.1%

Experiences with crises

The respondents were asked to recall three exceptional events (crises) in the Alps. Crises were defined as exceptional events associated with increased media attention, economic losses, injuries or deaths and that affected the tourism industry. The main events recalled were funicular and cable car accidents (53 mentions). Examples of these include the funicular accident in Kaprun, Austria 2001 and the Cavalese Cable Car disaster (Italy) in 1998. Floods including those in 2002 received 41 mentions, while avalanches such as the avalanches in Galtuer, Austria 1999 were mentioned 39 times. Other incidents recalled included tunnel accidents (19 mentions) such as the fires in the Tauerntunnel in Austria and the St Gotthard tunnel in Switzerland. Thunderstorms and mudflows received seven mentions.

A third of the respondents (35.3%) had experienced crises in their city or region since 1998, with 14 incidents (67.6%) recalled as occurring in 2002 and 11 incidents in the first third of 2003. In 81.1% of the cases, local citizens were among the victims of the disaster, 40.5% affected summer tourists, 40.5% affected winter tourists and a further 16.2% of the victims were 'off-piste' skiers or on a ski tour.

Most destinations reported that the main impact of disasters had been increased media interest (27.0) followed by increased information needs of tourists and locals (21.1%) and unexpected departures of tourists (8.1%). Long-term impacts did not appear to be significant although there were reductions in bookings (10.0% found the impact significant), cancellations (7.5%), loss of image (7.5%) and litigation (5.3%). Most of the impacts did not last longer than 6 months (58.3%). Financial loss was considered important by rescue services (30.3%), whereas financial losses due to reduced bookings, cancellations and insurance payments were not considered significant (6.3–9.4%).

In the example of Galtuer, no law suit was initiated. Most of the hotels responded positively to guests' concerns most likely to prevent further image losses. Nevertheless, the village is still shown in the media when examples of disasters are needed. Four days after the incident, a huge press conference was organized in the snow-bound village. After the conference, journalists were flown out, leading to sustained media criticism. The members of the avalanche warning commission were legally discharged from allegations raised by the media. Communication with guests and their relatives was maintained with a telephone hotline established through the Tyrolean Tourist Board immediately after the avalanche. It took the village about a year to re-establish normality.

Estimation of risks

In the estimation of probable risks (see Table 12.2), the risk of sports and mountain accidents ranked the highest, followed by traffic accidents, and flooding and mudslides. Terrorist attacks were not considered to be of a major concern.

An assumption of normal distribution is not supported when using the Kolmogorov–Smirnow test. Therefore, the Kruskal–Wallis test for differences in regions and the Wilcoxon test for differences in crisis experience have been applied. Whereas only the risk estimation for sports and mountain accidents (mean value South Tyrol 3.18, Tyrol 3.11 and Bavaria 2.50) and the risk for avalanches (Tyrol 2.26, South Tyrol 2.08 and Bavaria 1.64) showed significant differences among the regions, the estimation of risks according to the respondents' experience with crises varied significantly in the case of bus or train accidents, epidemics, tunnel accidents and bomb threats (see Table 12.2).

It was considered that the Galtuer avalanche was not predictable. However, because of the threat posed by avalanches, protection was

Table 12.2. Estimation of probable risks.

	Mean	Existing risk (3–5) (%)	Probable risk (4–5) (%)	Significant difference across regions (Kruskal–Wallis test)	Significant difference due to crisis experience (Mann-Whitney U-test)
Sports and mountain accidents	2.94	67.9	27.7	$\chi^2 = 7.325, P = 0.026$	NS
Other traffic accidents	2.78	60.2	19.5	NS	NS
Floods, mudflows	2.51	50.4	14.2	NS	NS
Fire accident	2.43	41.3	6.4	NS	NS
Bus or train accidents	2.09	28.8	1.8	NS	$U = 1044.500, P = 0.036$
Avalanches	2.00	27.4	8.8	$\chi^2 = 7.835, P = 0.020$	NS
Epidemics	1.66	8.3	1.9	NS	$U = 1014.000, P = 0.040$
Bombing threats	1.58	7.5	3.7	NS	$U = 1026.500, P = 0.077$
Tunnel accidents	1.52	13.0	2.8	NS	$U = 1033.500, P = 0.042$
Terrorist attack	1.50	7.5	3.7	NS	NS
Abduction	1.47	5.6	1.9	NS	NS

1 = no risk; 2 = low; 3 = neutral; 4 = high; 5 = very high.

improved, contingency plans developed and psychological training courses were established. A new purpose-built building, the Alpinarium, was constructed as a protection wall, and at the same time accommodates a library, training classes, exhibitions and other events connected with the Alps and their dangers. A centre for alpine security and information (ASI) and a new training centre for alpine security (ALPS) complete the improvement in alpine security initiated after the disaster. These developments were facilitated through strong regional political support.

Crisis awareness and precautions

Twenty-seven per cent of respondents had considered theoretical crisis scenarios including fire (11 responses), avalanches and traffic disasters (seven responses each). Thirty-one per cent of respondents had participated in simulated crisis scenarios in their destination or community, with fires (23 responses), avalanches (eight responses), major traffic accidents (eight responses) and mountain accidents (seven responses) being the most common scenarios. The fact that crises are usually unpredictable events (Glaesser, 2003) could be one explanation why tourism organizations seem reluctant to deal with the topic of crises and disasters. Still it is interesting to note that apparently more respondents have taken part in crisis simulations than actively considered theoretical crisis scenarios outside of the training they had participated in.

In the case of Galtuer, all victims were hit in a zone considered safe (green zone). Avalanche simulation models were developed before the disaster, considering 3 days of continuous snowfall, whereas the disaster had been preceded by 10 days of heavy snowfall (Heumader, 2000).

Fifty-four per cent of the respondents were members of crisis committees established to deal with crisis events. On average, crisis committees consisted of 11.2 persons, with teams ranging in size from two to 70 persons. In most of the cases reported, the mayors of local communities (62.3%) also had specific responsibilities when a crisis occurred. Mayors often chaired local crisis committees. Other groups of citizens who chaired crisis committees included country officials or the local fire brigade. Apart from community mayors (96.7%), the most important members of the crisis staff are the local fire brigade (98.4%), the mountain rescue service (65.6%), medical services (65.6%) and the police (63.9%) (see Fig. 12.1). During a crisis event, everyone, regardless of his/her position or occupation, assisted in some way. In Galtuer, between 20 and 30 doctors were among the guests and were able to assist in the medical care of the injured. It is surprising that tourism officials rarely served on crisis committees even though it is the tourism industry that is often the most affected sector when a crisis occurs in the study region. Furthermore, it is the role of the tourism officials to maintain internal communication with and provide information for the guests.

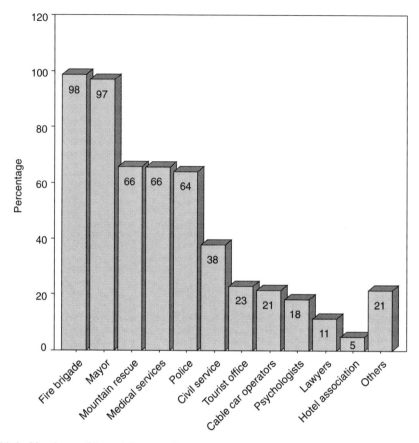

Fig. 12.1. Members of the crisis committee.

Another series of questions dealt with further preparations for crisis situations. Only 10.5% of the destinations had developed a crisis manual, 16.7% of the respondents had developed a public relations plan with guidelines for action and 17.1% had developed plans for an emergency hotline in the case of an adverse event. Planned PR tools that are most commonly used include press reports (77.8%), press conferences (66.7%) and Internet communication (55.6%). Sixty-five per cent of respondents had developed a list of relevant phone numbers and e-mail addresses for outbound communication during periods of crisis. Only 17.9% of the destinations had documented previous crises in the alpine region. Thirty-six per cent of respondents had developed strategies for enlisting legal assistance when it was required.

The most common measures taken in order to avoid or overcome crisis situations were: damage assurances (62.0%), regular cooperation with the avalanche warning services (48.1%), training for employees (44.3%), and the introduction of a compulsory means of communication with hoteliers and regular updates by the crisis committee (21.5% each).

Table 12.3. Preparation for crisis situations.

1.	Have you already gone through theoretical crisis situations in your mind?	Yes: 26.7%
2.	Have you already simulated crisis situations in your destination/ community?	Yes: 31.1%
3.	Is there a pre-defined crisis committee in the case of extraordinary events?	Yes: 53.8%
4.	Size of the crisis committee	Mean: 11.2 persons
5.	Who presides over the crisis committee?	Mayor: 83.6% Country officials: 9.8% Local fire brigade: 6.6%
6.	Who is the crisis committee's spokesperson?	Mayor: 78.1% Country officials: 7.3% Local fire brigade: 7.3%
7.	Who is responsible for coverage of the crisis (in the absence of a crisis committee)?	Mayor: 62.3% Local fire brigade: 11.3%
8.	Have you developed a crisis manual?	Yes: 10.5%
9.	Have you developed an address pool in case of a crisis situation?	Yes: 64.8%
10.	Have you developed a prepared PR plan for the outbreak of a crisis?	Yes: 16.7% Press releases: 77.8% Press conferences: 66.7% Internet/e-mail: 55.6% Interviews: 27.8% Gagging order: 22.2%
11.	Have you developed a hotline (free of charge) that can be used in the case of a crisis?	Yes: 17.1 (2.9%)
12.	Do you document crises in the alpine region?	Yes: 17.9%

Gerhard Walter, a tourism official who was in Galtuer when the avalanche struck, stated that although a pre-defined crisis plan had been established, the reaction to the crisis was totally different and driven by the actual situation. Whereas the establishment of a crisis plan is mandatory for a community, the compliance with that plan in a crisis situation is not. As a tourism official, his role in the crisis plan was to establish and/or maintain the internal communication within the village. The tourism office was reachable around the clock in order to reassure guests. Even after the disaster, Galtuer did not change its crisis plan.

Statements

The respondents were asked to respond to several statements (see Table 12.4) about their attitudes to aspects of crisis management and impacts on tourism. The respondents had a clear commitment to timely and extensive information for locals and tourists in the case of a crisis (statement 1) and against late information in order to avoid panic (statement 12). Still, the information needs of the media seems to be considered less important (statement 8) than the briefing of persons within the destination (statement 1). For a future crisis, extensive assistance from interest groups and politics is expected (statement 2), with South Tyrol (mean 4.25) and Tyrol (4.15) expecting more external help than respondents in Bavaria (3.80).

Concerning the increase of risks, respondents agreed to the statement that skiers and snowboarders were increasingly triggers of avalanches (statement 4), especially by the respondents who had not been concerned by crises in the last 5 years (mean 3.82). Respondents tended to agree that tourists are consciously taking higher risks while they are in the mountains than they used to (statement 5), and that the tourists' ignorance about alpine risks is increasing (statement 7), especially in Bavaria (mean 3.39) and Tyrol (3.31). On the other hand, the proposition that locals take higher risks than they used to (statement 11) was refuted. Responses stating that the increase of adventure sports would imply an increase of accidents (statement 9) were neutral. In the area of risk awareness of tourists, respondents were inclined to agree that tourists would increasingly consider security issues when planning their holiday (statement 6), particularly if they were considering visiting the Tyrol (mean 3.52). Respondents also believed that visitors had become more sensitive to crises in the last few years (statement 10). This seems true for the Tyrol (mean 3.47) as well.

The significance (statement 13) of crisis management within the tourism industry drew a variety of responses, indicating that more prominence was given to the issue after the crisis had occurred than in the period before a crisis was apparent. Most respondents agreed that they did not possess sufficient personnel resources to plan for crisis situations effectively (mean 2.41). For Gerhard Walter, the most important aspect is to have good people leading the crisis response organization.

Discussion and Outlook

The risk awareness of respondents does not seem high in spite of the crisis of the winter of 2000–2001 when there were 70 avalanches involving 201 people and resulting in 22 deaths in Austria alone. A large portion of those accidents happened in the Tyrol, with 45 avalanches involving 156 people of whom 80 were injured and 18 died (Mayr, 2001). Drabek (1995) argues that when being asked to assess risk that involves low probability events, even if they have a high risk of disaster, people mostly consider short-term horizons. Thus, people who had been recently affected by a catastrophe but were first-time visitors tended to estimate the likely future occurrence of the same event as being low. The results are consistent with Drabek (1995), who found that the majority of firms he investigated had only minimal planning, and that decision processes were incremental in nature, thus increasing the firms' vulnerability. The lack of clear responsibility can also be evidenced by the lack of crisis awareness within the alpine region. Although many communities are committed to a fixed crisis plan, there is

Table 12.4. Statements.

Statements	Mean	SD	Significant difference across regions (Kruskal–Wallis test)	Significant difference due to crisis experience (Mann–Whitney U-test)
1. At the outbreak of a crisis, locals and tourists have to be extensively informed	4.39	0.827	NS	NS
2. For an eventual crisis, we expect extensive assistance from interest groups and government	4.08	0.937	NS	NS
3. We don't possess sufficient personnel resources to consider crisis situations	3.68	1.293	NS	NS
4. Skiers and snowboarders are increasingly triggering avalanches	3.65	1.245	NS	$U = 1107.500, P = 0.095$
5. Tourists are consciously taking higher risks while they are in the mountains than they used to	3.25	1.042	NS	NS
6. Tourists increasingly consider security issues in their holiday decision	3.21	1.118	$\chi^2 = 7.158, P = 0.028$	NS
7. Tourists' ignorance about alpine risks is increasing	3.19	0.981	$\chi^2 = 5.625, P = 0.060$	NS
8. In the case of an exceptional event, we immediately inform the media	3.10	1.292	NS	NS
9. The increase of adventure sports implies an increase of exceptional damage/events	3.08	1.239	NS	NS
10. Tourists in our destination have become more sensitive to crises in recent years	3.02	1.058	$\chi^2 = 9.122, P = 0.010$	NS
11. Locals take higher risks while they are in the mountains than they used to	2.59	1.140	$\chi^2 = 12.827, P = 0.002$	NS
12. In order to avoid panic, it is better to inform the public about imminent crises as late as possible	2.26	1.126	NS	NS
13. In our business, crisis management is a permanent issue	2.16	1.116	$\chi^2 = 9.272, P = 0.010$	$U = 1110.000, P = 0.064$

1 = I do not agree at all; 2 = I rather disagree; 3 = neutral; 4 = I rather agree; 5 = I strongly agree.

an understanding that during the crisis people have to react flexibly based on the specifics of the disaster. Moreover, the Galtuer avalanche showed that local officials tend to rely on their regional or national superiors even though they possessed greater local knowledge and knew that immediate action is of utmost importance.

Destination image is a key factor that influences tourists' buying behaviour. Poor control of relations with the media during a crisis and after it can severely damage the industry, just as effective relations can have important positive effects (Cavlek, 2002). This understanding seems to prevail in the survey, as there seems to be a high commitment to timely and effective crisis communication and media involvement among the respondents. Still, media coverage is difficult to control. The image damage to Galtuer can probably be estimated to 5 years. Active media efforts to minimize damage can backfire and instead of positive results generate negative results, damaging the destination's image. Good relationships with the guests who should be aware of their principal contacts, honest information and a good understanding of whom to address at what stage of the crisis seem crucial to effective communication. The low level of involvement of tourism bodies in crisis planning could be a problem in this respect, at least for tourism-intensive regions.

Concerning the question of leadership and organization structure in a crisis situation, Walter states that 'if structures and processes perform well, they won't be in severe trouble during a crisis'. However, a crisis situation produces the unexpected that cannot be anticipated beforehand. This is particularly valid for media communication and PR, where crisis management authorities have little control over the content of news reports or the reaction of the public to PR.

The focusing of this study on a part of the European alpine region limits the ability to generalize the findings to other parts of the world, as the three regions are affected by natural disasters related to the mountainous landscape such as avalanches and floods, as well as accidents in tunnels or with cable cars. Crises due to terrorism or political instability are rare and so is the estimation of this risk by tourism organizations and, presumably, the population. However, these regions are highly dependent on tourism flows and income. Awareness of an increasing involvement in global industry networks and consequently the exposure to potential crises is slowly but steadily growing. Therefore, even in formerly unaffected regions, a thorough understanding of the impact that unexpected crises and disasters may have on tourism flows is important. Scenarios can be used as a platform to predict patterns and effects of events (Prideaux *et al.*, 2003). Accepting the inevitability of risk for crises and disasters, caused by man or nature, is the prerequisite for effective strategic crisis management. Crisis management only aims to prevent actual disasters or to focus on issues such as evacuation or rescue, but also aims to prepare destinations with a plan of action (Sönmez *et al.*, 1999). Thus, more of a focus ought to be on how to be pro-active in dealing with types of tourism crisis rather than on developing reactive post-crisis plans. The implementation of crisis disaster management long-term educational activities in university curriculae in tourism and hospitality administration has already been suggested (Drabek, 1995).

Acknowledgements

This project was co-financed by the European Union in the framework of INTERREG III A Italy/Austria 2000–2006. The authors wish to thank Mr Gerhard Walter, tourism official from Galtuer/Austria, for valuable insight during the interview on 8 January 2004.

References

Cavlek, N. (2002) Tour operators and destination safety. *Annals of Tourism Research* 29, 478–496.

Coombs, T. (1999) *Ongoing Crisis Communication: Planning, Managing and Responding.* Sage, Thousand Oaks, California.

Drabek, T.E. (1995) Disaster planning and response by tourist business executives. *Cornell Hotel and Restaurant Administration Quarterly* 36 (3), 86–96.

Dreyer, A., Pechlaner, H., Abfalter, D., Dreyer, D. and Rütt, K. (2004) Touristisches Krisenmanagement in Destinationen. In: Freyer, W. and Groß, S. (eds) *Sicherheit in Tourismus und Verkehr.* FIT, Dresden, pp. 119–142.

Faulkner, B. (2001) Towards a framework for tourism disaster management. *Tourism Management* 22, 135–147.

Faulkner, B. and Vikulov, S. (2001) Katherine, washed out one day, back on the track the next: a post-mortem of a tourism disaster. *Tourism Management* 22, 331–344.

Glaesser, D. (2003) *Crisis Management in Tourism Industry.* Butterworth-Heinemann, Oxford.

Heumader, J. (2000) Die Katastrophenlawinen von Galtuer und Valzur am 23. und 24.2.1999 im Paznauntal/Tirol. In: Forschungsgesellschaft für vorbeugende Hochwasserbekämpfung (ed.) *Veränderungen im Natur- und Kulturhaushalt und ihre Auswirkungen.* Interpraevent, Klagenfurt, pp. 397–409.

Mayr, R. (2001) Lawinenereignisse in Österreich – Winter 2000/2001, http:www.alpinesicherheit.at/tmp/lainenereignisse_in_oesterreich.htm (accessed 27 October 2003).

Pizam, A. and Mansfield, Y. (1995) *Tourism, Crime and International Security Issues.* Wiley, Chichester, UK.

Prideaux, B., Laws, E. and Faulkner, B. (2003) Events in Indonesia: exploring the limits to formal tourism trends forecasting methods in complex crisis situations. *Tourism Management* 24, 475–487.

Ritchie, B. (2004) Chaos, crises and disasters: a strategic approach to crisis management in the tourism industry. *Tourism Management* 25, 669–683.

Ritchie, B. and Crouch, G. (2003) *The Competitive Destination: a Sustainable Tourism Perspective.* CAB International, Wallingford, UK.

Santana, G. (1999) Tourism: toward a model for crisis management. *Tourizam* 49, 4–12.

Sönmez, S., Apostolopoulos, Y. and Tarlow, P. (1999) Tourism in crisis: managing the effects of terrorism. *Journal of Travel Research* 38, 13–18.

Steene, A. (1999) risk management within tourism and travel – suggestions for research programs. *Tourizam* 47, 13–18.

13 Taiwan's 921 Earthquake, Crisis Management and Research on No-escape Natural Disaster

TZUNG-CHENG HUAN

Introduction

The Taiwan earthquake of 21 September 1999 is known as the 921 earthquake or just 921. It killed 2400 people, injured 11,000 and left about 100,000 homeless (Tourism Bureau, Taiwan, 2000; The 921 Earthquake Post-Disaster Recovery Commission, 2003). Most of the serious damage occurred in or near the central Taiwan county of Nantou. The map of Taiwan (Fig. 13.1) conveys a variety of information. Large dots identify historic epicentres of earthquakes of magnitude 7 or greater. Certainly, there is a possibility of having another magnitude 7 quake in the Nantou region in less than 50 years. Still, it might be 100 years before another occurs. Having a magnitude 6 quake in the next 25 years is certainly likely (Table 13.1). However, what is your chance as a tourist of being in Nantou when an earthquake occurs? Even if there, if you are not in areas of significant movement, is there really much risk associated with being there?

The dam at Taichung was broken by the earthquake, with one of the two pieces being about 10 m above the other. The damage has resulted in a change in function of the dam to mainly a source of water for irrigation (see http://www.wracb.gov.tw/english/shih.htm). The breaking of the dam into two parts occurred in less than 30 s. If you were caught below the dam or were on the part that broke off you had virtually no chance to move to a safe location. The broken part of the dam has been preserved as a historic site commemorating the devastation that hit a large area of Taiwan. There was virtually no warning that a magnitude 7 earthquake would occur, therefore little opportunity to escape from buildings, from other structures that were heavily damaged, from landslides, etc.

As other chapters in this book make abundantly clear, a major component of most disaster management planning is planning what to do

Fig. 13.1. Map of Taiwan.

when disaster strikes. Certainly, having plans to deal with the consequence of an earthquake is important for Taiwan. This is because relatively high magnitude earthquakes are a common occurrence in Taiwan. An important matter that goes beyond planning to address immediate consequences of new earthquakes is minimizing the likely consequences of an earthquake by appropriate construction of infrastructure elements.

Problems with construction were the cause of many injuries in Taiwan (Tsai, 1999) and also in recent earthquakes in other parts of the world (Ting *et al.*, 1999).

There is discussion of conventional disaster management planning literature and of the literature on earthquake-related construction in an article by Huan *et al.* (2004). However, the theme of that article is that planning and management in relation to no-escape natural disaster must address some matters that relate uniquely to no-escape disaster. Consider the difference between being concerned about being hurt by a hurricane and being hurt by an earthquake. Now, not many decades ago you might have gone to a coastal area and 'all of a sudden' been caught up in a hurricane. Modern technology has changed that. There is abundant advanced warning of the likely impact of a hurricane, therefore escape is possible. Except for being caught in a flash flood when you have no reason to think that suddenly a small stream or dry gully will fill up with water, floods are predictable and thus a tourist being 'caught' in one need not occur. A tornado occurring is not necessarily so predictable that one has time to escape but, if someone is monitoring weather information, because of what they see around them, generally there is time to seek safe shelter. In this context, no-escape natural disasters can include avalanches, tsunami, land/mudslides, but do not include a tsunami when there is plenty of advanced warning to allow for evacuation.

There is an interesting parallel between being impacted by terrorism or other crime and no-escape natural disaster. It is well known that there will be more large earthquakes in Taiwan, Turkey, California, etc. In a way, making the decision to go to an area which may be subject to a high magnitude earthquake is no different from going to a destination where terrorists or bandits are known to present a risk. For tourists, whether one is concerned with danger from people or from nature, the degree to which one puts oneself at risk can be controlled. Even if one goes into an area where a high magnitude earthquake is likely, the risk of being hurt can be minimized by using accommodation that is designed to be safe when an

Table 13.1. The major earthquakes in Taiwan in the 20th century.

Year	Epicentre (county)	Magnitude	Casualties		Property damage	
			Deaths	Injuries	Destroyed	Damaged
1906	Chiayi	7.1	1,258	2,385	6,772	14,218
1935	Miaoli	7.1	3,276	12,053	17,907	36,781
1941	Chiayi	7.1	358	733	4,520	11,086
1946	Hsinchu	6.5	74	482	1,950	2,084
1951	Hualian	7.3	68	856	1,016	582
1959	Pingtung	6.9	17	68	1,214	1,375
1964	Tainan	6.5	106	650	10,502	25,818
1999	Nantou	7.3	2,455	11,305	38,935	45,320

Source: The 921 Earthquake Post-Disaster Recovery Commission, Taiwan (2003).

earthquake occurs. Also, one can enjoy an area without venturing into subareas which are particularly likely to be prone to high impact when an earthquake occurs. This is no different from avoiding areas where avalanches are likely when skiing. However, if it is likely to be 50 years until the next major earthquake impacts the Nantou area, you may see far less risk in being there than from skiing in an area where there are avalanches every winter.

In an area such as Natou, being hurt by an earthquake seems unlikely. Yes, you may have come to the area of the dam knowing that in the past there was a large earthquake that caused damage in the area. That is no different from going to San Francisco knowing that there have been large earthquakes that caused serious damage (Murphy and Wesnousky, 1995; Provost and Houston, 2003). However, consider that while you are calmly watching the water flow through the dam, the earth begins to shake, the dam cracks. What is missing in the 'broken dam' picture is a torrent of water flowing from the break in the dam (see Fig. 13.2). Alternatively, consider that you are not 'on location' but rather you see the consequences of the earthquake on television and in the newspaper. What happens to your 'interest' in going to Nantou? Certainly with aftershocks and damaged infrastructure, it is not likely to be the first choice for family recreation. What Huan *et al.* (2004) argue is that for many people making the decision to go to Nantou may be altered very differently than for a destination, for example, struck by a hurricane. Once hurricane damage is repaired, why not continue use 'as usual'?

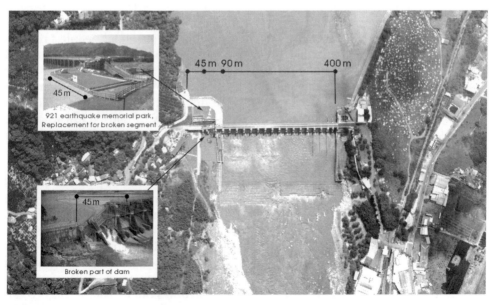

Fig. 13.2. Photograph of the dam. Sources: Agricultural and Forestry Aerial Survey Institute, Taiwan; Water Resources Agency, Ministry of Economic Affairs, Taiwan.

Now, consider that several years have passed since 921. The government of Taiwan has chosen to preserve the broken dam as a historic site. Actually, massive development and change have occurred because of 921. While by banning school trips to the Nantou area, the Ministry of Education supported the notion of there being serious risk from going there (Ministry of Education, 1999a, b), the Taiwan Tourism Bureau (TTB) and other government departments supported reconstruction and new development that encouraged tourism. There is little point in having a historic site if people are not encouraged to visit it. On the scale of the large region of Taiwan in which tourism-related infrastructure was heavily impacted by 921, according to the official record, the Ministry of Interior Affairs, expenditures in the area were 6,395,816,688 NT (US$188,112,256; 1 US $ = 34 New Taiwan Dollars (NT)) by 31 May 2004. Also, according to a political official interviewed (Mr Huang-Lang Tsai, legislator), private donations have played a large role in rehabilitation of the area.

Psychological Influences of No-escape Natural Disaster

There is literature on the psychological impact of earthquakes; Huan *et al.* (2004) cite some of this literature. However, to make this chapter special, the author visited the psychiatric/psychological facility in Tsao-Tun Psychiatry Center (TTPC), Nantou and talked to personnel concerned with treatment of people suffering from the consequences of 921. These personnel of the TTPC have written about their work, and some of that material is available in English (see Cheng *et al.*, 2001).

The purpose of talking to people involved with 'treatment' of people impacted by 921 was more than getting information about people suffering mentally because of what happened to them or their relatives. I wanted insights about continuing psychological consequences of the earthquake for people outside the Nantou area. Regarding the general matter of people around Taiwan having a persisting 'fear' of going to the Nantou area, the general opinion expressed was that as of 2004 those who have reservations about going to Nantou are better described as having concerns than truly being fearful. Still, as recent research has shown (Huan *et al.*, 2004), concern is impacting visiting Nantou. Some people who previously went to Nantou, as well as many who had not gone, do not feel comfortable about going there now. The proportion of people concerned about visiting Nantou has been reduced by recent developments aimed to combat risks. Earthquake-resistant construction of infrastructure has been a priority, supported by the 'Construction and Planning Agency, Ministry of the Interior' based in Taipei. Still, a new severe earthquake occurring could strongly influence those harbouring fear or concern if serious damage was done. However, if little damage was done, 'another 921' could foster confidence in being safe and therefore bolster tourism. The psychiatric professionals interviewed actually recognize that many

Taiwanese do not see 'another 921' as posing a risk that is of concern to them.

In summary, large and devastating earthquakes have psychological consequences. However, one must consider that different segments of a population are influenced differently by such disasters. Yes, some people who have visited an area may never go back. That may be a matter of fear or it may, as mentioned subsequently, be a consequence of how travel decision making occurs.

Trip Decision Theory in Relation to No-escape Natural Disaster

A theme of the article by Huan *et al.* (2004) is that travel decision theory implies that no-escape natural disaster will have special consequences for trip decision making. Without going into details and the literature covered in the article cited, the literature implies that an event like 921 can cause a destination area to move from being actively considered, from being in a set of destinations in contention for a trip, to one of several alternative sets. The move can be to a set such that when the area comes to mind one thinks about whether there is new evidence that it is safe to go there. Clearly, when the move is to such a set, marketing that is convincing about it being safe can cause a 'transition' of the destination back to active consideration. Alternatively, the mind may remove an area from consideration. With that transition, when you think about going somewhere on a trip and such thinking would ordinarily have involved considering going to the destination, the mind does not 'evoke' its consideration. When movement of a destination to such a set occurs, information about and marketing of it can be expected to be almost totally ignored. Presumably, action intended to cause it to be moved back into consideration when it is out of consideration must gain a person's attention in such a way that it prompts them to change whether a destination is considered. Months or years after Nantou was taken out of consideration because of an event such as 921, fear/concern may no longer play a significant role in evaluating Nantou against alternative destinations. However, it must come up for consideration for it to be in contention as a destination. For it to ever be considered may require 'turning off a flag' that says to the mind that Nantou is not up for consideration.

An important matter to keep in mind regarding the impact of no-escape natural disaster in comparison with many other disasters such as hurricanes is that not being able to escape can imply/invoke mental processes different from those that occur when escape is possible. When your favourite beach destination is hit by a hurricane, you do not worry about what would have happened to you if you were there because, if there was serious danger, you would have evacuated. If the hurricane struck and there was no serious damage to the infrastructure or it was damaged but not 'out of commission' for a long time, one expects that the destination is in the active evoked set as soon as visiting is reasonable (Walle, 1997; Jonas,

1999; Brunt *et al.*, 2000; Huan *et al.*, 2004). In other words, it is logical to think that, except for a period when the destination is being rehabilitated, the likelihood of visiting should not be influenced. Basically, fear/risk associated with the destination does not change as a consequence of a particular 'escapable' event. In contrast, with no-escape natural disaster, fear/concern is created that inhibits people going to a destination in the future. For some potential visitors, fear/concern can cause them to look for clear evidence that things are safe while for others it pushes the destination out of consideration, at least until something special brings it back into consideration.

A Context for 921 and Recovery

The author carried out research on how 921 influenced attitudes about Nantou very soon after the earthquake occurred. More than 3 years later, he has also carried out research on the continuing influence of it on selecting the Nantou area as a destination. This section specifically introduces the author's research as well as other research on the impact of 921.

Days after 921, the author was contacted by the Taiwan Institute of Economic Research and requested to examine the impact of 921 on tourists. As documented in Huan *et al.* (2004), the author thought about the problem and quickly mounted a survey rationalized on the basis of the image literature (Pike, 2002). The idea developed was that if the image of a destination was found to be negatively impacted and the nature of that negative impact was documented, one had a basis for taking some immediate ameliorative action. The study showed a big impact on people's attitudes. Because of that, the agency that requested the research found that the results of my initial research met its needs. However, when I started to pursue how the results could be used (e.g. in considering longer term future use), I found that there were many problems. This is when I started to collaborate with my colleagues to re-examine the way to study the impact of a natural disaster such as 921.

Consideration of the image of a destination provides a basis for thinking about how decisions are impacted. Image is an indirect, inferential way of approaching impact, and thus results are dependent on inferences that may not be soundly based on science or fact. A direct frontal approach on the impact of a disaster is obtaining information on how decisions to go to that destination have been influenced and are being influenced. The research of Huan *et al.* (2004) was a first step in research on decision making. It dealt with the tailoring of general decision-making literature to the impact of a no-escape disaster such as 921 occurring. Initial thinking focused on disasters. The literature in relation to natural disasters received special attention. However, as already shown, it soon became clear that not all natural disasters evoke the same influences on thought processes involved in selecting a destination to visit. It is at this juncture that we turned to serious thought about the implications of not being able to escape from a disaster. Logic led to the conclusion that no-escape natural disasters such as 921 had the potential to 'knock' a destination out of contention either: (i) by putting it into a state in which convincing evidence had to be provided that it was safe to go back; or (ii) by causing it to be moved into a state in which it was simply out of consideration unless special circumstances caused its viability as a safe destination to be reassessed.

Arriving at the ideas just introduced allowed consideration of the kind of research that was necessary to understand people's reactions to no-escape disaster; research that would yield results that would be effective in guiding planning and management decision making in relation to such disasters. The conclusion was that the research had to focus on fear or concern about such disasters and their actual occurrence influencing decisions to travel to particular destinations. Trying to obtain useful information about the impact of 921 very close to when it occurred was seen to be problematic. However, 2 or 3 years after 921, how a person felt and feels about going to the Nantou area can be reported on based on experience. If a person used to go to the Nantou area and does not go there any more because they still feel concerned for their safety, an important matter has been established. If the person does not even think about going where they went previously, this might only reflect that a fully satisfactory alternative destination was found. Still, it might also reflect that Nantou was moved into a set of destinations which simply do not receive consideration.

Verification that some potential travellers to Nantou altered the trip-making decision set that Nantou was in because of 921 was not verified in the 'theoretical' research just introduced. However, as made clear in providing the no-escape natural disaster ('NEND') theory for publication, the need for research on the validity of that theory was seen as very important. By 2003. I judged it appropriate to initiate research to test that theory. As of the summer of 2004, the formal results of that research are available (Huan *et al.*, 2004). Here, what it is important to note is that the 'follow-up' research confirmed that significant numbers of people moved the Nantou area into trip decisions sets associated with not going to that area. People who had not gone to Nantou, as well as those who had, placed it in trip decision sets which implied that they would not go as long as those placements remained.

Huang and Min (2002) have also studied the impact of 921. Their research is very different from the psychologically focused research that I have been involved in. Their research takes the form of a forecasting study. These authors give a variety of pieces of information about the impact of 921 on Taiwan. This includes information on expenditure for infrastructure rehabilitation. The main focus of their study is on what has happened to tourism to the Nantou region in terms of recovery. They conclude that although there was an initial heavy impact on tourism, just a couple of years after 921 tourism is getting back to its pre-earthquake level.

Now, whether concern is with getting back to where it was or to where it was expected to be without 921, establishing a positive trend is important. However, below you will see that there are many reasons for the positive trend that do not relate to 921, so drawing conclusions about what caused recovery to be almost complete by 2002 requires consideration of multiple factors.

What is Happening in Nantou and Research on the Impact of 921

After reviewing trip decision theory and research in relation to 921, it is useful to consider the present situation at Nantou and what it shows about the merits of past and future research. To obtain a new perspective on what is happening around the epicentre of 921, the author has conducted interviews with business people, politicians, facility managers and some tourists. These were in the summer of 2004 (when this chapter was written). Therefore, I have been getting perspectives on 921 for about 5 years after it struck.

There is consensus among those involved in tourism to Nantou that in 2004 more tourists are visiting Nantou than before 921. Prior to 921, Nantou was one of a few agricultural counties in Taiwan. On average, people were very poor yet there was tourism infrastructure. As noted above, the government has spent a lot of money on reconstruction at or near the central Taiwan county of Nantou. US$188 million was allocated through The 921 Earthquake Post-Disaster Recovery Commission and US$133 million through The 921 Earthquake Relief Foundation (The 921 Earthquake Post-Disaster Recovery Commission, 2003). This money went to the disaster area for urban regeneration, city image shaping, business district development, etc. Allocation of some money continues and the officials allocating it have a great deal of power (information is available at its website http://portal.921erc.gov.tw/english/). The director of the Tourism Bureau, Nantou County (Mr Tzung-Wen Wu) said that because the earthquake created such serious damage, people are accepting the need to construct earthquake-resistant hotels, restaurants and other tourism facilities. Also, the need to deal with bridge failures and road damage has led to safe bridges and general improvement in the transportation network.

Mention of transportation raises a matter that earlier research has not considered. Highway 3 is a divided four-lane expressway that was built to take pressure off Highway 1. It was planned and under construction prior to 921. Linking roads such as Highways 8 and 10 facilitate access to Highway 3 from Highway 1. Until Highway 3 access to Nantou was created, which occurred after 921, a reason to restrict trips to Nantou was problems involved in getting there (congestion, etc.). Based on interviews with both tourists and officials, before 921, Nantou was a good place for countryside tourism because of its beautiful scenery. Immediately after 921, people stopped going there because of serious damage and endless small earthquakes. During the last several years, more and more people are visiting Nantou because of more convenient access. The improved transportation system, particularly Highway 3, is very helpful. After exiting Highway 3, people can easily reach most 'Nantou' destinations in 1 or 2 h. Highway 3 encourages affluent travellers to come from Taiwan's two biggest cities, Taipei and Kaohsung (Fig. 13.1). Such visitors spend less than 4 h travelling to elegant destinations (2 h on four-lane highways and, at most, another 2 h on local roads).

Given that Highway 3 has played a big role in increased tourism to Nantou, there is a problem for research on the impact of 921. The highway's influence is confounded with that of rehabilitation. The rehabilitation could not have come at a better time. Extensive rehabilitation would not have happened quickly just because Highway 3 was completed through Nantou. The earthquake removed the need for making decisions to demolish poor infrastructure and replace it so as to capitalize on tourist flows along Highway 3. Nevertheless, the decision to build a major road (Highway 3) would not be likely to be driven by generating tourism to help an area hit by an earthquake.

Another factor complicating analysis of what is happening in Nantou is a government emphasis on leisure agriculture (farm tourism). Funding for and other encouragement of such tourism began in the early 1990s. The programme arose because the Council of Agriculture of Taiwan saw it to be necessary to encourage farmers to develop agricultural tourism to meet the challenge to their livelihood posed by imported agricultural products. Whether agricultural tourism is 'the new hope' for Taiwanese farmers is not of concern here. The programme has resulted in many Bed and Breakfast (B&B) establishments in the Nantou region. The initial viability of these is facilitated by government support that has nothing to do with 921. The potential actually to have tourists is greatly enhanced by Highway 3. It is also enhanced by having abundant new B&B and other 'farm tourism' offerings. Therefore, there is another confounding factor in assessing what is influencing post-921 tourism to Nantou.

The establishment of Sun Moon Lake National Scenic Area has certainly created a magnet for tourism to Nantou. A tourism boom is happening because of replacement of the tourism infrastructure that was destroyed by 921 by new infrastructure that meets a much higher standard. A local restaurant owner (Miss Show-Chu Lo) said that just after the earthquake, the Sun Moon Lake area was 'dead'. Local people did not stay overnight in commercial facilities because buildings were damaged. Those who stayed camped or stayed with relatives or friends (sometimes at a 'safe' distance away). After the earthquake, many officials visited this area. It was quickly promoted as 'Sun Moon Lake National Scenic Area' and infrastructure elements were reconstructed so that tourists need not see any of the damage caused by 921. A hotel manager noted that prior to 921, the hotel business was very competitive. Although, to his knowledge, no tourist died in a hotel in 921, most hotels were badly damaged so staying in them was not an option. Now, well-designed and well-constructed hotels have replaced the damaged hotels, and occupancy is high because of a 'flood' of visitors. Therefore, money is going into building new hotels. Generally speaking, the hotel occupancy rates are higher than before 921 and revenues much improved.

In considering what is going on in the Nantou region today, it is important to note that there is successful promotion by public agencies and private travel agents. For example, the Sun Moon Lake National Scenic Area Administration and local businessman have cooperated in organizing many festivals. Events include swimming activities, fireworks shows, concerts, etc. Now, the recreation and tourism facilities at Nantou are diversified and of good quality. This encourages people to visit there again and again. As for group package travellers, itineraries to Nantou are well designed. Visits to wineries in the area of Puli, Nantou exceed 1.5 million per year. Note that many tourist destinations in Taiwan would be pleased to get 1.5 million visitors. Pre-921 (1998) the wineries had only 0.7 million visitors (Statistics from Puli Winery Corp.).

In relation to the psychological treatment of victims in the disaster area, according to the report of the TTPC (Cheng *et al.*, 2001) most trauma victims recovered from serious problems within 2 years. The local people have confidence and hope for a good future because of robust economic development. Again, exogenous influences (e.g. Highway 3) as well as rehabilitation resulting from repairing 921 damage are intertwined in creating great opportunities and thus a positive environment for healing from a large catastrophe.

No-escape Natural Disaster Research and Nantou: Problems and Possibilities

As already suggested, there are problems with drawing inferences based on studies of 921. Nantou is a lovely mountain country setting that was disrupted by an earthquake. The earthquake damage was repaired in a way that encouraged tourism. From the published research, you may get the idea that the infrastructure was restored and tourism got 'back on track'. From the tourism research literature for Nantou you do not gain awareness that infrastructure development independent of any earthquake damage was rapidly changing the ease of access to Nantou. Infrastructure development that has taken place since the earthquake has made Nantou much more accessible than it was pre-quake. This complicates analysis of what has happened at Nantou.

There is certainly a vast pool of people in Taiwan who are not worried about going to Nantou. Highway 3 and connections between it and the earlier four-lane highway have facilitated access to Nantou. Whether in interpreting a forecasting study or in deriving consequences/implications of a study of the change in people's behaviour regarding selecting Nantou as a destination, improved access, as well as improved infrastructure, must be considered as greatly influencing use by markets that were hardly tapped prior to 921. The rapid growth in tourism in Nantou may be almost completely a consequence of people going there who did not go or rarely went prior to 921. The current level of visitors is then a consequence of a combination of good (improved) access and the broad range of improved services available. Given that Highway 3 was available but there had been no 921, more people would have come to Nantou with the improved access, and the infrastructure could have progressed toward current standards. Nevertheless, rapid growth in tourism to Nantou is consistent with: (i) some people who were going to Nantou prior to 921 no longer visiting because of 921 and (ii) others who would have gone, not starting to go because of 921. This is the case because growth has depended heavily on drawing visitors from very large latent markets that were tapped because there was better access.

To reach valid conclusions, research results must be taken in context. A forecasting model that deals with gross numbers does not elucidate the causes for tourist volumes catching up with past usage rates unless forecasts are made for 'new' segments (for which no data are available). In a similar vein, surveys about attitudes can show that some people will not go back unless their decision process changes. Unfortunately, the author's recent study (Huan *et al.*, 2004) about past behaviour and intentions is not large enough to yield definitive information about people changing their mind about going to Nantou. In particular, it was not formulated to consider the impact of new access. This is because when the survey was executed, I did not realize the importance of obtaining information on the impact of new access. I may still pursue this matter because it would be interesting to see the role change in access played in people's decision making. Furthermore, new enthusiasts for Nantou may be providing exactly the force need for others to decide to go to Nantou; to put it back in to their active consideration set. One can be quite certain that friends and relations are convincing others that it is safe to go to Nantou.

Public facilities such as the earthquake memorial museum and Taichung Dam historic site offer a basis for gauging what is going on. I spoke to public facility managers and to patrons, obtaining a variety of views. Just after the earthquake, some people went to the disaster area to see the damage. Now, destinations that commemorate 921 may be attractions. Their future depends on what they have to offer. How often do you go to a place with the same static displays unless the goal is recreation rather than information? The future of the public facilities devoted to information about 921 is hard to predict unless they move to being dynamic in what they offer. Some facilities that initially had lots of visitors now tend to attract mostly new, first-time, tourists (i.e. international visitors). Actually, some facilities that focused on 921 are already closed.

Officials and managers of 921-oriented facilities who wish to keep the Taiwanese market need to create value for repeat visitors. There is a real challenge for some government officials who would like to keep their jobs and budget for their facilities. Except for international visitors, those coming to Nantou now seem to have little interest in or concern about 921 or a another large earthquake. Still, among those who do not come, my recent research showed much concern about there being 'another' 921. Sustainable operation of earthquake-related facilities presumably depends heavily on offering something to cause return visits.

Discussion

This chapter is meant to highlight that valid thinking about the impact of no-escape natural disaster involves more than examining image, making forecasts or looking at how peoples' trip decision making was impacted by a no-escape natural disaster. Certainly, just after 921, the concern of the author and people he was talking to was with addressing the loss of tourism to Nantou. There was a disposition towards this line of thinking rather than towards recognizing that changes in access to Nantou meant a boom in tourism as long as certain infrastructure rehabilitation took place.

As for the matter of it being important to have a Nantou disaster management plan in place for dealing with the next 921 type earthquake, it now seems clear that two matters should be noted. First, appropriate action to eliminate infrastructure that will collapse in such an earthquake is what should occur rather than preparing to deal with infrastructure failing in the next big quake. As for preparedness to deal with the next 7+ magnitude earthquake, this earthquake will probably not be in Nantou (see Fig. 13.1 and Table 13.1). Therefore, the action plan (one could say disaster management plan) for such an earthquake has to be a Taiwan-wide plan. Given that no place on the large island that is most of Taiwan's land mass is more than 400 km from anywhere else, planning to mobilize resources to any earthquake zone is not a problem. Still, it is important to note that Taiwan's work on having earthquake-resistant buildings and on moving development away from areas where no affordable construction is safe may mean there will never be another disaster on the scale of 921.

The research of Huan *et al.* (2004) raised the matter of the impact of 921 on international tourism. Clearly, getting more international tourists is not a priority of most Nantou businesses. For them, money is money. However, for Taiwan, international tourism should be a priority given that it is only such tourism that brings in currency from abroad, thus helping to erase a balance of payments deficit. Therefore, I still see research on the impact of no-escape natural disaster on international tourist flows as very important. As suggested in my research with my colleagues (Huan *et al.*, 2004), such research need not be expensive and could be undertaken in cooperation with other countries (e.g. Turkey) for which the threat of no-escape natural disaster may significantly influence the benefits achieved from tourism.

Strangely enough, after an initial concern with a government-supported marketing action to influence tourism to Nantou positively, it now seems clear that the volume of domestic tourism rather than a lack of it is causing problems in Nantou. Unfortunately, things are happening in

Nantou that show that tourism being 'back on track' means some things are not going well. While new buildings are adequately earthquake resistant in construction and sited away from areas where major shifting or cracking will occur, this should mean that even with a magnitude 7+ earthquake there will not be a disaster resembling that arising from 921; however, disasters on a smaller scale are brewing and occurring. People have been killed and property destroyed. 921 created new potential for mud- and landslides (The 921 Earthquake Post-Disaster Recovery Commission, 2003). Removal of natural land cover for agriculture and recreational purposes has, in some cases, exacerbated dangerous conditions. Public safety requires more than construction being earthquake resistant and away from fault areas where the rise and shift in land in a new quake will damage or destroy virtually any building. Ecologically sound planning must occur. Other development problems that must be avoided are creation of too many facilities of one type or another. If businesses are going to be marginal or not viable, then eventually 'somebody' is going to need to deal with removing infrastructure that should never have been constructed. Given what has been presented, the current 'boom' in tourism in Nantou means that good development planning is much more important than any kind of major effort on preparing a Nantou-specific disaster management plan.

Conclusion

Just as you could not foresee the disaster if you were standing on the dam minutes before it occurred, you cannot properly comprehend what has followed without taking into account that Highway 3 was being built, that farm tourism was being encouraged and that Nantou had great tourism potential that would blossom with better access to its destinations. The disaster wrought by 921 presumably accelerated developments that would have occurred as a consequence of completion of Highway 3 and related transportation and infrastructure improvements.

It is easy to latch on to a theoretical framework, e.g. image, and study no-escape natural disaster by studying image. It is also easy to adopt the perspective that because there will be another no-escape disaster in a particular destination, X's guidelines for preparing a disaster management plan should be followed so that a plan is in place when the disaster occurs. This chapter has introduced you to the vagaries and complexities of dealing with a real disaster and future occurrence of such a disaster. You have seen why the need for special analysis considerations has been recognized. You have also seen that forecasting can be useful and that what is expected based on theory can be confirmed. However, forecasting results and theory must be applied considering the Nantou context if valid inferences are to be drawn.

Possibly most importantly, you have seen that what is happening in Nantou arises from it having a natural advantage as a tourist destination area that had not been very accessible. Quite possibly its quick recovery has been highly dependent on access improvement that was going on prior to 921, and that had nothing to do with 921. If another area had a '921' and it did not benefit from improved access, facilitating recovery could be more challenging. The benefits of appropriate theory-based research could be very useful in this context. In other words, in some circumstances, fairly simple follow-up research could yield important insights. On the other hand, exogenous forces following 921 have, in fact, made it easy to misinterpret what has happened. Therefore, key lessons from Nantou involve the need properly to conceptualize research problems and the need to recognize unique and powerful exogenous factors. One sees the limitations of research by recognizing that factors that have nothing to do with a no-escape natural disaster can combine with results of the disaster to yield consequences that are so intertwined that it is unlikely that research can sort out the specific contributions of causal factors.

Acknowledgements

Many people were kind enough to talk to me. Specific statements by the following are cited: Yi-Jen Tseng, Taiwan Institute of Economic Research; Grace Yeh, Tourism Bureau, Taiwan; Huang-Lang Tsai, Legislator (representative of Nantou County); Show-Chu Lo, general manager of Hsiang Ken Spa Resort, Taiwan; Tzung-Wen Wu, director of Tourism Bureau, Nantou County; Yih-Hsi Huang, director of Administration Office, Puli Winery Corp.; Shui-Chi Wu, vice director of Agricultural and Forestry Aerial Survey Institute, Taiwan; and Shih-Yuan Lin, Water Resources Agency, Ministry of Economic Affairs, Taiwan.

References

Brunt, P., Mawby, R. and Hambly, Z. (2000) Tourist victimization and the fear of crime on holiday. *Tourism Management* 21, 417–424.

Cheng, J.J., Tan, H., Chen, C.Y., Tung, P.L. and Wang, S. (2001) *Estimation of Psychological Impact After the 921 Earthquake in Nantou Area.* Tsao-Tun Psychiatry Center, Department of Health, Executive Yuan, Nantou, Taiwan.

Huan, T.C., Beaman, J. and Shelby, L. (2004) No-escape natural disaster: mitigating impacts on tourism. *Annals of Tourism Research* 31, 255–273.

Huang, J. and Min, J. (2002) Earthquake devastation and recovery in tourism: the Taiwan case. *Tourism Management* 23, 145–154.

Jonas, L. (1999) Making and facing danger: constructing strong character on the river. *Symbolic Interaction* 22, 247–267.

Ministry of Education (1999a) *Temporarily Do Not Go to Earthquake Disaster Area in Central Taiwan for Educational Sightseeing Activities.* Document No. Tai-Kao-III 88129577. Ministry of Education, Taipei.

Ministry of Education (1999b) *Try Not to Have Group Activities in Earthquake Disaster Area in Central Taiwan so as Not to Disturb its Rehabilitation Projects.* Document No. Tai-Jen-II 88125403. Ministry of Education, Taipei.

Murphy, J.M. and Wesnousky, S.G. (1995) A post earthquake reevaluation of seismic hazard in the San Francisco Bay region. *International Journal of Rock Mechanics and Mining Sciences and Geomechanics Abstracts* 32 (8), 361A.

Pike, S. (2002) Destination image analysis – a review of 142 papers from 1973 to 2000. *Tourism Management* 23, 541–549.

Provost, A. and Houston, H. (2003) Investigation of temporal variations in stress orientations before and after four major earthquakes in California. *Physics of the Earth and Planetary Interiors* 139, 255–267.

Ting, Y.C., Shi, M.X. and Yu, C.P. (1999) *On Experiences and Lessons Learned from Foreign Catastrophic Earthquakes and their Applications to Seismic Hazard Mitigation, Architecture and Building Research Institute*. Ministry of the Interior, ROC.

The 921 Earthquake Post-Disaster Recovery Commission, Taiwan (2003) *Achievement Report: Four Years of Reconstruction Following the 921 Chi-chi Earthquake (Taiwan)*. The 921 Earthquake Post-Disaster Recover Commission, Taipei, Taiwan.

Tourism Bureau, Taiwan (2000) *Annual Report on Tourism 1999, Republic of China*. Tourism Bureau, Taiwan, Taipei.

Tsai, H.F. (1999) Summarizing seven key reasons of buildings collapsed in the earthquake disaster area. *Commercial Times* 10 October

Walle, A. (1997) Pursuing risk or insight marketing adventures. *Annals of Tourism Research* 24, 265–282.

14 International Tourism and Infectious Disease: Managing the SARS Crisis in Singapore

JOAN HENDERSON

Introduction

Tourism's contribution to improved physical and emotional well-being is widely recognized, but many health hazards also confront international tourists. This chapter discusses the 2003 global outbreak of severe acute respiratory syndrome (SARS), a previously unknown and potentially fatal virus, which posed unprecedented problems for certain destinations at the centre of the epidemic. After an introduction to selected health risks linked to travel, SARS and its consequences for tourism are examined with particular reference to Singapore, which was one of the worst affected countries. A brief review of crisis management literature provides a theoretical framework for the discussion of circumstances in the republic, and the chapter concludes with some general observations about defining features of health-related tourism crises and the necessity for continued vigilance and preparation.

The case of Singapore and SARS illustrates how disease has the capacity seriously to disrupt international tourism. It also reveals the challenges of devising and implementing an effective response. Health issues emerge as a major public and private concern, and a central element in perceptions of tourist safety and destination choice, any threat to health constituting a potential crisis which requires management.

Health Risks

The World Health Organization (2002) cites numerous dangers to health encountered by overseas travellers, although understanding is personal and may be socially constructed (Carter, 1998; Lepp and Gibson, 2003). The US National Library of Medicine (National Center for Biotechnology

Information, 2003) provides an insight into some of the more prevalent illnesses, often connected to sanitation standards at destinations. Location and form of tourism are of relevance, and Rudkin and Hall (1996) describe how special interest tourists in South East Asia and the South Pacific are prone to certain infections. Vector- and water-borne diseases seem set to increase as more remote sites are opened up for tourism and foreign travel proliferates, but even controlled environments such as ships can prove unhealthy. Gastrointestinal illnesses, classified as outbreaks when at least 3% of those on board fall sick, are regularly logged by cruise lines (Centers for Disease Control and Prevention, 2003).

The agrifood sector has recently been the origin of several health emergencies, and avian influenza or 'bird flu' in Hong Kong, a strain of which can kill humans, discouraged tourist arrivals in the late 1990s. An extremely virulent variety erupted across Asia in 2004, although the worst fears of human-to-human transmission with devastating consequences for tourism were not realized. Bioterrorism has added to the spectrum of risk, with the possibility of terrorists using disease as a weapon by deliberately exposing individuals or communities to contamination.

International travel and other processes of globalization can accelerate the progression of communicable diseases, and many countries lack the necessary funds and health care services to battle against them successfully. Tourism crises arising from infectious disease thus vary in intensity depending partly on conditions at destinations, but also on the attitudes and anxieties of tourists. Any fears may be exaggerated, exemplified by pneumonic plague in India in 1994 and the ensuing 'global alarm which escalated in meteoric fashion' (Clift and Page, 1996, p. 3). Space devoted by the media to such scares is a key influence on images of places held by tourists and the tourism industry and their behaviour, as are travel advisories and health warnings circulated by governments and official bodies (Sharpley *et al.*, 1996). Well publicized incidences where a disease is portrayed as rampant have the capacity to become a major crisis for the tourism industry locally, nationally and even internationally.

Coping with these situations is a daunting task for everyone involved, but the likelihood of their occurrence has to be confronted. The European Centre for Disease Prevention warns of future health threats of a viral and microbial character, and the World Health Organization (WHO) also recognizes the gravity of epidemic-prone viral and bacterial diseases, emerging infections and drug-resistant pathogens. The World Tourism Organization (WTO) argues that member states must upgrade their competence in this area and formulate national policies on tourism health, including reporting systems (World Tourism Organization, 1991). Acceptance of responsibilities, transparency, assistance services, international cooperation and the alleviation of fear have been advocated as prerequisites for dealing effectively with tourism health crises (Caribbean Tourist Organization, 2003).

SARS and its Implications

SARS is a type of contagious pneumonia which first appeared in the southern Chinese Province of Guandong in late 2002, subsequently infiltrating other parts of Asia and beyond. Research is continuing into the coronavirus, which has been found to have a mortality rate of 14–15%, and lack of knowledge about it originally intensified public dread. There is no known cure and a vaccine has still to be developed, making it imperative to identify and isolate victims. A total of 8096 cases in 29 countries and 774 deaths had been recorded by July 2003 when the epidemic was over; most of these were in Asia and especially mainland China (World Health Organization, 2003). The first victims in Singapore were diagnosed in February, numbers rising steadily thereafter to reach final figures of 238 cases and 33 fatalities (Singapore Ministry of Health, 2003). There were later incidences, provoking worries about a second wave of infection, and scientific agreement that it might never be totally eradicated. Several new cases were reported in China in mid-2004, raising concerns that SARS could again cross borders, but fortunately these cases were contained.

A deadly disease about which little was understood and the unprecedented speed of its advance became a serious matter worldwide, generating extensive media publicity. There was a tendency amongst some reporters to dramatize events and overstate risks, given the comparatively small percentage of those who succumbed, provoking unnecessary agitation (Pacific Asia Travel Association, 2003). The resulting crisis was multidimensional and reverberated through economies and societies, but was exceptionally acute for the international tourism industries of those states most severely hit (World Tourism Organization, 2003). The virus was carried abroad by travellers, and air transport came to be perceived as particularly dangerous, together with visits to any afflicted areas, prompting a sharp downturn in demand.

Locations such as China, Hong Kong, Taiwan and Vietnam faced falls of over 50% in inbound tourism in the early months of 2003 (World Travel and Tourism Council, 2003), and heavy damage to Canadian tourism was predicted due to the presence of the virus in Toronto (Canadian Tourism Commission, 2003). Table 14.1 depicts the negative growth in Singapore's tourist arrivals from March onwards, with a drop of over 70% in May compared with the previous year. There were signs of recovery as time passed, but 2003 saw an annual reduction of 19.1%. Major generators performed differently, and the Japanese market contracted by 40% in contrast to that of Indonesia which had a 3.7% drop, raising interesting questions about the reasons for such variations. However, the decline in the first quarter was sudden and extreme across all origin countries, with repercussions for every component of the industry.

The International Labour Organization anticipated that countries experiencing an epidemic could lose a third of their travel and tourism employment, while those on the perimeter might register losses of 15% (International Labour Organization, 2003). Hotel occupancies

Table 14.1. Monthly international arrivals in Singapore 2002 and 2003

Month	2002	2003	Year-on-year change (%)
January	596,069	641,159	+7.6
February	597,415	612,897	+2.6
March	654,710	559,289	−4.6
April	621,957	203,282	−67.3
May	605,532	177,543	−70.7
June	601,599	315,878	−47.5
July	679,198	540,373	−20.4
August	671,154	601,819	−10.3
September	597,115	556,263	−6.8
October	638,237	586,016	−8.2
November	588,141	635,213	+8.0
December	709,143	690,761	−2.6
Total	7,560,270	6,120,493	−19.0

Source: Singapore Tourism Board Monthly Factsheets, 2002–2003.

demonstrate the extent of the problem, with five-star hotels in Singapore having average occupancies of 15% in April 2003 (*Travel Business Analyst*, 2003). Numbers were worse for some properties where rates below 10% persisted until June. Singapore's South East Asian neighbours were not exempt, and occupancies in Bangkok hotels were eroded by 20–30% in April, even though Thailand had only nine SARS cases and two deaths. The costs of lost business were heavy and estimated to be in excess of S$23 (US$13) million for Singapore's hoteliers (Singapore Hotel Association, 2003). Airlines serving Singapore were also forced to rationalize and abandon flights, and attendance at attractions plummeted, alongside retail spending (*The Straits Times*, 2003a). The pattern of an industry descending into crisis was repeated elsewhere, notably in Hong Kong (Chien and Law, 2003; Pine and McKercher, 2004) which was to record 5327 SARS cases and 299 deaths.

Modelling Crisis Management

Once neglected by the tourism industry, despite its widely accepted vulnerability to crisis (Cassedy, 1991), the subject of crisis management has acquired a heightened priority amongst practitioners and attracted increasing attention from researchers. Such a trend perhaps reflects a modern world of uncertainty and insecurity and the growing exposure of tourism to crisis originating from a diversity of external sources (Ritchie, 2004) besides natural disasters (Durocher, 1994; Faulkner and Vikulov, 2001; Huang and Min, 2002). The impact of political instability and terrorism on tourism has long been appreciated (Richter and Waugh, 1986; Scott, 1988; Richter 1992; Aziz, 1995), symbolized by 11 September 2001 (9/11) and its aftermath (World Tourism Organization, 2002; Blake and Sinclair, 2003).

Socio-economic upheavals may constitute a crisis for tourism, shown by the Asian financial crisis (Prideaux, 1999; de Sausmarez, 2003; Prideaux *et al.*, 2003), and examples of health emergencies have already been considered. While adverse developments in political, economic, social and environmental arenas may trigger corporate crises, small-scale incidents such as a transport accident may also have a similar effect (Regester and Larkin, 1998; Ray, 1999). Internal weaknesses connected to management or organizational deficiencies may also be a cause of a crisis.

Many studies assess reactions to a state of crisis by individual organizations and the industry and destination authorities acting collectively (Barton, 1994; Pottorff and Neal, 1994; World Tourism Organization, 1996, 1998; Sonmez *et al.*, 1999; Prideaux, 2003), one conclusion often being that crisis management planning is rarely well developed. Several purported crisis management plans are informal and undocumented, or confined to a narrow set of circumstances such as a hotel fire (Drabek, 1995). Practical recommendations to remedy these shortcomings include the establishment of a task force to take responsibility for crises, environmental scanning to anticipate problems, the formulation of prevention measures and documented action plans. The media's role in shaping popular perceptions of a crisis and the competency with which it is handled are stressed; good media relations are judged to be a major ingredient of any comprehensive crisis management strategy (ten Berg, 1990; Bland, 1998; Gonzalez-Herrero and Pratt, 1998).

Tourism researchers have adapted and applied more general theories of crisis management which describe the dynamics of crises in terms of a series of stages (Turner, 1976; Fink, 1986). The tourism disaster management model proposed by Faulkner (2001) is frequently cited and traces responses through principal phases labelled pre-event, prodromal, emergency, intermediate, long-term/recovery and resolution. Santana (2003) maintains that warning, signal detection, preparation and prevention are pre-crisis management functions, while crisis resolution encompasses containment, damage limitation, recovery and learning. However, it may be impossible to predict certain manifestations of crisis, and a time of realization when avoidance tactics are viable could be of extreme brevity or non-existent, exemplified by airline crashes (Henderson, 2003a) and terrorist attacks (Pizam, 2002).

SARS too, as both a public health and a tourism crisis, arrived and unfolded at great speed with little warning and few detectable signals. Preparation and prevention by the tourism industry were not realistic options so that crisis management essentially began at containment and damage limitation as depicted in Fig. 14.1, where the conventional pre-crisis stages have been compressed into a single onset of crisis period. The evolution of the crisis was closely tied to the progress of the epidemic which informed responses, optimism rising as the daily number of SARS cases fell and travel warnings were revised and ultimately revoked. Learning was ongoing and formed a series of feedback loops into the system of decision making.

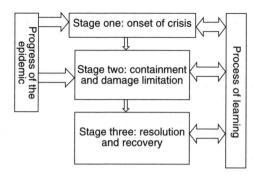

Fig. 14.1. The evolution of the SARS crisis.

Another striking feature of the SARS crisis was its scope and the numerous parties from which action was demanded, extending from managers and staff of single enterprises to intergovernmental organizations. Figure 14.2 attempts to capture the range of protagonists and, together with Fig. 14.1, affords the framework for the following analysis of reactions to the SARS crisis within the context of Singapore's tourism industry.

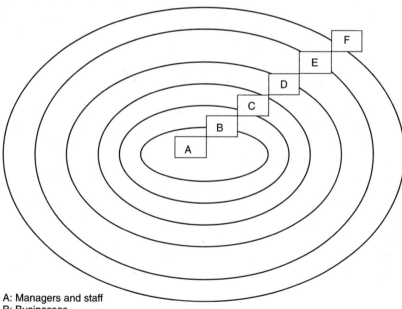

A: Managers and staff
B: Businesses
C: Industry sectors
D: National Tourism Organizations
E: National and local government authorities
F: International governmental and non-governmental agencies

Fig. 14.2. Layers of involvement in crisis management.

Stages 1 and 2: The Onset of Crisis, Containment and Damage Limitation

As already stated, the medical significance of SARS and its ramifications were not immediately obvious and the crisis for tourism commenced when this became apparent and there was no chance of evasion. Stage 1 was very brief (Fig. 14.1) and the crisis quickly moved to stage 2. Decisions on Singapore's response were based on information from a number of sources including government and non-government agencies.

The WHO distributed information about SARS and details of countries with local transmission, including Singapore, warning against visits and proposing health screening for departing international passengers. Instructions were prepared about how to handle possible infected air and surface transport passengers and those with whom they had come into contact when in transit. The thorough disinfection of aircraft and other vehicles was also advised.

Intergovernmental meetings of Asian tourism officials were held on a bilateral and multilateral basis in parallel with those attended by senior politicians and health ministers. The need for cooperation and coordination was accepted with regard to sharing data on SARS victims and their movements, and health checks on international departures, especially by air. Progress was made towards achieving these goals by the Association of South East Asian Nations (ASEAN), for example, although it was observed that an absence of resources could restrict implementation for some members. Officials from the APEC (Asia Pacific Economic Cooperation) grouping drew up an action plan which also sought to standardize approaches to the health screening of air passengers and information exchange.

Regional trade organizations expressed their concerns and support for the industry. The Pacific Asia Travel Association (PATA) claimed that it was endeavouring to educate the travel trade through its SARS information kit and help the public make properly informed choices. Press releases reminded audiences that the WHO had not blamed the tourism industry for the diffusion of SARS and that it was generally safe to visit the region. PATA representatives met with others from the APEC Tourism Working Group and World Travel and Tourism Council (WTTC), calling for the wider circulation of data and asserting the importance of keeping the media fully up to date. In addition, research studies into the longer term impact of SARS were conducted (Asia Pacific Economic Cooperation, 2003).

While the analysis here focuses on SARS as a disaster for states such as Singapore where it was spreading amongst the community, its relationship with inbound and outbound tourist flows could not be ignored by other governments and tourism industries. It was thus a crisis for generating markets and authorities of destinations where those who might be carriers of the virus were arriving, albeit one of lesser magnitude. Nations such as Australia, the USA and the UK cautioned their nationals about non-essential travel to places on the WHO list, while many tour operators, travel agents and MICE (Meetings, Incentives, Conferences and Exhibitions) organizers were reluctant to send customers there. Several international companies and organizations prohibited employees from journeying to SARS-affected locations and some insurance companies withdrew their cover. More stringent health checks on inbound passengers were also introduced in certain instances in a bid to avert the importation of the virus.

In the relatively small city state of Singapore, where there is not the same distinction between national and local institutions found elsewhere, the Singapore Tourism Board (STB) was one of the major official actors. Representing both government and the industry, it sought to maintain Singapore's credibility as a tourist destination by the provision of up-to-date information for markets and the industry at home and abroad. Favourable news stories of tourists continuing to visit and enjoying their stay were given prominence. However, there was an interruption in conventional marketing due to a sense that doubts about the means by which SARS was transmitted and negative global publicity would probably render this ineffective.

A Director of Emergency Planning and a 'Cool Team' task force were appointed, and steps were taken to safeguard the health of visitors and minimize the chances of infection. Practical schemes were initiated such as the COOL Singapore programme which granted COOL awards to hotels, shops and other sites which complied with an eight-point certification criteria (Singapore Tourism Board, 2003a). Tools employed were mass temperature taking of staff and visitors, fever being an easily observable symptom of the virus, and regular cleaning and disinfection of premises, with machinery for contact tracing should a SARS suspect be discovered to have visited a particular location. Ministry of Health instructions and complementary STB guidelines were also drawn up and adhered to.

The Board was supported in its efforts by the government which pledged to aid the tourism industry, unveiling a S$230 (US$131) million relief package to tide the hardest hit businesses over the crisis. A major portion was allocated to hotels, and constituted various forms of tax relief, bridging loans for small and medium enterprises, and training grants (Singapore Tourism Board, 2003b). The first priority of government was, nevertheless, to bring SARS under control, and nearly every department was expected to contribute. Pursuit of this aim led to constant health screening and schemes to enhance hygiene which impacted on the lives of both visitors to Singapore and residents. The regime meant that all air and sea international travellers were scanned thermally by machines capable of detecting those with a high temperature. Singapore is connected to Malaysia by a causeway, and those crossing by public transport or on foot were also scanned, with motorists subject to random testing by ear thermometers.

Sectoral agencies such as the Singapore Hotel Association (SHA), Association of Singapore Attractions (ASA) and National Association of

Travel Agents of Singapore (NATAS) were a forum for discussion and voiced industry forebodings. Their members and other businesses adopted policies of cost savings (especially regarding labour), reductions in capacity and lobbying for official aid. Prices were cut to stimulate demand and attempts made to retain the goodwill of customers choosing to cancel or postpone bookings. Much marketing was directed at Singaporeans in a move to enlarge the domestic market, formerly of little commercial interest (*The Straits Times*, 2003b). Infection control meant that great stress was placed on hygiene standards, with continuous cleaning and staff and customer temperature checks (Henderson, 2003b).

Stage 3: Resolution and Recovery

Singapore was eventually declared free of local transmission of SARS by the WHO at the end of May, an occasion which was a clearly defined turning point and allowed the crisis to enter recovery and resolution mode. Delisting by the WHO was a cause of great rejoicing, celebrated by the Singapore industry in a party which was publicized around the world. The focus of national and international parties then shifted from defensive and reactive to offensive and pro-active tactics, especially those of intensive advertising and special promotions which had an underlying theme of reassurance.

A statement issued by the WTO at an assembly devoted to recovery argued that it was safe to resume travel in Asia, except to Beijing which was still under a WHO advisory, and a marketing plan for Asia and the Pacific region was launched. PATA similarly urged a resumption of travel and revealed its global 'welcome back' campaign entitled Project Phoenix. Goals were to restore confidence and business, and establish a common Asian voice, making use of the power of the media to deliver consistent messages containing balanced information. While displaying good intentions, some industry observers were sceptical about the efficacy of such proposals given the comparatively small size of their budgets, short-term timeframe, widespread geographical coverage and competitive rivalries. Investment by National Tourism Organizations in the PATA scheme indicates limits to their commitment, with US$250,000 raised by July compared with US$50 million and US$115 million spent by Hong Kong and Singapore, respectively, on independent marketing (*Travel Business Analyst*, 2003; TTG Daily News, 2003).

The STB's own 'global recovery programme' comprised testimonial advertising, worldwide marketing, the promotion of packages devised jointly with industry and the hosting of travel trade and media personnel (Singapore Tourism Board, 2003c). A parallel project administered by the Civil Aviation Authority of Singapore disbursed financial inducements totalling S$10 (US$5.7) million amongst airlines, which raised their passenger volumes into Singapore (*The Straits Times*, 2003c). Renewed and aggressive marketing by sectoral bodies and individual companies was also conducted, with several examples of collaboration. The Singapore Association of Convention and Exhibition Organizers and Suppliers (SACEOS) commenced a S$10.2 (US$5.7) million public relations and promotion exercise, and the SHA and ASA partnered Singapore Airlines in selling 'Fabulous Offers' to overseas markets. Domestic tourists were not forgotten, with special hotel packages on sale during the school holiday period.

Improvements in international arrivals from June onwards indicated progress towards recovery; this was further evidenced by rising hotel occupancies, the restoration of cancelled airline services and attendances at attractions. Partial resolution was thus achieved, although fears of a return of SARS lingered, accompanied by an acknowledgement that the tourism industry was very much at its mercy. However, there was also a feeling that health authorities were strongly positioned to contain any more outbreaks after the measures conceived and executed during the first which were said to have been acclaimed worldwide (*The Straits Times*, 2003d, e).

The tourism industry also professed to have learnt from SARS. While learning is continuous throughout a crisis, resolution permits reflection and creates opportunities to make longer term changes with a view to being more ready and equipped for eventualities ahead. At the WTO meeting referred to above, participants vowed to unite in deriving lessons from SARS, be better prepared in the future and work closely with the media in an honest and transparent manner. In Singapore, the STB established a new Emergency Planning Division headed by the Director of Emergency Planning for SARS. Hoteliers spoke of SARS as an educational experience, leading to amendments to existing crisis management plans or the creation of new ones (Ng, 2004).

Finally, the challenges of 2003 disclosed the benefits of close relationships and the construction of alliances within and between the government and private sectors. The 'Cool Team' task force was accordingly transformed into a Tourism Consultative Council (TCC) of 25 members from 11 associations, four government agencies and seven individuals from the tourism and non-tourism industries elected by the STB. The TCC is intended to yield intelligence about and insights into critical issues facing the industry and assist in the pursuit of new strategic directions.

Conclusion

The outbreak of SARS in Singapore and its repercussions reveals international tourism's vulnerability to the actual and perceived dangers of infectious disease. A study of the case suggests some conformity to conventional crisis dynamics, although the opening phase was of limited duration and precluded preventive action with an immediate onset of crisis representing the first stage. The pace of the crisis was then dictated by the unfolding of the epidemic which was beyond the authority of tourism industry managers, such a loss of control imposing significant constraints which do not always prevail in situations of crisis.

Stage 2 of containment and damage limitation within Singapore sought to restrain the havoc being wreaked by the virus. The third and final stage of resolution and recovery comprised programmes centred on promotional campaigns. There was also time for review and the application of knowledge gained, reforms being introduced to ensure preparedness for a return of SARS or a similar virus. Communication was a vital function throughout, with many different audiences to address. The messages conveyed changed as the crisis evolved, but the circulation of accurate information and management of fear were core objectives.

It is clear that virulent infections do not respect territorial boundaries, and SARS became an international as well as a national problem, warranting official and commercial involvement. International actions were also determined by the phase of the crisis and the interests and agendas of the stakeholders, but tended to mirror those undertaken in the national sphere. While aspects of preferred solutions and the characteristics of the crisis demanded a coordinated approach, this may have been frustrated by the multiplicity of agents with a part to play and some conflicts of interest.

Nevertheless, it would seem that appreciation of the risks to tourism from known and undiscovered viruses have been heightened in Singapore and more generally, with a greater willingness to engage in cooperation at a domestic and trans-national level. Detection of warning signals of any future threats is likely to occur earlier than in 2003 because of the learning which accompanied the experience of the SARS crisis that year. This is suggested by the prompt recognition of the potential damage to tourism posed by avian influenza and the second Chinese outbreak of SARS in 2004, already made reference to, and the rapid assumption of a state of alert which could be seen as the adoption of a pre-crisis position.

Devising strategies to cope with outbreaks of infectious disease have acquired a new urgency in the modern world, and analysis of the Singapore and SARS case may help to inform and improve the planning process. The three-stage model depicted in this chapter provides one possible framework for understanding and dealing with health-related crises. However, the validity of the model requires further testing, and an additional preliminary stage prior to the onset of crisis could perhaps be incorporated in view of the growing awareness of viral epidemics and more sophisticated reporting machinery. Although prevention will often be impossible, delineation of such a period would allow for enhanced preparation and the restoration of tried systems and procedures. Unfortunately, there is a need for constant vigilance. SARS has not been defeated and there are predictions of the emergence of other viruses in the 21st century when the prevailing forces of globalization, one expression of which is mass travel, will facilitate their spread.

References

Asia Pacific Economic Cooperation (2003) *Tourism Risk Management for the Asia Pacific Region*. APEC International Centre for Sustainable Tourism, Griffith University, Queensland.

Aziz, H. (1995) Understanding attacks on tourists in Egypt. *Tourism Management* 16, 91–95.

Barton, L. (1994) Crisis management: preparing for and managing disasters. *Cornell Hotel and Restaurant Association Quarterly* April, pp. 59–65.

Blake, A. and Sinclair, T. (2003) Tourism crisis management: UK response to September 11. *Annals of Tourism Research* 30, 813–832.

Bland, M. (1998) *Communicating Out of a Crisis*. Macmillan Business, Basingstoke, UK.

Canadian Tourism Commission (2003) *SARS: the Potential Impact on the Domestic and Selected International Markets to Canada*. Executive Summary, Canadian Tourism Commission, Ottowa.

Caribbean Tourist Organization (2003) Tourism Sector Responsiveness to Health Crises. Caribbean Tourist Organisation website, <http://www.onecaribbean.org> (accessed 20 December 2003).

Carter, S. (1998) Tourists' and travellers' social construction of Africa and Asia as risky locations. *Tourism Management* 19, 349–358.

Cassedy, K. (1991) *Crisis Management Planning in the Travel and Tourism Industry: a Study of Three Destination Cases and a Crisis Management Planning Manual*. Pacific Asia Travel Association, San Francisco, California.

Centres for Disease Control and Prevention (2003) Vessel Sanitation Program. CDC website, <http://www.cdc.gov> (accessed 20 December 2003).

Chien, G. and Law, R. (2003) The impact of severe acute respiratory syndrome on hotels: a case study of Hong Kong. *International Journal of Hospitality Management* 22, 327–332.

Clift, S. and Page, S.J. (eds) (1996) *Health and the International Tourist*. Routledge, London.

de Sausmarez, N. (2003) Malaysia's response to the Asian financial crisis: implications for tourism and sectoral crisis management. *Journal of Travel and Tourism Marketing* 15, 217–231.

Drabek, T.E. (1995) Disaster responses within the tourism industry. *International Journal of Mass Emergencies and Disasters* 13, 7–23.

Durocher, J. (1994) Recovery marketing: what to do after a natural disaster. *Cornell Hotel and Restaurant Association Quarterly* April, pp. 66–71.

Faulkner, B. (2001) Towards a framework for tourism disaster management. *Tourism Management* 22, 135–147.

Faulkner, B. and Vikulov, S. (2001) Katherine, washed out one day, back on track the next: a post-mortem on a tourism disaster. *Tourism Management* 22, 331–344.

Fink, S. (1986) *Crisis Management*. American Association of Management, New York.

Gonzalez-Herrero, A. and Pratt, C.B. (1998) Marketing crises in tourism: communication strategies in the USA and Spain. *Public Relations Review* 24, 83–97.

Henderson, J.C. (2003a) Communicating in a crisis: flight 006. *Tourism Management*, 24, 279–287.

Henderson, J.C. (2003b) Managing a health-related crisis: SARS in Singapore. *Journal of Vacation Marketing* 10, 67–78.

Huang, J.H. and Min, J.C. (2002) Earthquake devastation and recovery in tourism: the Taiwan case. *Tourism Management* 23, 145–154.

International Labour Organization (2003) Press Release. ILO, 14 May.

Lepp, A. and Gibson, H. (2003) Tourist roles, perceived risk and international tourism. *Annals of Tourism Research* 30, 606–624.

National Center for Biotechnology Information (2003) PubMed. NCBI. National Library of Medicine, <http://www.ncbi.nlm.nih.go> (accessed 20 December 2003).

Ng, X.Y. (2004) Crisis management in the travel industry: the impact and management of SARS in the Singapore hotel industry. Unpublished academic dissertation, Nanyang Technological University, Singapore.

Pacific Asia Travel Association (2003) *People Should be Travelling: World Health Organisation*. PATA. Press Release, 2 May.

Pine, R. and McKercher, B. (2004) The impact of SARS on Hong Kong's tourism industry. *International Journal of Contemporary Hospitality Management* 16, 139–143.

Pizam, A. (2002) Tourism and terrorism. *International Journal of Hospitality Management* 21, 1–3.

Pottorff, S.M. and Neal, D.M. (1994) Marketing implications for post-disaster tourism destinations. *Journal of Travel and Tourism Marketing* 3, 115–122.

Prideaux, B. (1999) Tourism perspectives of the Asian financial crisis: lessons for the future. *Current Issues in Tourism* 2, 279–293.

Prideaux, B. (2003) The need to use disaster planning frameworks to respond to major tourism disasters: analysis of Australia's response to tourism disasters in 2001. *Journal of Travel and Tourism Marketing* 15, 281–298.

Prideaux, B., Laws, E. and Faulkner, B. (2003) Events in Indonesia: exploring the limits to formal tourism trends forecasting methods in complex crisis situations. *Tourism Management* 24, 475–487.

Ray, S. (1999) *Strategic Communication in Crisis Management: Lessons from the Airline Industry*. Quorum Books, Westport, Connecticut.

Regester, M. and Larkin, J. (1998) *Risk Issues and Crisis Management: a Casebook of Best Practice*. Kogan Page, London.

Richter, L.K. (1992) Political instability and tourism in Third World countries. In: Harrison, D. (ed.) *Tourism and the Less Developed Countries*. Belhaven Press, London, pp. 35–46.

Richter, L.K. and Waugh, W.L. (1986)

Terrorism and tourism as logical companions. *Tourism Management* 7, 230–238.

Ritchie, B.W. (2004) Chaos, crises and disasters: a strategic approach to crisis management in the tourism industry. *Tourism Management* 25, 669–683.

Rudkin, B. and Hall, C.M. (1996) Off the beaten track: the health implications of the development of special interest tourism activities in South East Asia and the South Pacific. In: Clift, S. and Page S.J. (eds) *Health and the International Tourist*. Routledge, London, pp. 89–107.

Santana, G. (2003) Crisis management and tourism: beyond the rhetoric. *Journal of Travel and Tourism Marketing* 15, 299–321.

Scott, R. (1988) Managing a crisis in tourism: a case study of Fiji. *Travel and Tourism Analyst* 6, 57–71.

Sharpley, R., Sharpley, J. and Adams, J. (1996) Travel advice or trade embargo? The impacts and implications of official travel advice. *Tourism Management* 17, 1–7.

Singapore Hotel Association (2003) SHA, *Hotelierclick*, 2 (7), June.

Singapore Ministry of Health (2003) Singapore Ministry of Health Press Releases, March–June, <http://app.moh.gov.sg> (accessed 6 June 2003).

Singapore Tourism Board (2003a) Singapore Tourism Board Media Release, 29 April.

Singapore Tourism Board (2003b) Singapore Tourism Board Media Release, 24 April.

Singapore Tourism Board (2003c) Singapore Tourism Board Media Release, 4 June.

Sonmez, S.F., Apostolopoulos, Y. and Tarlow, P. (1999) Tourism in crisis: managing the effects of terrorism. *Journal of Travel Research* 38, 13–18.

The Straits Times (2003a) It's not looking good. *The Straits Times* 8 April.

The Straits Times (2003b) Drive to get Changi Airport humming again. *The Straits Times* 3 June.

The Straits Times (2003c) Calling for Singaporeans. *The Straits Times* 14 May.

The Straits Times (2003d) Singapore's approach earns foreigners' trust. *The Straits Times* 25 April.

The Straits Times (2003e) SARS-free, now to fine-tune crisis-handling. *The Straits Times* 1 June.

ten Berg, D. (1990) *The First 24 Hours: a Comprehensive Guide to Successful Crisis Communications*. Basil Blackwell, Oxford.

Travel Business Analyst (2003) July.

TTG Daily News (2003) 10 July.

Turner, B.A. (1976) The organizational and inter-organizational development of disasters. *Administrative Science Quarterly* 21, 378–397.

World Health Organization (2002) *International Travel and Health*. World Health Organization, Geneva.

World Health Organization (2003) World Health Organization SARS website, <http://www.who.int/csr/sars> (accessed 6 June 2003).

World Tourism Organization (1991) Recommended Measures for Tourism Safety. World Tourism Organization, <http://www.world-tourism.org> (accessed 20 December 2003).

World Tourism Organization (1996) *Tourist Safety and Security: Practical Measures for Destinations*. World Tourism Organization, Madrid.

World Tourism Organization (1998) *Handbook on Natural Disaster Reduction in Tourist Areas*. World Tourism Organization, Madrid.

World Tourism Organization (2002) *Tourism after 11 September 2001: Analysis, Remedial Actions and Prospects*. World Tourism Organization, Madrid.

World Tourism Organization (2003) Findings of the WTO Secretariat Survey on the Effects and Management of the SARS Epidemic in the Field of Tourism. World Tourism Organization, <http://www.world-tourism.org> (accessed 4 August 2003).

World Travel and Tourism Council (2003) SARS Reports on China, Hong Kong, Singapore and Vietnam. World Travel and Tourism Council, <http://www.wttc.org> (accessed 13 June 2003).

15 A Proposed Model for Tourism Crisis Management: the UK's Foot and Mouth Disease Crisis Analysed

ANDREW LYON AND AMY WORTON

Introduction

The past few years have been turbulent ones for the travel and tourism industry, with crises that have included the Gulf Wars, the Bali bombings, 11 September 2001 (9/11), foot and mouth disease, hurricanes, earthquakes and floods all impacting on tourism. Policymakers in many destinations have realized the environment in which they operate is becoming increasingly uncertain and that they have to become progressively more competitive in the market for tourists. The damaging effects caused by the mismanagement of the industry can have long-term effects, leading to a possible decline in visitor numbers and local or regional structural problems in the economy.

If destinations are to manage the short-, medium- and long-term effects of unforeseen events, they need to become more pro-active in the way they handle such events. This chapter examines the distinctions between crises and disasters, and in particular examines the broader crisis management literature before proposing a model for crisis management for policymakers in tourism destinations. The proposed model examines the strategies that destinations could use to prepare for the unexpected, how to cope with the associated impacts of a crisis and how to manage effectively an integrated communication network. The UK's foot and mouth disease (FMD) crisis of 2001 is used as a case study to assess how the socio-political environment affects the decision-making process in crisis management. The proposed model is related to the FMD crisis to ascertain lessons which could be learned for future crisis management.

Disaster and Crisis Management

The literature on crisis and disaster management has been growing since the catastrophic events of 9/11. Before this, there has been a long history of disaster and crisis research particularly in the USA. Key authors such as Quarantelli and Drabek have contributed significantly to the debate on taxonomy, differentiation and management of both types of event. In the UK alone, the numbers of publications relating to FMD from various government departments, quasi-autonomous non-governmental organizations (QUANGOs), industry bodies and academics have been substantial. One of the key aspects which has come from the literature is a general agreement that crises and disasters need to be planned for and systematically managed in a much more coherent and structured way (Department of Culture, Media and Sport, 2001; Sharpley and Craven, 2001; Goodrich, 2002; World Tourism Organization, 2003).

In order to structure the way in which disasters and crises are managed, it is necessary to differentiate between the two. Faulkner (2001) argues that a disaster occurs when a destination or organization is confronted with sudden changes to the external environment within which that organization or destination operates. The effects of this are so severe that there can be little or no control over the consequences of the disaster. Natural disasters such as hurricanes, earthquakes and floods fit into this definition. Prideaux *et al.* (2003) state that disasters are unpredictable catastrophic events that can only be responded to after the event. Shaluf *et al.* (2003), in their comprehensive review of crises and disasters, affirm that there is still no universally accepted definition of a disaster, although they do examine the characteristics of disasters, stating that they can be natural, man-made or hybrid. The characteristics identified include: disasters only have negative effects; they can be of a sudden impact nature (air, rail, road accident) or high impact disaster (flood); they arise not because of a single factor, but due to accumulated unnoticed events; they cause large-scale damage to human life and to the physical environment; they have profound economic and social costs; and they involve management procedures which must be maintained and coped with under emergency situations, possibly involving threats of injury and loss of life. Quarantelli (1998) notes that it is not always useful to differentiate disasters from crises on the basis of the cause, for example natural versus man-made, and as Glaesser (2003) states it is the preparation for management of the event which is critical.

According to Prideaux *et al.* (2003) and Sapriel (2003), crises are man-made and are concerned with human mismanagement or inaction which has an impact on the future cause of events. Darling (1994, cited in Davis and Walters, 1998) stated that crises have an anatomy, where a combination of seemingly non-hazardous events can escalate into a crisis. For the crisis to develop, crucial signs of the crisis are missed and evidence is ignored or misinterpreted. Organizations dealing with the crisis then fall into the incompetence trap and all minor events relating to the crisis interrelate and accrue to allow the crisis to develop. Shaluf *et al.* (2003) add to the discussions, proposing three types of crisis; community, non-community; and corporate. They offer no universally accepted definition of the term, but argue that a crisis is a man-made event, can have positive and negative sides, has an anatomy and may result from economic and political issues as well as from disasters. A crisis is a situation in which a decision has to be made in a short time, and organizational crises can occur at any time, anywhere and to organizations of all sizes.

The scale, length and extent of the crisis will determine the impact of the event and, as a crisis develops, it is important to identify and understand the various stages crises go through in order that appropriate strategies can be developed. Although not all crises follow the same delineated pattern of the theoretical models, on examining work by Faulkner (2001), Fink (1986) and Roberts (1994), there are four common stages which can be applied to most crisis situations:

1. Pre-event: this is where a strategic management team can take a predetermined set of actions with responsibility for crisis management. Risk assessments of the likelihood of crisis occurrence can be made and necessary action taken.
2. Prodromal/emergency: this phase occurs when the crisis is inevitable and a point of no return is reached. Action therefore has to be taken for damage limitation to occur.
3. Intermediate phase: during this stage, short-term measures need to be taken to aim at the restoration of normality to the affected community as soon as possible.
4. Long-term planning/learning: these occur where items which could not be dealt with in the intermediate stage are addressed and a post-mortem on the crisis and its management are carried out, along with a review and reflective period to facilitate improved crisis management systems and procedures.

The effective management of these four phases of a crisis is imperative if destinations are either to avoid crises altogether or minimize the negative effects to stakeholders affected by the crisis.

Crisis Management and Tourism

As many crises are the result of inaction or mismanagement, it follows that more active management and better planning for tourism crises needs to be institutionalized into the tourism planning system in order that negative impacts are minimized. The World Tourism Organization (WTO) has expressed its concern over the (mis)management of crises and disasters affecting the travel and tourism industry and have issued guidelines to practitioners and governments alike (World Tourism Organization, 2003). The tourism industry is extremely dynamic, and the increasing uncertainty in the industry post-9/11 means that national, regional and local policy decisions cannot be taken in isolation and have to be made in the light of the global political economy (Meethan, 2001).

Tourism is not a remote or discrete industry and therefore it cannot sit aside from other economic sectors. Blake *et al.* (2002) examined the effects of FMD on the UK economy and, while the tourism-related sectors of the economy were the worse hit, so were retail distribution, leather goods, and recreational and welfare services. Another study by Blake and Sinclair (2002) on the effects of 9/11 on the US economy found that the two worst affected sectors were hotels and air transportation, but other sectors adversely affected included construction, fitness, sport and recreation clubs, drugs, and cleaning preparations.

Jeffries (2001) draws the link between the management of tourism destinations and public sector planning. Drabek (1996) castigated the tourism industry, especially local governments, for their often flagrant lack of preparedness at sites prone to disasters. In earlier work, it was found that while most tourism-related private sector organizations have undertaken some form of disaster planning in such areas, the dissemination of the plans along with inadequate staff training were evident (Drabek, 1991). Responsibility for action must be shared between key stakeholders, although it is the public sector that has the ultimate duty for the tasks of policy coordination, legislation and regulation. Godfrey and Clarke (2000) expand on this stating that tourism planning must be done in conjunction with and for the key stakeholders, including trade associations, regional and local government, local resident groups, key commercial organizations, special interest groups and external advisers.

Policies and strategies and management decisions on crises are formulated and implemented within a political and social process. In relation to policy, Kerr (2003, p. 28) makes a number of important observations:

> How governments use their powers, how they devise and implement policy, and assess its impact, will depend upon many factors including their political culture; socio-economic issues; environmental outlook; the political and economic power holders/brokers; and of course their perceptions of the tourism industry on their economy or society. Furthermore such policies will be influenced by the political philosophies and ideological preferences of the government of the day, and the minister in charge, combined with the wider political environment in which they find themselves. Public policy-making is also influenced by the economic; social; environmental; and cultural characteristics of society as well as by the formal and informal structures of government and society.

Hall (1994, cited in Hall and Jenkins, 1995), in his model of the elements in the tourism policymaking process, examined the role of the policy arena being influenced by significant individuals, interested groups, institutions and their leadership. How governments react to crises will therefore be influenced by the factors discussed above, with each response from policymakers being different. If the varying nature, scale and intensity of crises are brought into the equation, then there is increased difficulty in managing events that are difficult to predict.

The Foot and Mouth Disease Crisis in the UK

The FMD crisis in the UK is now examined in relation to the socio-political decision-making process throughout the crisis. The effects of FMD are well documented (Countryside Agency, 2001a, b; Culture, Media and Sport Committee, 2001; Department of Culture, Media and Sport, 2001; English Tourism Council, 2001; Haskins, 2001; Rural Task Force, 2001; Sharpley and Craven, 2001; Blake *et al.*, 2002; Department for Environment, Food and Rural Affairs, 2002; McConnell and Stark, 2002; Morris, 2002). The crisis was one of the worst to hit the UK's tourism industry for many years, with devastating effects for many rural areas, significant loss of income, job losses and an image problem for the UK as a nation.

Background to the crisis

The FMD crisis began on 20 February 2001 when a case of FMD was discovered in cattle at an abattoir in Essex in south-east England. FMD is a highly contagious disease which can be transmitted in numerous ways, through infected animals coming into contact with healthy ones, through animal products and even by the wind. The initial response from the UK government was: to ban the movement of all animals; to ban the export of live animals; and, by 23 February, the public was advised to avoid contact with livestock and from walking in farmland areas. As per European Union directives on the control of FMD, the government also focused its attention on the slaughter of infected animals. Livestock which had been in contact with those infected were also killed. The spread of the disease was rapid. By late March, almost 300 cases were confirmed in a single week.

The major policy decisions from the UK government that seriously affected the tourism industry were the closure of footpaths in the countryside, the closure of rural tourism attractions and to make Forestry Commission and National Trust land off limits to visitors. In effect, the whole of the British countryside was placed under quarantine. Overall, some 2026 premises were affected, with animals slaughtered at over 8000 farms. By the end of the crisis, over 6 million animals or over 6% of the nation's total livestock had been slaughtered (Department for Environment, Food and Rural Affairs, 2002). The crisis officially ended on 15 January 2002, when the UK was declared free of the disease.

The impacts of the crisis

Various reports have estimated the loss to the UK economy. According to the Department for Environment, Food and Rural Affairs (2002), the losses to agriculture and the food chain amounted to £3.1 billion, while they estimated losses to the tourism industry at between £2.7 and £3.2 billion. The Countryside Agency put the figure for tourism between £3 and £4.3 billion. Blake *et al.* (2002) in their study on the economy-wide effects of FMD using the CGE economic model estimated that the total fall in gross domestic produce (GDP) as a result of the crisis would be around £2.5 billion in 2001, with a further £1.46 billion in 2002. Significantly, the fall in GDP as a result of the fall in revenue from tourism was in the order of £1.93 billion in 2001 and £1.46 billion in 2002, highlighting the significance of tourism when compared with other sectors seriously affected, mainly agriculture. The House of Commons Committee of Public Accounts (2003) estimated the direst costs to the public sector of £3 billion, with the cost to the private sector at over £5 billion, with tourism accounting for around £4.5 billion of this and agriculture only £0.6 billion. In terms of the contribution to the UK economy, agriculture contributes considerably less in terms of revenue and employment than tourism. It is also evident that agriculture is an industry in decline while tourism is in assent (see Table 15.1).

If these factors were considered on their own merit, it would be logical to assume that the tourism industry should have had as much, if not more attention than the agricultural sector. This was, however, not the case. The British Tourist Authority (BTA) received £14.2 million pounds for public relations activities, while the agricultural sector received £1.4 billion in compensation (House of Commons Committee of Public Accounts, 2003).

The impacts on the tourism industry were considerable. Overseas visitor numbers declined by 7% during the period January to September 2001, and spending declined 11% compared with the same period in the previous year (English Tourism Council, 2001). Sharpley and Craven (2001) noted some of the main effects on the tourism industry including accommodation bookings which were down 58% in March 2001 from the same period the previous year. A number of sports events were cancelled, and restaurants, pubs and visitor attractions suffered a virtual collapse in business as day-visits and short break domestic tourism declined due to the effective closure of much of the countryside.

Table 15.1. Tourism and agriculture compared.

	Agriculture (all)	Tourism
Revenue per annum	£15.3 billion (total)	£64 billion
	£7.3 billion (livestock and livestock products)	
GDP	1%	4%
Foreign exchange	£8.4 billion (total)	£12.5 billion
Employment	1.5% of workforce	7% of workforce
Tax contribution	£88 million	£1.5 billion
Growth rate: 1996–1999	−21% in revenue	+26% in revenue

Source: English Tourism Council (2001) in Sharpley and Craven (2001).

The Response to the Crisis

In their review of the political issues surrounding FMD, McConnell and Stark (2002) identified four distinct phases of the FMD crisis and four key factors integral to understanding the government's response to the disease. The four phases identified were:

1. Diagnosis. Following the realization that FMD had broken out, the central government underestimated the potential severity of the crisis and gave the impression that they were in control.
2. 'Overkill'. From mid-March onwards, the response from government was heavy handed. The Prime Minister, Tony Blair, responded to multiple political pressures, particularly the imminent general election. The PM assumed control of the crisis, resulting in excessive and pre-emptive culling of livestock.
3. The peak. At the height of the crisis, the number of outbreaks of FMD increased rapidly. The government accepted the case for vaccination of animals, but the powerful National Union of Framers (NFU) did not accept the government's reasoning, thus causing a delay in the decision-making process. At this stage, the countryside was 'closed', the negative images of the cull were being relayed across the world by the media and a general election was looming. The Prime Minister realized that the government had a serious problem and went on a charm offensive, stating 'Britain was open for business and pleasure'. The cull was also relaxed. The crisis was hardly mentioned during the 4 weeks of electioneering in May/June and Labour was re-elected.
4. 'Sweeping up', In the final phase, there was a period after the election when even though there were still up to five new cases of FMD per day, the media and government hardly mentioned the crisis, until it finished at the end of September.

Four factors identified by McConnell and Stark that influenced the handling of crisis were:

1. The Government's extreme sensitivity to public opinion in the context of the general election: Tony Blair assumed control of the crisis, wanting to show strong leadership before the election. Many rural constituencies were marginal seats and there was a distinct possibility of Labour not being re-elected if the status quo was maintained.
2. Departmentalism and fragmentation of stakeholders. Within the UK, a system of a fragmented vertical and horizontal deterioration in communication across all the different agencies, conflicts between stakeholders (tourism versus agriculture) and regional devolution on policymaking all contributed to the mismanagement of the crisis. Throw in a general election, a media frenzy showing the UK as a giant barbecue, scientists not being able to agree on how to control the disease, and ultimately a recipe for disaster was in the making.
3. Pressure politics and the NFU. Initially the NFU and the Ministry of

Agriculture, Food and Fisheries (MAFF) were united in their approach to the crises. However, as the crisis deepened, rifts appeared. For example, farmers did not enforce the 24 hour cull policy and an internal revolt occurred within the NFU on the slaughter policy. Farmers needed appeasing with respect to compensation, and the debate over vaccination continued with little agreement, with the NFU effectively blocking the government's vaccination proposals.

4. The politics of international pressures. By focusing on slaughter and control of the disease, the wider socio-economic perspectives were ignored. Tourism in particular was neglected. The images shown abroad of the crisis seriously affected the image of the UK and the government's inability to cope with the crisis. Was the UK open or not, was a question often posed by journalists. The pressure from abroad therefore had an effect on the policy decisions made by the Prime Minister and his government.

These factors had a major influence on what happened during the phases of the crisis outlined above and relate to the points made earlier regarding how policy decisions are not made in a vacuum, but are affected by numerous factors. The FMD crisis highlights how significant individuals, the timing of the crisis in the political cycle, the relative strength of significant stakeholders and institutions, the political structures of the decision-making process and the perceived image of a country can have a major effect on how a crisis evolves and ultimately how it is managed.

The FMD crisis also uncovered the lack of strategies at a national, regional and local level to manage and overcome a crisis. This predicament is likely to stem from the fact that according to Faulkner (2001), there is little in the tourism literature to assist governments in preparing and managing the unexpected. An adapted crisis management version of Faulkner's model for disaster management is presented in Fig. 15.1. An adapted version is required due to the differences between crises and disasters outlined earlier. The proposed model is of use to policymakers at the national, regional or even local level of government. Specific mention is made of the tourism industry in the model, but it could also be used for other industries when considering crisis management. Due to the complex, multisectoral nature of many crises, it is envisaged that the model could also be applied to crises where more than one industry is involved, such as the FMD crisis which affected tourism and agriculture.

Explanation and Discussion

The four stages in the model in Fig. 15.1 will initially be explained and then related to the FMD crisis. While the analysis will focus primarily on the national government's response to the effect of the FMD crisis on the tourism industry, the agricultural sector will also be analysed to show the linkages between the two sectors.

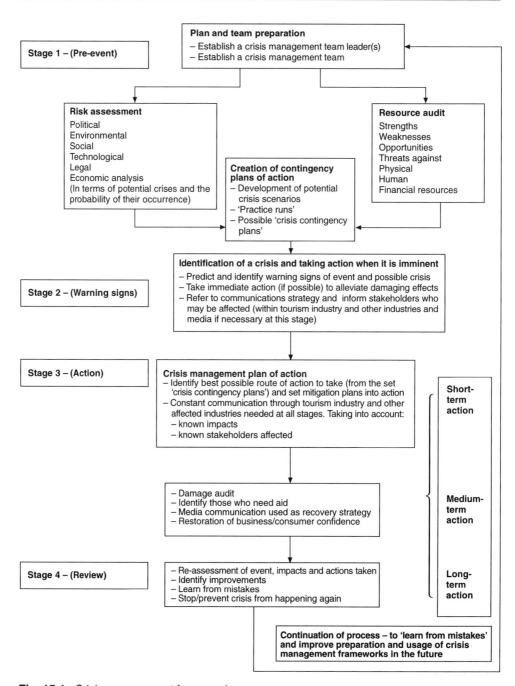

Fig. 15.1. Crisis management framework.

Stage 1. Pre-event

Most frameworks developed in the area of tourism crisis/disaster management emphasize the need for a 'team' and 'leadership' approach, to gain respect and control, and to enable effective management and coordination. It has already been established that in order for the tourism industry to be recognized and heard, there needs to be a united voice at government level able to take control and give guidance on policy formulation and matters of urgency. Turner (1994), Faulkner (2001) and Henderson (2003) stress the necessity of establishing a task force, to recognize potential areas of crisis, devising preventive measures and formulating coping policies for situations when they fail and actual crises take place.

These activities are all applied to the crisis management framework, under the 'pre-event' stage. Also in this stage of the crisis framework there is a need for risk analysis of the internal and external environments, creation of contingency plans of action, and a breakdown of resources, in terms of availability of finance, people and equipment.

The key to management of a crisis is preparedness, and the 'pre-event' stage calls for such awareness and strategic thinking. This is where assessments, audits, tasks and preparation of a contingency plan are carried out by a set 'crisis management team'.

Although many disasters/crises are not predictable and their disruptive effects are generally unavoidable, through the development of a management strategy, many potential hazards can either be foreseen, or at least their impacts can be minimized if swift action is taken in a coordinated way.

As mentioned previously, the socio-political environment needs to be considered when applying the model. This needs to be considered at the pre-event stage in the PESTLE and SWOT analyses in order for this to be taken into account in the establishment of key personnel and the development of scenario building.

Stage 2. Warning sign stage

The development of a strategy for crisis management is complex; how do you plan for the unexpected? The problem also lies with the fact that 'crises do not always follow a clearly delineated pattern of theoretical models because of their unpredictability and the speed at which they unfold' Henderson (2003, p. 3).

The first aim in successfully following a framework for crisis management is to identify warning signs of potential crises. This accords with the point at which an event or series of events appears to be developing into a crisis, the stage at which a crisis could be prevented, or the scale or magnitude at which the crisis could be placed on the spectrum as set out by Faulkner *et al.* (2000) of its level of impact or devastation. In the view of Fink (1986, cited in Faulkner, 2001, p. 137), 'the essence of crisis management becomes the art of removing much of the risk and uncertainty to allow you to achieve more control over your destiny'. Therefore, the 'warning sign stage' is probably the most crucial in the plan of the management of crisis. It is the time for dominant stakeholders to be pro-active through leadership and cooperation.

The 'warning sign stage' in the crisis management framework is a time where there is a need to be pro-active and to take initiative. It is a continuation of the 'pre-event'; a risk assessment will already have taken place in relation to a number of possible scenarios, the next task being to take immediate action in identifying mitigating impacts and to alleviate the potential damaging effects. The key here is to take control of the impacts of the crisis, before the crisis takes control of the industry. Mentioned earlier was the crucial need for cooperation, not only among those within the tourism industry, but with other stakeholders, including other industries and the media. This concept is explored further with the explanatory need for a communication network.

Stage 3. Action

The action stage in the crisis management framework requires action to be taken in the short, medium and long term.

Short term

Because of the characteristics of a crisis, different activities take place at each stage in the crisis management framework. High quality risk management in the previous stages will improve the success of the current phase. Risks must be identified and an assessment of their occurrence and likely impact should be made. Consideration should also be given to preventive or contingency measures that may be appropriate in a range of crisis situations. The most appropriate plan of action for a particular crisis should then be identified and implemented while allowing for changes to be made at short notice as the crisis develops. It is essential that throughout the whole process effective communications and cooperation occur between all stakeholders involved.

Medium term

Those businesses, organizations and departments that become adversely affected by the consequences of any type of crisis need to be considered by central government in a damage audit, with prioritization for those that need assistance to sustain their future operations. Support should be considered to providing financial assistance and other advice, to assist in reconstruction and re-establishment of the business.

Long term

Looking ahead to when activities are directed to re-establishing business activity, it may be necessary to establish a pre-crisis benchmark to determine the level of assistance required. Sometimes the chances of returning to the pre-event routine may not be possible. The Countryside Agency (2001a), for example, proposed that the speed and extent of recovery after a crisis will depend on the extent to which tourism enterprises are fundamentally profitable, and on any impacts that might accrue from any slow down in either the national or the global economies. Reviewing the situation can be a way of turning this negative position into a positive outlook, learning from mistakes and creating a sense of preparedness either to prevent destructive events occurring again or to mitigate the negative impacts.

Stage 4. Review

Mentioned throughout this chapter is the need for the continued cooperation of all stakeholders to ensure that any strategy, plan of action or framework is a success. The FMD crisis was a reminder of the fragmentation of the tourism industry and how it inter-relates with other industries. Sharpley and Craven (2001) suggest that rural policy and tourism policy should be synonymous, thus signifying the need for an integrated communication network, not only between tourism and agriculture/rural affairs, but also with many other industries and departments, such as transport, leisure, recreation and many more. Not only should it be on a national level, but local, regional and even international, through authorities, departments and trade organizations. Figure 15.2 highlights these key communication channels through a network of agencies from the national to the local level.

The 2001 Foot and Mouth Crisis: the Crisis Management Framework Applied

A number of stakeholders have indicated that they believed that the FMD crisis was badly handled (Countryside Agency, 2001a, b; Rural Task Force, 2001; Sharpley and Craven, 2001; House of Commons Committee of Public Accounts, 2003). If a more coherent approach to crisis management had been taken and all relevant parties and stakeholders had been better prepared and involved, more appropriate and timely action could have been taken. A number of reports and papers have been published on the lessons to be learnt from the crisis (Sharpley and Craven, 2001; Anderson, 2002; Department for Environment, Food and Rural Affairs, 2002; Frisby, 2002; Morris, 2002; National Audit Office, 2002; House of Commons Committee of Public Accounts, 2003). Key themes that have emerged from these reports include the following:

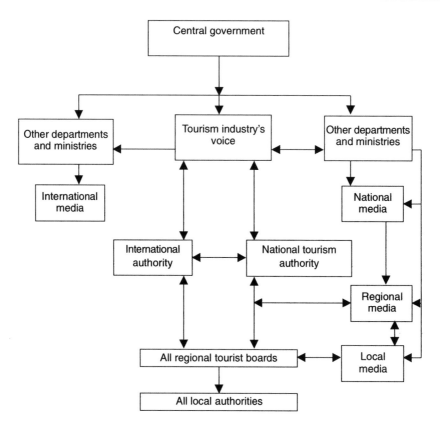

Fig. 15.2. Integrated communication network.

- The lack of crisis management preparation by the agencies involved, especially central government.
- Recognize socio-political environment of the policymaking arena.
- Risk assessments and scenario building need to take place.
- Key stakeholders have to be consulted prior to and during the crisis.
- Recognition that communication strategies need to be planned and coordinated.
- Swift action is needed once crisis signs are identified.
- A review process is required.

Something which began as a farming disaster had much wider impacts upon a wide range of industries, government departments and public authorities, including those responsible for the environment, public health, transport, the armed services, the countryside, leisure, sport, hospitality and not least tourism. The decisions by the government to 'close' the countryside was criticized by American Tourism Industry officials who stated that it was really an agricultural problem rather than a travel problem. Milligan (2001) made the point that it was blown out of proportion, with the media having a feeding frenzy; however, the reality was not nearly as bad as some of the impressions that were given by commentators.

The tourism industry was the major casualty of the British governments' actions and the media's negative coverage of the countryside. The damage caused by unilateral government decisions was not apparent until late on in the crisis when the tourism industry was severely affected. Even the government's recovery marketing campaigns could have been described by the tourism industry as 'too little, too late'.

An important point made by Cassedy (1991), Murphy and Bayley (1989) and Drabek (1992, cited in Faulkner, 2001) is that in a tourism context, the impacts of disasters on the market are often out of proportion with their actual disruptive effects due to exaggeration by the media. This also applies to crises and was specifically demonstrated during the FMD crisis. The role of the media in this situation turned out to have devastating consequences on the scale of the crisis for tourism. Ashcroft (1997) highlighted the need for effective public relations in handling a crisis, and examined the need for preparation and training for handling the media. Key personnel need to be identified, trained, briefed, available at key stages of the crisis, particularly stage 1, and above all they need to be armed with the right information. All this was clearly lacking in the FMD crisis as different spokespeople gave different accounts due to conflicting information coming from numerous sources.

The media can be used to advantage as a tool to restore a positive image. As the panellists at the first Travel and Tourism Marketing Conference stated, one of the keys to surviving a crisis is to react quickly to assure travellers that a travel product is open and safe (Deady, 1990). In the FMD crisis, the government's reaction lasted longer than necessary. The perception that the countryside was closed continued long after it had ceased to be the reality (Department for Environment, Food and Rural Affairs, 2002).

If a communication management framework such as that proposed in this chapter had been in place, there could have been alliances created that would enable more effective decision making between these stakeholders. A more extensive and comprehensive pool of knowledge would have been developed, allowing more informed decisions to be made.

The proposed framework would have enabled the introduction of a contingency plan of action which would have helped to prepare resources, assess the stability of the internal and external environments and allow possible warning signs to be detected. It would then specify the most appropriate actions to take, thus mitigating some of the impacts of the crisis. As things were, many of the actions taken at the time of the FMD outbreak were ill advised and the scale of the crisis was not realized for some time.

The review stage of the framework allows reflection and, with further research or benchmarking exercises, catastrophic events could be used as case studies. This thought is shared by Prideaux *et al.* (2002, p. 486) who suggest that 'crises offer some scope for prediction based on the premise that after a particular type of crisis has passed, analysis of its causes should enable greater predictability of similar problems in the future'. It is clear that there were many errors made in the handling of the FMD crisis and looking back at the taxonomy of the crisis these have enabled the development of a crisis management framework that may be used as an aid in the planning for future crises.

Conclusions

This chapter has focused upon the problems associated with the UK government's handling and management of the foot and mouth crisis in relation to the tourism industry. It concludes that much of the government's policy was neither sufficient nor appropriate, highlighting the reality that the government had very poor contingency and action plans to deal with a crisis of this scale.

The 2001 FMD crisis emphasizes the lack of recognition that the national government had for tourism and its value as an industry prior to the event. If they had taken into account the comparative value of farming and tourism at the beginning of the crisis, the outcome may have been different. Many of the actions and decisions made during the crisis had devastating effects on tourism. The decision to implement a widespread cull rather than vaccinate animals infected by the disease has been described as 'an inadequate response' and 'a government failure' by the media (Morris, 2002). The combined actions of the 'closure of the countryside' and portrayal of negative images in the media also resulted in tourists perceiving the wrong messages, subsequently causing a massive fall in much needed visitor numbers and revenue. In one example, accommodation bookings in the Lake District National Park experienced a 75% fall during the crisis (Culture, Media and Sport Committee, 2001). It has taken a crisis such as the FMD outbreak to point out the need for communication, cooperation and correct policy formulation by government to cope with emergency situations.

The foot and mouth crisis has been used as the medium in this chapter to show how little organized research has been carried out into understanding the management of crises in the tourism industry and, consequently, the lack of prepared frameworks to prepare, plan and manage for the impacts of such an event. The application of the advanced crisis management techniques in the emergency services, the military, chemical or oil industries could be explored by the tourism industry. The key stakeholders also need to speak with a more united and stronger voice, something which was missing in the FMD crisis. The industry's size, fragmented nature and the lack of cooperation during the foot and mouth crisis back up the need for such a strategy. In developing the crisis management framework, the need for an organized strategy for communication for use both within the industry and with other departments and ministries became apparent. Its use would enable stakeholders and those affected by such a crisis to communicate effectively, creating an improved pool of knowledge for decision making, and enabling correct information to be passed on to the media, using them to restore and create positive images rather than the reverse.

The proposed 'crisis management framework' and 'integrated communication network' are starting points in the understanding of crisis management and communication strategies, although it is clear that crisis management and communications strategies merit more detailed examination (Henderson, 2003). While the impacts of crises may not be totally avoided, improved planning and management procedures can assist in reducing their impacts. The next step into extending the research into crisis management should be the application of the framework suggested in this chapter to other case studies to test its relevance and assess its potential as a tool in the detection, preparation and management of crises.

References

Anderson, I. (2002) Foot and mouth disease 2001: lessons to be learned inquiry. The Stationery Office, London, <www.fmd-lessonslearned.org.uk> (accessed 13 October 2002).

Ashcroft, L.S. (1997) Crisis management – public relations. *Journal of Managerial Psychology* 12, 325–332.

Blake, A. and Sinclair, M.T. (2002) *Tourism Crisis Management. Responding to September 11.* Nottingham University Business School, Nottingham, UK.

Blake, A., Sinclair, M.T. and Sugiyarto, G. (2003) *The Economy-wide Effects of Foot and Mouth Disease in the UK Economy.* Nottingham University Business School, Nottingham, UK.

Cassedy, K. (1991) *Crisis Management Planning in the Travel and Tourism Industry: a Study of Three Destinations and a Crisis Management Planning Manual.* Pacific Asia Travel Association, San Francisco, California.

Countryside Agency (2001a) Foot and Mouth Disease: State of the Countryside Report. Countryside Agency, Cheltenham, UK, <www.countryside.gov.uk/stateofthecountryside> (accessed 5 December 2001).

Countryside Agency (2001b) *State of the Countryside 2001.* Countryside Agency, Cheltenham, UK.

Culture, Media and Sport Committee (2001) *Tourism – The Hidden Giant – and Foot and Mouth.* Culture, Media and Sport Committee, Fourth Report, Vol. 1. HMSO, London.

Deady, T. (1990) Travel firms warned: don't lie to press about crisis situations; panel stresses role of media in affecting the impact of disasters on tourism. *Travel Weekly* 49 (29), p. 29.

Department of Culture, Media and Sport (DCMS) (2001) Tourism Policy – Tourism Industry Seminar, <www.dcms.gov.uk> (accessed 5 December 2001).

Department for Environment Food and Rural Affairs (2002) Contingency Plans, Part 2 – preparing for a possible outbreak of foot and mouth disease, <www.ukresilience.info/foot_mouth.htm> (accessed 14 November 2002).

Drabek, T. (1991) Anticipating organizational evacuations: disaster planning by managers of tourist-oriented private firms. *International Journal of Mass Emergencies and Disasters* 9, 219–245.

Drabek, T. (1996) *Disaster Evacuation Behaviour: Tourists and Other Transients.* Institute of Behavioural Science, University of Colorado, Boulder, Colorado.

English Tourism Council (2001) Foot and mouth – taking stock. *ETC Insights* 13, 1–4.

Faulkner, B. (2001) Towards a framework for

tourism disaster management. *Tourism Management* 22, 135–147.

Faulkner, B., Moscardo, G. and Laws, E. (2000) *Tourism in the 21st Century – Lessons from Experience. Turbulence, Chaos and Complexity in Tourism Systems: a Research Direction for the New Millennium.* Continuum, London.

Fink, S. (1986) *Crisis Management.* American Association of Management, New York.

Frisby, E. (2002) Communicating in a crisis: the British Tourist Authority's response to the foot and mouth outbreak and 11th September 2001. *Journal of Vacation Marketing* 9, 81–88.

Glaesser, D. (2003) *Crisis Management in the Tourism Industry.* Butterworth-Heinemann, Oxford.

Godfrey, K. and Clarke, J. (2000) *The Tourism Development Handbook.* Cassell, London.

Goodrich, J. (2002) September 11, 2001 attack on America: a record of the immediate impacts and reactions in the USA travel and tourism industry. *Tourism Management* 26, 573–580.

Hall, C.M. and Jenkins, J.M. (1995) *Tourism and Public Policy.* Routledge, London

Haskins, C. (2001) *Rural Recovery after Foot and Mouth Disease.* Foot & Mouth Inquiry Panel, Cumbria, UK.

Henderson, J.C. (2003) Communicating in crisis: flight SQ 006. *Tourism Management* 24, 1–9.

House of Commons Committee of Public Accounts (2003) *The 2001 Outbreak of Foot & Mouth Disease, Fifth Report of Session 2002–2003.* House of Commons, London.

Jeffries, D. (2001) *Governments and Tourism.* Butterworth-Heinemann, Oxford.

Kerr, W.R. (2003) *Tourism Public Policy, and the Strategic Management of Failure.* Elsevier, Oxford.

McConnell, A. and Stark, S. (2002) Foot-and-mouth 2001: the politics of crisis management. *Parliamentary Affairs* 55, 664–681.

Meethan, K. (2001) *Tourism in Global Society; Place, Culture & Consumption.* Palgrave, Basingstoke, UK.

Milligan, M. (2001) Copland ponders world events (American Society of Travel Agent's president Richard Copland's forthcoming British Tourist Authority fact trip). *Travel Weekly* 60 (30), p. 2.

Morris, H. (2002) Rural tourism: post FMD will they come flocking back? *ETC Insights* 12, D21–D26

Murphy, P.E. and Bailey, R. (1989) Tourism and disaster planning. *Geographical Review* 79, 36–46.

National Audit Office (2002) The 2001 Outbreak of Foot & Mouth Disease. HMSO, London, <www.nao.gov.uk/publications/nao_reports/> (accessed 14 November 2002).

Prideaux, B., Laws, E. and Faulkner, B. (2003) Events in Indonesia: exploring the limits to formal tourism trends forecasting methods in complex crisis situations. *Tourism Management* 24, 475–487.

Quarantelli, E.I. (1998) *What is a Disaster: Perspectives on the Question.* Routledge, London.

Roberts, V. (1994) Flood management: Bradford paper. *Disaster Prevention and Management* 3 (2), 44–60.

Rural Task Force (2001) *Report of the Rural Task Force: Tackling the Impact of Foot and Mouth Disease on the Rural Economy.* DEFRA, London.

Sapriel, C. (2003) Effective crisis management: tools and best practice for the new millennium. *Journal of Communication Management* 7, 348–355.

Shaluf, I.M., Ahmadun, F. and Said, A.M. (2003) A review of disaster and crisis. *Disaster Prevention and Management* 12, 24–32.

Sharpley, R. and Craven, B. (2001) The foot and mouth crisis – rural economy and tourism policy implications: a comment. *Current Issues in Tourism* 4, 527–537.

Turner, D. (1994) Resources for disaster recovery. *Security Management* 1 August, pp. 57–61.

World Tourism Organization (2003) Crisis and disaster management guidelines. World Tourism Organization, <www.worldtourism.org/market_research/recovery/reports.htm> (accessed 15 June 2003).

16 Phuket: Tsunami and Tourism – a Preliminary Investigation

YETTA K. GURTNER

Introduction

With the prevalence of significant disasters affecting the tourism industry since the beginning of the 21st century, greater professional, academic and administrative attention has been given to the idea of managing risks, hazards and potential crisis situations. Numerous guidelines and models have been developed to determine and assess destination vulnerability, exposure, probability and any associated level of hazard risks. At the same time, many governments and organizations have been pressured to reconsider existing development patterns, warning systems, safety procedures and associated infrastructure. Yet in spite of such caveats and counsel, the existence of pertinent technology, and the inherent vulnerability of exposed coastal developments, the South Asia tsunami of 26 December 2004 impacted on an unprepared and unsuspecting population.

While the full human, social, environmental, economic and psychological costs may never be truly known, the immense level of devastation is indisputable. In reviewing the specific regions damaged and the unfortunate timing of the event, Francesco Frangialli Secretary – General of the World Tourism Organization (WTO) has described this tsunami as 'the greatest catastrophe ever recorded in the history of world tourism' (World Tourism Organization, 2005). Beyond the obvious and direct physical impacts, affected areas such as Southern Thailand have also been faced with the loss of their primary income – derived from tourism revenues. Amidst the immediate search, rescue and reconstruction efforts, Thailand has been challenged with the predicament of managing a serious tourism crisis.

Tourism Crisis Management – Establishing the Context

As an industry primarily based on consumer confidence, reputation and positive imagery, most destinations can ill afford to be associated with increased risk or adversity. Yet, despite the relative frequency and propensity of major natural, human and technological hazards, the development of appropriate crisis management strategies for the tourism sector is considerably recent. Beyond forecasting and risk management, tourism crisis management is offered as a pro-active, holistic approach to enhance operational capability and a capacity to resist, respond to and recover from potentially detrimental circumstances. In the past decade, there have been numerous models, guidelines and frameworks designed to conceptualize this process: Faulkner's (2001) 'Tourism Disaster Management Framework', the World Tourism Organization's (2001) 'Crisis Guidelines for the Tourism Industry', Pacific Asia Travel Association's (2003) 'The "Four Rs" of Crisis Management' and, more recently, Ritchie's (2004) 'Strategic Management Framework'. While each has made a significant contribution to the general awareness and understanding of effective tourism management strategies, most acknowledge the need for greater research and investigation into how the process is applied and affected on the practical level.

Case studies such as the recent tsunami in Southern Thailand demonstrate the importance of placing such tourism crises into the wider context. While it was never possible to prevent the advent of this tsunami, it is the historical, physical, social, cultural, economic and political development of this region that has really created the crisis. Tourism is both a product and an element of a complex interdependent, inter-related system comprised of destination and society. Consistent with the notion of sustainable tourism, effective destination crisis management needs to be coordinated and integrated with corresponding legislative, institutional and human resource development. This tangible experience of tourism crisis in tsunami-afflicted Phuket emphasizes the strategic importance of pro-active local government, community and stakeholder collaboration in hazard mitigation and destination resilience.

History of Tourism Development in Southern Thailand

Tourism for Thailand is not just a recent trend or temporary phenomenon. In addition to a reputation for good value, ease of travel and a friendly population, the country possesses an abundance of historical, cultural, physical and environmental assets, making it an attractive destination for any traveller. Prior to the 1980s, however, the provinces of Southern Thailand, particularly Phuket, were known more for tin mining, rubber plantations, rice farming and fishing than for the tourism industry (Tourism Authority of Thailand, 2005a; Wikipedia, 2005). While small-scale guest houses and cheap bungalow facilities were available, tourism was only promoted as a lucrative development opportunity for the area following a rapid drop in global tin prices. The early establishment and success of resorts such as Club Med and the Phuket Yacht Club were soon followed by more development and support services of varying size and quality (*Lonely Planet*, 2005).

The construction of the Phuket International Airport in 1976 further facilitated overseas access to the area, rapidly increasing the number of visitor arrivals (*Lonely Planet*, 2005). While local islands were featured in popular movies such as James Bond *The Man with the Golden Gun* (1974) and *The Beach* (2000) starring Leonardo DiCaprio, tourism in the region similarly focused predominantly around the beach, ocean and associated water activities. Images of pristine white sand, clear turquoise water, vibrant coral reefs and tropical weather were skilfully packaged with personal comfort and affordability. Consistent with such expectations and demands, accommodation and support services were developed as close as feasible to the coastline – in some cases businesses were established directly on the beach front. Although the region possesses many alternative types of physical and cultural attractions, tourist centres consisting of hotels, restaurants, tour companies, entertainment and souvenir shops were soon found at most sandy beaches along the west coast of Phuket – progressively extending north to Khao Lak and east to Krabi. By 2002, Phuket had become the major tourist province of Thailand, attracting over 4,000,000 visitors annually (Tourism Authority of Thailand, 2005a). Even in the wake of the attacks of 11 September 2001 (9/11), the Bali bombings and the regional severe acute repiratory syndrome (SARS) epidemic, this tourism sector continued to prosper.

Physical Vulnerability

While proximity to the oceanic Sunda trench and Sumatra fault line has meant that this area of Thailand had always been vulnerable and exposed to potential tsunamis, prior to the tragedy of 2004 there had been no significant events within existing local memory (Lambourne, 2005; Pacific Tsunami Warning Centre, 2005; Roach, 2005). Unlike the coastal communities of Japan, the Philippines and the Solomon Islands which have experienced numerous tsunamis, the people of Southern Thailand were generally ignorant of the risk and apparent warning signs. A history of poorly regulated building and development patterns also meant that many accommodation and support services were located directly in the coastal impact zone – exposed to any type of sea-based natural hazard. Cognizant of the perceptible risk to many coastal communities, in September 2004 Geoscience Australia had reinforced the need for a warning system similar to the Pacific Tsunami Warning Centre (PTWC) to be established in the Indian Ocean – unfortunately at this time the idea received minimal official support or interest (Geoscience Australia, 2004).

Even as the initial seaquake on 26 December 2004 registered at several seismic monitoring stations in the Pacific, the subsequent analysis, confirmation and communication of these readings created considerable time delays (Lambourne, 2005). It has been reported through several media sources that members of the Thai government did receive advance warning of a potential tsunami threat approximately 15 min prior to the first wave impact; however, there are a number of theories as to why this information was not directly relayed to the general 'at risk' public (*Bangkok Post*, 2005). While the matter has become the basis of an official government investigation, it has been suggested that if such a warning was issued and proved unsubstantiated, it would damage the sensitive tourist industry. Although an advance warning would have done little to reduce the extent of physical damage sustained, many lives may have been saved. Unfortunately, as the afflicted area also lacked the communication network/capability to issue any form of comprehensive warning message, the matter can only remain open to conjecture.

The Tsunami Impacts

In Phuket, the first natural indicator of the forthcoming tsunami occurred at approximately 7.59 a.m., the morning after Christmas, as an earth tremor was reported to be felt by many residents and holiday-makers on and around the island. As the shock waves were minimal, most dismissed the event as relatively insignificant. While many slept, the majority continued with customary activities such as going to work, eating breakfast or going down to the beach for a morning swim – oblivious to the impending danger. Without any official public warning or notification, the first of the turbulent tsunami waves had hit most of the region by 9.30 a.m. the same day – leaving extensive damage in its wake. Having impacted such a vast expanse of coastline (affecting a total of six Thai provinces), there have been many conflicting and even contradictory accounts regarding the timing of the first wave, the behaviour of the sea and even the height of subsequent waves. Apart from the obvious stress and immediacy of the situation, much of this variation can be attributed to differences in physical landscapes, direct obstacles and geographical location.

Despite the unbalanced media attention that has been given to the popular beach resort of Patong, the greatest damage was sustained in the low-lying areas of Khao Lak and on the relatively exposed island of Phi Phi Don – with waves in excess of 10 m (Tourism Authority of Thailand, 2005b). Along the west side of Phuket most of the waves were estimated at between 2 and 5 m – with the less developed tourist centre of Kamala Beach the worst physically affected. More than simply one large devastating wave, the earthquake had generated a series of waves that battered the coastline with both tremendous force and accumulated debris. In some low-lying areas, the deluge extended over 1 km inland, destroying or sweeping up anything in its path – including vegetation, humans, vehicles, building materials and even a Thai navy patrol boat. The only true refuge was to the higher ground; understandably many people perished.

As the waves finally withdrew, survivors were faced with scenes of death and destruction. Amidst such turmoil, many turned to plans for search and rescue operations – yet the uncertainty over further 'after shocks' or more waves remained. In the direct impact zones, power, water and telephones (land-lines) were disrupted, and the mobile network became quickly overburdened. Without adequate communications or information, few knew or really understood exactly what had happened. As the first attempts were made to help the injured and move them to the closest available medical facilities, much of the world remained ignorant to the plight of those affected.

Immediate Response Efforts

Although few could have anticipated the scale and magnitude of such a tragedy, the Thai government has had extensive experience in dealing with human disasters. Within hours, official operations were underway to help assist in the local search and rescue efforts. Much of the early progress was limited by blocked access and the substantial build-up of debris. As victims were extracted from the ocean, collapsed buildings and piles of wreckage, the medical facilities quickly became overwhelmed. While most of the hospitals were reasonably well established and resourced, medicine, trained personnel and adequate sterile space soon proved in short supply. Volunteers from all sectors of society, including tourists, rushed to provide assistance in any way possible.

In the unaffected provincial capital of Phuket City, an emergency operations centre (EOC) was established to centralize and coordinate the official response efforts. Victims, volunteers, businesses, residents, foreign aid workers and the media were all directed to this location. Temporary accommodation and basic first-aid was quickly provided for those who had been displaced. As many victims had lost all personal possessions and even family/friends, over subsequent days and weeks the Provincial Hall became the focus of foreign embassies (to assist search efforts and issue temporary identification), communication facilities (offering free Internet access and international phone calls), interpreters, food, water and donation tents, travel/flight assistance (offering free flights to Bangkok) and an unofficial notice area for the dead and missing. Smaller operation centres were established in other provinces to direct the rescue efforts and assist victims to the larger facilities.

In the immediate aftermath, most of the tourists who were not searching for lost friends and relatives expressed a desire to leave the region as soon as possible. As the international airport remained operational, extra flights were established to assist their evacuation, as incoming flights brought much-needed supplies and personnel. Prior to the tsunami, the hotels and businesses of the region had been experiencing the pinnacle of the peak tourist season. Even though the majority of such establishments on the island of Phuket had been unaffected by the waves (>80%), in many places occupancy rates quickly dropped to single figures. Beyond the extensive physical, emotional and psychological damage, the tsunami created an imposing tourism crisis for the tourist centres of Phuket and Southern Thailand.

Media Distortion

While this region was not the only area in the Indian Ocean to be affected by the tsunami – or even the most severely impacted – it appears to have received a disproportionate amount of media attention. In addition to the relative accessibility of the area, a high percentage of the immediate victims were international tourists – with the dead and injured representing over 35 different countries (Tourism Authority of Thailand, 2005b). As the massive extent of damage was quickly realized, and the death toll grew, foreign media from around the world sought to bring relevant news and images to their own populations. Through many of the travellers that were able to escape the damage, amateur videos and photographs of the event soon became widely and publicly available. Of the estimated 6000 plus people in Southern Thailand that have since been officially declared dead or missing, only about 250 were lost from Phuket – yet it has become perhaps one of the most renowned areas.

With the emergence of new footage or personal stories of loss and survival, the media continued to reinforce the sheer scale, chaos and tragedy of the event. While reality revealed that only a small proportion of the island of Phuket had been affected – rarely extending beyond three blocks from the beach front – headlines around the world proclaimed that the tropical island paradise of Phuket had been completely devastated and/or destroyed (*Phuket Gazette*, 2005). Although there was an extensive build-up of debris and many structures sustained heavy damage, clean water, food and access to basic amenities were never a serious issue. Away from the direct impact zone, electricity, communications and daily life remained relatively normal. Looting, scavenging, harassment, stand-over tactics and corruption had become evident (blamed on outside elements such as Burmese migrants and the Russian mafia), yet were far less prominent than the altruism of survivors. As victims and travellers continued to depart Thailand, most foreign governments issued blanket advisories to defer all travel to the affected region.

While search efforts continued, there also seemed to be a growing international concern regarding health conditions, the availability of antibiotics and the potential for disease outbreak and epidemics. As additional medical supplies soon became available, a pro-active provincial and national government took the immediate initiative of distributing bottled water to affected communities and spraying all stagnant water areas to prevent mosquito breeding. To date, no increased incidences of cholera, dysentery, malaria or dengue have been reported (*Phuket Gazette*, 2005). With existing morgue facilities inadequate to handle the growing number of corpses, adverse media reports served to raise a public fear of contracting diseases from the dead bodies. Given the tropical conditions, the increasingly desperate medical requests for dry ice, formaldehyde and refrigeration facilities were primarily to prevent putrefaction and assist victim identification rather than any real risk of disease.

Media coverage of the tsunami did achieve a number of objectives, including informing and increasing global awareness of the event, helping to contact and locate many missing persons and raising the profile of global tsunami appeals; however, a large proportion of the reporting has proven far from comprehensive, accurate or even consistent in the provision of facts and information. A media centre was created at the EOC in Phuket City – with regular official media releases – yet many journalists preferred to pursue dramatic images and personal stories. While the suspected kidnapping of a Norwegian boy survivor received international media attention and generated general concern and outrage, the subsequent discovery that this was simply a case of mistaken identity remained relatively unheralded (*Phuket Gazette*, 2005). Within Thailand, numerous credible statements and reassurances were issued by public spokesmen – including the King who had actually lost his own grandson in the tragedy – yet most of these seemed to receive little attention overseas.

Restoring Tourism

In southern Thailand and Phuket, it has perhaps been the tourism sector that has experienced the most damage from this tsunami – in terms of infrastructure, reputation, loss of patrons, staff and economic repercussions – yet the provincial and national tourism authority have remained efficient and productive throughout the ordeal. Contrary to the impressions of complete destruction, within 48 hours the local hotel association had produced (in print and on the Internet) a comprehensive operational status report of all accommodation providers in the afflicted region (*Phuket Gazette*, 2005). Working closely with businesses, government, private contractors and volunteers, heavy equipment was brought in to clean up the beaches and debris as soon as feasibly possible. Within days, most of the major beaches of Phuket had been cleared, with tourists, Jet Ski operators and umbrella sun loungers once again evident (although in far reduced numbers). Extensive investigations were also prompted to verify that minimal damage had been suffered by surrounding coral reefs, islands and associated resources (*Phuket Gazette*, 2005).

With the proliferation of Internet websites displaying adverse images and conveying frightening victim's stories, alternative pictures have been freely offered demonstrating community resilience and spirit, and the rapid reconstruction efforts (*Phuket Gazette*, 2005; Phuket Tourist Association, 2005). Public pleas for visitors to return have been supported by sponsored invited visits from celebrities, travel agents, journalists and foreign dignitaries, the hosting of large-scale international conventions and events, and extensive promotion demonstrating actual conditions in the region (Tourism Authority of Thailand, 2005a). There has been a clear and consistent request for travellers to support the local industry by returning to afflicted tourist centres. Through heavy discounting and incentives, further advertising has been targeted directly at the domestic and regional market segment. Public relations firms have also been contracted to recreate and re-establish the Thai tourism brand. Beyond the highly publicized international warning system that is to be established in the Indian Ocean, local authorities have also been trialling several locally based systems to provide greater interim safety and security for the community (*Phuket Gazette*, 2005).

In spite of the difficult experience and personal costs, the majority of directly affected accommodation providers, suppliers and associated businesses have proved inspirational in their reconstruction and recovery efforts. Within days, a small number of shop fronts had reopened along the Patong beach front, as nearby bars, restaurants and entertainment venues continued to open daily. Even though proprietors suffered significant damage and expense, most of the existing staff were retained to assist clean up activities and cater to the needs of the remaining tourists. In the immediate aftermath, accommodation, food, water and supplies were generally provided free of charge to survivors, and victims' families. Beyond merely coping with the loss of expected revenues, short-term strategies have primarily focused on the rehabilitation of affected services and motivating a return of consumer confidence (Tourism Authority of Thailand, 2005b). Although reconstruction of most of the damaged physical infrastructure was predicted to take between 3 and 6 months (with the exception of the worst affected resorts, Khao Lak and Phi Phi Island), the anticipated restoration of tourism industry is less certain.

Government and Local Initiatives

Criticism regarding risks and communication notwithstanding, the community, local, provincial and national governments of Thailand have proven relatively effective and efficient in coping with the Boxing Day disaster. Although the country is still generally classified as a developing nation, resource availability and existing infrastructure in Phuket rival those of many of the more developed nations. While a tsunami was never really considered to be a high level threat, the Thai Department of Disaster Prevention and Mitigation possessed the relevant skills, experience and flexibility to coordinate immediate response and relief efforts (*Bangkok Post*, 2005).

Utilizing an established network including the military, police, medical/forensic teams and local contacts, direct victim assistance was quickly mobilized and the centralized EOC created. As the sheer size and area of the disaster made specific details and facts difficult to ascertain in the first few days – particularly regarding the status of individuals – officials tried to remain honest and credible in their appraisals (*Bangkok Post*, 2005; *Phuket Gazette*, 2005). Within the week, a set procedure and series of databases with relevant contact numbers had been widely disseminated to inform and guide interested parties through appropriate actions. Volunteers and translators were also available at the airport, all medical facilities, makeshift morgues and coordination centres.

With the assistance and support of international search and rescue teams, emergency response efforts progressively wound down towards a greater emphasis on victim rehabilitation, identification and forensic science. As overseas families of the dead and missing expressed a desire to expatriate bodies and achieve some form of closure, DNA testing became the only recourse. Given the sheer number of samples to be processed, the Thai authorities chose to contract out much of this work to external laboratories (*Phuket Gazette*, 2005). Numerous official and unofficial memorials have since been held to honour the victims, survivors and volunteers – with overwhelming amounts of money and donations provided to assist those affected. The government has similarly committed significant financial and material resources to helping aid agencies with refuge camps and restoring damaged infrastructure such as schools, roads and homes.

Post-tsunami investigation has also led to a series of plans to help prevent and mitigate such future contingencies. Perhaps the most apparent issue has been the level and type of development along the directly exposed coastline. As much of this area now requires redevelopment, the government has formulated a series of legislative requirements aimed at greater sustainability and a reduction of overall vulnerability. Changes to zoning plans will mean that all future developments must be at least 100 m from the foreshore with an intervening landscaped parkland area to form a natural barrier between the ocean and buildings. Any facilities and infrastructure erected will have to conform further to minimum construction and safety standards (*Bangkok Post*, 2005; Tourism Authority of Thailand, 2005b). While an initial decision was made to keep the beach completely clear of any furniture or amenities to assist future evacuations, a compromise has since allowed the reintroduction of less hazardous plastic chairs, umbrellas and limited water craft in specially designated areas (*Phuket Gazette*, 2005). With greater appreciation of the value and fragility of the natural environment, the government has also committed to a greater regulation of illegal developments, marine park encroachment and conservation efforts.

At the community level, the government has introduced a series of initiatives including compensation, tax breaks and soft loans for afflicted businesses and families (*Phuket Gazette*, 2005). While most were uninsured, the King of Thailand has issued a personal call to brokers not to complicate or delay payment for damage and losses from legitimate claimants. As the majority of those directly impacted lived and worked within the coastal tourist centres, there has been extensive cooperation between the government, tourism authorities, public and private sectors to develop comprehensive short-, medium- and long-term recovery plans that incorporate community resilience and hazard mitigation (Tourism Authority of Thailand, 2005b).

Communicating Risks

The most publicly supported resolution from this event has been the necessity for a regional early warning system. While the potential value of such a system is undisputable, extensive research and experience reinforce the fact that warnings are only effective if the public understands and knows how to respond appropriately (Quarantelli, 1998). A consistent element in most stories to proliferate in the aftermath of the disaster was of people having felt the original earthquake. Although this event alone does not constitute a tsunami – when the sea later began to swell, bubble and then withdraw – an educated public would have known to seek higher ground immediately. In places such as Patong, it has been reported that as the tide initially withdrew, scores of people (locals and tourists alike) were attracted by curiosity and concern to the newly exposed ocean bed and stranded fish, oblivious and tragically exposed to the direct impact of the first devastating wave.

On another beach in Phuket, a 10-year-old British girl is credited with saving numerous lives by recognizing the precursors to a tsunami – taught in a recent school geography lesson. It seems logical to expect relevant local natural hazard education and awareness to be taught to 'at risk' populations; however, this is often not the case. Although they may not have appeared particularly notable at the time, there were other warning signs of the impending danger. Various local newspapers, interviews and anecdotal stories all describe how, prior to the first wave, animals were uncommonly restless and trying to move away from the seaside. Elephants, water buffalo and even dogs have been attributed with saving many lives as a result of their unusual behaviour; furthermore, few animal carcasses have been found following the inundation (*National Geographic*, 2005).

In terms of the general lack of tourist awareness, few destinations can expect that all travellers will be aware of and/or familiar with appropriate response actions in a hazardous situation. It has been widely acknowledge that tourists are in fact considered more vulnerable than the resident population, as they become more relaxed away from their usual environment (Faulkner, 2001). Such vulnerability is generally increased where significant cultural and language differences exist. In Thailand, the absence of any real local knowledge or understanding of tsunamis resulted in increased panic, chaos and confusion. Despite numerous reassurances from authorities over subsequent days and weeks, tourists, residents and hospitality staff alike remained unsure about the possibility of another devastating wave.

Good management practice suggests that beyond the inherent safety issues, tourist service providers should be prepared and informed about any local hazard risks. Additionally, it has been suggested that as responsible hosts, they assume a 'duty of care' and are obliged to educate and convey relevant knowledge to tourists and patrons in the event of an imminent threat. Although there have been some industry-specific concerns that open revelation of local threats and hazards may deter potential travellers, consumers should have the right to make an informed and educated assessment regarding personal risk. The growing popularity and demand for high risk, high adrenalin adventure activities demonstrates that informed risk does not necessarily undermine consumer confidence. It may not be possible to prevent an event like this tsunami, but precautions and effective communication may reduce the risks to humans.

Tourism Crisis and Socio-economic Reality

Irrespective of warnings, awareness or understanding, the Boxing Day tsunami was inevitable, and no amount of human intervention would have prevented its impact. Beyond the physical exposure, many of the coastal communities of Phuket and surrounding provinces of Phang Nga and Krabi were additionally vulnerable due to an over-reliance on tourism revenues. While global tourism is generally considered a buoyant and resilient industry, destinations afflicted with negative perceptions and/or lack of consumer confidence are not always as fortunate. The tsunami effectively triggered a tourism crisis for the popular coastal centres of southern Thailand – as visitor numbers dropped, so too did the socio-economic circumstances of most residents.

Many businesses within the tsunami impact zone sustained substantial structural damage and, without the appropriate insurance, necessary repairs have become beyond the financial means of existing owners. Without extensive monetary assistance, bankruptcy has become a distinct possibility for some. Others who experienced personal tragedy or intense emotional distress following the event no longer wish to work or operate within their former venues. As shops, resorts, restaurants and entertainment premises have closed for repairs and rebuilding, previous staff have suffered pay cuts, reduced working hours and even unemployment. It is not only these hospitality staff that have been affected – informal sector workers such as beach vendors and 'hostesses' have become increasingly competitive and desperate for paying customers. Local fishermen who have been able to repair damaged boats and overcome a new fear of the ocean have since been confronted with a downturn in demand for local seafood as many visitors are concerned that such fish may have consumed human bodies.

In a vicious cycle, the reduced consumer demand and interest in this region as a destination has resulted in the withdrawal of many airline carriers. Despite pro-active marketing and promotion, hotel occupancies and subsequent spending levels are well below the normal levels. Many of the businesses that have remained operational are struggling to outlast the tourism crisis. Planning forecasts and consumer-generated interest have been cautiously optimistic, yet as the threat of avian flu resurges and an uncertainty over future tsunamis continues to be foremost for potential travellers, visitor numbers are likely to remain reduced. Without a judicious recovery and return of significant tourism revenues, government strategies to introduce improved development standards and greater sustainability may become subjugated by economic rationalism.

A Preliminary Analysis

Consistent with the idea that effective tourism crisis management should be a self-appreciating continuum, it is necessary to review and evaluate the lessons of Phuket in this crisis situation in order to assist in the development of 'best practice' strategies. Based on this preliminary investigation, there are a number of clear issues that have direct relevance to the design and application of a generic crisis management framework:

1. Risk management with an 'all-hazards' approach.
2. Pro-active network and resource development.
3. Warnings, awareness and education.
4. Communication and media relations.
5. Resilience and vulnerability reduction.

Risk management with an 'all-hazards' approach

Lack of awareness, preparation and recent historical precedence suggest that prior to the tragedy, a tsunami was most probably considered a low risk probability for this region of Thailand. Even though the extensive coastal development meant that these tourist centres were exposed and vulnerable to any sea-related hazard, few would have anticipated a catastrophe of such magnitude or scale. While risk assessment (Faulkner, 2001), risk and hazard identification (Pacific Asia Travel Association, 2003), and risk analysis planning (Ritchie, 2004) may be useful in developing provisions for specific and probable hazards to the region, this experience advances the argument for a more generic 'all-hazards' approach in preparing for/mitigating potential crises and disasters (Quarantelli, 1998). Unfortunately, even with the best technology and intelligence, not all events may be accurately anticipated or forecast. In developing an effective tourism crisis management strategy, the World Tourism Organization (2001, p. 1) recommends 'to plan by imagining the worst-case scenario'.

Pro-active network and resource development

In preparing for tourism crises, another vital component identified by the majority of the management models is coordination with other agencies/organizations/stakeholders and resource management. The response/recovery process in Phuket demonstrates that even without a tsunami-specific crisis management plan, pro-active networking prior to an event can facilitate greater participation, collaboration and resource sharing.

As a consequence of recent threats such as regional terrorism, SARS and bird flu, the Tourism Association of Thailand (TAT), the Association of Thai Travel Agents (ATTA), the Thai Hotel Association (THA) and numerous airways had already established a reasonably cooperative marketing and promotional relationship prior to the tsunami disaster (Tourism Authority of Thailand, 2005b). Similarly, all levels of government had made a significant contribution to this tourism campaign in supporting and implementing the associated health, safety and security initiatives. While the rapid Thai government response on 26 December 2004 is testament to the experience and flexibility of the Department of Disaster Prevention and Mitigation, emergency response teams and other agencies, the establishment of the central EOC assisted and promoted the inclusion of greater tourism and community interests. Although confusion and inconsistencies were evident in the first few days, networks established prior to the disaster facilitated the identification and coordination of limited resources. Personnel, equipment, administration and tourist support services were quickly and effectively ascertained to direct initial evacuations, aid and inquiries. Even as the tourism industry was in damage control mode, it further assisted in the provision of food, accommodation, flights for survivors and additional resources.

Warnings, awareness and education

Perhaps Phuket's most obvious lesson for the rest of the world is to be better informed and organized. While an Indian Ocean early warning system is a certain outcome, greater community education and awareness may have significantly reduced the human toll. Natural hazard awareness should be integral to any community education, as all business and organizations including tourism service providers should be prepared and attentive to any potential threat to patrons, property and/or the destination. Where warning systems or alerts exist, it is vital for everyone to know how to respond appropriately. It is also necessary to note that not all crisis situations – particularly in the case of rapid-onset, sudden impact hazards (e.g. a terrorist attack) – have an obvious 'prodromal stage' (Faulkner, 2001; Ritchie, 2004) in which to initiate warnings, mobilization or evacuations, and all destinations should be prepared for this predicament.

Communication and media relations

Communication and effective public relations is a central tenet in tourism crisis management, particularly in minimizing negative perceptions and images generated by adversity. Although not entirely within the control of the Thai authority, there were several areas of this situation that may have been improved through better planning. The first apparent mistake was not publicly communicating the tentative tsunami warning issued by the seismologists. In the chaos and confusion in the immediate aftermath of the tsunami, there was still no openly available information or facts regarding the cause of the incident or even the chance of reoccurrence. Such lapses undermined the credibility of many later statements issued by the Thais.

Utilizing the widely accessible and available resource of the Internet, the regional tourism association in Phuket was extremely timely and efficient in conveying details of the actual damage sustained by hotels impacted by the tsunami. Despite such efforts, it took the industry more than a week to get the wider media – particularly internationally – to convey the fact that not all of Southern Thailand and Phuket were destroyed by the tsunami and that most services and amenities were unaffected. Even with a designated media centre, official press releases and recognizable spokespeople inaccuracies, misinformation and sensationalism were prevalent. Given the global interest generated by the number of foreign victims, it was impossible to prevent the continued images of death and destruction; however, such stories should have been placed in the broader geographical context and balanced with positive stories such as survivor altruism and family reunions.

Even though Thai authorities avoided censorship and tried to remain both honest and transparent, the communication and media handling seemed to lack sufficient command and control. Effective public relations and communications tactics should be integral to pro-active crisis planning. In adopting many of the specific strategies recommended by the World Tourism Organization (2001) and Pacific Asia Travel Association (2003) guidelines, it may have been possible to reduce the misinformation and damaging perceptions of total destruction.

Resilience and vulnerability reduction

Although generally considered outside the scope of most tourism managers and planners, the holistic conception and ultimate aim of good tourism crisis management is sustainability. The crisis in Phuket was clearly exacerbated by poor development practice and an over-reliance on tourism. While it is important to understand vulnerability, exposure and risks, greater efforts should be made to increase destination resistance and resilience. On the industry level, this implies greater community understanding, support and management integration. Education, legislation, insurance, alternative employment incentives, environmental protection and economic diversification are all tangible options. In the quest for enhanced recovery, Phuket and the other afflicted areas of Southern Thailand have already begun to implement some of these strategies. A more pro-active approach to destination crisis management would be to pursue greater sustainability before a crisis happens.

Conclusion

Prior to the tsunami, the coastal tourism centres of Phuket and surrounding provinces had experienced relative stability and prosperity. Associated development continued along the foreshore for decades, with little consideration of direct exposure and vulnerability to sea-based natural hazards. Although the tsunami was inevitable, the devastation and human tragedy in this region was exacerbated by a lack of warning, poor hazard awareness, inadequate development planning and an extensive local commitment to tourism. While subsequent response and rehabilitation efforts have generally received international praise, preliminary investigation of this tourism crisis recovery reveals a fairly integrated management approach. It is generally accepted that any tourism sector should be prepared to mitigate potential hazards, yet this experience suggests that effective destination crisis management strategies should be coordinated with the community, stakeholders, the media, emergency response agencies and all levels of government.

As the generation of a comprehensive tourism crisis management paradigm is still an ongoing endeavour, it remains essential to understand and review the lessons of such authentic crisis situations. Even though this analysis does not go beyond the response strategies initiated in the 3 months following the tsunami, it highlights several important issues. Perhaps one of the most valuable insights from this event is the significance of recognizing existing social, economic and environmental dynamics. Tourism development occurs within a broader community/destination context and, as such, associated planning, development and management issues also need to be instituted from this perspective. Although unprepared for the tsunami, Thailand's overall response has confirmed the value of pre-established networks, organizational relationships and resource sharing. Conversely, in the wake of this disaster, numerous regional deficiencies have also been identified in terms of the risk assessment process, general community awareness/education, communication procedures and subsequent media relations. Phuket's tourism industry has yet to recover from this crisis, yet the implications for other destination managers and authorities are clear – greater integration, holism and sustainability are the key to effective and efficient tourism crisis management.

References

Bangkok Post (2005) Bangkok Post News and Archives, http://www.bangkokpost.com/: 28 December 2004, Tsunami toll soars; 27 January 2005, Legal liability for failure to issue tsunami warning?; 21 February 2005, Upside to tsunami lawsuit; 23 March 2005, Khao Lak's long come back trail; 20 August 2005, Tsunami recovery work too slow.

Faulkner, B. (2001) Towards a framework for tourism disaster management. *Tourism Management* 22, 135–147.

Geoscience Australia (2004) Small threat but warning sounded for tsunami research. *Ausgeo News* September, pp. 4–7.

Lambourne, H. (2005) Tsunami. Anatomy of a Disaster. BBC News UK Edition. 27 March. <http://news.bbc.co.uk/1/hi/sci/tech/4381395.stm> (accessed 5 April 2005).

Lonely Planet (2005) Destination Phuket, <http://www.lonelyplanet.com/destinations/south_east_asia/phuket/index.htm> (accessed 5 April 2005).

National Geographic (2005) Did animals sense the tsunami was coming? <http://news.nationalgeographic.com/news/2005/01/0104_050104_tsunami_animals.html> (accessed 2 March 2005)

Pacific Asia Travel Association (2003) *Crisis. It Won't Happen to Us.* PATA, Bangkok.

Pacific Tsunami Warning Center (2005) About Tsunamis, <http://www.prh.noaa.gov/ptwc/abouttsunamis.htm> (accessed 25 March 2005).

Phuket Gazette (2005) Phuket Gazette – Online English Newspaper for Phuket. News Archives, <http://www.phuketgazette.com/>: 28 December 2004, Patong clean-up underway; 31 December 2004, Unidentified victims 'will not be cremated'; 3 January 2005, TAT Pushing hard for recovery; 5 January 2005, No disease outbreak in Phuket – health chief; 6 January 2005, Misleading reports about missing toddler; 15 January 2005, Beach chair operators oppose recovery plans; 3 March 2005, Patong gets disaster warning system; 18 March 2005, WTO calls for easier access to soft loans; 22 March

2005, Tourists 'will return in October'; 23 March 2005, Farewell to ghosts; 5 May 2005, Phuket 'badly needs a plan'; 14 May 2005, Time for Phuket 'to learn from mistakes'; 24 May 2005, B280m more needed to identify tsunami dead; 19 July 2005, Hotel occupancy rates rise 15pc; 2 August 2005, Patong Bay cleaner after the tsunami; 17 August 2005, Gov orders encroachers' homes demolished.

Phuket Tourist Association (2005) PTA. Tourism Recovery Centre, <http://www.phukettourist.com/> (accessed 29 March 2005).

Quarantelli, E.L. (1998) *Major Criteria for Judging Disaster Planning and Managing their Applicability in Developing Societies.* Disaster Research Centre, Delaware.

Ritchie, B.W. (2004) Chaos, crises and disasters: a strategic approach to crisis management in the tourism industry. *Tourism Management* 25, 669–683.

Roach, J. (2005) Tsunami Region Ripe for another big quake study says, National Geographic News, 16 March. <http://news.nationalgeographic.com/news/2005/03/0316_050316_sumatra.html> (accessed 20 March 2005).

Tourism Authority of Thailand (2005a) Provincial Guide. Phuket, <http://www.tourismthailand.org/province.php?id=74&region=south&gref=1> (accessed 5 April 2005).

Tourism Authority of Thailand (2005b) Andaman Tourism Recovery 2005 Homepage, <http://www.tatnews.org/ccc/2426.asp> (accessed 3 April 2005).

Wikipedia (2005) Wikipedia. The Free Encyclopaedia, <http://en.wikipedia.org/wiki/Phuket> (accessed 2 April 2005).

World Tourism Authority (2001) Crisis Guideline for the Tourism Industry. <www.world-tourism.org/market research/recovery/Crisis%20and%20Disaster%20Management%20Guidelines.pdf> (accessed 4 September 2002).

World Tourism Authority (2005) Address by Francesco Frangialli, Secretary-General of the World Tourism Organization, at the opening of the emergency session of the Executive Council of the World Tourism Organization, <http://www.world-tourism. org/tsunami/Phuket/DiscoursSG-E.pdf> (accessed 2 March 2005).

17 Tsunamis, Earthquakes, Volcanism and Other Problems: Disasters, Responses and Japanese Tourism

MALCOLM COOPER AND PATRICIA ERFURT

Introduction

The year 2004 was a difficult year for many Japanese communities. Natural disasters threatened most regions of the country during the year. The typhoon season and earthquakes on land and at sea brought devastation to northern regions of the country. Frequent earthquakes, tsunamis, volcanic eruptions, typhoons, the threat of further outbreaks of severe acute respiratory syndrome (SARS) and other natural and man-made problems resulted in the Japanese living under the continual threat of social disruption, loss of life and economic turmoil from disasters. On the economic side, the cost of disruption to commerce, and the insured aggregate values of Japanese cities are enormous and, even if the physical risk inherent in such disasters can be reduced through good planning and management, the potential for gigantic financial loss from a major disaster is therefore never far away.

As the world has once again found out (Bandar Aceh, 26 December 2004), earthquake-generated waves have been given the Japanese name tsunami because of their frequency, size and impact on countries around the Pacific Rim, especially on Japan. For potential tourists, the passing of this term into everyday speech in more than one language may reinforce the perception of Japan as a disaster-prone country best avoided. Natural disasters involving earthquakes and tsunamis striking Japan appear to affect perceptions of the desirability of visiting that country for the following reasons:

- They usually result from visible seismic activity on a rather large scale, e.g. earthquakes of high magnitude levels.
- They usually affect densely populated areas, especially the central island of Honshu.

- They are *expected* to happen due to the country's tectonic activity, geography, geology and its historical records of such disasters involving huge numbers of casualties/loss of life.
- A lack of real knowledge about the country and where the actual danger spots are. After the 1995 Kobe disaster, the press coverage involved typical comments such as: 'Tokyo – a disaster waiting to happen?', 'next one on the list', 'long overdue', 'overpopulated, a great disaster that could strike any time now' – and these rapidly become elements of the public perception of natural disasters and of Japan that may be transmitted to tourists though the media and by word of mouth.

As Japan has not yet become a common tourist destination for large numbers of international visitors whose actual experiences could reduce their impact, such perceptions may put potential visitors off travelling to the country. More specifically, as soon as the international media reports a major natural disaster, many potential travellers reconsider travelling to that area in case they themselves get caught in a major event, a very common fear according to Murphy and Bayley (1989) and Floyd *et al.* (2004). As a result, Japan has had a rather bad press over the years when it comes to inbound tourism; the reporting of major earthquakes and tsunamis uncovers an unpleasant fact about the country. In order to offset this at least partially, the government has recently launched an international campaign to attract foreign visitors (Ministry of Land, Infrastructure and Transport, 2003), who in turn are being asked to spread positive stories about their experiences in Japan (if they like what they see). However, this campaign does not mention the country's vulnerability to volcanism, earthquakes and flooding. The important point then is: what have the Japanese authorities actually done about disaster risk management, and is this known to potential tourists in order for them to undertake their own more realistic assessment of the likelihood of such a disaster while they are visiting? This chapter will examine these issues.

Japanese Natural Disasters

Japan is particularly vulnerable to natural disasters because of its climate, tectonic vulnerability and topography (http://www.infojapan.org/policy/disaster/21st/2.html), and level of development. Earthquakes are the most common natural disaster; the country experiences more than 5000 earthquakes per year, but they are by no means the only destructive force. Others range from tsunamis and typhoons to heavy pollution of the natural environment. A number of physical factors contribute to the high incidence of natural disasters in Japan, these being extreme climatic variations, rugged topography prone to disturbance, and its location on the circum-Pacific 'ring of fire' in which most of the world's volcanoes are located and where the Pacific Plate subduction zone (producing earthquakes; Fig. 17.1) is at its most active (Aramaki and Ui, 1982; *The Australian*, 2004).

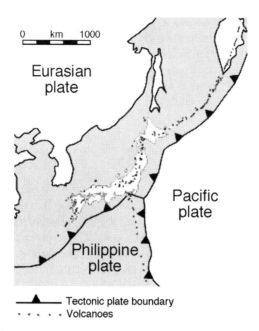

0   km   1000

Eurasian
plate

Pacific
plate

Philippine
plate

▲——— Tectonic plate boundary
• • • • • Volcanoes

Fig. 17.1. Location of volcanoes in and near Japan. Source: based on Aramaki and Ui (1982).

Furthermore, the fact that many earthquakes are combined with tsunamis adds another aspect to the complexity of disaster risk management.

Earthquakes and volcanism

The Great Kanto (Tokyo–Yokohama) earthquake of 1923 is recognized as perhaps the most devastating to hit a *developed* country in the past 100 years (Sorensen, 2002, pp. 125–127). The earthquake caused extensive damage in the cities of the region, destroying or damaging several hundred thousand homes and buildings, and the fires that followed caused more damage. The death toll is estimated to have been greater than 140,000, and over 44% of the urban area of Tokyo was destroyed by fire, with some 74% of all households affected (Watanabe, 1993). This damage was comparable with the human and infrastructural damage caused by the Second World War bombing in the same area, requiring a similar reconstruction effort. Town planning legislation was brought in to control re-development (Ad Hoc Town Planning Act, 1924) which had at its core a system of 'land readjustment', where all land was pooled in specific project areas, and land for public purposes (roads and parks – typically about 30% of the total) abstracted before individual building plots were reinstated. This system allowed reconstruction of road and other public services *before* housing, and therefore aided rationalization of the often chaotic building patterns of earlier periods. Of the 3636 ha of destroyed area in Tokyo, 3041 ha were divided into 65 project areas and rebuilt in stages between 1924 and 1930, financed by the central government and the land readjustment action of reserving public land (Sorensen, 2002, p. 112). However, land readjustment in the years following the earthquake also led to vastly greater suburban sprawl, as former residents of tightly built up Edo (central Tokyo) sought better housing on the fringes of the city.

In terms of the implications of disasters and their management for activities such as tourism, the Kanto earthquake established two important precedents for Japan's ability to deal with such events. The first was the system of land readjustment described above, and the second was the creation of the forerunner of an important class of public organization, the Mutual Prosperity Association (Dojunkai Foundation). The original public organization was formed in 1924 with the aim of supplying both housing and work for earthquake victims, but rapidly became known for innovations in self-help (upgrading of slum areas) and community approaches to new forms of housing (of greater strength to withstand new earthquakes). As is discussed below, such self-help organizations are an essential part of the Japanese local response to natural disasters, and their openness to including visitors (especially foreign tourists) needs to be examined in any analysis of how tourism may be affected by such events in Japan.

In order of disaster magnitude, the Tokyo earthquake was followed by the massive Kobe (Great Hanshin) earthquake of 17 January 1995. At 7.2 on the Shindo Scale[1] and lasting for only about 20 s, the Kobe earthquake extensively damaged infrastructure (800,000 houses were without water and gas supplies), left 300,000 homeless and killed in excess of 6400 people. The newly constructed port of Kobe was devastated by a widespread and severe liquefaction of the subsoil and permanent ground deformation, which destroyed over 90% of the 187 shipping berths and associated infrastructure. Over 350 fires contributed to the damage bill, mainly caused by ruptured gas mains. The total damage from the earthquake was estimated to be up to US$140 billion (http://www.dragon strike.com/mrk/disaster.htm). Buildings constructed before 1981 (largely with a concrete frame or wood) performed very poorly in the Kobe disaster. However, post-1981 buildings constructed with strong concrete shear walls performed well, and this indicates that the revised building codes progressively introduced after the enactment of the Disaster Countermeasures Basic Act 1961 have contributed to the protection of lives and property from this form of disaster.

More recently, in October 2004, a series of earthquakes in Niigata Prefecture north of Tokyo in central Japan killed or injured over 3200 people and made 100,000 homeless. Fifteen earthquakes at or above Shindo 5.0 were recorded over a period of 2 months, with four at over 6.0 during the 2 h after the first earthquake event. Damage to the region was compounded by the waterlogged soils from the series of typhoons of 2004. The temblors came just days after Japan's deadliest typhoon in more than a decade which left 78 people dead and dozens missing.

Compared with earthquakes, volcanic eruptions in Japan are a much lesser form of hazard. However, Japan has a long record of documented historic eruptions, starting with the eruption of Mount Aso (central Kyushu) in AD 710. Mount Aso is the country's most active volcano with more than 165 eruptions. Japan's largest historic eruption was at Mount Towada (Honshu) in AD 915, and, in 1792, the collapse of the Mayuyama lava dome created an avalanche and tsunami that killed an estimated 14,524 people (Simkin and Siebert, 1994). Most of these people were killed by the resultant tsunami. Japan leads the world's volcanic regions, with 1274 dated eruptions from 94 volcanoes. Japan also leads the world with 41 large explosive eruptions in the last 10,000 years. Pyroclastic flows, one of the deadliest volcanic hazards, have occurred at 28% of Japan's eruptions (Simkin and Siebert, 1994).

Mount Mayuyama is one of the dacite lava domes that form the Unzen Volcano complex in west central Kyushu, one of the areas affected by pyroclastic flows. In more recent times this has become a noticeably more active volcano. An eruption on 17 November 1990 marked the onset of the most recently active (phreatic) phase of the Unzen volcanic complex (http://volcano.und.nodak.edu/vwdocs/volc_images/img_unzen2.html). A volcanic dome made of dacite lava began to grow on 20 May 1991. This dome continued to grow for another 4 years. During this time, pyroclastic flows were frequently generated by the collapses of lava blocks from margins of the dome. During 1991–1994, approximately 10,000 pyroclastic flows were counted in the Unzen area. Landslides also generated large pyroclastic flows that travelled as far as 5.5 km from the dome. Forty-four people, including French and American vulcanologists, were killed by pyroclastic flows, and more than 2000 buildings were destroyed in the summer of 1993. However, it was not until April 1999 that scientific research at Unzen started, with drilling into the volcanic body in an effort to understand the eruption mechanism and magmatic activity at Unzen, and to mitigate volcanic disaster from future eruptions. Other historical volcano landslides are known to have generated tsunamis, including the following (http://volcano.und.nodak.edu/vwdocs/volc_images/img_unzen2.html):

- Landslides from the Kamagatake volcano on Hokkaido Island killed 700 people in 1640.
- A landslide from the Oshima-Oshima volcano on Hokkaido Island killed 1474 people on Hokkaido and northern Honshu in 1741–1742.
- A landslide from the Augustine volcano, Alaska, in 1883 triggered a tsunami that swept across Cook Inlet on to the Kenai Peninsula but caused no damage.

Tsunamis

One of the major natural disasters that can affect Japan is the tsunami. These occur frequently in the Japanese context because the country is prone to earthquakes and is completely surrounded by fairly shallow open water. The name is a Japanese word that is a combination of two words: 'ami' – wave, and 'tsu' – a particular point at the waterline; so a tsunami is a wave which approaches the shoreline, the term 'tidal wave' is an incorrect name for this phenomenon and is no longer used. These waves can reach over 30 m in height when they impact on the shore. The effects of a tsunami are illustrated by the tsunami which struck the northern island of Hokkaido on 12 July 1993. A 7.8 strength earthquake occurred off the west coast of the island in the Sea of Japan and within 15 min the resultant tsunami caused US$800 million in damage and killed more than 120 people. The worst tsunami disaster ever recorded is the one that hit the shores of the Indian Ocean in December 2004, killing an estimated 150,000 (Japan Times, 2005b). Prior to this, the worst tsunami disaster was the one that followed the volcanic eruption of the island of Krakatoa in 1883 when 35 m waves crashed into Java and Sumatra, drowning 36,420 people. In 1896, a large tsunami killed 27,000 in Japan. Destructive tsunamis of more recent times included one of Chilean origin in May 1960, which drowned 1000 people in Chile, Hawaii, the Philippines and Japan. From 1970 to 1997, tsunamis caused over 9000 deaths, including about 2700 on the Indonesian island of Flores in December 1992.

Damage mitigation

There is no way to stop a tsunami once set in motion, but there are ways to avoid damage. As Japan is a nation small in area and surrounded by seas, a potential threat of a destructive tsunami becomes a national event. The Japanese government has invested billions of dollars in coastal defences against tsunamis – for example, building concrete sea walls to blunt the impact of the waves and gates that shut to protect harbours – and has created an off-shore early warning system. The foundation of the tsunami warning system is a line of seismometers throughout the country: when monitoring detects a large, shallow earthquake under the ocean, they issue a warning. However, this method is plagued by false alarms, since not every earthquake necessarily triggers a tsunami. For example, since Hawaii's Pacific Tsunami Warning Centre was established in 1948, about 75% of warnings that resulted in costly evacuations turned out to be false alarms (http://www.pbs.org/wnet/savageearth/tsunami/html/sidebar1.html). To get around this, tsunami centres have turned to sensors that sit on the seafloor and detect a tsunami passing overhead. Japan has laid a series of such bottom-pressure sensors along a cable stretching out from its coastline and, when the sensors pick up a tsunami, the message is relayed to shore via satellite. The Japan Meteorological Agency, an agency of the national government, has the mandate to issue tsunami warnings. By using an archive of pre-calculated tsunami scenarios, the agency can forecast wave heights for all the coasts of Japan, when the magnitude and epicentre of the generating earthquake are known. Tsunami warnings and forecasts start from the cabinet level of the national government and are transmitted through the various layers of the national government, to the prefecture governments and eventually, in a matter of minutes, to the local government. Transmission of the warning and forecasts from local governments to the general public is done through a variety of media.

Other disasters

Japan has experienced a number of man-made disasters including the nuclear blast and subsequent fallout from the Hiroshima and Nagasaki atomic bombs during the Second World War, and pollution events such as Minimata disease where waste containing mercuric chloride (a catalyst in the production of plastics) was released into the bays of Minimata and Niigata in 1953 and 1960. These incidents revealed the perils of mercury poisoning to the world (Smith, 1975). Although only 52 people died as a result of immediate exposure to mercury in the Minimata case, hundreds of adults and children have since developed the degenerative neurological disorders characteristic of acute mercury toxicity, and there is an extraordinarily high cerebral palsy rate.

Another major natural disaster that affects the image of Japan is typhoons. Typhoon *Tokage* – the Japanese word for lizard – was the tenth major storm to make landfall in Japan in 2004 alone. At its peak, it stretched across an 800 km (500 mile) radius and reached speeds of 229 km/h (142 m.p.h.) as it battered the south-west of the country, forcing thousands to evacuate amid the threat of mudslides. The storm killed at least 69 people and left 21 missing, and was the deadliest typhoon to strike Japan since 1991 when 62 people were killed. Many of those killed were either drowned or buried in some of the more than 280 landslides in southern Japan alone. Near the city of Kyoto, 37 elderly tourists were rescued after spending the night on the roof of their bus, stranded by floods. Parts of southern Kyushu, especially Miyazaki Prefecture, were virtually shut down, with public schools closed and transport services suspended, and some 18,000 people were forced to evacuate their homes (http://www.reliefweb.int/w/rwb.nsf/).

Disaster Management and Tourism

As Murphy and Bayley noted in their seminal article on tourism and disaster planning (Murphy and Bayley, 1989), tourism is associated with *freedom* to enjoy, and tourists regularly quote safety and security as one of their primary concerns in the pursuit of this end (see also Poon and Adams, 2000). In seeking to understand the impact of this factor on tourist travel behaviour, the tourism literature has focused mainly on four major risk factors while neglecting a fifth to a large extent (Lawton and Page, 1997; Carter, 1998; Clements and Georgiou, 1998; Sonmez, 1998; Ioannides and Apostolopoulos, 1999; Pizam, 1999; Floyd *et al.*, 2004). The four factors are: (i) war and political instability; (ii) health concerns; (iii) crime; and (iv) terrorism; while the fifth, the impact of natural disasters on tourism, has largely been ignored (but see Faulkner, 2001; Mazzocchi and Montini, 2001; Prideaux, 2004). Political instability, health risks and terrorism have been identified as being very important determinants of travel propensity (Sonmez and Graefe, 1998), while travel patterns on a global scale clearly suggest that tourism demand decreases as the perception of risks associated with a destination increases (Sonmez *et al.*, 1999). Sonmez (1998) showed that tourists faced with the threat or perceived threat of terrorism tend to substitute risky destinations with safer alternatives but, importantly for the present discussion, also tend to generalize potential risks to a region or entire country.

On the other hand, the tourism industry (and some individual tourists), despite the regularity with which man-made and natural disasters occur around the world, continues to downplay the possibility of such events largely for marketing reasons (Murphy and Bayley, 1989; Cammisa, 1993; Hall, *et al.*, 2004, p. 3). Perhaps as a result, how the tourism industry (as distinct from actual tourists) adjusts to disaster or potential disaster situations has not received a great deal of attention in tourism management research, even though, as Faulkner noted in his seminal work on this topic, it is arguable that all destinations face the prospect of either a natural or human-induced disaster at some time in their history (Faulkner, 2001). The vulnerability of many tourist destinations to such disaster events has, however, been noted by several authors (Murphy and Bayley, 1989; Drabek, 1994; Burby and Wagner, 1996; Prideaux, 2004). Despite this, tourism businesses and organizations are generally unprepared for disaster situations even in high-risk areas (Cassedy, 1991; Drabek, 1992, 1994).

However, it is unlikely that tourism operators and associated organizations can easily 'plan' for natural disasters in order to offset their impact; this is generally a government (community) function (Santana, 2004). The fact that many tourism facilities including hotels and resorts, transport routes and the like are particularly vulnerable to natural disasters is more a function of what the industry is allowed to construct and where, not necessarily a failing of the individual companies themselves per se. Locational requirements, building construction and safety standards, and disaster coping strategies/relief planning and resources are generally the province of government in most countries. Where suitable standards and means of enforcement do not exist or are not policed, the effect of disasters can be compounded.

Risk management for natural disasters

In his introduction to 'Towards a framework for tourism disaster management', Faulkner (2001) makes the point that, to the casual observer exposed to the media that currently inform our daily lives, it appears that we live in a more complex, crowded and increasingly disaster-prone world. In addition to this factor, we now have more powerful technology that has a real capacity to generate disasters through unintended side effects, which complicates the process of isolating cause and effect relationships when disasters occur or when their likely occurrence is being planned for. For this reason, the boundaries between natural disasters and those induced by human action are becoming increasingly blurred, and this situational element needs to be taken into account in any analysis of such phenomena (Capra, 1996; Keown-McMullan, 1997). However, crises and disasters also have potentially positive (e.g. stimulus to innovation, recognition of new markets, etc.) as well as negative outcomes. This is in fact well illustrated by the recent SARS epidemic, which galvanized many tourism organizations in the Asia Pacific Region to advertise their attractions heavily, while calling for government to bring health-related safety measures up to date (Japan Association of Travel Agents, 2003). The reaction of potential tourists to this crisis was also positive in a sense; Japanese tourists have exhibited a propensity to shift travel away from areas of difficulty in the past and go elsewhere (but not stop travelling), and the domestic travel data for the period show that this was also true of the SARS crisis (Cooper, 2005).

On the positive side, governments (and their non-governmental organization (NGO) counterparts such as the World Health Organization) are increasingly concerned to try and predict the likelihood of occurrence of events having such severity and magnitude as to warrant major disaster *assistance* (Healy, 1989). However, while considerable progress has been made in minimizing the likelihood of *man-made* disasters through better use of technology and training, the impact of largely unpredictable sudden-impact natural disasters, the long-term environmental problems from natural disasters that are only now being addressed, and those events that occur at the interface between natural and man-made environments (Minimata disease, avian flu) remain to be fully understood and covered. Each of these has its own potential for risks to tourism, its appraisal and warning cycles, levels of impact, and recovery stages (Foster, 1980; Healy, 1989; Faulkner, 2001).

Foster (1980) developed a four-stage general model of disaster risk management planning that has subsequently been discussed in the tourism literature (Murphy and Bayley, 1989; Faulkner, 2001). In the first or appraisal stage, potential risks are identified and evaluated, while in the warning stage communities and operators are advised of the likely dangers and how perhaps to minimize their effects. During the third stage, that of actual impact, disaster-induced threats to life and property must be dealt with through public and private emergency service channels and rescue operations. In the fourth or recovery stage, the priority shifts to clean up, resettlement, and restoration of society and economy. Foster also noted the increasing importance of intermediation through news media, international agencies and 'sightseers' within these processes (an impact that perhaps culminated most recently in the 2003 media- and World Health Organization-induced SARS epidemic hype; Cooper, 2005).

Faulkner's Tourism Disaster Management Framework (Faulkner, 2001) elaborated on the conceptualizations of Foster and others to produce a six-stage model of a community's response to disasters. This model stresses coordinated team approaches, consultation and commitment in the disaster management process, but recognizes that natural disasters in particular are triggered by events over which victims have little or no control and that, therefore, their impacts are to some degree unavoidable. However, he does suggest that their impacts can be moderated by good planning and management practices, and this characterizes the Japanese situation above almost all other countries.

Japan's response to natural disasters

Even when significant problems exist in society, there is often no close correlation between these and appropriate policy responses (Reich, 1984). Such has been the case in Japan with respect to many environmental problems (Smith, 1975), although never with respect to natural disasters. A problem becomes an issue for government through two basic mechanisms: (i) where communities and private organizations/individuals are faced with a problem and force public recognition by government (outside initiatives); and (ii) where issues arise in government, are given official sanction, and are then expanded to include public support (the internal initiative; Hecko, 1974). The second of these mechanisms was how Japan first developed an environmental control law in the late 1960s. After several abortive starts in the 1950s, the bureaucrats finally saw the Diet pass the Basic Law for Environmental Pollution Control 1967. This was followed by a raft of laws covering water, air, toxic substances and noise, and the setting up of environmental institutions. Of particular interest to the present discussion was the pollution-related Health Damage Compensation Law 1973, which has attracted significant international interest for its coverage of natural disaster compensation based on the destruction of human life (Gresser, 1975) rather than that of property. The definition of critical environmental problems in this way meant that the environmental movement could count on significant political support for the realization of the democratic rights of unrepresented and injured citizens, while the government could respond more rapidly to actual natural disasters (Takabatake, 1975; Reich, 1984).

Relief programmes (including disaster planning and research)

Countermeasures against disasters in Japan fall into the following categories: (i) research into the scientific and technical aspects of disaster prevention; (ii) reinforcement of the disaster prevention system (facilities and equipment); (iii) construction projects designed to enhance the country's ability to defend against disasters; (iv) emergency measures and recovery operations; and (v) improvement of information and communications systems. Japan has in fact a long history of public relief programmes for the victims of natural disasters extending back into the Edo and early Meiji periods (Kase, 2004). After the Great Kanto (Tokyo–Yokohama) earthquake in September 1923 for example, many thousands of workers from Korea and other parts of Japan were employed on relief construction works. These were in two phases; immediate construction (requiring non-skilled labour; until autumn 1924), and urban planning reconstruction (requiring more skilled workers; 1925 onwards). In August 1925, the National Government's Agency for Social Affairs began an ongoing policy of public construction works as part of general social welfare provision in Japan, which has survived and been extended to the present day. In addition, some big cities (Kobe and Osaka) introduced mutual aid systems to supplement public reconstruction as a social safety net, while in recent years these provisions have been extended into all large population centres and many smaller cities.

As might be expected from these reactions, much research has been undertaken on natural disasters in Japan. This has ranged from research on long-term changes of the hydrological cycle due to global warming and their social impacts, through real-time analysis of the source process of large earthquakes, to greater understanding of hazard mechanisms caused by earthquakes, volcanic eruptions, landslides and floods, and the development of disaster mitigation technologies through observations, experiments and field surveys. A three-dimensional full-scale earthquake testing facility (E-Defence) is under construction in Miki City, north of the Kansai (Kobe–Osaka–Kyoto) area. When completed, E-Defence will be able to reproduce precisely the three-dimensional ground motion recorded during the Kobe earthquake in 1995 on a test table (http://www.infojapan. org/policy/disaster/21st/2.html). When coupled with data in real-time available from the nationwide networks of seismometers, strainmeters and tiltmeters, this facility will provide building code information and standards that will allow much more precise disaster mitigation regulations to be implemented.

The tenth anniversary of the Kobe (Great Hanshin) earthquake occurred on 17 January 2005 (*Japan Times*, 2005c). In the past decade, Japan's earthquake and other natural disaster countermeasures have changed enormously. Its earthquake observation system has become more sophisticated. Together with general observation and research, studies have made progress in understanding the active faults that cause inland underground earthquakes (*Japan Times*, 2004c). Since 2000 the government's Earthquake Research Committee has been calculating the long-term probability of an earthquake occurring in the 98 inland active fault zones of Japan. By the end of 2004 it had completed evaluation of 73 locations. At the same time, the committee has evaluated the probability of an undersea earthquake occurring off the coast and causing a major tsunami. On the basis of this evaluation, the government released in the spring of 2005 a series of National Seismic Hazard Maps showing the probability, in progressive coloured stages, of a region being struck by a strong tremor within a certain period (http://www.rms.com/Publications/Japan_EQ.pdf). For example, a strong earthquake has hit the area of Miyagi Prefecture, Honshu, about every 40 years, so the probability of a strong quake there within the next 30 years is high. Thus the area is shaded appropriately on the map.

Seismic activity forecast mapping, which is the result of earthquake research, as well as hazard maps compiled by local governments, serve as the foundation of national and local disaster prevention plans (Sorensen, 2002, p. 269). Hazard maps indicate the scale of damage that might be caused by a predicted earthquake based on estimates from specific data for each district in an area, such as the strength or weakness of the ground, the concentration of buildings, the deterioration of housing, and so on. However, although a seismic activity forecast map gives a kind of bird's-eye view of the whole, it is the hazard map that is important in actually helping to minimize damage and casualties. Local governments must draw up hazard maps, inform residents of them and encourage communitywide efforts to increase the earthquake resistance of buildings and formulate evacuation plans. In particular, it is essential that local governments prepare evacuation plans based on tsunami hazard maps. The Meteorological Agency is developing a system that would reduce the time taken to issue tsunami forecasts from the current 3 min after an earthquake to between 30 s and 1 min (*Japan Times*, 2005b). Yet the extra warning time will not have the desired effect of reducing damage and casualties unless there is a prompt and orderly evacuation.

The Japanese earthquake observation network has taken shape rapidly over the last decade. There are seismometers belonging to the Meteorological Agency, universities and research institutes at about 3800 places throughout the country, plus about 1200 GPS (global positioning system) observation points. It has become possible to keep constant watch on the movements of the Japanese archipelago and to analyse immediately what changes have occurred in the Earth's crust following an earthquake (*Japan Times*, 2005b). In the Niigata Earthquake, it is now known that a 20 km long fault shifted as much as 1.8 m. The integration of these observation data has also revealed the mechanism of earthquakes. Japanese research has attracted worldwide attention by throwing light on the slow-slip phenomenon – whereby the plate on the land side of an undersea quake moves slowly – and by revealing that the asperity, or roughness, along a plate's boundary becomes the focus of a quake.

Engineering and insurance

Both the Great Kanto (Tokyo) and Hanshin (Kobe) earthquakes, together with the effects of the Second World War bombing, accelerated the movement away from Japanese traditional housing styles into pre-fabricated houses and apartment blocks in Japanese cities (Waswo, 2002). This was because of widespread concern about the safety of traditional dwellings in such disasters. Suburban expansion on the fringes of the cities resulted, while areas of traditional housing in their centres were replaced by apartment blocks engineered better to withstand earthquakes. This change also encompassed a movement into private apartment rentals and away from private ownership in major cities. Considerable research has gone into engineering design, both for earthquake proofing of major facilities and for tsunami proofing of coastal settlements. This has in turn been reflected in strengthening of the building codes and planning regulations administered by national and local governments. Japan could therefore be said to be in one of the highest states of natural disaster readiness of any modern country.

This is also reflected in the availability of insurance and insurance underwriting for natural disasters in Japan. At the time of the Great Kanto earthquake in 1923, businesses had to write off quake-inflicted losses (Sawai, 1999). Today, adequate earthquake insurance is available, although it is very expensive because of high inner city land costs. This is illustrated by the 2004 earthquakes in Niigata Prefecture which caused catastrophic landslides and destroyed buildings. According to insurance specialists (*Japan Times*, 2004a), these events will not greatly damage non-life insurance firm balance sheets because of their high statutory reserves and the nation's financial safety net that protects them. Under this earthquake insurance system, established in 1966, the greater the damage, the more the government pays. If the total damage caused by the October 2004 Niigata earthquakes is assessed at ¥75 billion or lower, insurance companies will have to bear the full cost of payments. However, if damage reaches between ¥75 billion and ¥1 trillion, the government will split the cost with insurers, while damage beyond this amount will be covered by the government up to 95% of the difference. However, insurers' earnings are likely to suffer because of the record number of typhoons that hit Japan in 2005 because, unlike earthquakes, typhoon damage payments are not covered by the government (*Japan Times*, 2004a).

The impact on inbound and domestic tourism

What then is the effect of such natural disasters on tourism in and to Japan? Although there is very little published information on this question, several observations can be made. At a recent forum held to discuss Japan's difficulty in attracting foreign visitors and analyse what is needed to make the 'Yokoso Japan!' campaign a success, Yukio Okamoto, a diplomatic analyst, suggested that high prices were not the sole reason for Japan's unenviable reputation as a holiday destination, and said the problems for tourists in Japan begin immediately upon arrival. He cited long lines at the immigration counters at Narita, which can take 1 or 2 h to get through, and an inconvenient transportation system from the airport to the centre of Tokyo (another 2 h). Another critic argued a lack of shops that accept credit cards and difficulties for foreigners in using highways because of poorly displayed English signs have also harmed Japan's tourist potential. Other participants to the forum commentated on factors ranging from the reserve of the Japanese towards foreigners to the question of safety in natural events such as typhoons and the like (*Japan Times*, 2004b).

While none of the above-mentioned problems is beyond solving (and some do not even exist at all – such as concerns over how the foreigner might react in a natural disaster, if appropriate measures are in place to avoid them), the perception is growing that visitors may not receive the same assistance in a disaster situation as locals. Eyewitness accounts of the Kobe disaster report that the Japanese Self-defence Forces preferentially rescued Japanese citizens rather than foreigners in some cases, while a quarantine period was imposed on rescue dogs from Switzerland with the clear implication that this was a deliberate ploy to exclude foreign help in clean up operations (http://www.dragonstrike.com/mrk/disaster.htm). Comments such as those by Tokyo Governor Ishihara, who suggested in April 2000 that the Self-defence Force might be needed to control foreigners in the event of a major disaster in Tokyo further illustrate this point. *Sankokujin*, the word he chose for foreigners, has particularly racist overtones, dates from the pre-war period (Reed, 1999) and was designed to sow doubt in the minds of the general public about the suitability of having foreigners in their communities. On the other hand, the evidence shows that there is generally very little panic during such events in Japan even by foreigners, and virtually no looting, which makes the task of rescue authorities much easier (http://www.dragonstrike.com/mrk/disaster.htm).

That such anti-foreigner attitudes are not held by all Japanese may be evidenced by the fact that in the aftermath of the recent Niigata earthquakes, the Kyoto City International Foundation began raising money to help offer counselling services assistance to foreign residents and visitors affected by the earthquakes. The Foundation plans to use the cash raised to provide foreigners in the area with psychological care, as many of them have been left shell-shocked by the seemingly non-stop temblors that rocked the region during the last months of 2004.

According to the Nagaoka City International Association, some 2018 foreign residents were living in the main city of Niigata Prefecture as of the end of September, 2004. Many of those had come from China, Brazil and the Philippines to study or work in mills and factories. Though the 390 foreign residents forced to stay in evacuation centres after the October earthquakes struck have now returned home, many are still suffering daily from stress. Some foreign workers even lost their jobs because of damage to workplaces and business operations after the earthquakes (Japan Times, 2004b).

The existence of a difficult language barrier in these situations was very recently acknowledged in a report that local governments and radio and television stations might broadcast disaster warnings and information using children's-level Japanese so that foreigners could understand them (*Japan Times*, 2005a). The announcements have been printed in a manual that will be distributed mainly to the disaster preparedness departments of Prefectural governments and broadcasters. The manual, written in a level of Japanese which would otherwise be suitable for elementary school second- and third-year pupils, was compiled by a group led by a professor of socio-linguistics. Tsunami warnings, for example, will be broadcast as:

Tsunami wa totemo takai nami desu. Umi no chikaku wa abunai desu (Tsunamis are very high waves. It is dangerous near the sea). Also, instead of *hinansho* (shelter), the term *nigeru basho* (place to flee to) will be used. Why the authorities cannot provide translations of disaster warning and advice documentation in all the main languages currently used in Japan as a matter of course (or even in Japanese and English as now standard on public transport), remains a mystery!

Conclusions

The consensus in the literature is that it is difficult to predict the likely impact of natural disasters on tourism, as tourists go by sentiment as much as by perceived realities. If a tourist likes a destination, then it is entirely possible that he or she will discount the potential for natural disasters to affect travel to it. Conversely, if not, then the potential for disasters could assume a higher order of negative importance for the tourist than is warranted by actual experience. For a destination it is of course possible to exercise a considerable degree of hindsight in describing the actual impact of any disasters that have occurred there in the past, and also to overemphasize preparedness for the next disaster. Nevertheless, for any destination, even if natural hazards cannot be avoided, their dramatic consequences can be reduced through appropriate preparations and risk reduction measures. This brief outline of the nature and extent of natural disasters which have affected Japan since the beginning of the 20th century indicates that Japan is in fact one of the most prepared nations in the world in this respect. That typhoons, earthquakes and volcanism still manage to impact on the country and on its tourism merely indicates how difficult it is to guard against all possible impacts.

Japan suffered a record ten landed typhoons in 2004, breaking the earlier record of six, plus a series of strong earthquakes, prompting Salvano Briceno, Director of the International Strategy for Disaster Reduction (ISDR), to make the following statement: 'The tragic series of natural hazards that has recently hit Japan reminds us that all countries, rich or poor, are subject to increasing threats from social vulnerability and natural hazards' (Leoni, 2004). The impact on tourists is less easy to ascertain, though the words of the Japanese Prime Minister's policy speech to the opening day of the 162nd Diet Session on Friday, 21 January 2005 perhaps indicate that there is less to be concerned about here than might be assumed. Prime Minister Koizumi noted that an additional 900,000 visitors had come to Japan in 2004, for the first time ever bringing the yearly total to over 6 million (*Japan Times*, 2005c). Certainly, tourists do not appear to be overly concerned with the implications of such reports as *Megacities–Megarisks* published in January 2005 (Munich Re Group, 2005), in which the Tokyo–Yokohama conurbation is calculated to have a natural hazards risk index rating of 710, followed by San Francisco (167), Los Angeles (100) and Kobe–Osaka–Kyoto (92). A score of this magnitude is a reflection of when, not if, a natural disaster will occur in the Tokyo Metropolitan Area, but again it is not as real a measure of impact to the tourist as the prices they may have to pay for goods and services in the Tokyo area and/or in Japan as a whole, and therefore does not influence travel decision making quite as directly (Santana, 2004).

To offset such measures of vulnerability, the Japanese earthquake, typhoon and tsunami observation and defence networks have been considerably upgraded over the last decade. There is no doubt that the country is one of the safest to be in during a major disaster in terms of its readiness and ability to respond to such events. This may be reflected in the fact that both domestic and international tourists flock to Kobe only 10 years after the 1995 earthquake disaster, and wherever there is a similar disaster in Japan or abroad Kobe residents go to help where they can. Perhaps this is where we have to leave any analysis of the impact of a natural disaster on tourism, with the enduring experience of its victims and, in the Japanese context, their willingness to place their experience at the disposal of other communities when such events happen elsewhere. Kobe's physical reconstruction has largely been completed and the population has now climbed back to the 1995 level of 1.5 million, and, if anything, tourism to Kobe has grown, not decreased, despite the high likelihood of further earthquakes in the region.

Note

[1] The Shindo scale is a scale of intensity, like the Mercalli Scale. It provides information related to the severity of shaking at the earth's surface, where it affects structures. In contrast, the Richter Scale of magnitude of an earthquake describes the energy released by the earthquake.

References

Aramaki, S. and Ui, Y. (1982) Japan. In: Thorpe, R.S. (ed.) *Andesites*. John Wiley & Sons, New York, pp. 259–292.

The Australian (2004) Tasmanian tremor a possible catalyst for Aceh disaster says Geoscience Australia. *The Australian* December 27.

Burby, R.J. and Wagner, F. (1996) Protecting tourists from death and injury in coastal storms. *Disasters* 20, 49–60.

Cammisa, J.V. (1993) The Miami experience: natural and manmade disasters 1992–93. In: *Expanding Responsibilities: a Blueprint for the Travel Industry*. Proceedings of the 24th Annual Conference of the Travel and Tourism Research Association, Whistler, BC, pp. 294–295.

Capra, F. (1996) *The Web of Life*. Harper Collins Publishers, London.

Carter, S. (1998) Tourists and traveller's social construction of Africa and Asia as risky locations. *Tourism Management* 19, 349–358.

Cassedy, K. (1991) *Crisis Management Planning in the Travel and Tourism Industry: a Study of Three Destinations and a Crisis Management Planning Manual*. PATA, San Francisco, California.

Clements, M.A. and Georgiou, A. (1998) The impact of political instability on a fragile tourism product. *Tourism Management* 19, 283–288.

Cooper, M.J. (2005) Japanese outbound tourism and the SARS epidemic of 2003. *Journal of Travel and Tourism Marketing* 19 (2/3), 119–133.

Drabek, I.E. (1992) Variations in disaster evacuation behaviour: public response versus private sector executive decision-making. *Disasters* 16, 105–118.

Drabek, I.E. (1994) Risk perceptions of tourist business managers. *The Environment Professional* 16, 327–341.

Faulkner, W. (2001) Towards a framework for tourism disaster management. *Tourism Management* 22, 135–147.

Floyd, M.F., Gibson, H., Pennington-Gray, L. and Thapa, B. (2004) the effect of risk perceptions on intentions to travel in the aftermath of September 11, 2001. In: Hall, C.M., Timothy, D.J. and Duval, D.T. (eds) *Safety and Security in Tourism*. The Haworth Hospitality Press, Binghampton, New York, pp. 19–38.

Foster, H.D. (1980) *Disaster Planning: the Preservation of Life and Property*. Springer Verlag, New York.

Gresser, J. (1975) The 1973 Japanese law for the compensation of pollution-related health damage: an introductory statement. *Law in Japan: an Annual* 8, 91–135.

Hall, C.M., Timothy, D.J. and Duval, D.T. (2004) Security and tourism: towards a new understanding? In: Hall, C.M., Timothy, D.J. and Duval, D.T. (eds) *Safety and Security in Tourism*. The Haworth Hospitality Press, Binghampton, New York, pp. 1–18.

Healy, R.J. (1989) *Emergency and Disaster Planning*. John Wiley & Sons, New York.

Hecko, H. (1974) *Modern Social Politics in Britain and Sweden: From Belief to Income Maintenance*. Yale University Press, New Haven, Connecticut.

Ioannides, D. and Apostolopoulos, Y. (1999) Political instability, war and tourism in Cyprus: effects, management and prospects for recovery. *Journal of Travel Research*, 38, 51–56.

Japan Association of Travel Agents (2003) *6th JATA Survey on Travel Market Trends: Overseas*. JATA, Tokyo.

Japan Times (2004a) Deadly quakes unlikely to devastate insurers. *Japan Times* 29 October.

Japan Times (2004b) The foreign angle. *Japan Times* 16 November.

Japan Times (2004c) Disaster panel pores over three Tokyo earthquake scenarios. *Japan Times* 19 November.

Japan Times (2005a) Disaster alerts to be in 'easy' Japanese. *Japan Times* 15 January.

Japan Times (2005b) Editorial: research to ameliorate disaster. *Japan Times* 17 January.

Japan Times (2005c) Koizumi repeats postal reform line. *Japan Times* 22 January.

Kase, K. (2004) Unemployment policy in pre-war Japan: how progressive was Japanese social policy? *Social Sciences Japan Journal* 7, 199–221.

Keown-McMullan, C. (1997) Crisis: when does a molehill become a mountain? *Disaster Prevention and Management* 6, 4–10.

Lawton, G. and Page, S. (1997) Evaluating travel agents' provision of health advice to travellers. *Tourism Management* 18, 89–104.

Leoni, B. (2004) Natural disasters: rich countries also pay their toll, UNISDR/2004/08, <http://reliefweb.int/w/nsf> (accessed 19 December 2004).

Mazzocchi, M. and Montini, A. (2001) Earthquake effects on tourism in central Italy. *Annals of Tourism Research* 28, 1031–1046.

Ministry of Land, Infrastructure and Transport (ed.) (2003) Kanko Rikkoku Ni Muketa Seifu no Torikumi, <http://www.mlit.go.jp/sogoseisaku/kanko/top.htm> (accessed 19 December 2004).

Munich Re Group (2005) *Megacities–Megarisks*. Munich Re Group, Berlin.

Murphy, P. and Bayley, R. (1989) Tourism and disaster planning. *Geographical Review* 79, 36–46.

Pizam, A. (1999) A comprehensive approach to classifying acts of crime and violence at tourism destinations. *Journal of Travel Research* 3, 23–28.

Poon, A. and Adams, E. (2000) *How the British Will Travel 2005*. Tourism Intelligence International, Bielefeld, Germany.

Prideaux, B. (2004) The need to use disaster planning frameworks to respond to major tourism disasters: analysis of Australia's response to tourism disasters in 2001. In: Hall, C., Timothy, D.J. and Duval, D.T. (eds) *Safety and Security in Tourism*. The Haworth Hospitality Press, Binghampton, New York, pp. 281–298.

Reed, S.R. (2000) Elections in Japan 1999. *Social Sciences Japan Journal* 3, 251–260.

Reich, M.R. (1984) Mobilising for environmental policy in Italy and Japan. *Comparative Politics* 16, 379–402.

Santana, G. (2004) Crisis management and tourism: beyond the rhetoric. In: Hall, C.M., Timothy, D.J. and Duval, D.T. (eds) *Safety and Security in Tourism*. Binghampton: The Haworth Hospitality Press, New York, pp. 299–321.

Sawai, M. (1999) Noda Shoichi and Roku-Roku Shoten, a machine tool manufacturer. *Social Sciences Japan Journal* 2, 107–122.

Simkin, T. and Siebert, L. (1994) *Volcanoes of the World*. Geoscience Press, Tucson, Arizona.

Smith, E. (1975) *Minamata*. Holt, Rinehart, and Winston, New York.

Sonmez, S. (1998) Tourism, terrorism and political instability. *Annals of Tourism Research* 25, 416–456.

Sonmez, S. and Graefe, A.R. (1998) Influence of terrorism risk on foreign tourism decisions. *Annals of Tourism Research* 25, 114–144.

Sonmez, S., Apostolopoulos, Y. and Tarlow, P. (1999) Tourism in crisis: managing the effects of terrorism. *Journal of Travel Research*, 38, 13–18.

Sorensen, A. (2002) *The Making of Urban Japan*. Routledge, London.

Takabatake, M. (1975) Citizens movements: a new model for creating citizen movements in Japan. *Japan Interpreter* 9, 315–323.

Waswo, A. (2002) *Housing in Post War Japan: a Social History*. Routledge Curzon, London.

Watanabe, S. (1993) *The Birth of 'Urban Planning' – Japan's Modern Urban Planning in International Comparison*. Kashwashobo, Tokyo.

Internet sites Consulted

http://www.dragonstrike.com/mrk/disaster.htm (accessed 19 December 2004).

http://www.infojapan.org/policy/disaster/21st/2.html (accessed 19 December 2004).

http://www.reliefweb.int/w/rwb.nsf/ (accessed 19 December 2004).

http://volcano.und.nodak.edu/vwdocs/volc_images/north_asia/japan_tec.html (accessed 14 January 2005).

http://www.edlotterman.com/Litigation.htm (accessed 19 December 2004).

18 The 'Perfect Storm': Turbulence and Crisis in the Global Airline Industry

DAWNA L. RHOADES AND ROSEMARIE REYNOLDS

Introduction

In October of 1991, a so-called 'Perfect Storm' hit the east coast of the USA. This storm and the fate of one fishing boat, the *Andrea Gail*, was the subject of the 2000 film of the same name. This unnamed storm was the result of the combination of three separate weather events, each serious in its own right, which combined to create an event more dangerous and deadly than any single event could have produced. The global airline industry has been experiencing the effects of its own 'Perfect Storm' caused by the confluence of four distinct factors (Air Transport Association, 2003).

Two of these factors have a long history of creating problems for the industry – economic recession and war. The other two factors are new: the 11 September 2001 (9/11) terrorist attacks, and severe acute respiratory syndrome (SARS). Together these factors have created a crisis that has resulted in worldwide airline losses greater than all the profits made in the industry since the 1903 flight at Kitty Hawk (Gahan, 2002).

The crisis in the airline industry is not sending ripples through the economies of the world; it is creating waves. Airlines are attempting to deal with their crisis by passing losses on to aircraft manufacturers, airports, leasing companies, employees and suppliers, including travel agents and tour providers. As air travellers shifted their travel consumption to destinations closer to home, airlines experienced a decline of 2.6% in international tourism receipts for 2001. This was the first decline in international tourist arrivals since the Second World War (World Tourism Organization, 2002). This crisis created a cascading effect on a broad array of interconnected industries, and has government officials, business leaders and employee groups pondering changes both big and small in an attempt to bring long-term stability to a vital constellation of related industries.

This chapter will examine pre-existing problems in the airline industry caused by economic and historical factors, as well as the four recent events that led to the current 'Perfect Storm'. The chapter will conclude with a discussion of efforts at the government, industry, firm and individual level to deal with the crisis in the air transportation industry.

Air Transportation in Economic Perspective

Following the Second World War, the level of passenger traffic in the USA, the world's biggest air transport market, grew explosively. Passenger traffic tripled in the 1950s and 1960s, nearly doubled in the 1970s, slowed to an 80% increase in the 1980s, and posted a modest 35% increase in the 1990s (O'Connor, 2001). At first glance, it would seem difficult to believe that an industry that has witnessed this level of growth could possibly struggle; however, there are a number of economic characteristics that contribute to the state of the industry today.

Intermediate good

First, air transportation is considered to be an intermediate good by economists, since few, if any, consumers fly merely for the sake of flying. Air travel is a means to an end, whether for a business meeting or a vacation. As an intermediate good, the demand for air travel is affected by many factors, only some of which are under the control of airline management.

Elasticity of demand

The demand for air travel also shows elasticity to both price and income. Elasticity refers to the sensitivity of consumer demand to changes in price or income. In a wider context, the income elasticity of demand for air travel in poorer countries is relatively low, while the elasticity of demand in more prosperous nations may be high; in effect, a 5–10% increase in the income of consumers in a prosperous nation will more probably be spent on luxury items such as travel, while the same increase in a poorer nation will go toward meeting basic needs. Of course, the reverse is also true; a 5–10% decrease in income in a prosperous nation will be reflected in declines in luxury spending, including travel (O'Connor, 2001).

Variability of demand

Airlines can control price to some extent, given the competition within their markets, but they have less control over the variability of the demand for travel resulting from consumer preferences for season, day of the week or hour of the day. Airlines can adjust or adapt their flight schedules to cater to these demands, but as the air traveller consumer crisis in the USA in 1999 demonstrated, the air traffic system is not designed to handle the 'bunching' of flights around peak, preferred times of departure and arrival. This bunching resulted in increasing flight delays and rising consumer complaints (Department of Transportation, 2000).

S-curve theory

Another economic factor contributing to the congestion and chronic overcapacity experienced in the industry is the belief in the S-curve theory, which suggests that marginal flights (those generating revenues covering out-of-pocket but not fully allocated costs) result in greater than proportional gain (or loss) of market share. If true, the S-curve would argue that carriers are justified in adding flights (capacity) in a highly competitive market as long as they cover marginal costs because they will attract more passenger traffic than the actual capacity increase.

This same logic also makes competitors reluctant to cut capacity, even in cases where the marginal benefit is questionable. Given the long lead-time between aircraft purchasing and delivery and the long-term difficulty in predicting economic recession, it is easy to see how an airline could find itself with more capacity than passenger demand. The problem is further compounded as each individual carrier makes the 'individually rational decision' to add capacity.

Perishable and undifferentiated product

Two final factors add to the problems of airlines. These are the fact that the airline seat is a perishable product that cannot be stored for future sale, and that this seat is also seen as an undifferentiated product by most consumers (O'Connor, 2001). In fact, industry experts fear that 'a very real risk exists that the flight will be reduced to a commodity status and that the individual choice of airlines will be factored out of the buying process' (Fraser, 1996, p. 61). Price will then drive the market in an industry that is increasingly capital intensive (subject to pressure for new, faster aircraft and more sophisticated technology) and severely impacted by rising fuel costs (O'Connor, 2001).

Air Transportation in Historical Perspective

Historically, governments around the world have viewed air transportation as a special case in industrial activity. It not only contributes to the economic growth and development of the general economy and the broad tourism and hospitality sector, but it also serves a security and defence function; civilian air fleets are routinely used in time of conflict as additional airlift capability for troops and supplies. When these two factors are added to the national pride associated with the airlines that carry a nation's flag around the world, governments find it difficult to resist the urge to intervene. During the 1930s and early 1940s, almost all nations intervened either directly or indirectly to encourage the development of a stable air transportation system, with colonial powers intervening on behalf of the nations under their jurisdiction (Rhoades, 2003). Tight systems of regulation were established that limited the danger of overcapacity (by controlling entry into the market), established prices that insured carrier profitability, and enforced standards for safety and service quality.

This system began to change as governments first deregulated their domestic markets, and then turned their attention to international ones. The USA was the first nation to deregulate its air transportation industry in 1978, based on a series of studies that suggested that regulation often resulted in fares that were 50% higher than those on unregulated routes of similar length. These studies also concluded that regulation forced carriers to accept uneconomical load factors, raised labour costs, protected inefficient carriers and prevented carriers from growing (either internally or through acquisition) and establishing economies of scale that would allow them to lower unit costs (Caves, 1962; Jordan, 1970; Kahn, 1971; Douglas and Miller, 1974).

Beginning in the 1990s, a number of other countries began to initiate air transport deregulation, including Australia (1990), Peru (1990), the UK (1993), Thailand (1995), Kenya (1995) and Morocco (2000). Most, but not all, of these countries experienced a significant increase in capacity following deregulation; however, many have failed to generate new entrants capable of sustaining domestic competition and insuring greater consumer choices and lower fares (Williams, 2002).

Almost as soon as the USA announced plans to deregulate its air transportation industry, it began pursuing a policy designed to create its vision of open international skies for aviation. The US vision sought to create a world where market forces determined fares, capacity, frequency and the number of carriers serving a particular international route. The vision did not include access to domestic market traffic, which would continue to be reserved for 'national carriers'. In the nations of Europe, deregulation and liberalization were carried out more gradually through a series of three packages; the end result would be the establishment of a single aviation market across the entire European Union (Rhoades, 2003).

While governments continue to maintain control over a number of aspects of air transportation, deregulation and the increasing influence of global organizations such as the World Trade Organization limit the level of intervention that can (and does) take place in the industry; market forces now play a much greater role in determining the health of individual carriers and national transportation systems.

Recent Impacts on the Industry

Of the four factors leading to the current 'Perfect Storm', two have historically had a severe impact on air transportation markets – economic recession and war. The other two factors are new – the 9/11 terrorist attacks and SARS.

Economic recession

In the USA, which has experienced the longest period of deregulation, economic recessions in the early years of each decade resulted in industry losses. By the beginning of 2001, the airline industry was already beginning to feel the effects of the latest economic recession. Economic recession exposes the overcapacity in the market, leading to declines in prices as carriers scramble to fill seats and retain market share. Financially weak (or bankrupt) carriers create further downward price pressure in their attempts to generate revenues (Wruck, 1990; Wolf, 1995). The last major recession in 1990–1991 combined with the other perennial enemy of commercial aviation, war (the first Gulf War), to create industry losses in the US alone of over US$10 billion (Rosen, 1995).

These crises led to a variety of responses by the industry. Financial crises in the 1980s led to industry consolidation and the creation of hub-and-spoke systems. In the 1990s, crisis encouraged the development of complex holding structures, the expansion of non-airline services and/or discrete services and the creation of international alliance structures designed to create global seamless service (Rosen, 1995).

In addition to these actions, carriers pursued strategies designed to reduce costs, including eliminating marginal routes, outsourcing non-critical functions or activities, reducing labour costs through lay offs or restructured labour contracts, and reducing the level of services provided to consumers. The result of these reduction efforts was a US airline industry that was more cost competitive than all but several of the lower wage nations of Asia (Oum and Yu, 1993).

War

According to the Air Transport Association (2003), the Gulf War was directly or indirectly responsible for the following problems in US commercial aviation:

- Traffic – down 15% internationally.
- Daily flights – cut by 350, reducing service to hundreds of communities.
- Employment – 25,000 total lost jobs.
- Fuel costs – up 45% for increased costs of US$1.5 billion.
- Net losses – US$13.1 billion over 4 years.
- Bankruptcies – seven carriers filed for bankruptcy, four liquidated.

The Air Transport Association (2003) has estimated that the Iraq War could eventually cost US carriers anywhere from US$10.7 to US$13 billion. These losses would be the result of two key factors – declining passenger traffic and rising fuel prices. Declining passenger traffic often means that carriers fail to meet the breakeven costs of operation. Likewise, fuel costs constitute between 10 and 15% of an airline's cost. It is estimated that every 1 cent increase in the cost of a gallon of fuel costs the airline industry US$180 million; the spot price of jet fuel rose 108% between February 2002 and February 2003, going from 57 cents to US$1.20 a gallon (Air Transport Association, 2003).

9/11

The airplane has long been associated with warfare, but not since the kamikaze pilots of the Second World War have planes been used as the principal weapon in the sense they were used in the 9/11 attack. The shutdown of the US aviation system following 9/11 produced losses for the industry in excess of US$330 million per day (Air Transport Association, 2003). The 'fear factor' immediately following the attacks resulted in a 74% decline in bookings for US carriers in 4 days; international bookings were down 19% (Morrell and Alamdari, 2002).

As aviation insurance and new security taxes soared, carriers struggled to attract passengers (Air Transport Association, 2003). Worldwide monthly traffic figures prior to 9/11 had shown little change over the same period in 2000 despite the beginning of economic slowdown, but figures for the entire year show a drop of 3% in passenger traffic and a 2% drop in passenger load factors (International Civil Aviation Organization, 2002). The North America market still lags behind the rest of the world in terms of passenger and cargo traffic recovery (International Air Transport Association, 2003). American Airlines, the world's largest carrier, announced a modest third-quarter net profit of US$1 million dollars in 2003, its first since 9/11 (Reuters, 2003).

SARS

The area of the world least affected by the 9/11 attacks was Asia. The carriers in this region had recovered from the economic slowdown associated with the financial crisis that swept Asia following the devaluation of the Thai baht, and were predicted to return to pre-financial crisis growth. Unfortunately, SARS resulted in devastating declines in travel to Asia in 2003.

Even months after the initial outbreaks in Hong Kong and China, carriers such as Cathay Pacific were reporting passenger levels at only half of their pre-SARS levels (Asia Pacific Airline Daily, 2003). Overall Asia Pacific traffic figures for August 2003 remained 4.5% below the levels for the previous year (International Air Transport Association, 2003).

Responding to Crisis

The 'Perfect Storm' has provoked responses at all levels of the air transportation system, including national governments, industry, individual carriers and employees.

National governments

In the USA, where carriers were hit hardest by the events of 9/11, the US government provided US$5 billion in direct and immediate aid while making another US$10 billion available for loan guarantees (Morrell and Alamdari, 2002). War has given the US government further reason to support US carriers through the Civil Reserve Aircraft Fleet (CRAF) programme, in which airlines commit their aircraft to support military operations. In exchange for the commitment, the airlines are given access to government markets with over US$2 billion per year in revenue (Graham, 2003). According to the study of Graham, 40% of the revenue comes from Department of Defense's passenger and cargo business, while the remaining 60% is from air travel for government employees travelling on official business. The timely payment of CRAF funds did provide another funding source for cash-strapped carriers. In some ways offsetting this assistance, taxes now levied on a US ticket have risen to an average of US$51.00 (Air Transport Association, 2003).

In Europe, the European Commission approved compensation to carriers for the additional costs of insurance as well as approving actions by several individual member nations to 'assist' their national air carriers. The Commission has also relaxed rules to permit greater coordination between carriers on schedules and fares, and indicated that it would look more favourably on airline mergers. There have been similar moves by various Asian nations to support ailing carriers (Morrell and Alamdari, 2002).

Industry

At the industry level, bankruptcy and consolidation have returned. To date, Scandinavian Airlines (SAS) has received approval to acquire Norwegian carrier Braathens, the merger of Japan Airlines and JAS has been accelerated, Air France and KLM have announced a new holding company, and British Airways has suggested a deal similar to the Air France–KLM arrangement between British Airways and Iberia (Morrell and Alamdari, 2002; Associated Press, 2003). In the USA, US Airways and United entered bankruptcy protection in an effort to reduce costs. With an overall debt load of almost 93% of every dollar, and credit ratings in junk bond territory, the prospects are excellent for further shakeout in the US airline industry (Air Transport Association, 2003). In fact, it appears likely that one or more of the current US carriers will follow legends such as Eastern and Pan Am into liquidation (Zellner and Arndt, 2004).

Airlines

At the individual carrier level, airlines have responded the way they historically have to industry crises; they have cut operating expenses, reduced capacity through flight schedule cutback and aircraft retirement, cut capital expenditures and laid off employees. The only difference between this crisis and previous ones is the magnitude of the downturn and the response. As Morrell and Alamdari (2002) have noted, few carriers have changed their longer term strategy. In fact, 'the major carriers are continuing their strategies of operating as network carriers, assisted by alliance groupings' (Morrell and Alamdari, 2002, p. 19).

Meanwhile, the low cost carriers have accelerated their growth throughout the world by continuing to offer consumers low fares and largely no-frills service. These carriers are projected to represent over 40% of the US market and 25% of the European market within the near future (Binggeli and Pompeo, 2002; Haddad and Zellner, 2002; Velocci, 2002).

Employees

From August 2001 to December 2002, employment in the US airline industry declined by 13% while employment in Europe fell almost 10% (Morrell and Alamdari, 2002; Air Transport Association, 2003). In addition, employees have faced mergers and acquisitions. In a service industry, the impact of stress on employees cannot be ignored.

It is estimated that stress cost US industry as a whole US$150 billion per year in terms of accidents, lost workdays, worker compensations claims and increased health insurance premiums. In a survey by Northwestern National Life, 72% of the participants reported frequent stress-related physical or mental conditions that they believed added to health care costs (Murphy, 1995). The current estimate is that stress causes an average of 16 sick days per year for employees with stress-related illnesses, and contributes to three-quarters of all industrial accidents (Gibson *et al.*, 2003; Hellriegel and Slocum, 2004). The National Institute for Occupational Safety and Health (NIOSH) has listed psychological disorders caused by stress as one of the top ten leading work-related diseases and injuries (Murphy, 1995).

Different Answers

To date, the parties interested in air transportation have responded as they always have to crises, but the long-term success of these responses is questionable. Other possible responses focus on empty core theory, the role of governments, the size of the industry and the shape of the players.

Empty core theory

The airline industry has been cited as an example of Telser's empty core. According to core theory, excess competition in an industry can create a lack of a stable equilibrium. In fact, Telser (1994) has used the word 'chaos' to describe a situation where consumers want and are willing to pay more for a product yet price cutting continues to drive down prices so that few in the industry are making a profit. Various authors have identified conditions under which the core may be empty, including: sizable fixed avoidable costs, large sunk costs, variable demand, discontinuous supply and unrestricted ability to contract and re-contract (Sjostrom, 1989; Pirrong, 1992; Telser, 1994).

All of these conditions exist in the air transportation industry. It must carry large sunk cost investment in aircraft fleet and high avoidable costs, including fuel, labour and maintenance. There are also substantial adjustment costs associated with changing output because of prior commitments to fleet planning. Airline demand varies by season, time of day, day of the week and local events. The cost conditions on the supply side are such that cost per mile falls as the number of miles increases, but distance flown can be increased only by reducing aircraft capacity (payload). In deregulated markets, buyers and sellers are free to enter into contracts without outside interference.

If the core of the airline industry is indeed empty, then one goal of any 'solution' should be to create a stable air transportation system capable of generating long-term sustainable profits. Before a solution can be found, industry players must formulate answers to three key questions. The first question is 'what role should governments play in determining the shape (and creating the stability) of the air transport industry?' The second question is 'how many players should exist in the industry to insure industry stability and consumer benefit?' Finally, 'what should the players look like?'

The role of government

At the extreme, the industry can turn back to the pre-deregulation, pre-liberalization days of the 1950s–1970s. Governments can control domestic air transportation by tightly regulating air carrier entry and exit into the market and into specific routes. Fares can be fixed at levels that ensure 'fair profit' for operating carriers. Service and safety quality standards can be established and enforced. With the exception of the USA, most nations lived with a single 'international' carrier who was partially or fully owned by their government who protected them from international competition by restrictive bilateral air service agreements. These national carriers owned and maintained their own fleet, managed their own employees, operated their own marketing and reservation systems, and performed their own catering; they were a classic vertically integrated firm.

The other extreme would call for governments to pull out of air transport regulation even further, allowing not only more domestic mergers and acquisitions, but also foreign carrier entry and ownership of air carriers. Competition in many markets would increase and inefficient carriers would be allowed to die quickly. Airlines would be free to continue the trend of outsourcing non-essential or non-core functions, retaining only those elements or functions where they saw strategic value and profitability.

The old system did create stability, but at the cost of higher fares and fewer choices. Unfortunately, as the system has moved toward the other end of the spectrum, it has yet to find any long-term stability. Warren Buffet, the Chairman of Berkshire Hathaway and one of the world's most famous investors, has said that he does not invest in aviation because 'the money that has been made since the dawn of aviation by all the country's airline companies was zero. Absolutely zero' (Loomis and Buffet, 1999, p. 219). In an effort to create stability, the industry has used computer reservation systems to 'signal' other sellers and manage revenues. It has created frequent flyer plans to limit re-contracting and fought to increase hub market share, driving out competitions and limiting choice. It has sought to serve international markets while limiting competition through global alliances (Raghavan, 2003). Large carriers have attempted to get larger, then added 'carriers within a carrier' to serve special segments of the population (Delta and Song, British Airways and Go, Qantas and Australian). Whether an industry further freed from government interference could find stability is questionable.

Industry size

The question about the number of players is also a question about size. Does size confer certain advantages to a competitor? It is believed that expanding the operation of a firm could lower its cost of doing business by creating economies of scale. Economies of scale can also act as a barrier to entry by forcing 'the entrant to enter at a large scale, risking forceful retaliation from incumbents or to come in at a small scale, usually in a niche market but at a cost disadvantage' (Levine, 1987). Economies of scale can be derived from technological, managerial, financial, marketing, commercial, and research and development sources (Bized, 2002). Size can also create complexity – vertically, horizontally and geographically. It can become a disadvantage if a firm lives in a rapidly changing environment with younger, faster competitors (Ashkenas *et al.*, 1995; Galbraith, 1995). There are also economies of scope that result when resources can be shared across units or activities, and economies of density or growth that allow better utilization (O'Connor, 2001).

Shape of the players

Economies of scope or density-directed growth rather than simply an overall increase in size is one option. There is some research that shows that consumers generally favour an airline that serves a large number of cities (Tretheway and Oum, 1992). Hence, airlines must expand to serve more cities themselves or enter into alliances to serve them by extension. Yet, why should a consumer care if 'their airline' serves 500 cities when they only want to go to ten of these cities? Is the idea of having access to 500 cities worth the additional fare for flying a large, international carrier over a smaller regional carrier who serves the ten cities normally visited?

Vertically integrated companies also tend to be large; their size is a function of the decision to own rather than contract out for the resources and services necessary to create their product or service. Decoupling is the reverse of the vertically integrated model. It is based on the notion that firms will choose an activity in the value chain that they perform best, based on expertise, knowledge or strategic vision, and outsource the remaining activities to other firms who have made similar choices (Galbraith, 1995). In a decoupled world, it would be possible to have a virtual airline.

- The virtual airline owns no aircraft – they are leased.
- The virtual airline employs no cockpit or cabin crew – they too are leased.
- The virtual airline has no engineering facility – maintenance is contracted out.
- The virtual airline does no ground handling – that too is contracted out.
- The virtual airline also contracts out accounting and reservations and may use electronic ticketing (International Civil Aviation Organization, 1997).

What is left of the 'airline' in such a system might be nothing more than a small corporate office whose task would be to coordinate the activities of the airline. Of course, a virtual airline cannot exist without firms willing to undertake each of the separate activities and do so on a scale to match the 'airlines' demand.

The Maintenance Repair and Overhaul (MRO) industry is experiencing a wave of consolidation and focusing on ways to lure away in-house MRO activities (Croft, 2003; Phillips, 2003). The Internet is changing the face of airline distribution with a new breed of consolidators such as Expedia whose forecasted 2003 growth was projected to be 55% (Mullaney and Grover, 2003). If consolidators can make more headway in the business class market, then airlines might be relegated to selling a few 'walk-up' tickets. Aircraft leasing is an increasingly popular option for airlines. If leasing companies could also be convinced to handle aircraft fuel, then individual carriers could potentially be freed of three of their largest expenses – aircraft, fuel and distribution.

The remaining major cost is labour. Unfortunately, this may be the most difficult issue to solve given the very likely resistance of labour unions and employee groups. Airlines remain heavily unionized and most carriers have a history of contentious labour relations. While Southwest Airlines has an excellent history of cooperation, the record at other carriers leaves much to be desired. So while it would seem that the industry could benefit from genuine efforts to increase productivity and reduce costs, these are unlikely to occur (Blasi and Gasaway, 1995; Wever, 1995). In short, it is relatively easy to imagine a start-up carrier as a virtual airline; it is difficult to imagine a carrier the size of United Airlines as a virtual carrier or to envisage a path that would take it from traditional carrier to virtual.

Conclusion

The confluence of war, recession, terrorist attacks and SARS has created what many in the media and the air transport industry are calling the worst crisis in aviation history; but debate is raging over what can and should be done to protect individual carriers, employees, local/national/international customers, travel-related business and broad national economies. In truth, if we define organizational crisis as 'a low-probability, high-impact event that threatens the viability of the organization and is characterized by ambiguity of cause, effect, and means of resolution as well as by a belief that decisions must be made swiftly' (Pearson and Clair, 1998, p. 60), then perhaps the current events do not qualify.

Certainly, the so-called legacy carriers who trace their roots back to the early days of aviation do not appear to be experiencing any ambiguity over how to resolve their problems; they are responding to this crisis the way they have always responded to crisis – tighten your belt, cut out more costs even at the expense of service quality, and hope to outlast your competitors. The question is whether these historic responses will be enough.

Dorothy Leonard-Barton (1992) has outlined another way to examine the capabilities and possibilities of firms and industries; she looks at the ability of firms to change and adapt to new conditions in markets or technology. According to Leonard-Barton (1992), a firm that is unable to adapt to changing conditions because of its attachment to core practices and customers is suffering from core rigidity. This concept is different from the economic notion of empty core, but no less damning. Responding to a crisis of this magnitude may well require individual carriers and the industry as a whole to re-examine the basic tenets under which they and it have operated for decades.

While the traditional carriers are engaged in their standard response to crisis, low cost carriers around the globe are gaining ground as never before. James Hlavacek, Executive Vice President and Chief Operations Officer of ATA Airlines, has even suggested that in the foreseeable future there will be only one class of service in the US domestic markets

(Hlavacek, 2003). Where this vision leaves the traditional, international carriers is less certain, as is the effect of such a shift on the larger travel and tourism industry. It could lead to major expansions in passenger traffic and open opportunities for traditional and online firms to consolidate the travel experience, or it could continue to depress an industry that is vital to the economies of many nations.

These questions, as well as questions such as how carriers will respond to future crises such as the avian flu as the next potential SARS-like crisis, must be addressed. Crises can be managed much more effectively if there is a plan for dealing with them; the core of crisis resolution is sensing potential problems before they happen through the use of strategic forecasting, contingency planning, issues analysis and scenario analysis, rather than simply reacting to them after they occur (Kash and Darling, 1998).

References

Air Transport Association (2003) *Airlines in Crisis: the Perfect Economic Storm*. Air Transport Association of America, Washington, DC.

Ashkenas, R., Ulrich, D., Jick, T. and Kerr, S. (1995) *The Boundaryless Organization: Breaking the Chains of Organizational Structure*. Jossey-Bass Publishers, San Francisco, California.

Asia Pacific Airline Daily Centre for Asia Pacific Aviation (2003) Cathay Pacific, <www.centreforaviation.com> (accessed 10 June 2004).

Associated Press (2003) British Airways chief says merger with Iberia is possible. 5 October, press release,

Binggeli, U. and Pompeo, L. (2002) Hyped hopes for Europe's low-cost airlines. *The Mckinsey Quarterly* 4, electronic version.

Bized (2002) Economies of Scale, <www.bized.ac.uk> (accessed 11 July 2004).

Blasi, J. and Gasaway, J. (1995) The great experiment: labor–management cooperation at Eastern Airlines. In: Cappelli, P. (ed.) *Airline Labour Relations in the Global Era: the New Frontier*. ILR Press, Cornell, New York, pp. 184–200.

Caves, R. (1962) *Air Transport and Its Regulators: an Industry Study*. Harvard University Press, Cambridge, Massachusetts.

Croft, J. (2003) A business in need of repairs. *Air Transport World*, pp. 40–45.

Department of Transportation (2000) *Air Travel Consumer Report*. DOT Office of Consumer Affairs, Washington, DC.

Douglas, G.W. and Miller, J.C. (1974) *Economic Regulation of Domestic Air Transport: Theory and Policy*. The Brookings Institution, Washington, DC.

Fraser, D. (1996) A personal approach, airline. *Business*, pp. 58–61.

Gahan, M. (2002) Aviation's Continuing Crisis, BBC News Online, 13 August. <www.bbcnews.com> (accessed 11 July 2004).

Galbraith, J.R. (1995) *Designing Organizations: an Executive Briefing on Strategy, Structure, and Process*. Jossey-Bass Publishers, San Francisco, California.

Gibson, J., Ivancevich, J., Donnelly, J. and Konopaske, R. (2003) *Organizations: Behavior, Structure, Processes*. McGraw-Hill Irwin, Boston, Massachusetts.

Graham, D. (2003) *Sustaining the Civil Reserve Air Fleet Program*. Institute for Defense Analysis, Washington, DC.

Haddad, C. and Zellner, W. (2002) Getting down and dirty with the discounters. *Business Week* 28 October, pp. 76–77.

Hellriegel, D. and Slocum, J. (2004) *Organizational Behavior*. South-Western College Publishing, Canada.

Hlavacek, J. (2003) Keynote presentation, Aviation Suppliers Association Annual Meeting, 23–24 June, Naples, Florida.

International Air Transport Association (2003) Traffic recovery trend confirmed in August, Press Release, International Air Transport Association.

International Civil Aviation Organization (1997) *Launch of the Strategic Action Plan 1997.* 22 May, ICAO, pp. 1–9.

International Civil Aviation Organization (2002) Events of 11 September had Strong Negative Impact on Airline Financial Results for 2001. Press Release, International Civil Aviation Organization.

Jordan, W.A. (1970) *Airline Regulation in America: Effects and Imperfections.* Johns Hopkins University Press, Baltimore, Maryland.

Kahn, A.E. (1971) *The Economics of Regulation.* Wiley, New York.

Kash, T. and Darling, J. (1998) Crisis management: prevention, diagnosis, and intervention. *Leadership and Organization Development Journal* 19, 179–186.

Leonard-Barton, D. (1992) Core capabilities and core rigidities. *Strategic Management Journal* 13, 111–125.

Levine, M.E. (1987) Airline competition in deregulated markets: theory, firm strategy, and national regulatory policy. *The Yale Law Journal* 74, 1416–1447.

Loomis, C. and Buffet, W. (1999) Mr. Buffet on the stock market. *Fortune* 140, 212–220.

Morrell, P.S. and Alamdari, F. (2002) *The Impact of 11 September on the Aviation Industry: Traffic, Capacity, Employment, and Restructuring.* International Labour Office, Geneva.

Mullaney, T.J. and Grover, R. (2003) The web mogul. *Business Week* 13 October, pp. 62–70.

Murphy, L. (1995) Managing job stress: an employee assistance/human resource management partnership. *Personnel Review* 24, 41–50.

O'Connor, W.E. (2001) *An Introduction to Airline Economics*, 6th edn. Praeger, Westport, Connecticut.

Oum, T.H. and Yu, C. (1993) *Winning Airlines: Productivity and Cost Competitiveness of the World's Major Airlines.* Kluwer Academic Publishers, Boston, Massachusetts.

Pearson, C.M. and Clair, J.A. (1998) Reframing crisis management. *Academy of Management Review* 23, 59–76.

Phillips, E.H. (2003) MRO in transition. *Aviation Week and Space Technology* 14 April, pp. 64–66.

Pirrong, S.C. (1992) An application of core theory to the analysis of ocean shipping markets. *Journal of Law and Economics* 25, 89–131.

Raghavan, S. (2003) Application of core theory to the airline industry. Paper presented at the Air Transportation Research Society Conference, Toulouse, France, 12–15 July.

Reuters (2003) AMR narrows 3Q loss. *CNNMoney*, 22 October.

Rhoades, D.L. (2003) *Evolution of International Aviation: Phoenix Rising.* Ashgate Publishing, Aldershot, UK.

Rosen, S.D. (1995) Corporate restructuring: a labour perspective. In: Cappelli, P. (ed.) *Airline Labour Relations in the Global Era: the New Frontier.* ILR Press, Cornell, New York, pp. 31–40.

Sjostrom, W. (1989) Collusion in ocean shipping: a test of monopoly and empty core models. *Journal of Political Economy* 97, 1160–1179.

Telser, L.G. (1994) The usefulness of core theory in economics. *Journal of Economic Perspectives* 8, 151–164.

Tretheway, M.W. and Oum, T.H. (1992) *Airline Economics: Foundation for Strategy and Policy.* The Centre for Transportation Studies, University of British Columbia, Canada.

Velocci, A.I. (2002) Can majors shift focus fast enough to survive? *Aviation Week and Space Technology* 18 November, pp. 52–54.

Wever, K.S. (1995) Revisiting the labour–management partnership. In: Cappelli, P. (ed.) *Airline Labour Relations in the Global Era: the New Frontier.* ILR Press, Cornell, New York, pp. 164–183.

Williams, G. (2002) *Airline Competition: Deregulation's Mixed Legacy.* Ashgate, Aldershot, UK.

Wolf, S.M. (1995) Where do we go from here: a management perspective. In:

Cappelli, P. (ed.) *Airline Labour Relations in the Global Era: the New Frontier.* ILR Press, Cornell, New York, pp. 18–23.

World Tourism Organization (2002) Facts and Figures, <www.worldtourism.org/marketresearch/factsandfigure> (accessed 4 April 2003).

Wruck, K.H. (1990) Financial distress, reorganization, and organizational efficiency. *Journal of Financial Economics* 27, 419–444.

Zellner, W. and Arndt, M. (2004,) Big airlines: not much runaway left. *Business Week* 4 July, p. 50.

19 Responding to the Crises of 2001: the Australian Experience

BARBARA ANDERSON, BRUCE PRIDEAUX AND GRAHAM BROWN

Laws and Prideaux (2005) define the term 'crisis', as it applies to tourism, as an event of any magnitude that disrupts the orderly operation of the tourism industry. In recent years, the impact of crisis and crises has received increasing attention from scholars; however, broadly agreed methods of coping with crisis remain elusive. The size of the impact of a crisis often depends on the location, magnitude and type of the event(s) that precipitate the crisis. Effects of a crisis will not necessarily be felt equally by all those affected and it is often possible to identify winners as well as losers in any crisis situation. For example, a hurricane that devastates coastal tourism resorts in Florida will be viewed as a disaster by the industry in Florida but may be a boon for operators in California if they can persuade travellers to substitute California for Florida. In a business sense, there are a large number of possible implications of crises, ranging from negative to positive impacts.

This chapter reports on the findings of research undertaken in 2002 to investigate the impacts of three major crises on firms servicing Australia's tourism industry. Factors that either moderated or exacerbated the effects of these crises were identified together with the short- and medium-term responses made by participating organizations. Other aspects investigated include the broader operating environment, the nature of organizational learning that had taken place and a comparison of the events of 2001 with other 'crises' experienced by the industry. The study is significant as there has been little previous research carried out as to the manner in which organizations have responded to such events.

Extraordinary events, defined as crises, in the external environment present challenges that force tourism operators to respond quickly in order to maximize business opportunities or minimize losses. Externally generated crises are unforeseen and may suddenly engulf organizations (Booth, 1996). In 2001, the Australian tourism industry faced three major crises, the failure of the HIH Insurance Company, the World Trade Center attacks on 11 September 2001 (9/11) and the almost simultaneous collapse of Ansett Airlines, on 14 September 2001. HIH was a major Australian insurance company dealing in liability insurance, while Ansett Airlines was Australia's second largest domestic airline and owner of Traveland, a large national chain of retail travel agents. The collapse of Ansett disrupted airline travel for months and severely reduced capacity into a number of destinations such as Cairns and the Whitsundays. While the events themselves were not related, their consequences were, and posed threats to the viability of numerous organizations. Thus while the collapse of HIH and the World Trade Center attack shared no common cause, their combined impact on insurance premiums was significant. The impact of these crises was often determined by particular operators' market focus. Thus while destinations and firms reliant on international passengers suffered a decline as a result of 9/11, other firms not trading in the international market were relatively sheltered unless they were affected by the collapse of Ansett Airlines (Prideaux, 2004).

Prior to the crises of 2001, Australian tourism operators had suffered a number of external crises such as the Asian Financial Crisis, the first Gulf War and before that the oil crisis of the 1970s. The only major domestic crises that had significant impacts on tourism were the 1989 pilots' strike which resulted in the curtailment of most domestic air services for a period of several months, and the recession of 1991.

Review of the Literature

It has previously been stated that terrorist incidents such as the World Trade Center attack may have significant impacts on tourist behaviour. Faulkner (2001) observed that tourists have become soft targets and are at risk from hijacking and terrorism. Other studies have shown that tourists substitute risky destinations with safer choices, demonstrate a delayed reaction to terrorism and exhibit cultural differences in their reactions to risk (Sonmez, 1998, pp. 427–428). For example, as a result of terrorist activity in 1985, 1.8 million Americans changed their foreign travel plans the following year (Sonmez and Graefe, 1998). Consequences of terrorism may include a decline in visitor flows and an increase in costs, particularly from the provision of additional security measures and increased insurance premiums. The collapse of airlines and other transport operators also affects visitor flows particularly when capacity into destinations is reduced. When a number of crises occur in a very short time period, the collective impacts may be greater than the individual impacts as effects cascade through the industry and influence consumer confidence.

In response to a crisis, firms are forced to make urgent management decisions that are not part of the organization's normal operating procedures. Pearson and Mitroff (1993, p. 59) suggested that 'the purpose of crisis management is not to produce a set of plans; it is to prepare an organization to think creatively about the unthinkable so that the best possible decisions will be made in time of crisis'. Faulkner (2001) suggests that good management means having strategies for coping with unexpected events over which organizations have no control. Crisis situations also mean that reliable information has to be obtained and valuable resources have to be protected and effectively used (Heath, 1998).

Crises of the nature of those that occurred in 2001 create critical periods of learning readiness in organizations. This period of learning has three phases: defensiveness, openness and forgetfulness. When faced with a crisis, managers and employees may feel defensive and be moved to protect themselves. However, once the immediate threat or incident has passed, they may be open to understanding their organization's vulnerabilities and to assessing its performance in managing the crisis. It is in this phase of openness when most learning can take place. However, the extent to which organizational members are open to learning and the duration of this phase are largely dependent on the behaviour of senior management. After the crisis, operations must be restored as soon as possible. The sense of urgency that motivates a desire for change is often lost at this point, and all the superficial learning is forgotten (Kovoor-Misra and Nathan, 2000, p. 32). These authors suggest that 'healthy forgetfulness involves moving on, but only after the necessary lessons have been learned'.

Senior managers play a critical role in determining the extent to which their organizations learn from a crisis. Strategies that are often employed by these managers include the minimization of defensiveness, the avoidance of laying blame and focusing on the lessons to be learnt; leading by example; and building of trust between managers and employees (Kovoor-Misra and Nathan, 2000).

Although there is the potential to learn from crises, it is apparent that many organizations do not incorporate such learning in their standard operating procedures (Kovoor-Misra and Nathan, 2000; Roux-Dufort, 2000). Roux-Dufort (2000, p. 26) suggests that 'the organization's priority is to come back and maintain the status quo as soon as possible, rather than exploring the extent to which the crisis is a privileged moment during which to understand things differently'. Confirming this view, Henderson (1999) reports that the results of a survey of leading tourist attractions in Singapore investigating the consequences of the Asian financial crisis indicated that there was no crisis management planning although there was a need for such planning. This finding confirms the observation made by Cassedy (1991) that many tourism organizations do not include the possibility of disasters in their strategic plans.

One of the difficulties facing organizations has been the lack of theory development and, where available, the ability to implement it. Faulkner's work is one of the few tourism models developed to guide crisis management. Moreover, there are only a few examples of researchers probing other literatures for new theory on crisis management (Prideaux *et al.*, 2003).

This brief literature review highlights the volatile environment in which many tourism organizations operate. While extraordinary events are becoming a routine part of everyday business, there is little evidence that organizations have learnt from past events and incorporate crisis management planning in their normal business plans. A further difficulty faced by many firms is that corporate knowledge is lost when managers familiar with crisis management leave.

Methodology

To identify the methods adopted by managers to deal with the crises of 2001, the authors of this chapter undertook a series of interviews with senior managers of a range of tourism companies in Australia. The respondents represented organizations in a range of tourism sectors, including, accommodation, business tourism, entertainment, tourism management and transportation (including car hire and tour operators) at a number of representative locations throughout Australia (Adelaide (A), Alice Springs (AS), Sydney (S), Melbourne (M), Cairns (C) and the Gold Coast (GC)). By conducting interviews in different sectors of the tourism industry and at a number of locations, an understanding of how a variety of tourism operators in a number of destinations around Australia responded to the events of 2001 could be ascertained. A profile of the interviewees is found in Table 19.1.

Some of these organizations had operations in more than one sector and geographical location. The interviews, lasting between 30 and 45 min, were audio-taped and later transcribed. Interviewees' names have been changed to preserve their anonymity when quoted. At the end of each quotation, the following information is provided as follows: (pseudonym of interviewee, tourism sector, location: total number of employees when provided).

The semi-structured interview research design was adopted in preference to the more common quantitative survey approach as it allowed respondents to discuss their views on a range of issues and it also allowed the researchers to probe for additional information where appropriate. As a consequence, quantitative tables are not provided; rather responses are

Table 19.1. Profile of interviewees.

Industry sector	Adelaide	Alice Springs	Melbourne	Sydney	Cairns	Gold Coast
Accommodation	2	3			3	
Business tourism	2	1	1		1	
Entertainment						2
Tourism management		1				
Transportation	4	3	1	2	1	2
Total	8	8	2	2	5	4

reported either in full or in part, and verbatim, to give the reader a greater insight into the views of the respondent. For the purposes of this chapter, many of the responses are abridged and because of space constraints others are not reported.

It should also be acknowledged that the nature of the responses is partly determined by the positions/responsibilities of the interviewees. As the majority of interviewees were either general managers or sales and marketing executives, it is recognized that their responses to some questions, for example the impact of the collapse of HIH Insurance Company, may be different from those that may have been provided by finance managers. It should also be mentioned that the phenomenon of 'self-presentation' was observable amongst a number of interviewees. General, broad, sanitized answers were frequently given.

Interview Findings and Discussion

The semi-structured interviews provided rich sources of data. The analysis of these data revealed that the impact of the events of 2001 on organizations had been influenced by a variety of factors, which included patterns of demand, nature of the market and business alliances. Organizations adopted a variety of short-term responses to the impact of these events, which included information gathering, financial, marketing and human resource strategies. The medium-term responses focused on financial and marketing initiatives. On the basis of this preliminary analysis, a conceptual framework for data analysis and discussion was developed (see Fig. 19.1).

The analysis of the interview findings commences with the identification of the range of factors that influenced the impact of the events of 2001 on participating organizations. The actual impacts of these events on the participants in the study are then examined. The short- and medium-term responses to these events are outlined. The broader operating environment is then discussed in terms of the role of organizational policies in these responses; the organization learning which has taken place and comparisons of the events of 2001; perceived benefits of these events to the tourism industry; and comparison with other crises experienced by the tourism industry.

Factors influencing the impact of events of 2001

The complexity of the environment in which tourism organizations operate is highlighted by the variety of factors that influenced the impact of the events of 2001. These factors, discussed below, have been identified as:

- The patterns of demand (seasonality).
- The market mix.

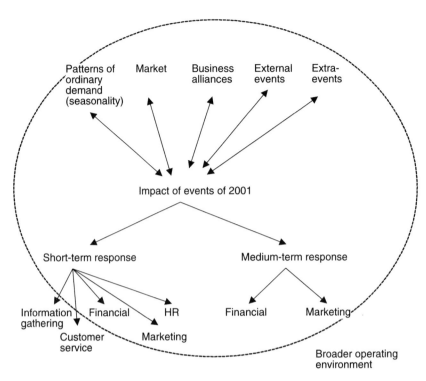

Fig. 19.1. Conceptual framework for data analysis and discussion.

- The nature of business alliances.
- Other external events.
- Business-specific events.

The patterns of demand (seasonality)

The pattern of demand at the time of any crisis will moderate or exacerbate the impact that is felt. The normal seasonal variations in Australia meant that the events of September 2001 impacted differently on organizations represented in this study. For example, the effects of 11 and 14 September were moderated in one hotel in Adelaide, and the hotel manager indicated that there had been no retrenchment of staff as the events had occurred at a busy time. However, a car hire manager in Cairns reported that: 'because it [Ansett collapse] fell on the school holidays period and ... I might have lost 20% or 15–20% of the business ... for that 10 day period' (Trent, car hire, C: 4). In contrast, an Adelaide transportation manager suggested that it was unfortunate that these events had coincided with their peak season, meaning that extra casual staff had to be used to cope with the increased demand. A hotel manager in Cairns discussing the impact of these events in the following months, mentioned that 'October, November and most cases, to December, was tough, and then to add to the problem, its a general consumer perception in Australia that you don't come to North Queensland during the summer months' (Nigel, accommodation, C).

The market mix

Certain segments of the international tourist market were more affected by 11 September than other sectors, as reflected in these comments:

> ... Sept 11, with that and then Ansett, for us, for the Japan market, it was a very big hit, because over November, December, January, that 4–5 month period, is when the bulk of Japanese and China groups move, especially school groups, all of that was cancelled overnight. 99% of that was cancelled basically within 3 weeks of Sept 11 and Sept 14 with Ansett.
>
> (Martin, charter company, S: 500)

> ... after Sept 11th, a lot of airfares dropped in the States and domestically to get people moving, if you're just a back-packer or an independent traveller, a lot of people see that as a good opportunity to travel, whereas groups won't touch that with a barge pole ... .
>
> (Martin, coach company, S: 500)

Differing responses to 11 September between the Japanese and American, and European markets were acknowledged by another interviewee:

> We also ran an international conference a week after [11 September], ... it was interesting to see the segmentation that in fact didn't turn up. All the European contingent turned up, in traditional style. Asia and America ... there were very large withdrawals ... .
>
> (Trevor, business tourism, M: 500)

The impact of different markets on tourism destinations was clearly demonstrated in tropical north Queensland.

> About 50% of the business going to Port [Douglas] would be domestic. The other 50% was split between Europe and USA, so of course as soon as September 11 hit, we then found that the in-bound traffic from North America dried up as did most of the in-bound traffic from Europe. The problem was exacerbated for the ... traffic that continued to flow be it at a much-reduced rate, is that once they got to Australia, they couldn't get around ... Qantas just couldn't up-lift, and there just wasn't enough capacity.
>
> (Nigel, accommodation, C)

The importance of having an appropriate mix of markets is under-scored in the following comment:

> If we'd have been dealing with just Japan market, which we were 10 years ago, ... we would have probably been out of business now, ... but fortunately the domestic market, (has) grown enough in the last 3 or 4 years to cover the drop from the in-bound market in the last 12 months.
>
> (Martin, coach company, S: 500)

Business alliances

While the value of trade alliances/preferred provider relationships have been widely endorsed, some alliances compounded the negative effects of the collapse of suppliers such as Ansett Airlines. Brad (tour operator, M) stated that the flow-on effects of the collapse of Traveland group of companies caused a significant loss of business. Similarly Pat (tour operator, GC: 100) stated that her business was seriously impacted because several of her clients' clients had cut deals with Ansett.

Business-specific events

Several interviewees reported that they only experienced minimal impacts from the events of 2001 due to unique situations in their own organizations.

Ian (accommodation, AS: 350) was not affected because the business was undergoing rebuilding, while Ray (entertainment, GC) had ceased the business relationship with Ansett 18 months before the airlines collapse and suffered only limited impacts.

In normal periods, seasonal variations may either moderate or exacerbate the effects of the events such as 2001. The nature of the market mix and existing business alliances also influenced the impact of these events. External events, such as the economic down-turn in the USA and Europe, were also considered to have compounded the impact of 9/11. In some cases, business-specific events moderated the impact of these events.

The impact of events of 2001

There was general agreement among interviewees that the demise of Ansett Airlines had the greatest impact on their organizations, while the collapse of the HIH Insurance Company was reported as having the least short-term effect impact. Interviewees' responses also highlight the interdependence between various sectors of the tourism industry, such as accommodation, business and leisure tourism.

> ... Ansett was ... 2 things – it was a customer to us, but it was also a ... way for people to get to South Australia, that's suddenly turned off.
>
> (Stuart, tour operator, A: 3)

> From the Ansett collapse and then World Trade Center, the conferencing market was affected, we found that the room blocks that we had for places like the Convention Center were shrinking, ...
>
> (Michael, accommodation, A: 130)

> Ansett ... had one of the biggest effects to our business, simply because, Sept 11 ... created big changes to international travel, and people wanting to go overseas for their holidays, so we naturally assumed that we'd change our direction ... to domestic side of the holidays. But the Ansett collapse had major implications for us, first of all, because, we couldn't get the seats we wanted. ...
>
> (Peter, transportation and tours, A: 6)

Other interviewees suggested that the events of September 2001 had equal impact. A hotel manager in Adelaide indicated that the two events compounded each other, meaning that business was affected severely.

A number of interviewees reported an increase in business immediately following the collapse of Ansett Airlines, although this was often short-lived.

> Ansett was interesting because, for the first 6–8 weeks after the collapse, we acted as a substitute to airlines, which is not normally our role, because we're too slow for that. But we were jam packed for those 6–8 weeks after Sept 13th, the Ansett crash.
>
> (Lachlan, transportation, A: 300)

> We found that September 14 was more of an impact than September 11, in the immediate sense. Post-September 14, for the first month, or the first part, we went from having a quiet September, to having an extremely busy September, and an extremely busy beginning of October.
>
> (David, car hire, AS: 8)

> so that's just something to adjust to … .
>
> (Renata, tour operator, S)

Short-term responses

A sense of helplessness was detected in the one interviewee's short-term response to these events, 'just pulled our hair out, played more golf, there was nothing we could do' (Trent, car hire, C: 4). However, in responding to these events, a number of interviewees acknowledged the need to be flexible, as can be judged from these comments:

> And, and our requirement at that time … was to become flexible, to not hold clients responsible when numbers drop and they did come, and not hold them responsible for contractual obligations as normally … they would prevail. We'd say, we'll go work with you, until we all find we're back to normal.
>
> (Trevor, business tourism, M: 500)

> … one lesson out of those 2 events was that … we need to have that flexibility to be able to … turn or make some changes with the direction of the company … .
>
> (Paul, accommodation and tours, S)

> … if a business can't act quickly, then you're not going to be there. And I think it's a cultural thing … that is something that has to be embedded in the culture of the company … .
>
> (Renata, tour operator, S)

The short-term responses made by organizations generally focused on information gathering, the maintenance of customer service and a range of financial, human resource and marketing strategies. The need for responses to be made on the basis of accurate information was highlighted by a number of interviewees:

I think it took quite a while before people came to terms with what was a reasonable strategy and quite some time, for me, was anything up to 2–3 weeks. I think people … reacted like a lot of us, too quickly, in trying to, trying to assess this and the following scenario within the next 7–8 days … I don't think anyone would have been able to give you a reasonable opinion within seven days … .

(Trevor, business tourism, M: 500)

first one was to rapidly … increase our intelligence-gathering information, so to ensure that the decisions we were making were based on fact, not on reaction. Two, we always have immediate response plans, and those immediate response plans happened automatically. So as a result, short-term, not a lot, on the basis that we don't want to be acting from fear, we want to be acting from certainty.

(Ray, entertainment, GC)

well the very first thing we had to do was to try to establish what effect it was going to have on those traditional feeder markets because it caught us totally unawares.

(Nigel, accommodation, C)

Customer service

There was recognition of the need to provide excellent customer service during these troubled times:

the first reaction after Ansett, just really making sure that we were on one hand, looking after people, and secondly, just not exposed to any of the extra costs that we would have done, caused by cancellations.

(Stuart, transportation, A: 3)

There was absolutely nothing we could do … we had a look at all our bookings and we found out … if they were Ansett reservations, we never cancelled them, we kept those bookings for those people … we tried to look after our customers, which at the end of the day, was also looking after selfishly our interests, as well.

(Mark, car hire, AS: 9)

The first thing we did, we reacted by trying to reassure everybody that it was OK, e-mail, direct telephone calls and we actually got over and met our clients … .

(Reg, business tourism, A)

Financial, human resource and marketing responses

Organizations, irrespective of size, sector and location, responded to these events by adopting a range of financial, human resource and marketing strategies. Budgets were closely scrutinized and costs reduced wherever possible, as seen in the following comments:

We also took the view that if there was a reduction in the business that was coming through the door, obviously we would review our costs and review our staffing levels.

> (Michael, accommodation, A: 130)

... we sat back and tried to re-evaluate what was going to happen. Did a number of things in the fleet levels and costings and things like that. Like any business that realises that life's going to be tough, you start to look at ... everything.

> (Mark, car hire, AS: 9)

from an organization point of view, it [September 11/14] really was just a rallying point ... to go back in and re-look at our strategies and our forecasts and our budgets, and really try and break it down to a very short term, you know, almost 3 month, quarterly focus, so we really look at the quarter, um, now as a result, rather than in the longer term.

> (Paul, accommodation and tours, S)

the short-term was like a lot of businesses, we battened down the hatches, we pulled out the budgets and looked at our costs and made adjustments where possible. ... So we contained costs.

> (Brad, tour operator, M)

... we cut back a lot of expenses, quite viciously ... we cancelled all sorts of things, the management took a cut, 20% pay cut ... and went on to a very stringent, low cost budget.

> (Renata, tour operator, S)

In the area of staffing, there was a widespread reluctance to retrench staff as it was acknowledged they would be needed when the industry recovered from its decline.

we tried to cut costs as much as possible ... the first thing that comes to mind is retrenchment which we wouldn't do, we tried to push people out on holidays.

> (Martin, coach company, S: 500)

Nobody lost their job, and ... that's why the management volunteered to take a 20% pay cut, because they wanted to have their staff there, so that when business picked up, they wouldn't have lost all crucial staff ... .

> (Renata, tour operator, S)

management team got together and said, in terms of staffing, first, well last on, first off. ...

> (Pat, tour operator, GC: 100)

Many interviewees acknowledged the importance of keeping staff informed of what was happening and involved them in decision making about employment options:

[w]e kept them very much informed of what was going on within the market. I also made a commitment to them that ... there would not be any knee-jerk reactions to what was transpiring and that we would keep them informed as to what ... .

> (Michael, accommodation, A: 130)

> I spoke to my staff and I had 2 choices, either put some off ... or cut back their hours.
>
> (Peter, transportation, A: 6)

> We did not have to go through a redundancy programme in any way, shape or form ... it takes a long time to get them (staff) being a very important person for our clients.
>
> (Trevor, business tourism: 500)

Cairns, which experienced a 27–30% increase in tourism as a result of the events of September 2001, was the exception:

> In fact, we had to up-man, because we had more Japanese ... and it seems quite strange to say, but we had one of the strongest years this year, than what we've had for about the last four years.
>
> (Nigel, accommodation, C)

Differing marketing strategies were adopted by organizations in response to the events of September 2001. Some organizations reduced their marketing budgets and activities. For example, a hotel manager in Adelaide indicated that there was no point in advertising. Other made reductions in their marketing budgets (Brad, tour operator, M). However, other organizations increased their activities in response to these events. Lachlan (transportation, A: 300) increased his advertising budget to attract more domestic customers. Nigel (accommodation, C) increased his marketing budget in North America and into Europe, to see if more interest could be generated in Cairns.

While formal business alliances had, in some cases, exacerbated the effects of the Ansett collapse, informal alliances or trade relationships were used by a number of interviewees to market their products as effectively as possible. Brad (tour operator, M) brought more partners into his firm's marketing to spread the cost. Paul (accommodation and tours, S) increased his firm's focus on trade channels and trade relationships to ensure that his product was sold widely. Another operator (Renata, tour operator, S) introduced a new product to the domestic market.

A number of interviewees recognized the need to change their marketing strategies and to protect their existing clientele. For example, several organizations quickly focused on the drive market:

> ... we immediately deployed the same selling strategies as we deployed during the pilots' dispute, where we quickly went to the drive market ... .
>
> (Ray, entertainment, GC)

> ... in November, ... we did a market analysis and we changed our total market direction overnight ... we built a prison wall around our 60% repeat factor, client base, so we protected that first ... .
>
> (Douglas, business tourism, A: 600)

Many organizations recognized the need for flexibility and the maintenance of excellent customer service, focused on gathering appropriate information to enable them to make sound decisions as to financial, human resource and marketing strategies to be adopted in response to these events.

Medium-term responses

The medium-term responses adopted by the majority of interviewees focused on sales and marketing strategies, such as maintaining current marketing strategies, heavy promotional activities and changing markets:

> I think this year's the medium and we're certainly seeing a slump – sales and marketing is really, really the key to it.
>
> (Stuart, transportation, A: 3)

> I think if you've got sound sales marketing strategies in place, you just continue with those … .
>
> (Michael, accommodation, A: 130)

> from our sales and marketing point of view, is just to maintain that presence in the brochures, particularly in the international markets, … .
>
> (Paul, accommodation and tours S)

Several interviewees reported changing their market focus:

> It's just a matter of re-directing where we spend our marketing dollars, like there's no use marketing much in America, 'cause they're not flying.
>
> (Mark, car hire, AS: 9)

> … we're aiming more at the local market, we had actually looked at trying to do the short haul market, being Singapore, Malaysia, but with Bali, that's put a hold on that area … so we're looking more at domestic.
>
> (David, car rental, A: 8)

Once again, the importance of organizational flexibility was highlighted:

> … I think the key issue is … actually based upon our strategic framework … in other words, what is our business doing relative to the market?
>
> (Ray, entertainment, GC)

Hence, medium-term responses focused on the use of appropriate sales and marketing strategies.

Broader operating environment

A number of aspects of the broader operating environment were discussed with interviewees. These aspects included the role of organizational policies in guiding responses to the events of 2001; the organizational learning which had taken place; and the perceived benefits, if any, to the tourism industry of these events.

One interviewee acknowledged the need for plans in the following comment: 'I just think that businesses the size of ours have to have plans in place, because in fact, that [crises] happens everyday, all you're looking at is the magnitude' (Ray, entertainment, GC). Another interviewee commented: 'I don't think anybody could have planned what they were going to do … being honest, … we literally ran around for a couple of weeks wondering what the hell we were going to do ... the normal business practices did not seem to apply' (Nigel, accommodation, C).

Indeed, the majority of interviewees indicated that there had not been any policies in place to guide their response to the events of 2001, as seen from the following comments:

We didn't have any plans in place ... .

(David, car hire, A: 8)

No.

(Ian, accommodation, AS)

... policies, that presupposes we have a long-term vision and plan. No, no, we're a small business ... we decided that to be aggressive, we've been aggressive in the market now for 2 years ... .

(Lachlan, transportation, A: 300)

While other organizations did not have any formal policies to guide their responses to the events of 2001, the organizational learning gained by long-term managers during the prolonged Australian pilots' strike of 1989 was acknowledged to have guided their actions. Mark (car hire, AS: 9) drew on his experience of the pilots' strike to develop a strategy for the Ansett collapse. Martin (coach company, S: 500) listed the Gulf War and the pilots' strike as crises that provided a precedent for management.

Organizational learning

Respondents were asked to identify if organizational learning had taken place as a result of the events of 2001. Responses ranged from satisfaction with the strategies they adopted to others who indicated that in a future crisis they would respond differently:

I just think that that what happened actually probably reinforced the way we went around doing our business, that we basically had in place the necessary procedures to actually alter the business accordingly to what was happening at the time.

(Michael, accommodation, A: 130)

The Ansett thing, I think we handled that one very well, in terms of just looking after people, looking into our forward business.

(Stuart, transportation, A: 3)

I don't think they should change anything, they did a good job.

(Kate, car hire, AS: 7)

no, I don't think so. No, because we, we came through about as well as we could have come through it.

(Renata, tour operator, S)

Other interviewees reported that certain lessons had been learned from these events:

... it's made us much more cautious than what we were previously ... if we'd
had our time over again ... a number of things I would have done differently
... there were a lot of promotional activities that we ... took part in, that we
would not have done.

(David, car hire, A: 8)

Our yield management is more sophisticated now, so that would work better.
But no, I wouldn't change much.

(Lachlan, transportation, A: 300)

... I think though, the reduction which were made in advertising, we'd
possibly review that, ... put a bit more money back into that.

(Brad, tour operator, M)

Another interviewee suggested that the timing of another crisis would
dictate his organization's response:

... I would say that if that happened within the next year and business
dropped, we'd probably have to retrench staff.

(Martin, coach company, S: 500)

Perceived benefits of the events of 2001 to the tourism industry

The interviewees were asked what, if any, were the benefits of these events
to the tourism industry. The majority of interviewees saw these events as a
refining process, reflected in comments such as these:

I think it sorts out the men from the boys ... .

(Ian, accommodation, AS)

sure, I think it benefits, because when any ... reverse happens to any industry,
the weak, inefficient ones fall out and if, if you're not ... very quick on your
feet, you don't survive.

(Renata, tour operator, S)

I think these events ... they are such large shocks, is that it does rip you out of
your complacency ... . You find out who are the performers and who aren't
and, I think, in that context, a lot of the pretenders, pretenders seem to fall
off.

(Paul, accommodation and tours, S)

A number of interviewees highlighted the value of organizational
learning as a result of these events:

everything that happens has to have a benefit of some sort ... if it's acted on
and learnt from ... .

(Stuart, transportation, A: 3)

I think the operators get a chance to sit down and really look at what their
business is all about ... it forces people to also explore other markets that they
probably wouldn't have explored in the first place.

(Michael, accommodation, A: 130)

you can always try, you can do things better, and certainly, we've probably been able to improve our product, you just try a bit harder.

(Peter, transportation, A: 6)

I just think from a management point of view, it makes you react without panicking.

(Mark, car hire, AS: 9)

the benefits are … just working out smarter ways of doing business, being more efficient… .

(Brad, tour operator, S)

side-benefits should always be that we increase our level of understanding and the knowledge and intelligence … .

(Ray, entertainment, GC)

One interviewee suggested that the industry should raise their profile in government:

I would probably suggest that if we as an industry, do not learn from the lack of profile that we had in government. We're too fragmented.

(Nigel, accommodation, C)

In summary, few of the strategies adopted by companies were guided by existing policies. However, the learning gained by managers who had experienced the pilots' strike provided guidance for those who were in the industry at that time. Limited organizational learning appears to have taken place in the majority of organizations. The benefits of these events were said to accrue from the process of refining that accompanies such times and the fact that organizations were forced to 'work smarter'.

Comparisons of the events of 2001 with other 'shocks' experienced by the tourism industry

When asked to compare the impact of these events with other 'shocks' experienced by the tourism industry, the pilots' strike of 1989 and the 1991 Gulf War were regularly mentioned as comparative 'shocks':

The killer to the tourism industry was the airline strike.

(Ian, accommodation, AS)

The other one was the Gulf War, and a similar thing – so Americans stayed home, so we saw a significant reduction.

(Brad, tour operator, M)

the worst other shock that we had was the pilots' dispute, followed by the Gulf War.

(Renata, tour operator, S)

The impact of these events on the tourism industry were also compared with the impact of the widespread drought in Australia and the absence of a unified industry body to lobby governments.

The Sydney Olympic Games in 2000 were also viewed as a significant 'shock', some interviewees suggesting that that year had been a financial disaster:

the Olympics was a shock, was an absolute financial disaster.
(Lachlan, transportation, A: 300)

our worst year of all was 2000, because we were on the ground during the whole of the Olympics. Every departure ... either international or Australian that overlapped the Olympics had to be cancelled through lack of interest.
(Renata, tour operator, S)

the impact that like the Olympics had for us, was that we did not have one convention in September.
(Ailsa, business tourism, C: 150)

that's what happened in 2000 is that people stayed home and if the internationals came in they just came for the Olympics.
(Brad, tour operator, M)

On the other hand, another interviewee suggested that the Olympics did not constitute a 'shock':

no I wouldn't [call Olympics a shock] because we knew it was happening.
(Nigel, accommodation, C)

Another view was expressed by one interviewee that events such as those of 2001 should no longer be considered as abnormal:

the simple answer from my perspective, is that neither September 11, Ansett, HIH or anything else is no longer seen as out of the ordinary, in fact we operate in an environment, we expect that to happen. So if anything really all that did, is re-affirm the basic principles that we just live by and that is that we live in an uncertain world, and that organizations need to have a greater sense of dynatism and resilience.
(Ray, entertainment, GC)

In summary, it can be said that these interview findings confirm the seasonality of the tourism industry mentioned by Borooah (1999) and Lim and McAleer (2001), and demonstrate how this phenomenon can either moderate or exacerbate the impact of crises, such as those experienced in 2001. The observation of Pearson and Mitroff (1993) that the purpose of crisis management is to prepare organizations to think creatively about their responses to such events was confirmed by a number of organizations that acknowledged the need to be flexible in their approach and ready to change their market mix. However, such decisions had to be based on accurate information, confirming the suggestion made by Heath (1998) that reliable information had to be obtained on which to base decisions for future action. The determination of organizations to retain their staff, if at all possible, during these crises reflects their desire to protect this valuable resource, a strategy also advocated by Heath (1998). There was little evidence that organizational learning had taken place, confirming the observations of Roux-Dufort (2000), indeed, a number of organizations desired to return to the status quo. Similarly, there was little evidence that crisis management planning had taken place in participating organizations, confirming the observations of Cassedy (1991).

Conclusion

The increasingly volatile environment in which tourism organizations are now operating means that events such as those occurring in 2001 should no longer be seen as 'shocks', but part of everyday, normal business life. Although the exact timing of such events is beyond the control of tourism organizations, it is imperative that firms become flexible and creative in their responses. Since 2001 there have been further events that have affected tourism in Australia particularly in the outbound market but also in the inbound market, including the war in Iraq, SARS (severe acute respiratory syndrome), the Bali bombings and the 2004 Boxing Day tsunami. We know that further crises will occur, but not when, where and what impact will occur. The lessons learnt in 2001 indicate a need for organizations to prepare for crisis as a normal rather than abnormal part of their business environment.

This research has identified a range of responses used by operators to cope with the business pressures caused by the crises of 2001. These include the need to develop good information-gathering networks that not only enable firms to respond appropriately on the basis of accurate information, but also provide some warning of an impending event and allowing pro-active actions to be taken, where appropriate. Having the flexibility to build new business alliances rapidly is another strategy that has merit. Alliances formed prior to a crisis have been shown to be both advantageous and deleterious to participants, and so organizations should be alert to the need to re-negotiate or develop new alliances as the situation demands. The need to retain key staff was highlighted by a number of respondents. Staff are the human capital of a firm and are the keepers of corporate knowledge both formal and informal. Keeping staff adds to knowledge, while releasing key staff is akin to disposing of valuable asserts at below replacement cost. In the recovery phase, corporate knowledge allied with loyalty both to the firm by employees and to employees by the firm are key elements underpinning a successful recovery and return to prosperity.

The need for sound financial management was also a matter that required considerable attention by management, including both in the period immediately after the crisis and during the later recovery phase. Being able to rapidly renegotiate financial commitments or reduce exposure to non-performing business strategies was essential. Rapid reassessment of company marketing strategies in both the short and long term was also noted. The ability to diversify into new markets and reduce exposure in existing markets was seen as a useful strategy. Further, developing a range of products to reduce exposure to any one market was identified by respondents as a beneficial response. Finally, it is obvious that organizations should devise ways in which to document the organizational learning that has taken place, to ensure that this is not lost and is used to inform future decision making.

Acknowledgements

The authors wish to thank the Sustainable Tourism Co-operative Research Centre, Australia for financial assistance in the preparation of this chapter.

References

Booth, S. (1996) Crisis management. In: Warner M. (ed.) *International Encyclopedia of Business and Management*, Vol. 1. Routledge, London, pp. 897–903.

Borooah, V. (1999) The supply of hotel rooms in Queensland, Australia. *Annals of Tourism Research* 26, 985–1003.

Cassedy, K. (1991) *Crisis Management Planning in the Travel and Tourism Industry*. Pacific Asia Travel Association, San Francisco, California.

Faulkner, B. (2001) Towards a framework for tourism disaster management. *Tourism Management* 22, 135–147.

Heath, R. (1998) *Crisis Management for Managers and Executives*. Financial Times Management, London.

Henderson, J. (1999) Managing the Asian financial crisis: tourist attractions in Singapore. *Journal of Travel Research* 38, 177–181.

Kovoor-Misra, S. and Nathan, M. (2000) Timing is everything: the optimal time to learn from crises. *Review of Business* Fall, pp. 31–36.

Laws, E. and Prideaux, B. (2005) Crisis management: a suggested typology. *Journal of Tourism and Travel Marketing* 19 (2/3), 1–8.

Lim, C. and McAleer, M. (2001) Monthly seasonal variations in Asian tourism to Australia. *Annals of Tourism Research* 28, 68–82.

Pearson, C.M. and Mitroff, I.I. (1993) From crisis prone to crisis prepared: a framework for crisis management. *Academy of Management Executive* 7 (1), 48–59.

Prideaux, B.R. (2004) The need to use disaster planning frameworks to respond to major tourism disasters: analysis of Australia's response to tourism disasters in 2001. *Journal of Travel and Tourism Marketing* 15, 281–298.

Prideaux, B., Laws, E. and Faulkner, B. (2003) Events in Indonesia: exploring the limits to formal tourism trends forecasting methods in complex crisis situations. *Tourism Management* 24, 511–520.

Roux-Dufort, C. (2000) Why organizations don't learn from crises: the perverse power of normalization. *Review of Business* Fall, pp. 25–30.

Sonmez, S.F. (1998) Tourism, terrorism, and political instability. *Annals of Tourism Research* 25 (2), 416–456.

Sonmez, S.F. and Graefe, A.R. (1998) Influence of terrorism risk on foreign tourism decisions. *Annals of Tourism Research* 25, 112–144.

20 Restoring Kenyan Tourism in Crisis: Kenyan Tourism's Response to Negative Travel Advisories 2003

DAVID BEIRMAN

The Kenyan tourism industry is a major element of the Kenyan economy. It is the third largest source of the country's foreign exchange earnings (after coffee and tea) and one of Kenya's principal providers of employment. The Kenyan tourism industry experienced steady growth of inbound tourism during most of the 1990s. This growth was severely disrupted following a major terrorist bombing in August 1998 which destroyed the US Embassy in central Nairobi. This catastrophe effectively halted tourism growth, especially from the important US market during the late 1990s. On 28 November 2002, an assault by Islamist suicide bombers against the Israeli-owned Paradise Hotel in Mombassa resulted in the death of 12 Kenyans and three Israelis, and the destruction of the hotel. Simultaneously, Islamist terrorists made a failed attempt to shoot down a Tel Aviv-bound Israeli charter jet carrying 250 passengers (Whittaker *et al.*, 2002).

Publicity in the Western media highlighting the perceived danger of travel to Kenya precipitated a severe slump of Western tourism to Kenya during 2003. The Kenyan tourism industry and the tourism authorities of the recently elected Kenyan government led by President Mwai Kibaki forced Kenya to treat the recovery of the nation's tourism industry as top priority in order to maintain tourism as a key element of the fragile Kenyan economy (Kenyan Tourism Board, 2003).

The development and implementation of a strategy to save the Kenyan tourism industry became the over-riding concept for all sectors of the Kenyan tourism industry from April 2003. This chapter examines the development and implementation of a workable strategy derived from the author's own research in the field of destination crisis marketing based on the experience of many other tourism destinations obliged to respond to the threat and actuality of terrorism.

Introduction

Tourism is a strategically important sector of Kenya's national economy and Kenya's third largest source of foreign exchange earnings. Since Kenya gained independence from Britain in 1963, economic growth has been undermined by endemic government corruption, crumbling infrastructure and inefficiency. These problems have had their own impacts on the tourism industry. Road and railway links are frequently in a poor state of repair, and airport and seaport facilities are of variable quality. Utilities, including electrical and water services, are not always reliable. In May 2003, severe storms and flooding damaged dams and water supply pipelines servicing the capital Nairobi, resulting in water shortages in the city (Akumu, 2003). Similar problems occur periodically (Sindiga and Kanuna, 1999).

Kenya's most compelling tourism attractions are its natural assets which include an abundance of wildlife, much of it protected in national parks. Kenya's outstanding scenic attractions are dominated by the dramatic lakes and valleys of the Great African Rift Valley in the country's west. Mount Kenya, Africa's second highest peak, is the world's only snow-capped mountain straddling the equator. Kenya's largely unspoilt Indian Ocean coastline is a popular sun and sea destination for Europeans. Most of Kenya's people live on a high plateau or in mountainous regions which provide a relatively mild climate for an equatorial country.

Kenya is one of the few parliamentary democracies on the African continent, although political opposition was severely curtailed during the presidency of Daniel Arap Moi whose KANU Party ruled between 1978 and 1992. The nation has suffered many social and economic problems, while corruption and inefficiency became entrenched in Kenyan public and economic life (Phombea, 2002). Kenya has one of the world's highest mortality rates from malaria, AIDS (acquired immune deficiency syndrome) and other epidemics. Despite the high mortality rate from epidemic diseases, the population is amongst the fastest growing in Africa. Kenya's economy is heavily dependent on agriculture, especially low priced cash crops such as coffee and tea. There are few mineral-based natural resources, and most of its industrial output is for local consumption. A single party, KANU, dominated national politics from Kenya's independence in late 1963 until the elections of December 2002, resulting in the first democratic change of government in Kenya's history as an independent state and one of the few democratic changes of government in Africa.

By the beginning of the 21st century, global international financial institutions including the International Monetary Fune (IMF) and the World Bank refused to extend loans to prop up Kenya's faltering economy largely due to Kenya's inability to meet debt repayments and the endemic corruption. Former US Ambassador to Kenya, Smith Hempstone, observed that Western loans and grants tended to cushion the lifestyle of Kenya's power elite at the expense of the infrastructure projects for which the loans were approved to finance (Hempstone, 1998). Kenya's economic malaise exacerbated serious social problems including high levels of unemployment, poor educational standards, poverty, and crimes of violence and theft. Kenyan society was beset with religious, racial, tribal and ethnic tensions. Europeans and Asians, while relatively small minorities in Kenya, owned much of the productive wealth and were often resented by the majority of impoverished Kenyans.

The election of the Rainbow Coalition government led by Mwai Kibaki in December 2002 gave rise to high and often exaggerated expectations of dramatic changes and instant reforms in Kenyan society. Such expectations had to be reined in by the new government in recognition of the fact that many of the country's social and economic problems were deeply entrenched and required long-term solutions.

Inbound tourism grew unsteadily during the 1990s. Despite Kenya's social and political problems, it remained one of the most stable countries in sub-Saharan Africa. Most of the country's major tourist attractions, especially the Indian Ocean beach resorts and its wildlife refuges and national parks, were insulated from the social problems of mainstream Kenyan society. Resorts, major hotels and tour operators ensured that tourists were largely unaffected by the social problems which afflicted much of Kenya's urban society. Most hotels and resorts employed their own security staff and some had independent electricity and water supplies.

Kenya's high rate of inflation and overall economic instability led to a situation during the 1990s in which inbound tourism numbers grew but receipts actually fell in terms of US dollars. According to Clivedon, income from tourism in 1990 was valued at US$443 million, grew to US$627 million in 1994 and had plummeted to US$257 million by 2000. Yet, inbound tourism numbers had risen from 814,000 in 1990 and peaked in 1994 at 928,000. In 2000 there were 900,000 international tourist arrivals (Clivedon, 2002). A contributing factor to the contradictory link between inbound tourism growth and income reduction was a growing proportion of inbound tourists arriving from neighbouring states on short visits and a corresponding reduction in the number of more profligate European and North American tourists during the late 1990s. This trend was exacerbated after the terrorist bombings of the US embassies in Nairobi and Tanzania's capital Dar es Salaam in August 1998. The other major contributing factor to Kenya's reduced tourism income has been the growing preponderance of low cost charter package tourism centred on Mombassa and the Indian Ocean coastal resorts. The growth of low cost tourism was at the expense of Kenya's more upmarket safari tourism sector. One cannot ignore the fact that since the demise of Apartheid in South Africa in 1994, many tourists from Western countries have eschewed Kenya for alternative Safari destinations and opted for South Africa as a wildlife safari destination based on the perception that South Africa is deemed safer and more 'Westernized' than Kenya in addition to offering a price competitive range of luxury and Safari tour product options.

Terrorism Threats, Negative Travel Advisories and their Impacts on Kenyan Tourism

Kenya's tourism industry has experienced threats to its viability from several sources since 1990. Kenya experiences one of the world's highest incidence of human immunodeficiency virus (HIV) AIDS, thousands die from malaria and other diseases, and the tourism infrastructure is occasionally affected by flood and drought. Crime directed against tourists is an ongoing risk tourists and the tourism industry factor into their contingency management planning. However, the incidence and the threat of terrorism have had the most severe impact on high yield Western tourism to Kenya in recent years. The most serious terrorist incident in Kenya's recent history occurred on 7 August 1998 when a massive explosion destroyed the US Embassy in the centre of Kenya's capital city, Nairobi. Simultaneously, the US Embassy in Dar Es Salaam, the capital of neighbouring Tanzania, was also destroyed. Both attacks were attributed to the Islamist terrorist group Al Qaeda, whose leader Osama bin Laden publicly claimed responsibility. The Nairobi bombing was particularly devastating. The large complex housing the US Embassy was reduced to rubble and damage to the surrounding urban area was extensive. There were 213 confirmed deaths, almost all of whom were Kenyans, and over 5000 people who happened to be in the vicinity were wounded (Fisher-Thompson, 1998).

The impact on tourism was immediate. The US State Department and most Western governments advised their citizens either to leave Kenya or to defer travel to Kenya. The global media extensively covered the attack and focused attention on Kenya's vulnerability to terrorism. The Kenyan government's alleged failure to prevent attacks or to arrest prime suspects magnified the perception of insecurity. However, it is reasonable to assert that the failure of US intelligence and security to prevent massive attacks against two of its East African embassies was as least as much a reflection of the inadequacies of US intelligence as it was of Kenya's.

Despite the attack on the US Embassy, inbound tourism to Kenya following the 1998 catastrophe experienced a relatively small numerical decline (see Table 20.1) but a massive revenue cut in terms of US dollars. The principal impact of the 1998 US Embassy bombing was in the decline of high yield, upmarket visitors. In 1994, Kenya attracted 928,000 international visitors spending US$627 million dollars. In 2000, Kenya received 899,000 international visitors who spent US$257 million, representing a 59% reduction in tourism receipts. The economic impact of such a large loss of revenue on a small economy so heavily dependent on tourism revenues represents a national economic crisis (Clivedon, 2002).

Kenya's tourism recovery from 2000 to 2002 was hampered by the continuing threat of global terrorism represented by the 11 September 2001 (9/11) attacks against the World Trade Center and the Pentagon in the USA which negatively impacted on global tourism and air travel. The linkage between Al Qaeda and the terrorists responsible for the 9/11 attack

Table 20.1. Inbound tourism and tourism receipts to Kenya 1990–2002.

Year	International arrivals (thousands)	Change from previous year (%)	International receipts (US$ million)	Change from previous year (%)
1990	814	+10.7	443	+10.8
1991	805	−1.1	423	−4.5
1992	782	−2.9	394	−6.9
1993	826	+5.6	359	−8.9
1994	928	+12.3	627	+74.7
1995	896	−3.4	496	−22.5
1996	925	+3.2	448	−7.8
1997	907	−1.9	385	−14.1
1998	857	−5.5	290	−24.7
1999	862	+0.6	304	+4.8
2000	899	+4.3	257	−15.7
2001	925	+3.9	314	+22.7
2002	927	+0.2	257	−22.7
Average annual change		+2.0		−3.9

affected Kenya largely because Kenya shares borders with Somalia and Sudan which each are alleged to have large cells of Al Qaeda supporters.

On 28 November 2002, Islamist terrorists, allegedly linked with Al Qaeda, mounted a suicide car bomb attack against the Israeli-owned Paradise Hotel just outside the Indian Ocean port city of Mombassa. Three Israelis and 12 Kenyan members of a dance troupe performing a welcoming ceremony for arriving guests were killed. The hotel was totally destroyed. Simultaneously, an attempt was made by members of the terrorist group to shoot down an Israeli Arkia charter jet carrying 250 passengers which had just taken off from Mombassa's international airport en route to Tel Aviv. Fortunately for the passengers and crew of the Israeli aircraft, the shoulder-launched SAM 7 (strella) missiles narrowly missed their target and the plane and its passengers landed safely in Israel (CNN World, 2002).

The Paradise Hotel attack in Kenya occurred 6 weeks after the bombing of the Sari nightclub on the Indonesian island of Bali that killed 202 people from 22 countries including local Balinese. Almost half the dead were Australian tourists. Both incidents were attributed to Islamist extremist groups and, in both cases, Islamist groups claimed responsibility. The prime distinction between them was that the Bali bombing was generically targeted at Westerners while the Kenyan attack was targeted specifically at Israelis. The fact that most of the casualties in Mombassa were Kenyan nationals was unintended. The Bali outrage resulted in an immediate drop of tourism from most of Bali's source markets while, the impact of the Kenyan attack primarily impacted on the relatively modest (6000 passengers per annum) Israeli market. However, its broader impact was once again to cast doubts over Kenya's ability to prevent terrorist attacks.

In December 2002, Kenya's national elections resulted in the election of the opposition Rainbow Coalition led by Mwai Kibaki. The election outcome represented the first democratically elected change of government in Kenya's history as an independent state. Daniel Arap Moi, President of Kenya for 25 years, officially retired from the Presidency in November 2002 and his KANU party faced the electorate in disarray with a record of corruption, a floundering economy and a national infrastructure in terminal decline. International aid agencies and financial organizations such as the IMF and the World Bank had ceased extending financial aid to Kenya on the grounds that most of the funds were embezzled by a small elite of corrupt government officials (Phombeah, 2002).

The Kibaki government pledged itself to wage a war on corruption. One of its first acts was to extend free elementary education to all Kenyans. The resumption of international financial aid was almost immediately forthcoming from the IMF, the European Community and the World Bank. The Kenyan tourism industry had placed considerable hope in the new government's stated intention to improve Kenya's poorly maintained road, rail and airport infrastructure. In February 2003, the government-controlled Kenyan Tourism Board published a 5-year marketing plan aimed at heightening awareness of the country's unique attractions to its principal source markets and targeted potential source markets. The plan focused extensively on promoting a series of safari images which highlighted Kenya's key attractions, specifically the Indian Ocean, wildlife, culture, mountains lakes, desert, sport, human history and food. As is often the case with government tourism master plans, it contained few, if any, contingency plans to account for negative events.

In March 2003, the Kibaki government made a political decision believed by some Kenyan tourism industry leaders to have ignited a tourism crisis. The US and British governments marshalled international political support for their policy to wage war against Saddam Hussein's regime in Iraq. Kenya's government publicly opposed US and British policy. In the context of Kenya's immediate domestic and regional political interests, its position was quite understandable. Kenya shares borders with Sudan and Somalia, two states with weak central governments and active Islamist terrorist cells. Although Kenya has generally enjoyed cordial diplomatic relations with the US and strong trade and historical ties with Britain, the newly elected government sought to distance itself from expressing overt support for an attack on Iraq which would complicate relations with at least two of its regional neighbours. Domestically, the new government also sought to avoid arousing opposition from Kenya's large Muslim minority comprising 20% of the population.

In May 2003, the governments of the USA and Britain issued travel advisories which cautioned their citizens to defer non-essential travel to Kenya. By the end of April, the British government took the unusually drastic step of ordering British-owned commercial airlines to cease all services between Britain and Kenya. The official reason for these measures was that the British and US governments had received what they described as 'credible terrorist threats' against tourism-related targets in Kenya. The alleged threats were issued concurrently with the end of the British, American, Australian coalition's military invasion of Iraq and the overthrow of Saddam Hussein's regime. It is noteworthy that France (Kenya's third largest European source market and a country opposed to the US-led coalition against Iraq) issued no travel advisory to deter its citizens wishing to travel to Kenya (Graf, 2003).

The Kenyan tourism industry responded with outrage at what they considered to be an unjustified singling out of Kenya as a terrorist target. From a commercial perspective, the British and US advisories severely compromised Kenya's numerically largest source market (Britain) and its highest yielding market (the USA which has the largest per capita spend). Kenya's Minister of Tourism Raphael Tuju described the US and British advisories as an unjustified attack against the Kenya tourism industry (Graf, 2003). The private sector of Kenya's tourism industry sought to present an united front in response to the advisories. The Kenyan Tourism Federation, the Kenyan Association of Tour Operators, Kenya Air, the Kenyan Association of Hoteliers and the Kenyan Association of Travel Agents and other organizations entered into an informal alliance to respond to the challenge of negative advisories. On 21 May 2003, the author[1] was invited to run a 1-day seminar in Nairobi's Serena Hotel involving 65 people representing Kenya's tourism industry leadership. The aim of the seminar was jointly to develop and implement a strategic marketing approach for responding to the challenge of terrorism-related negative travel advisories. The Kenyan Association of Tour Operators which convened the seminar invited all major private and government stakeholders. Significantly, it took the hitherto unprecedented step of inviting representatives of the diplomatic corps from six of Kenya's principal source markets, Britain, Germany, Italy, the USA, France and Australia.

The May 2003 seminar dealt with all aspects of crisis and restoration marketing. However, the most lively and significant exchange was between the tourism industry delegates and diplomatic representatives of Britain, France, Germany and Australia. At the time of the seminar, the British, Australian, German, American and Israeli governments had all issued advisories recommending their citizens defer travel to Kenya. The most significant aspect of this first ever dialogue in Kenya between the travel industry representatives and the diplomats was that the diplomats explained the process of travel advisory formulation. Conversely, the leaders of the Kenyan tourism industry were able to describe the impacts of the advisories on their industry and a society so dependent on tourism.

Open discussion between the travel industry leaders and the diplomats was followed by further discussions at government–government level. Jake Grieves-Cook, President of the Kenyan Tourism Federation, and Tom Fernandes, President of the Kenyan Association of Tour Operators, played a significant role in ascertaining the actions required by the industry in conjunction with the Kenyan Ministry of Tourism and the security services to address the concerns of the governments of key source market countries. By early June 2003, the British and German governments had toned down their travel advisories for Kenya. Significantly, the British government revoked their ban on British-owned passenger airline flights to Kenya. In June 2003, Italian airline Alitalia announced the commencement of direct flights to Kenya from Italy, which opened up the potential for significant growth in the Italian market, already Kenya's fifth largest source of non-African foreign tourists. On the negative side, despite acknowledging Kenyan efforts to upgrade tourism security significantly, between May and July 2003 the US government maintained its hardline travel advisory which continued to advise its citizens to defer travel to Kenya.

The broad strategic approach adopted by the Kenyan tourism industry and the Kenyan Ministry of Tourism to stimulate market recovery involved the following:

1. The Kenyan government, primarily through Tourism Minister Raphael Tuju, would actively lobby Britain, the USA and Germany to moderate travel advisories applying to Kenya.

2. Kenyan security services, airport authorities, Kenya Air and the travel industry would act to address specific security concerns outlined by the British, US and German governments. Security at the major international gateway airports in Nairobi and Mombasa was substantially upgraded, as were security measures at domestic airports servicing tourist traffic.

3. The Kenyan tourism industry and the Kenyan Tourism Board would address security concerns as an integral part of its marketing programme.

4. The Kenyan Tourism Board and the private sector of Kenya's tourism would seek to broaden its marketing base in order to reduce dependence on the US and British markets. Consequently, the Italian and French markets were more actively courted. Kenyan Airways also commenced new services to Bangkok and Hong Kong, inaugurated in September 2003, facilitating access between the potentially lucrative South East Asian, Japanese and Chinese markets and Kenya.

5. The Kenyan Tourism Board and the private sector of Kenya's tourism industry would jointly focus on raising Kenya's profile amongst consumers and the travel industry in strategically significant source markets.

6. The Kenyan tourism industry initiated discussions with travel insurers which would cover acts of terrorism (Grieves-Cook, 2003).

In addition to the six approaches outlined above, the Kenyan tourism industry sought to strengthen its marketing alliances with neighbouring countries including Tanzania and Uganda in order to pool resources for marketing East Africa in common source markets. The Kenyan strategy represented a strong example of alliance marketing involving the cooperation of all key segments of the tourism industry.

The Kenyan Tourism Board, the government's tourism marketing body, and the Kenyan Tourism Federation, the private sector's travel industry representative body, sought to coordinate a balance between a recovery marketing strategy targeted at the consumer markets and the travel industry in source markets. A significant element of the strategy was the attempt to broaden Kenya's base of source markets. The negative travel advisories issued by the US, British and German governments severely impacted on inbound tourism to Kenya primarily because of the high level of dependence on these three source markets which between them accounted for 37% of total tourist arrivals in 2000 and close to 50% of non-African arrivals. A significant downturn in arrivals from the USA, Britain and Germany had the potential to cripple Kenya's inbound tourism industry. The vulnerability of Kenya's tourism industry to negative perceptions from these three markets had to be addressed as a matter of urgency.

Despite the Kenyan government's implementation of the majority of US recommendations for security upgrades, the USA not only maintained a negative travel advisory for Kenya but had effectively closed its Embassy in July. The official reason given by the US government was that threats were being made by Islamist groups against American interests in Kenya. A known Al Qaeda operative, Fazul Abdullah Mohammed, alleged 'mastermind' of the attack against the Israeli-owned Paradise Hotel in Mombasa on 28 November 2002, was believed to be active in or near Kenya. In June 2003, Kenyan police arrested four people suspected to have been involved in the Mombasa attack and allegedly linked to Mohammed.

The lack of specificity of the alleged anti-US terrorist threat in Kenya has led some Kenyan tourism leaders and politicians to suggest that the US travel advisory is unrelated to any security threat and is a politically punitive measure against Kenya's refusal to be part of President George W. Bush's 'coalition of the willing'. The evidence to support this claim is more circumstantial than conclusive. However, when President Bush visited a number of African states in July 2003, he made a point of visiting Kenya's neighbour Uganda, a country vulnerable to the same potential security threats as Kenya but not subject to a negative US travel advisory and ruled by a government which was a *de facto* part of the 'coalition of the willing'. Despite being one of Africa's few genuine democracies, Kenya was noticeably excluded from President Bush's African agenda. One of the few Western countries which continued to advise its citizens to defer travel to Kenya by July 2003 was Australia, one of the USA's most active allies in the invasion of Iraq. In October 2003, Kenya's President Kibaki made a state visit to Washington. The US travel advisory was a key issue raised at the official meeting with US President George W. Bush. Although the Kenyan leader and his entourage was warmly welcomed to the White House, the US President made no commitments to alter the American government's travel advisory (Thome, 2003).

The strategy of diversifying Kenya's source markets was becoming increasingly evident by August 2003. Although the British market was recovering, there was a growth in arrivals from Italy, France, Germany and the Persian Gulf States. Direct air services between the Gulf States and Kenya facilitated the arrival of more tourists from this region. Kenya Airways' establishment of flights between Nairobi, Bangkok and Hong Kong is intended to facilitate a push into the Eastern Asian market. The major barrier to capitalizing effectively on these new air routes is the limited marketing budget of the Kenyan Tourism Board. Although there is an intention expressed in their marketing plan to establish an office in Tokyo in association with Kenyan Airway's new routes into Bangkok and Hong Kong, there is no funding allocated to it. The private sector of Kenya's inbound tourism industry and Kenya Airways is increasingly relied upon by the government to provide the bulk of financial support for marketing destination Kenya in new and potential growth markets. The Kenyan Tourism Board's 2003 marketing plan made no meaningful financial provisions for advertising and left many unanswered questions regarding marketing representation in new source markets.

Kenya's tourism industry leadership has become increasingly outspoken on the issue of negative travel advisories, and some industry leaders have claimed that Western government advisories are an exercise in neo-colonialism in order to impose controls over Kenya's tourism industry and society. This is a concept which has been advanced and supported by several tourism scholars including C. Michael Hall, who has also added that the Western media acceptance of such advisories directed at developing countries has exacerbated the potency of advisories in shaping negative destination perceptions in Western tourism-generating markets (Hall, 2002). There is insufficient research on this issue to make any conclusive empirical observations of the veracity of this argument. However, it is relevant to make the observation that negative travel advisories in 2003 have necessitated a radically altered marketing approach by Kenya's tourism industry.

Conclusion

It is too early to judge the success of Kenya's response to negative travel advisories imposed during mid-2003. From a marketing perspective, there is no doubt that the Kenyan tourism industry leadership acted quickly to address the issue. The most significant development was the relatively rapid moderation of the British and German advisories which impacted on Kenya's two numerically largest source markets. The determination by Kenya's airport authorities and security services to address Western security concerns facilitated this change. The Kenyan tourism industry and Kenyan Airways established an alliance which re-prioritized the source markets and facilitated the development and growth of new source markets. The move to diversify source markets was an important step towards reducing Kenyan vulnerability to the moods of a small number of critical source markets. The US and Australian governments only relaxed their travel advisories in April 2004, without ever having explained to the satisfaction of the Kenyan government and tourism stakeholders why negative travel advisories were maintained for over 9 months after Britain and Germany had relaxed them.

The major challenge for Kenya's tourism industry and the Kenyan Tourism Board is to translate the opportunity for market diversification into significant inbound tourism growth resulting in increased numbers of tourists and per capita yield. Although the Kenyan government and its tourism ministry have been quick to express rhetorical support for a more intensive marketing campaign to promote Kenya globally, there is little evidence that the words have translated into a commensurate financial commitment by the Kenyan government. In fact, Kenya's Tourism Minister Raphael Tuju announced in October 2003 that the Kenyan Tourism Board would reduce funding for some of its marketing representatives in Europe and the USA. His reasons (with justification) were that many of these agencies were costing the Kenyan government large sums of money, little of which was directed to marketing Kenya. However, as Kenyan private sector leaders readily state, this problem arose from mismanagement by the Kenyan Tourism Board which failed to establish and enforce marketing programmes and accountability guidelines to its overseas marketing representatives. By the end of 2003, the private sector of Kenya's tourism industry continued to bear most of the operational and financial burden of restoring the image and marketability of Kenya.

Postscript March 2005

During 2004, Kenya's tourism industry experienced significant recovery. This was due in part to the fact that strategies discussed in the chapter actually took effect. It was also a reflection of the global resurgence in the travel industry during 2004. The private sector of Kenya's tourism industry focused considerable attention on the high yield, safari tourism market and, during late 2003 and 2004, leading operators including Abercrombie and Kent and Wildlife Safaris brought large groups of travel journalists and senior travel agents from the USA, Australia, Western Europe and East Asia on familiarization tours to experience the Kenyan Safari product first-hand.

Although Kenya's government tourism statistics have yet to reveal the statistical impact of these activities, the many Kenyan tour operators the author dealt with in Nairobi revealed that their Kenyan business picked up substantially during 2004. The eventual relaxation of the US and Australian government travel advisories assisted in facilitating this growth, but the direct push marketing campaign had achieved more for market recovery than a direct confrontation over travel advisories would ever had achieved.

Kenya's tourism industry was largely unaffected by the Indian Ocean tsunami of 26 December 2004. Although the tsunami struck Kenya's Indian Ocean coastline, virtually all resort areas had been evacuated prior to the arrival of the tsunami wave. There was a single fatality in Kenya and some damage to coastal settlements, but Kenya's large distance from the epicentre of the Sumatra earthquake enabled authorities to act on reports of damage from other affected countries and evacuate local citizens and tourists from areas of potential danger.

Note

[1] The author interviewed a wide range of Kenyan tourism industry leaders in preparation for the May 2003 seminar in Nairobi conducted by the author. Interviewees including John Glenn, Tom Fernandes, Trevor Fernandes of Wildlife Safaris and Jake Grieves of Cook Travel.

References

Akumu, G. (2003) Expect worse effects of climate change. *The Nation* Nairobi. May 16, p. 2.

Clivedon, R. (2002) *Travel and Tourism in Kenya Country Report*. Mintel International Group. Travel and Tourism Intelligence, London.

CNN World (2002) 29 November.

Fisher-Thompson, J. (1998) Allbright offers a reward for capture of terrorists in East African bombings. US Intelligence Service Washington File. 10 August.

Graf, P. (2003) MSN News. Kenya seeks to reassure britain it is safe. *Reuters* 27 May.

Grieves-Cook, J. (2003) Kenyan Tourism Federation Memo to all Kenyan Tourism industry associations. 11 June.

Hall, C.M. (2002) Travel safety, tourism and the media. *Current Issues in Tourism* 5, 458–466.

Hempstone, S. (1990) *Rogue Ambassador*. University of the South Press, Sewanee, Tennesssee.

Kenyan Tourism Board (2003) *Kenyan Tourism Marketing Plan 2003–2007*. Deloitte Touche, Kenya, February.

Phombeah, G. (2002) Moi's Legacy to Kenya. BBC World. 5 December.

Sindiga, I. and Kanuna, M. (1999) Unplanned tourism development in sub-Saharan Africa with special reference to Kenya. *Journal of Tourism Studies* 10, 25–39.

Whittaker, B., Henke, D. and Evens, R. (2002) Al Qai'da tape lays claim to Kenyan attack. *The Guardian* 9 December, p. 2.

21 A Comparison of Pre- and Post-9/11 Traveller Profiles: Post-crisis Marketing Implications

STEPHEN W. LITVIN AND JOHN C. CROTTS

Introduction

The impact of the events of 11 September 2001 (9/11) on the world's tourism economy was immediate and far reaching, forcing most destination marketers to revise their marketing strategies in an attempt to recover from the tragedy of that fateful day. All knew that there would be fewer people willing to travel internationally after 9/11, but the crisis management literature offered little insight as to which market segments would be the quickest to recover, and virtually no aid in predicting who these more intrepid travellers may be.

To aid in our understanding of post-crisis travel, the research presented is a study comparing US travellers who travelled internationally before 9/11 with those who journeyed abroad following the tragedy of that day. Proof of the impact that 9/11 had upon US outbound tourism flows is in the numbers. Table 21.1 summarizes US citizen overseas travel for the years 2000 and 2001 (Office of Travel and Tourism Industries, 2003). The data reflect the industry's malaise prior to 9/11, generally attributed to a weakening US economy (Daneshkhu, 2001). In fact, third quarter 2001 international travel, even before 9/11, had declined from the previous year. The attacks of 11 September, however, brought an entirely new set of industry challenges, as overseas travel for the month of September 2001 fell 30% versus the previous year, and stayed weak for the balance of the year. Once the immediate shock of the day had passed, marketers knew they had to continue to promote their product to overcome consumers' proclivity not to travel overseas. While they recognized that fewer people would travel, what they did not know was what those people who would travel might look like.

There is a growing body of research dealing with post-9/11 tourism marketing. By way of example, Hopper (2002) examined how London positioned and promoted the city following 9/11. Frisby (2002) presented a similar case study that reflected the post-crisis actions of the British Tourist

Table 21.1. Overseas air travel by US citizens (000s).[a]

	2000	2001	Change (%)
January	1,685	1,846	+10
February	1,695	1,742	+3
March	2,242	2,297	+2
First quarter	5,622	5,885	+5
April	2,076	2,168	+4
May	2,427	2,424	0
June	2,827	2,906	+3
Second quarter	7,330	7,498	+2
July	2,826	2,754	−3
August	2,431	2,439	0
September	2,202	1,540	−30
Third quarter	7,459	6,733	−10
October	1,966	1,422	−28
November	1,860	1,483	−23
December	1,815	1,730	−5
Fourth quarter	5,641	4,635	−18
Year	26,052	24,751	−5

[a] Source: Office of Travel and Tourism Industries (2003), US Department of Commerce, International Trade Administration. Includes all international travel except to Mexico and Canada.

Authority. Litvin and Alderson (2003) reviewed and evaluated the post-crisis response of the Charleston (South Carolina) Area Convention and Visitors Bureau, and Fall (2003) reported survey results from an extensive sample of US Convention and Visitors Bureaux (CVBs) to determine 9/11's effect upon their choice of marketing media. While each of these studies added value to our appreciation of the challenges faced and responses taken by various marketing organizations in the face of the crisis, none of these efforts, nor others reviewed, focused upon post-tragedy traveller psychographics. By comparing a random sample of pre-9/11 US overseas travellers with a similar sample of post-9/11 US travellers, this research attempts to close this research gap. This is important. Tourism marketers learned or were reminded of the importance of crisis management plans following the tragedy (Litvin and Alderson, 2003). However, clearly 9/11 was not the last tourism crisis organizations are likely to face. Hopefully these organizations will now revisit their plans and reflect upon the lessons they personally learned and will also incorporate into their revised plans the wealth of knowledge shared by others who have studied the event, to include the results of this study.

Theoretical Background

Two theoretical streams we believe contribute to such an analysis. These are: why do elements of society engage in terrorist activities against tourists and what can be done about it? Secondly, why do tourists voluntarily place themselves in unfamiliar situations where occasionally they can become targets? These seldom-integrated theoretical streams draw from wide spectra of the literature involving criminology, social psychology and the leisure sciences, and contribute to our understanding as to the motivation and tactics of criminal elements and the impact that their actions may inflict on a destination.

Two of the more popular theories of criminology are Routine Activity Theory and Hot Spot Theory (Crotts, 2003). Though these have generally been applied to predatory crime, it can be argued that terrorist activity is no more than a subset of criminology. The Routine Activity Theory (Felson and Cohen, 1980) draws heavily from the study of human ecology. This theory assumes criminals to be rational beings who attempt to satisfy needs by taking something of value from others. According to Routine Activity Theory, for a criminal act to occur, three elements must converge in both time and place. These are: a suitable target; a motivated offender; and lack of a guardian capable of preventing the interaction between the two.

The Hot Spot Theory centres on the criminology of place. The theory suggests, within a given locale, that relatively few places will be associated with a high percentage of crime. These places, or hot spots, provide convergent opportunities in which crimes can and most often do occur. For example, more than seven of ten violent crimes committed against Florida tourists occurred in three location types, with 42% of violent crimes reported along highway roadways, 18% in parking lots and garages, and 12% in hotels and motels (Shieber *et al.*, 1995).

International tourists, in unfamiliar situations and highly visible due to their dress, language and the types of places they stay and visit, are often the target of routine crime (Crotts, 2003). Despite this, many continue to travel abroad. This is perhaps best explained by the Ulysses factor; one's need to know what is 'over the next mountain', a motivational theme of much leisure travel literature (Cohen, 1984; Bello and Etzel, 1985; Snepenger, 1987). For many, routine environments fail to provide an optimal level of arousal, thus motivating individuals to seek a degree of novelty in their vacation choices. Variations in novelty-seeking behaviours, however, should be expected (Cohen, 1984). These appear to be derived from two innate but dichotomous traits of human personality: the search for optimal levels of arousal versus the desire for safety or self-preservation (Crotts, 1993). The conflict between these provides a theoretical basis for explaining why some people will choose to travel abroad in spite of terrorist advisories and warnings, while others will not. Significant fear obviously triggers one's self-preservation response. However, for lesser degrees of emotion, early experimental research has established that excitement that produces mild emotional disturbances is generally considered desirable. The optimal amount of such disturbance (tension, fear, etc.) is determined by a purely individual threshold, but, as a rule, if disturbance is short of one's threshold these otherwise negative feelings create a positive, even pleasurable, response (Hebb and Thompson, 1954). This explains: why individuals under experimental conditions, when given the choice between the familiar and unfamiliar, will tend to choose the unfamiliar (Montgomery, 1952; Hebb and Thompson, 1954); why the dog that has been frightened by a strange object will nevertheless be apt to return to it again, balanced by a need to view the object more closely and a preparation for flight (Melzack, 1952); why children who have been frightened tend to ask to be shown again the object that caused their fright (Valentine, 1930); and probably why many of us enjoy the thrill of a rollercoaster.

In the leisure science literature, the balance of the need for psychological security and novelty seeking in leisure experiences is deemed the Optimal Arousal Theory (for a literature review, see Iso-Ahola, 1980). The theory suggests that when a leisure (or travel) environment is perceived as providing too much risk, the individual will tend to avoid or withdraw from that setting. On the other hand, when the individual perceives an environment as too familiar, he/she will quickly tire of the setting and will seek more arousal through novel and/or more complex situations. Therefore, 'Leisure behaviour is a dialectical and optimizing process in which two opposite forces simultaneously influence the individual: the need for stability and the need for change' (Iso-Ahola, 1981, p. 121).

The above focuses on well established theories related to general crime, but each is applicable in the case of terrorist activities. While the Routine Activity Theory generally finds criminals seeking economic gain from their victims, in the case of terrorism violence can be construed as a routine activity. This is performed with the goal of taking something intangible, but held precious, from their victims, i.e. a sense of security, normalcy of economic activity, etc. Threat of such violence should have an impact upon travel behaviour. While the Hot Spot Theory suggests that knowledgeable tourists can avoid certain locations likely to be stalked by criminals, the events of 9/11 suggest that there may be no place safe from terror, no identifiable 'hot spot' to be avoided. Finally, the Optimal Arousal Theory informs that with an increased degree of risk and uncertainty, or at least perception of such post-9/11, the more risk-adverse travellers would be likely to reach the threshold at which the prospect of foreign travel would no longer be pleasurable, thus resulting in withdrawal from the activity. Such an assumption would be in line with the finding of Piotrkowski and Brannen (2002) that three of four Americans felt less secure and less able to control forces that influenced their lives following 9/11.

Thus, the research question addressed herein: we know there were fewer US international travellers post-9/11, but were those that travelled abroad subsequent to that fateful date measurably different psychographically from those who had travelled before? The hypothesis, based upon the above theory, is that such differences should be evident.

Research Method

To explore the question, data from the 2000 and 2001 'Inflight Survey of Overseas Arrivals to the USA' were purchased from the US Department of

Commerce. Annually, the Department surveys approximately 30,000 US residents on regularly scheduled flights with self-administered questionnaires distributed in-flight by the flight crews of participating airlines following departure from the USA. Employed is a random cluster sampling procedure where all passengers on randomly selected flights on randomly selected days are administered the survey instrument. Currently, 61 US and foreign flag carriers cooperate with the survey. Response rates are generally quite high, averaging 58% (Tourism Industries, 2001).

Survey results may be purchased by tourism providers and researchers. For the current research, two subsamples were purchased. These comprised 700 randomly selected outbound travellers from the fourth quarter of 2000, and an additional 700 travellers randomly selected from the same period a year later – the 3 months immediately following 9/11. The instrument was unchanged between years. Selection parameters were imposed to limit the selected subjects to overseas travellers whose primary trip purpose was discretionary travel (i.e. holidays, leisure, recreation, or visiting friends and relatives). Such sample limitation was deemed appropriate, as discretionary travel would seemingly be most impacted by the perceived risk associated with post-9/11 travel. The two samples proved a good demographic match. The year 2000 sample was 58% male, with an average age of 47.6, and an income level of 5.7 (based upon an 11-point scale with a range of $1 = <US\$20,000$ to $11 = >US\$200,000$). The post-9/11 sample was on average 46.2 years of age ($t = 1.582$, $P = 0.114$), 54% male ($\chi^2 = 2.654$, $P = 0.103$), and reported an income level of 5.9 ($t = 1.034$, $P = 0.301$). Based upon the sample sizes, the results are within a precision level of 95% of the population of American overseas leisure travellers.

Research Findings

The comparison of US overseas leisure travellers from a 'normal year' (2000) with those who ventured abroad following 9/11 reflected few variations. Variables reviewed included: travellers' trip planning; travel and their travel party characteristics; travel activities; the travellers' critical evaluations of various aspects of their journey; and finally a single question related to their changed travel plans in light of security issues. Following is a comparison of the two samples.

Pre-trip sources used to gather information (Table 21.2)

While 60% of 2000 travellers utilized the services of a travel agent for their travel planning, this had fallen to 48% for post-9/11 travellers, reflecting a 20% decline in usage in a single year. Mirroring this trend, the percentage of travellers that utilized Internet searches increased from 27 to 37% in 2001 versus 2000. In addition, for both cohorts, the role played by government tourist offices in the planning process was extremely limited. Only 4–5% of both samples indicated they had obtained information from these sources.

Travel booking and trip characteristics (Table 21.3)

Nine variables related to travel booking and trip characteristics have been considered. Each has been previously identified as reflective of a traveller's degree of risk aversion by Money and Crotts (2003) in a multinational study exploring travel behaviours cross-culturally based upon Hofstede's (2001) risk-aversion dimension. Money and Crotts (2003) indicated that risk avoiders (as opposed to risk takers): travel alone less often; visit fewer destinations during their journey; stay away from home for a shorter period of time; and include more pre-booked accommodation in their itineraries. Surprisingly, the current research found no differences in any of these behaviours when comparing pre-9/11 travellers with the post-9/11

Table 21.2. Source of travel information.[a]

	2000 (%)	2001 (%)	χ^2 [b]	P [c]
Travel agent/tour operator	60	48	16.952	0.000[d]
Internet	27	37	15.179	0.000[d]
Friends and relatives	20	18	0.377	0.539
Government tourist offices	5	4	0.457	0.499
TV/radio/newspaper ads	5	5	1.292	0.256

[a] Respondents could indicate multiple sources. Other sources of less than 5% not listed.
[b] Cochran's test of homogeneity – relationship between two dichotomous variables.
[c] Two-tailed probability.
[d] Statistically significant at 0.100, i.e. two samples were 'different'.

Table 21.3. Travel booking and trip characteristics.

	2000	2001	Test score	P [a]
Respondent travelling alone (%)	20	22	$\chi^2 = 1.368$ [b]	0.242
Travelling with children (%)	9.2	9.7	$\chi^2 = 0.070$ [b]	0.791
Travel party size (adults and children)	2.9	2.6	$t = 2.020$ [c]	0.043[d]
Trip duration (days)	15.0	14.3	$t = 0.604$ [c]	0.546
Number of destinations visited	2.0	1.9	$t = 0.687$ [c]	0.492
Accommodation reservations made pre-trip (%)	70	72	$\chi^2 = 0.839$ [b]	0.360
Pre-paid package component to trip (%)	27	21	$\chi^2 = 5.787$ [b]	0.016[d]
Days before trip decided to travel	116	110	$t = 0.861$ [c]	0.389
Days before trip made air reservations	74	76	$t = 0.294$ [c]	0.804

[a] Two-tailed probability.
[b] Cochran's test of homogeneity – relationship between two dichotomous variables.
[c] *t*-test score for equality of means.
[d] Statistically significant at 0.100.

sample. Similarly, while Money and Crotts (2003) suggested that risk-adverse travellers plan their travel and book their airline reservations further in advance than do the less risk adverse, again no intersample differences were reflected in the current data. Finally, Money and Crotts (2003) indicated that risk aversion would result in a larger travel party size, more children in the party and a greater dependency upon pre-paid package tours. It was noted herein, however, that post-9/11 travellers travelled in significantly smaller parties (2.6 versus 2.9 travellers), while the percentage travelling with children remained unchanged between the two samples. The percentage utilizing pre-paid packages decreased from 27% to 21% between the years.

Activities during vacation (Table 21.4)

Respondents were provided a list of 25 leisure activities and asked to tick all in which they planned to partake during their trip. Table 21.4 lists the ten most frequent responses of the two samples. Of the 25 options provided, the same ten activities comprised both years' lists, albeit with several minor ordinal changes. For both samples, the two top behaviours remained dining and shopping.

Ratings of airline, airport and security (Table 21.5)

Respondents were asked to evaluate various components of their trip based upon a 5-point scale that ranged from 1 = poor to 5 = excellent. Of 15 evaluative items assessed, ten reflected no significant differences. Travellers were no more or less critical, post-9/11, of the food served

Table 21.4. Top ten activities planned during trip.[a]

	2000 (%)	2001 (%)	χ^{2}[b]	P[c]
1. Dining	82	86	4.854	0.028[d]
2. Shopping	76	81	3.818	0.051[d]
3. Visiting historic places	61	56	3.403	0.065[d]
4. Sightseeing in cities	49	49	0.003	0.957
5. Visiting small towns and villages	45	48	1.150	0.284
6. Touring countryside	41	39	0.428	0.513
7. Visiting heritage sights	37	39	0.596	0.440
8. Enjoying water sports	34	40	6.494	0.011[d]
9. Nightclubs and dancing	30	29	0.031	0.861
10. Art galleries and museums	30	27	1.854	0.173

[a] Ordinal rank based upon 2000 responses.
[b] Cochran's test of homogeneity – test of relationship between two dichotomous variables.
[c] Two-tailed probability.
[d] Statistically significant at 0.100.

Table 21.5. Ratings of airline, airport and security.[a]

	2000	2001	t[b]	p[c]
Flight schedule	4.0	3.9	1.648	0.100
Ticket price	3.5	3.4	1.252	0.211
Reservation service	3.7	3.6	1.848	0.065[d]
Check-in waiting time	4.0	3.8	2.676	0.008[d]
Check-in personnel	4.1	4.0	1.935	0.053[d]
On-time departure	3.7	3.8	−1.582	0.114
Food and beverage quality	3.6	3.5	1.214	0.225
Flight attendant quality	4.1	4.2	−0.726	0.468
Seat comfort	3.4	3.3	1.289	0.198
Carry-on space	3.7	3.7	0.292	0.770
Terminal convenience	3.5	3.7	−1.877	0.061[d]
Airport security	3.3	3.7	−5.006	0.000[d]
Overall flight	4.0	3.9	0.867	0.386
Overall airline	4.1	4.1	−0.382	0.703
Overall airport	3.7	3.7	−0.160	0.873
Carrier loyalty[e]	1.7[e]	1.7[e]	0.324	0.746

[a] Based upon a 5-point scale ranging from 1 = poor to 5 = excellent.
[b] t-test score for equality of means.
[c] Two-tailed probability.
[d] Statistically significant at 0.100.
[e] Determined by the question: 'Would you choose or recommend this airline for your next trip on this route?', with a scale from 1 = definitely would, to 4 = definitely would not.

aboard their flight, flight attendant quality, carry-on luggage space or seat comfort. Post-9/11 travellers, however, were less satisfied with the amount of time they spent waiting to check in to their flights and with the personnel who checked them in, but were less critical of the terminal and of airport security.

Concerns over personal safety

Responses to the question 'Did concerns for your personal safety cause you to change your travel plans?' indicated that 3.2% of post-9/11 respondents had altered their travel plans. This reflected a statistically insignificant increase from the 2.1% of year 2000 travellers surveyed ($\chi^2 = 1.550$, $P = 0.220$).

Discussion

The hypothesis that the events of 9/11 would significantly change the travel behaviours and attitudes of US overseas travellers is not supported. In fact, with but few exceptions, there was little to distinguish between the pre-9/11 and post-9/11 travellers. Interpretation of the literature suggested that people would feel less comfortable venturing abroad following 9/11, wishing to avoid 'hot spots' and concerned over the prospect of leaving the security of 'known guardians'. Yet, post-9/11 travellers were substantially unchanged from those who had travelled abroad the previous year.

It may be that the same travellers, though fewer, travelled during the two periods and that the events of 9/11 did not affect their attitudes and behaviours. It is speculated, however, that this is not the case. Rather, a more likely explanation for the lack of change is that while the more risk-adverse traveller probably decided to stay home following 9/11, those other less fearful souls who made the decision to venture abroad post-9/11 had their normal psychographic tendencies moderated by the uncertainty of the times. The net effect of these two factors, nervous travellers staying home and less nervous travellers becoming more cautious (as one would expect), seems to have resulted in post-9/11 traveller behaviour that was strikingly similar to that exhibited by the average traveller during 'normal' times.

That said, there were several behaviours of post-9/11 travellers which were of particular interest. Among these was the significant reduction in the percentage who took pre-packaged tours (Table 21.3). Plog (1991) has noted that more risk-adverse travellers, those exhibiting psychocentric tendencies, are attracted to the security of pre-packaged tours. In this case, however, travellers turned away from packages, with a possible explanation being their desire not to travel in conspicuous numbers during a time of uncertainty.

In today's market, the reduced use of travel agents is a well documented trend (Litvin, 1999). In the current case, travel agent use fell 20% between years (Table 21.2.). Fall (2003), in a study geared toward US domestic travel, indicated that post-9/11 marketing would be more relationship oriented as travellers sought increased 'connectivity' with travel providers. Fall's thesis would suggest the use of travel agents as a relationship-oriented travel distribution channel. It was surprising that the uncertainty of the times failed even temporarily to stem the tide away from the use of travel agencies. Of equal interest was the lack of increased use by post-9/11 travellers of government tourism offices (Table 21.2), again a relationship-oriented information source. In both samples, the percentage of travellers who availed themselves of these resources was relatively minor.

Another point of interest – as noted above, there was no change in the travellers' timeframe for either when they decided to travel or when they booked their airline reservation (Table 21.3). On the one hand, as noted by Tversky and Shafir (1992), buyers who face hard decisions often delay in making those decisions. Certainly during the volatile months following 9/11 one would expect that people would have postponed travel decision making as long as possible. Conversely, previous research (Money and Crotts, 2003) has found that risk takers generally purchase international airline tickets further in advance than do the more risk adverse. The net result was that post-9/11 travel behaviour was unchanged from the previous year.

As a general comment, the travel activities of the two groups of travellers remained substantially unchanged, as the ordinal listing of the ten most frequent activities was identical between the years (Table 21.4). However, four of these activities reflected statistical intersample change. The two that reflected the largest percentage change were of particular interest. First was the decline in the percentage of post-9/11 travellers planning to visit historic sites. Perhaps these attractions were seen as potential targets for terrorists, and thus avoided. Secondly was the larger percentage of 2001 travellers who planned to partake in water sports, perhaps a reflection of the pent-up stress of the time and the need for a relaxing escape.

The ratings of the airlines, airport and security (Table 21.5), while substantially unchanged between samples, are interesting to consider. Hofstede's (2001) cross-cultural work provides an interesting backdrop. According to Hofstede, a psychographic continuum that ranges from *masculinity* to *femininity* reflects the distribution of emotions between the genders. This ranges from 'tough' masculine to 'tender' feminine. Studies by Crotts and Erdmann (2000) found that members of a feminine society were less likely to criticize travel services and demonstrated a higher degree of consumer loyalty than those exhibiting more masculine tendencies. One might presume that the shared experience of 9/11 would have the carryover effect of making people in general more sensitive and forgiving towards others, i.e. more feminine. Such a presumption would be supported by the psychological study of Fredrickson *et al.* (2003), which reported that post-crisis, in the face of worry and trauma, people often experience heightened love and closer personal relationships – again, feminine traits. However, as with the previous variables, such a trend was not reflected in the data, as the overall ratings generally remained unchanged between the two samples.

A final surprising behaviour was the lack of change in the percentage of families that travelled with children following 9/11 (Table 21.3). Leaving the children at home, or families with children postponing their trips, seemed an intuitive reaction to the events of 9/11. Perhaps that no behavioural change was noted in this variable is a strong validation of the overall findings that post-9/11 traveller behaviour was not significantly different from that of 'normal' travellers.

Conclusion

The Hot Spot Theory and Routine Activity Theory both seem to indicate that post-crisis international travellers, such as those that travelled abroad following the tragic events of 9/11, would be more risk adverse than those who had enjoyed the pleasures of such travel before the crisis. This is supported by the Optimal Arousal Theory that would predict that post-crisis travellers would adjust their personal arousal versus security fulcrum to give greater weight to the latter when faced with the uncertainty that follows a crisis. However, this research noted an interesting dichotomy –

that while far fewer Americans travelled internationally in the wake of 9/11, those who made the journey in the fourth quarter of 2001 were remarkably similar, psychographically and behaviourally, to those who had done so in the year prior to the attack. This insight is important for tourism organizations facing future crises. Tourism marketers can anticipate, following a crisis, that visitor arrival numbers will fall, and that such a decline in demand may require that they seek new market segments. Facing a declining market, they may even recognize a need to craft new marketing messages to induce visitation. However, these findings provide reassurance that their target market's behaviours and attitudes will not fundamentally change and that those travellers they do attract will be very similar to those they have served in the past. They can expect their post-crisis travellers to partake in the same activities, with little change in their trip planning, expectations, perceptions and travel behaviours. These are comforting and useful findings as crisis management plans are recrafted and refined in the wake of 9/11.

References

Bello, D.C. and Etzel, J.E. (1985) The role of novelty in the pleasure travel experience. *Journal of Travel Research* 12, 20–26.

Cohen, E. (1984) The sociology of tourism: approaches, issues and findings. *Annual Review of Sociology* 10, 373–392.

Crotts, J. (1993) Personality correlates of the novelty seeking drive. *Journal of Hospitality and Leisure Marketing* 1, 7–29.

Crotts, J.C. (2003) Theoretical perspectives on tourist criminal victimization. *Journal of Tourism Studies* 14, 92–98.

Crotts, J.C. and Erdmann, R. (2000) Does national culture influence consumers' evaluation of travel services? a test of Hofstede's model of cross cultural differences. *Managing Service Quality* 10, 410–419.

Daneshkhu, S. (2001) Hotels forced to accommodate US gloom. *Financial Times (London)* 21 August, p. 4.

Fall, L.T. (2003) Using Grunig's situational theory of publics to investigate how convention & visitors bureaus across the nation are employing communication tactics in the wake of September 11. *Iowa Journal of Communication* 35, 121–141.

Felson, M. and Cohen, L.E. (1980) Human ecology and crime: a routine activity approach. *Human Ecology* 8, 389–405.

Fredrickson, B.L., Tugade, M.M., Waugh, C.E. and Larkin, G.R. (2003) What good are positive emotions in crises? A prospective study of resilience and emotions following the terrorist attacks on the USA on September 11th, 2001. *Journal of Personality and Social Psychology* 84, 365–376.

Frisby, E. (2002) Communicating in a Crisis: the British Tourist Authority's responses to the foot-and-mouth outbreak and 11th September, 2001. *Journal of Vacation Marketing* 9, 89–100.

Hebb, D.O. and Thompson, W.R. (1954) The social significance of animal studies. In: Lindzey, G. (ed.) *Handbook of Social Psychology*. Addison-Wesley, Reading, Massachusetts, pp. 228–234.

Hofstede, G. (2001) *Cultural Consequences*, 2nd edn. Sage Publications, Thousand Oaks, California.

Hopper, P. (2002) Marketing London in a difficult climate. *Journal of Vacation Marketing* 9, 81–88.

Iso-Ahola, S.E. (1980) *The Social Psychology of Leisure and Recreation*. Wm. C. Brown, Dubuque, Iowa.

Iso-Ahola, S.E. (1981) The social psychology of recreational travel. In: Goeldner, C.R. (ed.) *Proceedings of the Twelfth Annual*

Conference of the Travel and Tourism *Research Association TTRA.* Las Vegas, Nevada, pp. 113–124.

Litvin, S. (1999) The minefield of the middle: real problems facing the mid-size travel agent. In: Moisey, R.N., Nickerson, N.N. and Klenosky, D.B. (eds) *Navigating the Global Waters, 30th Annual Conference Proceedings TTRA.* Boise, Idaho, pp. 118–133.

Litvin, S.W. and Alderson, L.L. (2003) How Charleston got its grove back: a CVB's response to 9/11. *Journal of Vacation Marketing* 9, 188–197.

Melzack, R. (1952) Irrational fears in dogs. *Canadian Journal of Psychology* 6 (3), 141–147.

Money, R.B. and Crotts, J.C. (2003) The effect of uncertainty avoidance on information search, planning, and purchases of international travel vacations. *Tourism Management* 24, 191–202.

Montgomery, K.C. (1952) Exploratory behaviour and its relation to spontaneous alteration in a series of maze exposures. *Journal of Comparative Psychology* 45, 50–57.

Office of Travel and Tourism Industries (2003) Basic Market Analysis Program U.S. Citizen Air Traffic to Overseas Regions, Canada & Mexico, <http://tinet.ita.doc.gov> (accessed July 2003).

Piotrkowski, C.S. and Brannen, S.J. (2002) Exposure, threat appraisal, and lost confidence as predictors of PTSD symptoms following September 11, 2001. *American Journal of Orthopsychiatry* 72, 476–485.

Plog, S.C. (1991) *Leisure Travel: Making it a Growth Market … Again.* John Wiley & Sons, New York.

Shieber, S., Crotts, J.C. and Hollinger, R. (1995) Florida tourists vulnerability to crime. In: Pizam, A. and Mansfield, Y. (eds) *Tourism, Crime and International Security.* John Wiley & Sons, London, pp. 37–50.

Snepenger, D.J. (1987) Segmenting the vacation market by novelty-seeking role. *Journal of Travel Research* 26 (2), 8–14.

Tourism Industries (2001) *Inflight Survey of Overseas Arrivals to the USA.* US Department of Commerce, International Trade Administration, Washington, DC.

Tversky, A. and Shafir, E. (1992) Choice under conflict: the dynamics of deferred decision. *Psychological Science* 3, 358–361.

Valentine, C.W. (1930) The innate basis of fear. *Journal of Genetic Psychology* 37, 394–419.

22 Crisis Communication Response Strategies: a Case Study of the Irish Tourist Board's Response to the 2001 European Foot and Mouth Scare

SIOBHAN TIERNAN, JOSEPHINE IGOE, CONOR CARROLL AND SINEAD O'KEEFE

Introduction

The tourism industry is constantly under threat from any number of negative triggering event(s), which may decimate their industry. Events such as 11 September 2001 (9/11), the Bali bombings, the Turkish earthquake, SARS (severe acute respiratory syndrome) and bird flu can potentially destroy prospective visitors' confidence in a tourist destination. Potential visitors may not travel or travel elsewhere due to safety concerns. In light of these potentially damaging events and their increasing frequency, tourist destinations must put in place effective crisis management recovery strategies to maintain and restore visitor confidence in a destination, after a crisis event. Such an event occurred in Ireland in 2001, when the UK foot and mouth epidemic threatened the Irish tourist industry. This chapter sets out to portray the communications response strategy employed by the Irish Tourist Board (ITB) in New York. It attempts to provide key learning points for the management strategies during a crisis.

First, the chapter will give an overview of the key theoretical literature on crisis management. Much of the research to date in this field has been practitioner oriented. This study will compare the strategies employed by the ITB with normative literature prescriptions. Secondly, an overview of the tourism context will be given, to emphasize the key importance of the tourism industry to the Irish economy. Finally, the case findings are presented. The use of a case study methodology is in line with previous research methodologies employed in this field. Crisis management has a strong tradition in case-based research. These cases prove to be sources of

© CAB International 2007. *Crisis Management in Tourism*
(eds Eric Laws, Bruce Prideaux and Kaye Chon)

learning for the management of other crisis situations. This chapter attempts to add to this learning, through documenting the response of the ITB in New York to the UK foot and mouth crisis. While providing key learning points for practice, it also integrates the most recent academic literature to develop key recommendations for dealing with such a crisis situation in the future.

Conceptual Understanding of a Crisis

The word 'crisis' is commonly misconstrued and is constantly quoted in the turbulent modern business environment. It is now commonly used to describe any *'problem'*, *'scandal'*, *'disaster'*, *'threat'*, *'accident'* *'jolt'*, *'scare'* and *'catastrophe'*, with no attempt made to delineate the scope or severity of a given problem (Reilly, 1993; Fishman, 1999). One main tier of academic work on crises has been the definition of what is meant by the word crisis. Such a simple word is difficult to define, due to contextual differences, coupled with differing perceptions of the nature of a crisis held by the individual, group or organization. One of the seminal definitions is offered by Herman (1969, pp. 29–30) who argues that there must be three conditions for a crisis to exist. First, there must exist a threat that hinders the achievement of a unit's goals. Secondly, the decision time to alter the situation must be short, and thirdly the event is a surprise to decision makers (Billings *et al.*, 1980). However, the element of threat is the only variable which has received constant empirical support as a necessary element of a crisis (Billings *et al.*, 1980). Shrivastava (1987) states that corporate crises can be triggered by both internal and external environmental factors. Crises do not necessarily have to threaten the survival of the firm, but merely interfere with organizational objectives.

Some key commonalities in the definitions emerge, namely that of a triggering event, a turning point for an organization, surprise or non-routine, damage to reputation, and a threat to survival or goals of the company. Organizational crises are highly ambiguous events that require a decision, or judgement, which will result in change that is either positive or negative (Pearson and Clair, 1998). Faulkner (2001) attempted to synthesize the contributions of Weiner and Kahn (1972), Fink (1986) and Keown-McMullan (1997) by suggesting that there are several essential characteristics of a crisis situation, outlined as follows:

- A triggering event occurs, which is so significant that it may affect the very survival of the organization.
- A sense of urgency, surprise and high threat are present, leaving a short decision time period.
- A feeling of an inability to cope with the situation is present amongst those affected.
- Decisive change is imminent which may have positive or negative consequences.
- The crisis situations are dynamic, fluid and unstable.

Given the sheer variety and array of crises that can affect an organization, it is important to delineate between crisis categories. A variety of crisis typologies exist. Crises can range from those that incur minimal damage in terms of lost sales, profit and reputation, to those that have profound repercussions for its stakeholders, and those that threaten its very survival. Mitroff (1988) created a comprehensive inventory of the types of crisis that could affect a company. Although not exhaustive, it provides a useful summation of typical crises that interfere with normal business operations, and that could possibly impinge on a firm's reputation or status, and ultimately affect its bottom line.

Many authors have used a wide variety of dimensions in their classification schema for crises including; internal/external, violent/non-violent, intentional/unintentional, severe/normal damage, technical/socio-political failure, remote/relevant environment, high/low deniability and concrete/diffuse victims (Marcus and Goodman, 1991; Egelhoff and Sen, 1992; Newsom et al., 1992; Pearson and Mitroff, 1993). The list of potential matrices and frameworks for the analysis and classification of crises is infinite. This further adds to the complexity of attempting to define the boundary or scope of a crisis in developing a successful crisis management response strategy.

Crisis Management: Communication Strategies

Crisis management by its very nature is multidisciplinary, involving numerous and varied fields of enquiry such as economics, sociology, psychology, political science, public administration, public relations, environmental science, chemical engineering, computer science and communication (Preble, 1997). In the crisis management literature, there are typically two strands of literature, those that focus on the 'preventive' aspects (how can crises be prevented from occurring), and those that focus on the 'reactive' aspects, once a crisis event occurs. Effective crisis management can reduce the crisis life cycle, returning organizations to normal operations. This in turn prevents lost sales, limits damage to reputation, precludes the development of public policy issues, saves resources and protects lives, health and the environment (Higbee, 1992; Barton, 1993). Crises are events that can threaten the very existence of an organization (Barton, 1993). A crisis can have huge impact on a firm such as: a huge legal liability, lost sales, lost profits, lost productivity, be accused of social irresponsibility, be vulnerable to attack from competitors, drain resources, but above all damage the reputation and prestige of the organization (Barton, 1993; Mitroff and Pearson, 1993; Shrivastava, 1994; Siomkos, 1999; Tsang, 2000).

There exists a growing volume of research dedicated to communication strategies during a crisis and post-crisis, such as Marcus and Goodman (1991), Allen and Caillouet (1994), Hearit (1994, 1995), Benoit (1995, 1997), Coombs (1995, 1998, 1999a, b), Hobbs (1995) and Zerman (1995).

Research on crisis communications can be focused upon two succinct areas, that of *form* (i.e. how the crisis response is presented), and that of *content* (i.e. the actual messages used in the response) (Coombs 1999a). Coombs (1999a, p. 128) defines crisis communication strategies as all 'actual verbal and nonverbal responses an organization uses to address a crisis'. Stakeholders assess all aspects of an organization's crisis communications response. Coombs (2000) contends that three basic informational needs exist: background information on the crisis event; how stakeholders will be affected; and, finally, what precautionary measures stakeholders need to take. Blame and responsibility are crucial issues for affected stakeholders during a crisis or disaster (Harrison, 1999). If an organization is perceived to have failed in its responsibility, this in turn has repercussions for the firm's reputation, damaging their credibility and reliability.

Crisis communication, according to Heath (1994, p. 259) is seen as 'the enactment of control (or at least its appearance) in the face of high uncertainty in an effort to win external audiences' confidence, in ways that are ethical'. The remit of this definition should be extended, so that crisis communications targets both the internal and external audiences of an organization. Effective crisis communications strategies are crucial in ensuring that positive relationships with stakeholders are maintained (Fishman, 1999). Crises create uncertainty for stakeholders and they need to minimize this uncertainty through the provision of information which is pertinent to the crisis (Birch, 1994). Many commentators believe that the primary objective of crisis management is to maintain an organization's image, the public perception of an organization (Pearson and Mitroff, 1993; Sturges, 1994).

Case Study Findings

The ITB was forced to implement a crisis management strategy designed to prevent a widespread collapse of the American market to Ireland. The crisis management team implemented a two-phased strategy in the form of a 'Reassurance and Recovery Campaign' to deal with the situation. Each strategy focused on publicity, advertising and relations with trade members and tour operators. The outcome of this strategy was that the decline in tourism numbers for April–June was only 6.8% as opposed to much larger projections. In 2000, a total of 297,000 passengers travelled compared with 274,000 in 2001 during the April–June period. This case will describe in detail how the ITB formulated and implemented its two-phased strategy in response to the crisis.

The tourism context

International tourism has expanded at such a pace that it can be truly considered as a global business. Annually in excess of 700 million international trips are made, generating €500 billion in annual receipts. The tourism industry sustains over 70 million jobs worldwide and currently accounts for 4% of global gross domestic produce (GDP) (Bord Failte, 2003). Growth in the international tourism sector has been driven by economic wealth, mass communication, affordable travel, availability of leisure time and travel opportunities opened by new technology.

In Ireland, tourism plays a critically important role in national and regional wealth creation. The industry itself is a major driver of economic activity, generating €4 billion in foreign revenue earnings, which amounts to 4.4% of gross national produce (GNP). It supports 140,000 jobs and is by far the largest Irish-owned internationally traded sector of the Irish economy. It has a knock-on effect on demand for a variety of other products and services provided by a wide range of enterprises, which are predominantly Irish owned and small to medium size in nature. The importance of tourism to Ireland is unquestionable.

In early 2001, the Irish tourism industry achieved unprecedented annual growth rates that had been present throughout the previous decade. Visitor numbers to Ireland grew well ahead of global rates throughout the 1990s, increasing by an average of over 7% each year compared with 4.3% globally. In terms of receipts, Irelands performance has also exceeded global rates. Table 22.1 depicts the trends in visitor numbers and foreign revenue earnings from 1990 to 2002.

The best performance source markets for Irish tourism have been the USA and the UK. In terms of per capita spend, North America is significantly higher than any other geographic region of the world, as shown in Table 22.2. A direct consequence of this situation is that a downturn in the American market has a disproportionate effect on the overall revenue stream.

The ITB in New York

A strong attachment has always existed between the USA and Ireland, as is evidenced by the huge number of Americans who visit Ireland every year (895,000 tourists travelled from North America in 2003). Emigration was the major factor leading to both political and personal links between the

Table 22.1. Visitor numbers and foreign revenue € million earnings 1990–2002.

Area	1990	1995	2000	2001	2002
UK	1785	2285	3482	3340	3452
Europe	744	1101	1435	1336	1378
Germany	178	319	319	285	288
France	198	234	283	280	298
North USA	443	641	1056	903	844
Total revenue	1446	2132	3637	3922	3985

Source: Tourism Policy Review Group (2003, p. 30).

Table 22.2. Overseas visitor spend per capita (€) 1990–2002.

	1990	1995	2000	2001	2002
UK	237	279	317	362	372
Mainland Europe	425	447	506	610	629
North America	477	545	652	795	840
Other areas	483	601	684	801	933
Total overseas	326	386	434	505	522

Source: Tourism Policy Review Group (2003, p. 31).

USA and Ireland. In 2000, a total of 1,158,000 tourists travelled from North America to Ireland. Ireland is now ranked eighth in the most popular North American holiday destinations in Europe. The potential role for tourism was anticipated in Ireland as early as the 1950s when it was recognized that Ireland could benefit from the mounting growth in global tourism. As early as 1925, the Irish Tourist Association (ITA) had been established. An Irish tourism marketing organization was established – Bord Failte Eireann – in 1955, following a government decision that a single organization should be responsible for the development and marketing of the Irish tourism industry. Tourism steadily grew in the 1960s, with a 47% increase in tourism revenues.

There are currently two main state agencies involved in the development and promotion of the tourism sector in Ireland. Failte Eireann, The National Tourism Development Authority, was established in 2003 after a structural reorganization of the former Bord Failte. Tourism Ireland was also established as part of the agreement reached in the peace agreements concluded in Belfast in 1998. It is designed to promote tourism to the whole of the island of Ireland in contrast to the previous situation where the roles were performed independently by Bord Failte and the Northern Ireland Tourist Board.

To develop and promote tourism further, Ireland has Tourist Board Offices located throughout the country and also abroad. There are 100 tourist offices in the Republic and 30 in Northern Ireland. The ITB's mandate is 'to market Ireland as a tourist destination, to help the Irish industry develop and to provide information for decision-making' (Tourism Policy Review Group, 2003). The ITB's head office is in Dublin and it is represented in Northern Ireland and 20 overseas markets. The organization employs a total of 239 staff members.

Following the first transatlantic flight by Aer Lingus, the Irish state airline, in 1958, a New York tourism office was created by Bord Failte in partnership with the airline. Today, the ITB's North American headquarters is still in New York. The North American market is divided into five different regions, the Mid-West, West Coast, South, East Coast and Canada; each region is represented by a regional marketing manager. The ITB in New York is focused on promoting Ireland while undertaking general product marketing to support the industry's own tactical marketing activities.

The Marketing and Promotions Department in the ITB in New York work together to promote Ireland on two different levels:

- *Destination marketing*: Ireland is promoted as a general holiday destination through brand advertising. These may include car touring or heritage vacations, with overnight stays at castles or manor houses.
- *Sports/activity based*: Ireland is promoted as a top destination in Europe for golf vacations, angling, and walking and equestrian pursuits.

The Public Relations Department of the ITB in New York focuses on quality coverage to reinforce messages sent out to the public from the Advertising Department. The main objective of the Public Relations Department is to generate national awareness and exposure for Ireland, with an emphasis on niche markets of golf, equestrian, walking, cultural or heritage travellers.

The crisis begins

February 2001 saw the outbreak of foot and mouth disease (FMD) at a slaughterhouse in Northumberland, UK. Quarantines and mass killings of livestock were soon common across the UK. By 8 March, 45,000 animals had been destroyed in the UK. To prevent FMD spreading to Ireland, immediate disinfectant procedures were implemented at all points of air and sea arrivals. These measures were essential once confirmed cases of FMD were announced in Northern Ireland. Sporting events, public meetings and even the St Patrick's Day parades were all cancelled.

An action group representing the Department of Tourism, Sport and Recreation, the ITB and the tourist industry was established in Dublin to monitor the FMD situation. They strived actively to manage issues including holidays already booked, and limit the amount of negative publicity towards Ireland on a global scale. The objective was to minimize long-term damage to Ireland's image as a holiday destination while considering Ireland's future prospects in overseas markets. Field sports including hunting, shooting, fishing and equestrian activities, and promotional activities such as advertising sporting events were cancelled on 6 March. This acted as a death knell to the ITB's strategy of sports/activity-based tourism marketing strategies. City and urban touring products and facilities were promoted, as were museums, castles and heritage sites. Restrictions to those travelling to the UK were clearly stated, while short-term tactical advertising across the UK was cancelled.

Communications response strategies

The outbreak of FMD in the UK received enormous publicity in the North American media. At this initial stage, management at the ITB in New York should have drafted a Crisis Management Plan. Such measures would have given management time to consider various marketing and publicity campaigns, if FMD were to strike Ireland, while also dealing with the negative publicity in the long term.

Americans spoke of FMD in Europe as opposed to specific areas hit by the epidemic. Headlines such as 'Foot-and-Mouth grips Europe' appeared in *San Antonio Express News* with a circulation of 375,294 people on 4 March 2001, and this was representative of the typical US media coverage. The Public Relations Department's aim was to broadcast that Ireland was free of FMD in the early stages of the UK's outbreak. Some newspaper articles were misleading if not actually incorrect. Such articles included the *New York Times* on 3 March, as the headline read 'Foot and Mouth is bad luck of the Irish'. The article did state that Ireland was free of FMD; however, one needed to read the whole article to establish this.

Network television stations across the USA carried the foot and mouth crisis as their main news bulletin on 12 March, focusing exclusively on the cancellation of the St Patrick's Day parades in Ireland. One of the most dominant features concerning the negative publicity attached to the foot and mouth crisis in Ireland was that it occurred at a time when potential holidaymakers are very impressionable and engaged in the process of selecting holiday destinations, as shown in Fig. 22.1.

The ITB felt that this was a crucial period in potential tourist decision making and, if tourists were faced with possible restrictions on what they could do in Ireland, they may have decided to discount Ireland as a destination. During these weeks in early March, calls to the New York office, the 1-800 North American phone number and to the Public Relations Department increased. North American's were assured that Ireland was free of FMD by ITB staff in each of these departments. The ITB's websites which service North American tourists as well as the ITB's global site and www.shamrock.org, which serves members of the travel trade in North America, were updated on a daily basis. Each of these websites gave exact details on precautionary measures being undertaken by the Irish government to ensure Ireland remained free of foot and mouth.

A list of the closed tourist attractions was made available, and updated cancellations of sporting events were also posted. Faxes and e-mails were sent daily to 186 of the ITB's main trade contacts giving details of closures.

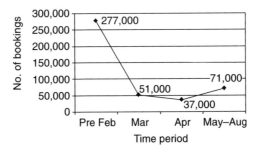

Fig. 22.1. Decision/bookings season. Source: Irish Tourist Board in New York.

Communications began with 18,000 retail agents who promote European holiday destinations and included regular e-mail and updates regarding both FMD and other tourism-related news concerning Ireland.

On 12 March, management met to discuss a strategy for the North American market. The immediate aim was to combat negative publicity by portraying Ireland as free from FMD. As there was no structured crisis management team within the ITB's management structure, an initial crisis management structure was implemented. The Chief Executive of ITB in New York assumed the role of crisis management team (CMT) leader. It was necessary for all departments to work together to encourage Americans to travel to Ireland. The team discussed in detail the scale of FMD in Europe and its possible impact on the North American consumer. It was crucial to assess the potential impact of FMD, and its severity once contracted. Experts were consulted at this stage. Members of the CMT met with members of the US travel trade in the following days to outline a possible strategy to encourage consumers to continue making holiday plans to travel to Ireland.

On 22 March, the Republic of Ireland's first case of FMD was discovered in County Louth, despite the efforts of the Irish government and the public to prevent the disease entering Ireland. One specific editorial in the *Atlanta Journal* read 'Dublin – Ireland – the first cases of Foot and Mouth Disease were confirmed today in the Republic of Ireland ...' (2001, p. 1). This gave the impression that FMD was in Dublin, Ireland's most popular tourist destination, instead of outlining a single secondary case confirmed in County Louth.

Once FMD was announced in the Republic of Ireland, the CMT held a lengthy meeting. This was the crucial stage in management's operational planning system to ensure that Ireland's image as a tourist destination experienced as little negative publicity as possible. The ITB in New York was already receiving messages of concern from trade members due to vacation cancellations occurring on a daily basis. The CMT at the ITB went from conceptualization to implementation within days. It analysed the impact of the outbreak of FMD in Ireland on tourism from North America on two fronts: first, the cancellations experienced by trade members and, secondly, the national negative publicity regarding travel to Europe. They then set about designing a 'Reassurance and Recovery Campaign'.

When a crisis occurs suddenly, the allocation of funding is often a problem for management. Funds had to be taken away from existing budgets, to counter the threat of the crisis. In addition, the Irish government allocated US$2.2 million to the Reassurance and Recovery Campaigns. The budget allocation is presented in Table 22.3.

Implementation of the Reassurance Campaign: 26 March–7 April

A general staff meeting was called on the afternoon of 22 March. All staff members were informed of the situation in Ireland and the ITB's position

Table 22.3. Irish government budget allocation to the reassurance and recovery campaigns.

Budget allocation	Amount (US$)
Advertising phase 1	1,600,000
Advertising phase 2	1,600,000
Minister's visit	60,000
Task force	60,000
Postcard mailing	300,000
Other direct mail	100,000
Public relations	85,000
Trade advertising	50,000
Radio advertising	60,000
Delta in-flight advertising	40,000
Travel	40,000
Total	3,995,000

Source: Irish Tourist Board in New York.

towards the media. Each department head briefed staff members as to their particular role throughout the crisis situation. This was an essential measure that should be part of all crisis strategies. At this early stage, there were no accurate predictions as to the extent of the disease and whether FMD would spread further in the Republic of Ireland. The CMT implemented a two-phased strategy in the form of a Reassurance and Recovery Campaign to deal with the crisis (O'Keefe, 2002). Each campaign focused on three areas:

- publicity;
- trade members and tour operators;
- advertising.

Publicity

Public Relations Departments help a company manage change, which can often be difficult in a crisis situation. The ITB in North America has a long-standing relationship with both the public and the media in the USA and Canada. This was of critical importance particularly in a crisis situation. This relationship, combined with management negotiating abilities, helped to deal with deadlines and find potential solutions to the problem at hand. The Public Relations Department also interacts with more internal and external audiences than any other department within the company's structure.

Management failed to appoint one key spokesperson to deal with media enquiries. The CMT leader spoke to many of the key publications and the head of public relations oversaw all press releases and interviews. Staff members in the Public Relations Department and those dealing with the 1-800 phone number were issued guidelines. Phone line operators were given basic facts about the company's situation while diverting all media calls to a designated spokesperson. At some stages of the crisis, there was uncertainty as to who was authorized to answer questions.

The Public Relations Department worked closely with numerous journalists throughout this period. A number of positive articles about Ireland unrelated to the FMD outbreak were published. Each year the ITB's Public Relations Department conducts spring press trips where North American journalists travel to Ireland with a view to publishing articles on their vacation experiences. Spring press trips in 2001 were postponed until the summer months. The crisis management team decided to hold the annual St Patrick's Day radio interviews, which were broadcast live to over 350 radio stations throughout the USA. These interviews were an opportunity to tell Americans that Ireland was still open to tourists regardless of some closures of tourist attractions and the cancellation of St Patrick's Day parades throughout the Republic of Ireland.

The services of Lou Hammond and Associates were employed for 2 months commencing on 20 March to assist the ITB's Public Relations Department in organizing media interviews and to issue media releases on a regular basis. A constant stream of positive news about amenities and activities was sent to the media to reinforce the 'the business as usual with loads to do in Ireland' message. The Public Relations Department also employed the services of Luce Clippings Co. to monitor all references of FMD in the US-mediated States.

Dealing with trade members and tour operators

One of the main aims of the Promotions Department was to reassure members of the North American travel trade that Ireland was not closed to tourism during the foot and mouth crisis. On 23 March, ITB staff members began meetings with cross-sections of the US travel trade to discuss strategy and proposals for reassurance and recovery plans. A letter of reassurance was sent to 5300 Retail Travel Agents who previously attended ITB spring seminars. It was also sent to 827 Shamrock Club members. Agent training programmes in association with Consortia and Associations were intensified.

Advertising

It was necessary to buy advertising space in newspapers, and airtime on television and on the radio throughout North America to convey the message that Ireland was open for visitors regardless of FMD. A reassurance letter signed by the Chief Executive of the ITB in New York was published in the travel section of *USA Today* (circulation 2.639 million) on 30 March. A more ethnic version of this letter was published in the *Irish Voice* and *Irish Echo* newspapers in New York on 3 and 7 April, respectively.

A direct mail initiative aimed at the 52,000 most recent enquirers through the irelandvacations.com website and callers to the 1-800 number were mailed a pack containing the main Ireland vacation planner and tour packages along with a letter of reassurance. Reassurance e-mails were sent to 40,000 enquirers who logged on to www.shamrock.org. The crisis management team was forced to act quickly at a time when emotions were high and the Irish tourist industry was threatened. The crisis management process was maintained throughout the summer months and they were then able to implement a recovery campaign once the incubation period lapsed in County Louth and Ireland was declared free of FMD.

Implementation of the Recovery Campaign: 7 April Onwards

The CMT implemented a recovery campaign to increase awareness that it was safe to travel to Ireland. An incentive marketing drive was undertaken to measure the American market, encouraging those holidaying in the autumn to travel to Ireland. Moving from the reassurance campaign to a recovery campaign was an effective mechanism of progression once Ireland was clear of FMD. However, the CMT should have taken the time to analyse the crisis management plan, altering possible ineffective procedures. Feedback from trade members and media representatives is an effective way of gaining positive and negative opinions for consideration in designing the recovery campaign and future crisis management operations.

Publicity

Irish President Mary McAleese played an important part in spreading the message that Ireland welcomed visitors when she visited Texas in April. President McAleese attended an ITB reception for travel trade members, the media and the Irish American community in Dallas. Commencing on 22 April, the Minister for Tourism, Sport and Recreation Dr James McDaid undertook an extensive visit to the USA. The Minister's visit was a major step in promoting Ireland as a holiday destination through extensive media interviews in each city. Lou Hammond and Associates played an important role in getting the Minister face time on television, and coverage on radio and in print.

Dealing with trade members and tour operators

Members of the Board of Directors, Regional Presidents of ASDA and media representatives travelled to Ireland on 22 April on a fact-finding mission to give personal testimonies on their return. A week-long promotion 'Agent Appreciation Week' was undertaken from 21 to 25 May, and 30 suppliers who participated in the 2000–2001 Marketing Ireland Seminars attended. An hour-long trade show followed by dinner and entertainment took place in Boston, Garden City, Los Angeles, Chicago and Washington, DC.

Advertising

Direct mail during the reassurance campaign included e-mailing previous enquirers about details of new fares and tour operator packages. Postcards were sent to enquirers via the 1-800 number, and 75,000 e-mails were sent to enquirers from the site reiterating the message that 'Ireland is open for business'. Advertising on cable television channels was scheduled for 3 weeks commencing 23 April. However, travel trade members requested that this be brought forward and began on 7 April. Advertising was carried out on 11 cable channels and carried price/product messages. Aer Lingus special fares were promoted through the ITB's in-house voice recording system. Trade advertisements appeared in *Canadian Travel Press* and *Canadian Travel Courier* along with consumer advertising in two Toronto publications on 14 and 15 April.

Discussion and Conclusions

This case highlights key features of a 'Crisis Communications Response Strategy'. Key lessons pertaining to the overall management of a crisis situation are also evident. These include: the need to be aware of the informational needs of a variety of stakeholders; the importance of the dispersion of timely and accurate information; that organizations must deploy adequate resources to counter the impact of a crisis; that multiple methods of communications must be exploited; and finally that a single messenger should be used in dealing with media enquires.

Billings *et al.* (1980) surmised three basic responses to a crisis: inaction; routine solutions; and original solutions. By not responding, the media is allowed to define the situation. Organizations need to prepare for the many types of crisis that they may be exposed to or vulnerable toward. If a company fails to appreciate the magnitude or seriousness of a crisis, it may turn into a potential disaster for the company. There is a huge opportunity cost if the company fails to respond and deploy resources to contain the impact of the crisis. They must understand the implications of failing to act and if the affected stakeholders see their response as inadequate.

Crisis communications is crucial to ensuring that positive relationships with stakeholders are maintained (Fishman, 1999). The diversity and complexity of examining varied stakeholder's calls for research that focuses on one particular stakeholder. For example, if consumers are exposed to negative information/stories about a firm, it greatly affects consumers' consumption-related beliefs and attitudes (Griffin *et al.*, 1991).

Three key lessons can be identified from the ITB response to the foot and fouth crisis:

- To have in place a structured action plan, even before the crisis hits, as time is at a premium during a crisis.
- To have a structure in place, where members of the team know their role in the recovery campaign.
- Most importantly, the identification of key stakeholders is critical to the entire strategy, in terms of knowing who to communicate with, how and when. Knowing your target audience is vital to a successful crisis communications strategy.

The CMT at the ITB went from conceptualization to implementation in a matter of days. The communications strategy proved vital to damage limitation of the crisis. Crucial to its publicity success was the fact that the ITB has a long-standing relationship with both the public and the media in the USA and Canada. However, one structural issue that should be acknowledged is that the ITB management failed to appoint one key spokesperson to deal with media queries. This led to confusion within the team as to who should answer certain questions, and potentially could have led to conflicting publicity if not recognized up front.

Organizations should employ a combination of marketing communications methods to communicate their message during and after a crisis event. The types of methods available can be divided into those which are required for immediate delivery of corporate 'messages' and those that are used in the long run, helping to rebuild stakeholder confidence in the product brand or corporate brand. Immediate delivery mediums can be classified as methods which allow for the rapid design and transmission of a company's response to a crisis issue to the affected stakeholder. The term 'rapid' means that they can be implemented in less than 24 hours of the crisis occurring or being discussed in the public domain. The relationship with journalists was vital in communications with the consumer. Having a single media contact is vital in ensuring consistency of messages and so as to avoid confusion of media representatives. A point of strategic success was the decision to broadcast live interviews from television stations on St Patrick's Day. This in turn was built on the strength of the relationship that has existed throughout history between the Irish and the North Americans.

The other key stakeholder group, beside the consumer, is trade members. The ITB sent staff to meet with cross-sections of the US travel trade. Letters of reassurance were sent to 5300 Retail Travel Agents. Letters were also sent to 827 Shamrock Club members. Agent training programmes were intensified. The media have a role in reporting and commenting on a story. The media processes a company's message and disseminates this information to the company's various stakeholders. The interpretation that they place on an event or a company's response to a crisis will have enormous repercussions on how the message is communicated. Thus media relations are of critical importance and the multifaceted targeting approach employed by the ITB in New York proved critical to the success of the campaign. It was vital that the ITB maintained Ireland's product image throughout North America. The strong relationship the ITB has built up with the trade members and the end-consumer proved absolutely critical to the trust that existed between the stakeholders throughout the crisis. In summary, an integrated structured communications response strategy was essential to the success of the 'Reassurance and Recovery Campaign'.

While the number of case studies in managing crises in tourism is growing, the difficulty for researchers and practitioners is that no one crisis is the same, due to unique contextual variables that may exist. Crises, by their nature, present a multitude of challenges for researchers and practitioners. The exploration of newer cases helps to enrich our understanding of the nature of crises and improve the design of effective response strategies. This case study helps our understanding of the role of crisis communication response strategies, and explores the implementation of such a strategy. The study highlights the importance of speed, pro-active media relations along with recognition of the varied stakeholders' informational needs. Recognition of the two distinct phases, 'reassurance' and 'recovery', was essential in dealing with the complex context during the crisis. Other structural elements such as the appropriate allocation of sufficient resources (i.e. manpower, money and management) to combat the effects of crisis, and the usage of a coordinated integrated marketing communications plan were also essential to the success of the campaign.

References

Allen, M.W. and Caillouet, R.H. (1994) Legitimate endeavours: impression management strategies used by an organization in crisis. *Communication Monographs* 61, pp. 44–62.

Barton, L. (1993) *Crisis in Organizations: Managing and Communicating in the Heat of Chaos.* College Divisions South-Western Publishing, Cincinnati, Ohio.

Benoit, W.L. (1995) *Accounts, Excuses, and Apologies: a Theory of Image Restoration.* State University of New York Press, Albany, New York.

Benoit, W.L. (1997) Image repair discourse and crisis communication. *Public Relations Review* 23, 177–180.

Billings, R., Milburn, T. and Schaalman, M.L. (1980) A model of crisis perception: a theoretical and empirical analysis. *Administrative Science Quarterly* 25, 300–316.

Birch, J. (1994) New factors in crisis planning and response. *Public Relations Quarterly* 39, 31–34.

Bord Failte (2003) New horizons for Irish tourism – an agenda for action. *Report of the Tourism Policy Review Group to the Minster for Arts, Sport and Tourism.* Dublin.

Coombs, T. (1995) Choosing the right words: the development of guidelines for the selection of the 'appropriate' crisis response strategies. *Management Communication Quarterly* 8, 447–476.

Coombs, T. (1998) An analytic framework for crisis situations: better responses from a better understanding of the situation. *Journal of Public Relations Research* 10, 177–192.

Coombs, T. (1999a) *Ongoing Crisis Communication – Planning, Managing, and Responding,* Sage Series in Public Relations, Sage, London.

Coombs, T. (1999b) Information and compassion in crisis responses: a test of their effects. *Journal of Public Relations Research* 11, 125–142.

Coombs, T. (2000) Designing post-crisis messages: lessons for crisis response strategies. *Review of Business,* pp. 37–41.

Egelhoff, W.G. and Sen, F. (1992) An information-processing model of crisis management. *Management Communication Quarterly* 5, 443–484.

Faulkner, B. (2001) Towards a framework for tourism disaster management. *Tourism Management* 22, 135–147.

Fink, S. (1986) *Crisis Management.* American Association of Management, New York.

Fishman, D. (1999) ValuJet flight 592: crisis communication theory blended and extended. *Communication Quarterly* 47, 345–375.

Griffin, M., Babin, B.J. and Attaway, J.S. (1991) An empirical investigation of the impact of negative publicity on consumers attitudes and intentions. *Advances in Consumer Research* 18, 334–341.

Harrison, S. (1999) Media liaison: lessons from the front line. In: Harrison, S. (ed.) *Disasters and the Media.* Macmillan Press, London, pp. 203–209.

Hearit, K.M. (1994) Apologies and public relations crises at Chrysler, Toshiba, and Volvo. *Public Relations Review* 20, 113–125.

Hearit, K.M. (1995) From 'We didn't do it': to 'It's not our fault': the use of apologia in public relations crises. In: Elwood, W.N. (ed.) *Public Relations Inquiry as Rhetorical Criticism.* Praeger, Westport, Connecticut, pp. 117–134.

Heath, R. (1994) *Management of Corporate Communication: From Interpersonal Contacts to External Affairs.* Lawrence Erlbaum, Hillsdale, New Jersey.

Herman, C.F. (1969) *Crises in Foreign Policy. A Simulation Analysis.* The Bobbs-Merril Company, New York.

Higbee, A.G. (1992) Shortening the crisis lifecycle: seven rules to live by. *Occupational Hazards* 54, 137–138.

Hobbs, J. (1995) Treachery by any other name: a case study of the Toshiba public relations crisis. *Management Communication Quarterly* 8, 323–346.

Keown-McMullan, C. (1997) Crisis: when a does a molehill become a mountain? *Disaster Prevention and Management* 6, 4–10.

Marcus, A. and Goodman, R.S. (1991) Victims and shareholders: the dilemmas of presenting corporate policy during a crisis. *Academy of Management Journal* 34, 281–305.

Mitroff, I. (1988) Crisis management: cutting through the confusion. *Sloan Management Review* Winter, pp. 15–20.

Mitroff, I. and Pearson, C. (1993) *Crisis Management: a Diagnostic Guide for Improving your Organization's Crisis-preparedness.* Jossey-Bass, San Francisco, California.

Newsom, D., Scott, A. and Turk, J.V. (1992) *This is PR: the Realities of Public Relations,* 5th edn. Wadsworth, Belmont, California.

O'Keefe, S. (2002) Crisis Management at the Irish Tourist Board New York. Final year project submitted at the University of Limerick, Ireland.

Pearson, C. and Clair, J. (1998) Reframing crisis management. *Academy of Management Review* 23, 59–76.

Pearson, C.M. and Mitroff, I.I. (1993) From crisis prone to crisis prepared: a framework for crisis management. *Academy of Management Executive* 7, 48–59.

Preble, J.F. (1997) Integrating the crisis management perspective into the strategic management process. *Journal of Management Studies* 34 769–791.

Reilly, A. (1993) Preparing for the worst: the process of effective crisis management. *Industrial and Environmental Crisis Quarterly* 7, 115–144.

Shrivastava, P. (1987) *Bhopal: Anatomy of a Crisis.* Baltinger, Cambridge, Massachusetts.

Shrivastava, P. (1994) Rereading Bhopal: anatomy of a crisis through feminist lens. *Journal of Management Inquiry* 3, 278–285.

Siomkos, G. (1999) On achieving exoneration after a product safety crisis industrial crisis *Journal of Business and Industrial Marketing* 14, 17–29.

Sturges, D. (1994) Communicating through crisis: a strategy for organizational survival. *Management Communication Quarterly* 7, 297–316.

Tourism Policy Review Group (2003) Report prepared for the Department of Tourism, Dublin, Ireland.

Tsang, A. (2000) Military doctrine in crisis management: three beverage contamination cases. *Business Horizons* September/October, pp. 65–73.

Weiner, A. and Kahn, H. (1972) Crisis and arms control. In: Hermann, C. (ed.) *International Crises: Insights from Behavioural Research.* Free Press, New York, p. 21.

Zerman, D. (1995) Crisis communication: managing the mass media. *Information Management and Computer Security* 3 (5), 25–28.

23 The Regional Effects of Terrorism on Tourism: an Empirical Analysis

BRIAN W. SLOBODA

Introduction

On 11 September 2001 (9/11), terrorists hijacked four American commercial aircraft and crashed two of them into the World Trade Center, one into the Pentagon and the fourth in a rural area in Pennsylvania. As a result of these incidents, the World Trade Center towers collapsed, a slice of the Pentagon was decimated and many lives were been lost. In the wake of this tragedy, the travel and tourism industry experienced a substantial decline in airline travel, hotel stays fell, tourism industry workers were laid off and many downstream industries experienced a sharp decline in revenue. Over time, the tourism industry and commercial aviation have recovered despite the uncertainty of future attacks

Airlines, travel and tourism, accommodation, eating places, postal service agencies and the insurance industry are highly susceptible to increased terrorism attacks. In fact, regions and economies where tourism is a major industry often experience economic decline if a catastrophic terrorist event strikes anywhere in the world. As a consequence, such regions and economies face a reduction in return on capital, and future investment is discouraged. After the Bali tragedy in October 2002, tourist arrivals in Indonesia declined by 2.2%. As tourism accounts for 3.4% of its gross domestic product (GDP), market analysts had projected its GDP to decline by 1% (Euroweek, 2002). After the tragic events of 9/11, international tourist arrivals fell by 0.6%, the first year of negative growth in this sector since 1982.

This chapter will assess the impact of terrorism on tourism in the USA and other countries by use of the Seemingly Unrelated Regression (SUR) model by extending the model of Drakos and Kutan (2003) to incorporate a greater variety of countries in order to understand more fully the interdependencies of terrorism on tourism. To model these interdependencies, this analysis will assess the following hypotheses:

1. Hypothesis 1: terrorism does not have any impact on tourism of a country; therefore, it does not have any effect on the relative market shares.
2. Hypothesis 2: the effect of own-country terrorism on own-country market share is uniform across all countries.
3. Hypothesis 3: terrorism of one country does not have any impact on its competitors for tourism.

The rationale for using the SUR model is that it enables cross-correlations of the disturbance terms between countries which can be given in the standard ordinary least squares (OLS) models, and this becomes more important if there is substitutability of countries by consumers after a terrorist incident.

Review of the Literature

In the consumer maximization model, consumers are faced with an optimization problem given many constraints or the need to allocate scarce resources among many choices. Thus, consumers want to maximize their utility, subject to budget and time constraints. Terrorists also behave in a rational way since they want to maximize their goals subject to constraints that include resources and risks imposed by authorities[1] (Sandler *et al.*, 1983; Atkinson *et al.*, 1987; Im *et al.*, 1987; Sandler and Scott, 1987; Sloboda, 2003; H.E. Lapan and T. Sandler, 1987, unpublished manuscript).

Enders and Sandler (1991) and Enders *et al.* (1992) provide an empirical framework for a sample of European countries concerning the link between terrorism and the tourism industry. Enders and Sandler (1991) find significant negative, immediate impacts, i.e. a 2–3 month impact on Spanish tourism arrivals after an incident. Enders *et al.* (1992) used the sample of European countries for the period 1974–1988 previously used by Enders and Sandler (1991). They modelled the share of tourism in these European countries using quarterly data for the number of terrorist incidents and tourist receipts, and estimated that the aggregate losses in revenue for Austria, Greece and Italy were US$4.467 billion. They concluded that terrorist incidents have an adverse effect on tourism revenues in Europe; in addition, tourists often change their countries to minimize their risk of being involved in a terrorist incident.

Tremblay (1989) also studied the impact of terrorism on the tourism sector and concluded that the effect can occur up to 3 months after the event and last up to 9 months after the event. In fact, the results of Tremblay (1989) agree with the results of Enders and Sandler (1991) and Enders *et al.* (1992). Pizam and Fleischer (2001) studied the effects of the frequency of incidents of terrorism on tourism in Israel from May 1991 to May 2001. They concluded that the frequency and regularity of terrorist incidents rather than the severity of the attacks resulted in a decline for the tourism sector. Enders and Sandler (1996) quantified the impact of terrorism on foreign direct investment, concluding that terrorism had a significant and persistent negative effect in Spain and Greece. In addition, smaller countries that face a constant threat of terrorism may incur economic costs by attracting less investment, which impedes economic growth. The combined effects of less outside investment and lower growth rates would result in sectors of the economy such as tourism being underdeveloped.

Drakos and Kutan (2003) extended the analysis of Enders *et al.* (1992). Using monthly data for the period 1991–2000 and using the SUR method, they investigated the effects of terrorism in Greece, Israel and Turkey on each other's market share since these countries have experienced high terrorist incidents in recent years, and earlier analyses focused only on European countries. Also they incorporated Italy as a control country because it represents the remaining country in the Mediterranean region. Their results indicate that there are substitution effects. Also, their results revealed that the tourism industry in Israel and Turkey was more sensitive to terrorism than in Greece. In a similar analysis, Aly and Strazicich (2000) examined the effects of terrorism on the tourism sector for Egypt and Israel. More specifically, they examined the time paths of the shocks to determine if the time paths were permanent or transitory. In their analysis, they utilized a two-break minimum Lagrange multiplier (LM) unit root test as developed by Lee and Strazicich (1999). In contrast to similar augmented Dickey–Fuller (ADF)-type endogenous break tests, Lee and Strazicich (1999) has shown that the one-break minimum LM unit root test estimates the break point correctly and does not have spurious rejections.

The Theoretical Development of the Analysis

Because the analysis is examining the effects of terrorism on market shares of tourism, total market share is defined as the total receipts of tourism of all countries in the analysis. Additionally, the relative market share is defined as the ratio of a country's receipts to the total receipts of all countries in the analysis. Also the market shares sum to unity, so one of the countries would be a residual country. The selection of this residual country is examined in here.

The theoretical framework followed in this analysis assumes the consumers maximization problem which states that consumers take into account terrorist incidents when deciding which country to visit. Moreover, consumers are assumed to select between expenditure on tourism or other goods based on the price of tourism and other goods. Finally, a consumer's purchase decisions on tourism products are assumed to be constrained by the consumer's level of income. If the country selected by the consumer experiences a terrorist incident(s), the consumer will most probably substitute their choice for another country. On the other hand, the consumer may forgo travel and purchase other goods. The present theoretical foundation of consumer maximization used in this analysis follows the approach suggested by Enders *et al.* (1992) and Drakos and Kutan (2003).

For each country in the analysis, its market share is dependent on a set of variables denoted by the vector X. This vector contains variables such as infrastructure investment, number of tourists and special events. In this analysis, it is assumed these variables are held constant since the focus is on the effects of terrorism on tourism. The general equation for each country is:

$$MS_i = f_i(X_i | T) \tag{1}$$

where MS denotes the market share for the ith country at a point in time and T is the number of terrorist incidents experienced by the country. To measure the effects of terrorism on domestic tourism, the first derivative of Equation 1 is used. For example, if Italy is of interest, the result of the first derivative is the effect of terrorism on tourism flows in Italy. Mathematically, this impact is measured by φ_{Italy} or:

$$\frac{\partial MS_{Italy}}{\partial T_{Italy}} = \varphi_{Italy} \tag{2}$$

Equation 2 is associated with Hypothesis 1. Given the terrorist incident in a country, this model can be extended to examine the direct and indirect effects of terrorism on other countries, and these effects can be generalized as follows:

$$\frac{\partial MS_{Italy}}{\partial T_{Italy}} + \left(\frac{\partial MS_{Spain}}{\partial T_{Italy}} * \frac{\partial MS_{Italy}}{\partial T_{Italy}} \right) + \left(\frac{\partial MS_{Greece}}{\partial T_{Italy}} * \frac{\partial MS_{Italy}}{\partial T_{Italy}} \right)$$
$$+ \dots + \left(\frac{\partial MS_{UK}}{\partial T_{Italy}} * \frac{\partial MS_{Italy}}{\partial T_{Italy}} \right) = \varphi_{Italy} + \varphi_{Spain} + \dots + \varphi_{UK} \tag{3}$$

The first term in Equation 3 is the direct effect of terrorism in a country as given in Equation 1, and the subsequent terms will be the indirect effects of the terrorism on the market shares of other countries. The results of Equation 3 as given by $\varphi_{Italy} + \varphi_{Spain} + \dots + \varphi_{UK}$ capture the effects of terrorism on the remaining countries. The analysis can then be assessed by assessing the effects of terrorism on domestic market share. Intuitively, the latter can be represented as

$$\frac{\partial MS_{Italy}}{\partial T_{Italy}} \neq 0 \tag{4}$$

Intuitively, if the first order derivative equals zero, then terrorism would not have any effect on tourism. Equation 4 would be associated with Hypothesis 2. The final part of the modelling process is the assessment of the substitution between countries after a decline in market share in a country results in an increase in the market share of other countries after a terrorist incident. From Equation 3, each of the terms in parentheses is tested.

$$\left(\frac{\partial MS_{Spain}}{\partial T_{Italy}} * \frac{\partial MS_{Italy}}{\partial T_{Italy}} \right) \neq 0 \tag{5}$$

If the term equals zero, terrorism in Spain does not have any impact on the market share of Italy. Equation 5 would be associated with Hypothesis 3.

Empirical Methodology and Data Sources Empirical Methodology

Each country in the analysis can be represented by Equation 3. Thus, this will generate a system of equations that can be estimated by the SUR model. The SUR method estimates the parameters of the system of equations when all the right-hand side variables are assumed to be exogenous and the error terms are heteroscedastic and contemporaneously correlated.[2] Moreover, the equations appear to be 'seemingly unrelated', but there still exists a possibility of correlation among the error terms of the equations. The model for this analysis can be generalized as:

$$MS_{Gre} = \alpha_{Gre} + \beta_{Gre} MS_{Gre,t-1} + \varphi_{Gre,TUR} T_{Gre,t} + \varphi_{Gre,It} T_{It,t} + \varphi_{Gre,US} T_{US,t}$$
$$+ \varphi_{Gre,Eg} T_{Eg,t} + \varphi_{Gre,IS} T_{IS,t} + \varphi_{Gre,UK} T_{UK,t} + \varphi_{Gre,Gre} T_{Gre,t}$$

$$MS_{It} = \alpha_{It} + \beta_{It} MS_{It,t-1} + \varphi_{It,TUR} T_{It,t} + \varphi_{Ite,It} T_{It,t} + \varphi_{It,US} T_{US,t}$$
$$+ \varphi_{Ie,Eg} T_{Eg,t} + \varphi_{It,IS} T_{IS,t} + \varphi_{It,UK} T_{UK,t} + \varphi_{It,Gre} T_{Gre,t}$$

$$MS_{UK} = \alpha_{UK} + \beta_{UK} MS_{UK,t-1} + \varphi_{UK,TUR} T_{Gre,t} + \varphi_{UK,It} T_{It,t}$$
$$+ \varphi_{UK,US} T_{US,t} + \varphi_{UK,Eg} T_{Eg,t} + \varphi_{UK,IS} T_{IS,t} + \varphi_{UK,UK} T_{UK,t} + \varphi_{UK,Gre} T_{Gre,t}$$

$$MS_{IS} = \alpha_{IS} + \beta_{IS} MS_{IS,t-1} + \varphi_{IS,TUR} T_{IS,t} + \varphi_{IS,It} T_{It,t} + \varphi_{IS,US} T_{US,t} + \varphi_{IS,Eg} T_{Eg,t}$$
$$+ \varphi_{IS,IS} T_{IS,t} + \varphi_{IS,UK} T_{UK,t} + \varphi_{IS,Gre} T_{Gre,t}$$

$$MS_{Eg} = \alpha_{Eg} + \beta_{Eg} MS_{Eg,t-1} + \varphi_{Eg,TUR} T_{Eg,t} + \varphi_{Eg,It} T_{It,t} + \varphi_{Ege,US} T_{US,t}$$
$$+ \varphi_{EGe,Eg} T_{Eg,t} + \varphi_{Eg,IS} T_{IS,t} + \varphi_{Eg,UK} T_{UK,t} + \varphi_{Eg,Gre} T_{Gre,t}$$

$$MS_{Tur} = \alpha_{Tur} + \beta_{Tur} MS_{Tr,t-1} + \varphi_{Tur,TUR} T_{Tur,t} + \varphi_{Tur,It} T_{It,t} + \varphi_{Tur,US} T_{US,t}$$
$$+ \varphi_{Tur,Eg} T_{Eg,t} + \varphi_{Tur,IS} T_{IS,t} + \varphi_{Tur,UK} T_{UK,t} + \varphi_{Tur,Gre} T_{Gre,t}$$

$$MS_{US} = \alpha_{US} + \beta_{USr} MS_{US,t-1} + \varphi_{US,TUR} T_{Tur,t} + \varphi_{Ur,It} T_{It,t} + \varphi_{USr,US} T_{US,t}$$
$$+ \varphi_{US,Eg} T_{Eg,t} + \varphi_{US,IS} T_{IS,t} + \varphi_{US,UK} T_{UK,t} + \varphi_{US,Gre} T_{Gre,t}$$

In each equation, the market share or the dependent variable is lagged by one period since the effects of terrorism could have an impact on tourism up to a year later. In this analysis, the coefficients of φs represent the impact of terrorism on the market shares of the given countries. To facilitate the assessment of impacts from terrorism from the SUR model, the coefficients as given by $\varphi_{i,j}$ represent the cross-country impacts of terrorism, and the expected sign of the coefficient could be positive or negative. A positive sign would indicate that a terrorist incident or a higher level of risk will cause individuals to substitute one country for another; therefore, the substituted country will receive the increased benefits. On the other hand, a negative coefficient will indicate that a terrorist incident in a country will result in a loss of benefits for both countries. Put another way, a terrorist incident in a country will cause individuals to cancel all travel plans in response to a terrorist incident. As an example, the coefficient of $\varphi_{US,IS}$ represents the impact of terrorism in the USA on the market share of Israel. Additionally, the coefficients of $\varphi_{i,i}$ represent the own-country effects of terrorism, say $\varphi_{Greece,Greece}$, on its market share, and the expected sign of the coefficient would be negative.

Data sources

The annual data on terrorist incidents or the independent variables are derived from the chronology incidents of Mickolus (1980, 1993), Mickolus *et al.* (1989) and Mickolus and Simmons (1997, 2002). These chronologies are the only publicly available sources and rely heavily on articles available in the press, with key sources including the Associated Press, United Press International, *The Washington Post*, *The New York Times*, *The Washington Times*, the Foreign Broadcast Information Service Daily Reports and the network television news. Because the data sourced come from newspaper accounts, analysts must be aware of the shortcomings of under-pressure reporting. On the other hand, these sources are usually better at chronicling the actions of terrorists than reports from government officials. Additionally, these sources pick up newsworthy terrorist incidents, so some bias may exist in the decision about which terrorist events are reported. Unfortunately, this bias worsened in 1996 when the FBIS Daily Reports was no longer available, so, in the time series, there could be some differences in the number of recorded terrorist incidents.

As for the dependent variable, the data on tourist receipts are taken from the International Monetary Fund's *Balance of Payments Statistic*. The line items of Passenger Services: credit (line item 1C1A4) and Travel: credit (line item 1D.A4) are summed for each country to represent an approximate measure of the total receipts from tourism. Additionally, the series Merchandise Exports (line 1A.A4) contains purchases made by tourists which cannot be disaggregated from non-tourist purchases. Thus, this series was incorporated into the measure of tourist receipts. The International Monetary Fund (IMF) reports its balance of payment (BOP) data in terms of SDRs (special drawing rights), so it is not necessary to convert these estimates into a standardized currency before proceeding with the analysis.

Empirical Results

The market share for each country is defined as the ratio of the country's tourist receipts to the total tourist receipts of all countries used in this analysis, and this market ratio of the tourist receipts data from the *Balance of Payments Statistics* is represented by the value of the tourist receipts for each country over the total sum of a country's tourist receipts. The descriptive statistics for the market shares for each of the countries are presented in Table 23.1.

The descriptive statistics reveal that the USA has the biggest market share of approximately 39%, while Egypt has the smallest market share of approximately 1%. Regarding the standard deviation, the USA has the most variation, which indicates that its market share is subject to greater changes. Egypt has the smallest variation, which indicates a more stable market share. For further insight into the market share data among countries, Table 23.2 shows the bivariate correlations.

Those correlations along the diagonal of the matrix represent the own correlation of the same country, while the off-diagonal elements assess the market shares between countries. For example, the correlation measure of −0.85160 (the correlation between Italy and the UK) indicates a negative correlation. Put another way, if there is a terrorist attack in the UK, individuals would choose to substitute Italy as a travel destination. In contrast, the correlation measure of 0.71088 (the correlation between Egypt and the UK) indicates a positive correlation, meaning that consumers view these two countries as complements.

The system of equations as given in Equation 1 is estimated via the SUR method. Figures 23.1 and 23.2 provide the plot of the actual market shares for each of the countries used in the modelling process, while Figs 23.3 and 23.4 show the actual terrorist incidents for each of the countries.

Table 23.1. Descriptive statistics for market shares.

Variable	Mean	SD
Italy	0.17453	0.03620
USA	0.39863	0.07845
Spain	0.18433	0.01721
Egypt	0.01705	0.00459
Israel	0.0219	0.00411
UK	0.02879	0.01452
Turkey	0.14760	0.05112
Greece	0.02712	0.00829

Table 23.2. Pearson correlation coefficients, $n = 22$, probability $> |r|$ under H_0: Rho = 0.

	MS_IT	MS_US	MS_S	MS_Eg	MS_IS	MS_UK	MS_TUR	MS_Gre
MS_IT	1.00000							
MS_US	−0.83225	1.00000						
	<0.0001							
MS_S	−0.11334	−0.37114	1.00000					
	0.6155	0.0890						
MS_Eg	−0.63333	0.67785	−0.30902	1.00000				
	0.0016	0.0005	0.1617					
MS_IS	0.45237*	−0.50982	0.00853	−0.04040	1.00000			
	0.0345	0.0154	0.9700	0.8583				
MS_UK	−0.85160	0.93040	−0.22321	0.71033	−0.49562*	−1.00000		
	<0.0001	<0.0001	0.3180	0.0002	0.0190			
MS_TUR	0.72981	−0.96681	0.40059	−0.68906*	0.42597	−0.92525	1.00000	
	<0.0001	<0.0001	0.0647	0.0004	0.0481	<0.0001	<0.0001	
MS_Gre	0.85956	−0.84825	0.01982	−0.53534	0.60063	−0.81701	0.75586	1.00000
	<0.0001	<0.0001	0.9302	0.0102	0.0031	<0.0001	<0.0001	

MS is an abbreviation for market share; IT = Italy, US = USA, S = Spain, Eg = Egypt, IS = Israel, TUR = Turkey, and Gre = Greece.
Correlations denoted in italics are significant at the 1 and 5% levels.
Correlations denoted with an asterisk are statistically significant at the 5% level.

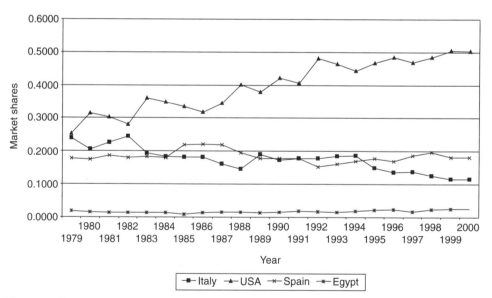

Fig. 23.1. Plot of market shares for Italy, the USA, Spain and Egypt.

Before the SUR modelling can proceed, the time series of the variables must be stationary since a time series often has an upward as well as a downward trend. By definition, a stationary series will have a constant mean, variance and autovariances over time. Given the plots in Figs 23.1–23.4, none of the time series follows the definition of stationary;

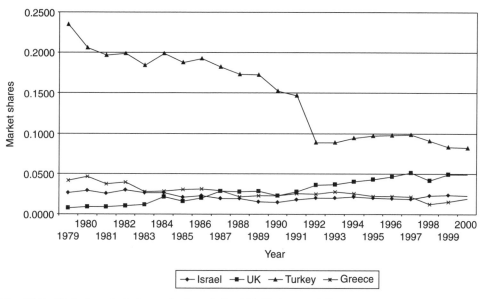

Fig. 23.2. Plot of market shares for Israel, the UK, Turkey and Greece.

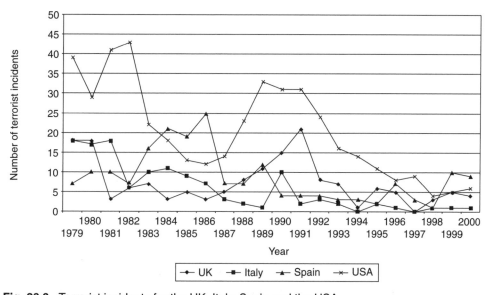

Fig. 23.3. Terrorist incidents for the UK, Italy, Spain and the USA.

consequently, each series must be transformed.[3] Once the time series has been transformed, the estimation of the SUR model can proceed. Since the analysis has eight countries in an SUR, the estimation only requires the estimation of the seven countries since the last country is simply a residual from the remaining countries. In the preliminary models, a country was left out, and the diagnostics of the model were assessed to determine the

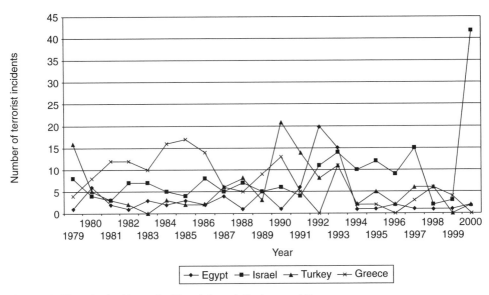

Fig. 23.4. Terrorist incidents for Egypt, Israel, Turkey and Greece.

best model. Table 23.3 represents the best model specification in which Spain is omitted from the estimation process.

The results of the diagnostics indicate that the residuals satisfy the assumptions of the OLS.[4] The results of the model coefficients of the model are now assessed. As for the effects of terrorism, each of these countries has a negative coefficient that indicates that market shares would decline after a terrorist incident in the country where it occurs. For example, the USA had a coefficient of −0.0344 or about −0.0344% decline in its market share. As for the cross-country effects of terrorism, some of the coefficients were positive while others were negative. Recall that the positive coefficients indicate that an individual would substitute one country with another country, assuming these two countries are substitutes for each other, while the negative coefficients indicate that a terrorist incident results in losses for both countries. As an example, the coefficient of $\varphi_{IT,IS}$ shows that if a terrorist incident occurs in Italy, Israel's market share will increase by 0.3129% and Italy's market share will fall by 0.3129%. In the model, many of the variables also show insignificant *t*-statistics, but its marginal explanatory value (MEXVAL) showed that the omission of these variables would be significant.[5,6] The first coefficient in each of the equations shows the one-period lag to be positive, indicating that after 1 year, the effects of terrorism still had an impact on market share, which fell in the range of −0.0105 for Egypt to −0.6712 for Israel. In fact, not only are these variables statistically significant as reported by the *t*-statistics, but each of the MEXVALs also shows the importance of these variables in assessing the impacts on market shares.

Before providing the results of the test, each hypothesis and its conceptual underpinning is presented.

Table 23.3. Estimation results of the seemingly unrelated regression (SUR) model.

Greece	Constant	$\varphi_{Gre,t-1}$	$\varphi_{Gre,TUR}$	$\varphi_{Gre,It}$	$\varphi_{Gre,US}$	$\varphi_{Gre,Eg}$	$\varphi_{Gre,IS}$	$\varphi_{Gre,UK}$	$\varphi_{Gre,Gre}$
Coefficient	-0.0002	-0.5818	.0014	-0.0028	0.0004	0.0010	0.0007	-0.0020	-0.0008
t-statistic	-0.0222	-6.6026	1.0071	-1.5657	0.0398	0.8086	0.0297	-0.7574	-0.7039
MEXVAL	0.642	190.853	29.070	45.200	1.150	23.343	0.8590	21.866	20.2940

Italy	Constant	$\varphi_{IT,t-1}$	$\varphi_{IT,IT}$	$\varphi_{IT,TUR}$	$\varphi_{IT,US}$	$\varphi_{IT,Eg}$	$\varphi_{IT,IS}$	$\varphi_{IT,UK}$	$\varphi_{IT,Gre}$
Coefficient	-0.15952	-0.43864	-0.0152	0.01540	0.1611	0.0078	-0.3129	-0.0315	-0.0063
t-statistic	-3.6931	-5.6953	-2.2047	2.7022	3.7071	1.4469	-3.0416	-3.1687	-1.3123
MEXVAL	106.608	161.542	63.645	78.00	107.16	41.791	87.804	91.542	37.886

UK	Constant	$\varphi_{UK,t-1}$	$\varphi_{UK,IT}$	$\varphi_{UK,TUR}$	$\varphi_{UK,US}$	$\varphi_{UK,Eg}$	$\varphi_{UK,IS}$	$\varphi_{UK,UK}$	$\varphi_{UK,Gre}$
Coefficient	0.0555	-0.5540	-0.0013	-0.0023	-0.0492	0.0006	0.1208	-0.0001	-0.0039
t-statistic	3.2353	-2.931	-0.5467	-1.1192	-2.9477	0.3061	2.9743	-0.0317	-2.1298
MEXVAL	93.397	84.613	93.397	15.762	32.309	85.095	8.833	85.862	61.483

Israel	Constant	$\varphi_{IS,t-1}$	$\varphi_{IS,IT}$	$\varphi_{IS,TUR}$	$\varphi_{IS,US}$	$\varphi_{IS,Eg}$	$\varphi_{IS,IS}$	$\varphi_{IS,UK}$	$\varphi_{IS,Gre}$
Coefficient	-0.0181	-0.6712	-0.0017	0.0015	0.0184	0.0006	-0.0391	-0.0040	0.0003
t-statistic	-3.141	-7.130	-1.929	1.990	3.207	0.8989	-2.856	-3.139	0.6180
MEXVAL	90.687	205.848	55.687	57.706	92.856	25.950	82.446	90.625	17.842

Egypt	Constant	$\varphi_{Eg,t-1}$	$\varphi_{Eg,IT}$	$\varphi_{Eg,TUR}$	$\varphi_{Eg,US}$	$\varphi_{Eg,Eg}$	$\varphi_{Eg,IS}$	$\varphi_{Eg,UK}$	$\varphi_{Eg,Gre}$
Coefficient	-0.0012	-0.0150	0.0013	0.0005	-0.0001	-0.0009	-0.0016	0.0029	-0.0007
t-statistic	-0.209	-0.0555	1.315	0.6910	-0.0168	-1.2103	-0.1139	2.1182	-0.7318
MEXVAL	6.039	1.603	37.985	19.948	0.4880	34.941	3.289	61.149	21.128

Turkey	Constant	$\varphi_{TUR,t-1}$	$\varphi_{TUR,IT}$	$\varphi_{TUR,TUR}$	$\varphi_{TUR,US}$	$\varphi_{TUR,Eg}$	$\varphi_{TUR,IS}$	$\varphi_{TUR,UK}$	$\varphi_{TUR,Gre}$
Coefficient	0.0972	-0.6355	0.0011	-0.0059	-0.0920	-0.0130	0.1979	0.0013	0.0111
t-statistic	3.893	-11.037	0.2629	-1.770	-3.657	-4.1354	3.3260	0.2114	3.979
MEXVAL	112.536	318.627	7.591	51.110	105.575	119.379	96.015	6.104	114.884

Continued

Table 23.3. *Continued*

USA	Constant	$\varphi_{US,t-1}$	$\varphi_{US,IT}$	$\varphi_{US,TUR}$	$\varphi_{US,US}$	$\varphi_{US,Eg}$	$\varphi_{US,IS}$	$\varphi_{US,UK}$	$\varphi_{US,Gre}$
Coefficient	-0.0447	-0.5687	-0.0163	-0.0076	-0.0344	0.0059	-0.0879	0.0390	-0.0209
t-statistic	-0.8224	-5.185	-1.775	-1.024	-0.6294	0.8488	-0.6778	2.957	-3.480
MEXVAL	23.743	149.707	50.260	29.564	18.170	24.504	19.567	85.382	100.464

Diagnostics	Adjusted R^2	D–W[a]	Standard error of estimate (SEE)
Greece	0.4408	1.70	0.0024
Italy	0.6313	1.81	0.0096
UK	0.0437	2.18	0.0035
Israel	0.4487	1.87	0.0012
Egypt	0.034	1.76	0.0013
Turkey	0.8615	1.71	0.0056
USA	0.3908	1.95	0.0130

The Durbin–Watson (D–W) statistic is used to check for the problem of autocorrelation in the residuals of the model. In general, if the value of the D–W is less than 1.5, the problem of autocorrelation must be corrected. Since each of the equations has a lagged dependent variable, the standard D–W statistic cannot be used. Instead, the Durbin H statistics was used and is reported in the table.

The *F*-statistic is not reported for each of the equations in the model since it is counterproductive, i.e. the *F*-test shows that the coefficients other than the constant are all zero, and very often the results indicate that the *F*-statistic would be highly significant. In addition, these highly significant results would give us false assurances that the results are astounding without examining the model in detail.

1. Hypothesis 1:[7] terrorism does not have any impact on tourism of a country; therefore, it does not have any effect on the relative market shares. Rejecting this hypothesis would indicate that consumers do incorporate terrorism in a country into their decision to travel to a particular countries.

2. Hypothesis 2:[8] the effect of own-country terrorism on own-country market share is uniform across all countries. Rejecting this null hypothesis would suggest that there is a country-specific cost for terrorism.

3. Hypothesis 3:[9] terrorism of one country does not have any impact on its competitors for tourism. Rejecting the null hypothesis would indicate that terrorism does have an impact on its competitors or results in an increase in the market share by other countries.

The test results for these hypotheses are presented in Table 23.4.

For Hypothesis 1, the results indicated that the null hypothesis is rejected and that incidents of terrorism exert an effect on the tourism sector for each of the countries. Additionally, the results of this test appear to be valid given the global decline in tourism after 9/11. Individuals fearing the possibility of an attack adjusted their travel plans. For Hypothesis 2, the results indicated that the null hypothesis is rejected, and there are country-specific costs of terrorism. Such conclusions seem plausible since the fear of terrorism in recent years has caused individuals to cancel their travel plans even within their own countries. Instead, individuals may opt for local travel, and such decisions have been noticed in the decline of tourism demand after 9/11. Finally, for Hypothesis 3, the

Table 23.4. Results of the hypothesis testing.

Null hypothesis	Wald test statistic (*P*-values)
H_1	34.239 (0.0000)*
H_2	18.792 (0.0000)*
$H_{3,Greece}$	8.63 (0.1952)
$H_{3,Italy}$	34.47 (0.0000)*
$H_{3,UK}$	19.06 (0.0041)*
$H_{3,IS}$	16.68 (0.0105)**
$H_{3,Eg}$	10.53 (0.1040)
$H_{3,TUR}$	28.65 (0.0000)*
$H_{3,US}$	17.37 (0.0001)*
$H_{3,Joint}$	22.41 (0.0000)*

Those test statistics denoted with a single asterisk are significant at the 1 and 5% levels of significance and those denoted with a double asterisk are significant at the 5% level. The Wald test statistic is an *F*-test that tests the restrictions as imposed in each of the hypotheses. For greater analytical details concerning the Wald test statistic, the reader should consult Greene (2001).

For the joint hypothesis, it is simply that all of the hypotheses of the countries under Hypothesis 3 are equal to zero.

joint null hypothesis was rejected and, upon examination of the results of the individual countries, Turkey and Italy serve as the main drivers for the rejection of the joint hypothesis. However, Greece and Egypt were not rejected, suggesting that cross-country terrorism does not affect the competitors' market shares in every case. The results from the hypothesis testing make sense since the coefficients of the SUR model reveal that the effects are not as significant for other countries. As for the remaining countries, the rejected null hypotheses indicate that cross-country incidents of terrorism did affect the market shares.

Conclusions

This analysis examined the effects of regional terrorism on tourism. Much of the earlier empirical assessment measured how the tourism industry in a particular country is affected by terrorist attacks taking place in that country, i.e. these analyses failed to assess interdependencies between different countries' tourism industries and the effects of terrorism.

A terrorist incident(s) in one country may provide a deterrent effect since tourists may not choose to visit the country after such an incident and could also fear that terrorism could spill over into countries previously not involved. Thus, they would choose other destinations for travel, or not travel at all.

The results suggested from the present analysis support the conclusions of earlier works that terrorism does have an impact on tourism. On an interesting note, earlier empirical works have often shown that Greece was sensitive to terrorism, but the empirical results of this analysis and that of Drakos and Kutan (2003) do not support this conclusion. The rationale for the lack of sensitivity of Greece to terrorism is that in the 1980s, Greece experienced many terrorist incidents but in the 1990s did not have as many events. Consequently, the Greek government may have adapted to these events through better policymaking to combat terrorist activities. The coefficients for the USA may appear to be high, so care must be used in their interpretation, i.e. unlike other countries, the terrorist incidents for the USA contain many incidents of attacks on US interests overseas. Moreover, if individuals are aware of a high threat level or of numerous terrorist incidents, they may consider this when they decide to travel, i.e. the individuals may be likely to choose less risky countries or be more risk averse.

Finally, for this analysis, tourist receipts data are only provided as annual data; consequently, the data for terrorist incidents also need to be annual.[10] The data used are annual data since the only frequency domain for both series is available annually. A drawback of using annual data is the problem of aggregation bias since the aggregation of the data removes variability within the data. If the data are available quarterly or, even better, on a monthly basis, the present analysis could examine the seasonality effects of terrorism on tourism, if any.

Notes

1. A terrorist's willingness to risk dying does not constitute being irrational. Think of it this way: those involved in public safety, i.e. policemen, firefighters and others, face the probability of death. More importantly, if they are provided with remuneration that compensates them for the added risks that the job entails, they will do the job.

2. Contemporaneous correlation, unlike autocorrelation for single equation models, allows for correlation to exist. For SUR models, the existence of contemporaneous correlation is more efficient for estimating all of the equations jointly rather than estimating each equation separately using OLS.

3. Because of space limitations, the transformed models are not provided.

4. Other diagnostics were conducted on the residuals, and these additional analyses are available from the author upon request.

5. The marginal explanatory value (MEXVAL) of each variable is simply the percentage by which the standard error of the estimate (SEE) of the equation is affected if the variable is omitted from the equation and is not replaced with another variable, i.e. the MEXVAL shows the importance of each variable to the fit of the model.

6. The *t*-statistic is the ratio of the regression coefficient and its standard error, and the goal of the *t*-statistic is to show the significance of the variable in the model. The application of the *t*-test to the variable in the model requires many assumptions which may not be indicative of the significance of the variable to the model. For the analytical details concerning MEXVAL, the reader is referred to Almon (1990).

7. For Hypothesis 1, each of the cross-country coefficients is set equal to zero. For example, $\varphi_{Gre,TUR} = \varphi_{TUR,Gre}$ and other coefficients are all set equal to zero.

8. For Hypothesis 2, the null hypothesis is formally expressed as follows. H_2: $\varphi_{Gre,Gre} = \varphi_{IT,IT} = \varphi_{TUR,TUR} = \varphi_{UK,UK} = \varphi_{Eg,Eg} = \varphi_{IS,IS} = \varphi_{US,US}$.

9. The hypotheses for each country for Hypothesis 3 are given as follows:

$$\text{Greece}, H_{3a}: \varphi_{Gre,Tur} = \varphi_{Gre,It} = \varphi_{Gre,US} = \varphi_{Gre,Eg} = \varphi_{Gre,IS} = \varphi_{Gre,UK} = 0$$

$$\text{Italy}, H_{3b}: \varphi_{It,Tur} = \varphi_{It,Gre} = \varphi_{IT,US} = \varphi_{It,Eg} = \varphi_{It,IS} = \varphi_{Ie,UK} = 0$$

$$\text{UK}, H_{3c}: \varphi_{Uk,Tur} = \varphi_{UK,It} = \varphi_{UK,US} = \varphi_{UK,Eg} = \varphi_{UK,IS} = \varphi_{UK,Gre} = 0$$

$$\text{Israel}, H_{3d}: \varphi_{IS,Tur} = \varphi_{IS,It} = \varphi_{IS,US} = \varphi_{IS,Eg} = \varphi_{IS,Gre} = \varphi_{IS,UK} = 0$$

$$\text{Egypt}, H_{3e}: \varphi_{Eg,Tur} = \varphi_{Eg,It} = \varphi_{Eg,US} = \varphi_{Eg,Gre} = \varphi_{Eg,IS} = \varphi_{Eg,UK} = 0$$

$$\text{Turkey}, H_{3f}: \varphi_{TUR,Gre} = \varphi_{Tur,It} = \varphi_{Tur,US} = \varphi_{Tur,Eg} = \varphi_{Tur,IS} = \varphi_{Tur,UK} = 0$$

10. The data for terrorists' incidents are also disseminated as quarterly, but tourist receipts are only given as annually. Thus, the frequency domain among the time series must be consistent in doing empirical analysis.

References

Almon, C. (1990) *The Craft of Economic Modeling*. Ginn Press, Needham Heights, Massachusetts.

Aly, H.Y. and Strazicich, M.C. (2000) *Terrorism and Tourism: Is the Impact Permanent or Transitory? Time Series Evidence from Some MEAN Countries*. Department of Economics, Ohio State University Working Paper Series.

Atkinson, S.E., Sandler, T. and Tschirhart, J. (1987) Terrorism in a bargaining framework. *Journal of Law and Economics* 30, 1–21.

Drakos, K. and Kutan, A.M. (2003) Regional effects of terrorism on tourism in three Mediterranean countries. *Journal of Conflict Resolution* 47, 621–641.

Enders, W. and Sandler, T. (1991) Causality between transcountriesal terrorism and tourism: the case of Spain. *Terrorism* 14, 49–58.

Enders, W. and Sandler, T. and Parise, G.F. (1992) An econometric analysis of the impact of terrorism on tourism *Kyklos* 45, 531–554.

Enders, W. and Sandler, T. (1996) Terrorism and foreign direct investment in Spain and Greece. *Kyklos* 49, 331–352.

Euroweek (2002) Bali blast fractures Southeast Asian economic hopes. *Euromoney*. International Investor PLC, London, 18 October.

Greene, W.H. (2001) *Econometric Analysis*, 4th edn. Prentice Hall, Upper Saddle River, New Jersey.

Im, E.I., Cauley, J. and Sandler, T. (1987) Cycles and substitutions in terrorist activities: a spectral approach. *Kyklos* 40, 238–255.

Lee, J. and Strazicich, M. (1999) *Minimum LM Unit Root Test with Two Structural Breaks*. Department of Economics, University of Central Florida Working Paper Series.

Mickolus, E. (1993) *Terrorism, 1988–1991: a Chronology of Events*. Greenwood Press, Westport, Connecticut.

Mickolus, E. and Simmons, S.L. (1997) *Terrorism, 1992–1995: a Chronology of Events and a Selectively Annotated Bibliography*. Greenwood Press, Westport, Connecticut.

Mickolus, E.F., Sandler, T. and Murdock, J.M. (1989) *International Terrorism in the 1980s: a Chronology of Events*, Vol. 1 (1980–1983) and Vol. 2 (1984–1987). Iowa State University Press, Ames, Iowa.

Mickolus, E. and Simmons, S.L. (2002) *Terrorism, 1996–2001: a Chronology*, Vols I and II. Greenwood Press, Westport, Connecticut.

Pizam, A. and Fleischer, A. (2001) *Severity vs. Frequency of Acts of Terrorism: Which Has a Larger Impact on Tourism Demand?* The Center for Agricultural Economic Research, Rehovot, Israel, Working Paper No. 20117.

Sandler, T. and Scott, J.L. (1987) Terrorist success in hostage-taking incidents. *Journal of Conflict Resolution* 31, 35–53.

Sandler, T., Tschirhart, J. and Cauley, J. (1983) A theoretical analysis of transnational terrorism. *American Political Science Review* 77, 36–54.

Sloboda, B.W. (2003) Assessing the effects of terrorism on tourism by use of time series methods. *Tourism Economics* 9, 179–190.

Tremblay, P. (1989) Pooling international terrorism in Western Europe. *Annals of Tourism Research* 16, 477–491.

24 Sabah's Responses to 11 September: a Tourism Analysis[1]

AWANGKU HASSANAL BAHAR PENGIRAN BAGUL AND
WAN SHAWALUDDIN WAN HASSAN

Introduction

The fragility of the tourism industry is due to its vulnerability to human-caused disasters, either social or political, such as terrorism, war, regional tensions, riots or political upheaval, and natural disasters such as torrential rains, hurricanes and volcanic eruptions (Glaesser, 2003). These crises then create difficult situations and threaten the normal operations and conduct of the tourism industry, damaging tourist destination's reputation for comfort, safety and attractiveness, and, in turn, causing a downturn in the local tourism industry. This was clearly manifested when the USA became a direct victim of an act on 11 September 2001 (9/11), leaving a dent in the tourism industry. It is known that the tourism industry has developed an extraordinary resistance to crises and a capacity to adapt and survive. Nevertheless, a single year of significant decline in the tourism industry caused by 9/11 made this an important case study.

This chapter is based on a case study focusing on the tourism experience and responses to 9/11 with particular focus on Sabah. Content analysis was used to obtain the information relating to the effects of 9/11 and the relevant management instruments employed including organizational responses to 9/11. The secondary research involved a chronological analysis of the 9/11 effect, the importance of tourism in relation to the effects of 9/11 and clarification of the concept and theories of crisis management. The primary research involved informant interviews, which included the key players and stakeholder of Sabah's tourism industry. This chapter explores the effects of 9/11 and examines the external influences contributing to the effects. Sabah's experience in the 9/11 events reflected an effective approach to crisis management and demonstrated the resistance to crises in the long term in the tourism industry.

Scenario of 9/11

The 9/11 attacks on the World Trade Center and the Pentagon resulted in more than 3000 people killed and left a devastating impact on the economy, with a loss of more than US$120 billion in total. In the words of Booth and Dunne (2002, p. 1): 'in the case of the attacks on the World Trade Center and the Pentagon, it is as if we instantly understood that the meanings of these events were global, beyond locality, and out-of geography experience'.

Since the attack was linked with the Al Qaeda group under the leadership of Osama bin Laden, the USA began a new chapter in its foreign policy declaring a 'war on terrorism'. This was followed by the defeat of the Afghanistan's Taliban regime, which had been providing shelter to Al Qaeda, in late 2001. Despite the defeat, Osama bin Laden's Al Qaeda remains intact. The Taliban still maintains a strong networking with other Islamic extremist groups in South Asia, South East Asia and the Middle East.

In South East Asia, the Jemaah Islamiah (JI), the Moro Islamic Liberation Front (MILF), Kumpulan Militan Malaysia (KMM) and Abu Sayaff were said to have links with Al Qaeda. After 9/11, South East Asia had to take much greater cognizance of the threat of international terrorism and its links to domestic Muslim terrorist or separatist elements. Terrorism threats encouraged almost all countries in South East Asia including Malaysia to work closely with the American government in dealing with the problem. Some analysts believe that South East Asia is a second front of the Americans in its war again terrorism (Sodhy, 2003).

Repercussion of 9/11 on the global tourism industry

The 9/11 attacks have had a more dramatic impact on the global tourism industry than any other crisis in recent years. The tourist reaction at that time was to return home as soon as possible. Massive cancellations followed, especially for long-haul trips from North America, Asian countries and Western Europe, although this phase passed quickly, and at the end of October, the industry was reporting gradual recovery. However, some airlines were immediately threatened by bankruptcy, such as Swissair and Sabena. Midway Airlines unfortunately confirmed its closing soon after the attacks. The International Association of Travel Agents (IATA) announced that global airline losses in 2001 were between US$10 billion and US$12 billion (World Tourism Organization, 2001). The crisis basically had severe effects on long-haul tourism, airlines, hotels and the business travel sector. With the existing weakened international economy, businesses were closed, capacity and working hours were reduced, and a sizeable number of jobs were lost. Another effect that was quite significant to South East Asia including Malaysia was that a number of Western governments issued travel warnings to their citizens against travelling to countries perceived to have links with terrorists. This has negative repercussions, as many countries in the region are heavily dependent on the tourism industry.

Tourism in Malaysia and Sabah

Profile of Malaysia

Malaysia is a country with a constitutional monarchy, with 13 states and three federal territories. It is a multisector economy with growth exclusively driven by export, with Japan and the USA as top export destinations. It is a secular Muslim country populated by 24.4 million people and has moved towards a pluralist culture based on a vibrant and interesting fusion of Malay, Chinese, Indian and indigenous cultures and customs. It is South East Asia's principal tourist destination, offering pristine white beaches, brilliant natural scenery and spectacular wildlife.

Profile of Sabah

Sabah is located at the northern part of Malaysian Borneo, covering an area of 73,620 km^2 (Department of Statistics, Malaysia, 2000). With a population of about 2.9 million (Department of Statistics, Malaysia, 2000), it is a virtual melting pot of many different cultures and traditions. It is known as one of the 12 mega-diversity sites in the world owing to its rich living heritage.

Its close proximity to the southern Philippines, where Abu Sayaff rebel groups maintain their presence, makes Sabah prone to problems especially related to terrorism. The Abu Sayaff group was responsible for the kidnapping of tourists and locals at Sipadan Island and Pandanan Island in Sabah's East Coast in 2000. Many Abu Sayaff leaders trained in terrorist camps in Afghanistan were believed to be the key plotters of 9/11. It is also believed that bin Laden has been funding Abu Sayaff through the International Islamic Relief Organization since 1992 (Kurlantzick, 2001) and provides sanctuary and other forms of assistance for foreign Islamic militants. It is no surprise that Western governments issued a negative advisory regarding Sabah and Malaysia in general.

The importance of tourism for Malaysia and Sabah

Malaysia has always been keen on the tourism industry, which is now the second biggest contributor to foreign revenue of the country and still shows more potential for expansion. Malaysia received RM17.3 billion in

2000, a 40% jump from the RM12.3 billion in 1999, with corporate tax of RM2 billion in addition to RM500 million in service tax from it, putting the real earnings from tourism at RM20 billion (Kong, 2003).

Sabah's tourism industry is relatively young, with its rapid growth beginning in 1995. Tourism is crucial to Sabah as the state government sees it as an avenue to diversify the state's economy. Sabah's economy has always been heavily dependent on the export of its primary and minimally processed commodities (Outlines Perspective Plan Sabah, 1995). Tourism is also seen as important by the Federal government, as shown by the doubled allocation for Sabah tourism projects from RM5.36 million under the Sixth Malaysia Plan (Economic Planning Unit, 1991–1995) to RM11.1 million under the Seventh Malaysia Plan (Economic Planning Unit, 1996–2000). Sabah has repositioned itself from a 'value for money' destination to a 'nature adventure' destination. It has world-class tourism products such as the pristine Sipadan Island, one of the top diving sites in the world, and the Kinabalu Park, Malaysia's first World Heritage Site. Tourism receipts amounted to RM1,091 million in 2002, which is a significant contribution to Sabah's economy (Sabah Tourism Board, 2004). Tourists spend 35% of their total expenses on accommodation, followed by 19% on food and drinks, 20% for shopping and the rest for transportation, visits and others (Bernama, 2003a). The importance of the tourism industry to Sabah's economy was highlighted when the events of 9/11 occurred.

Effects of 9/11 on Sabah's Tourism

In general, the figures of inbound and outbound tourism for Malaysia have been decreasing due to an avoidance of long-haul travel caused by 9/11. Tourism arrivals fell 3%, although the decrease was not as drastic as some of Malaysia's neighbouring countries such as Singapore experienced, due to the aggressive promotional activities by the Malaysia tourism board. The weak currency of Malaysia was a positive factor for inbound tourism, while making outbound tourism more expensive. Incoming arrivals increased to approximately 13.3 million in 2002, increasing at about 4%. This represents a slow down in the growth rate of 25% of the previous year due to the resounding aftermath effects of the 9/11 events carried over from the previous year (Euromonitor, 2004).

Pre-9/11 in Sabah

Before 9/11, the World Tourism Organization estimated that world tourism would increase 3–4% that year. The Sabah tourism environment in 2001 started with excitement, hope and expectations. Sabah had made tremendous efforts hosting the World Premier Expedition Race and Eco-Challenge Sabah 2000, and filming of one of the world's top TV shows,

Survivor, at Pulau Tiga. The Sabah tourism industry also hoped to eradicate the negative publicity of the Sipadan and Pandanan Islands kidnapping incidents, and expected to see new growth in the US market. The positive tourism environment had continued until the events of 9/11.

When the events of 9/11 occurred, tourism, being a very sensitive industry, was affected quite badly, although the effects were not equal in every destination (World Tourism Organization, 2001). Tourism destinations were battling the fears of flying and negative travel advisories. In general, places heavily reliant on visitors from the USA and Muslim countries felt the most severe effects.

Effects of 9/11 on Sabah

Sabah has experienced a decline of visitors from the USA and other Western destination since 9/11, as shown in Table 24.1. There was a decrease of 1.3% in worldwide arrivals at Sabah (Sabah Tourism Board, 2004). Sabah, being one of the states in Muslim-dominated Malaysia, suffered the negativity of the Islamic terrorism image brought about by 9/11. Some resorts had reported cancellations from American and UK groups (Bernama, 2003b). Besides the adverse image, the fear of flying due to imminent danger that came with it also strongly discouraged potential tourists. It is interesting to observe that the events of 9/11 have created a chain of effects, such as the cancellations of flights leading to other cancellations in accommodation sectors and overland/water transportation, and in turn has affected the food and beverage industries and business including tourism-related services and souvenirs.

The American market saw a decline from 11,010 arrivals in 2000 to 6076 in 2001, 6010 in 2002 and 2063 in 2003. However, this is seen as a negligible effect on the Sabah tourism industry as the number of American tourist arrivals to Sabah is small, which is related to the great distance between the USA and Sabah, and lack of direct flight availability, among other factors. Meanwhile, tourists from the UK and Ireland, which make up the bulk of the Western visitors to the state, have also been constantly decreasing after 9/11, from 18,544 arrivals in 2000 to 19,690 in 2001, 18,263 in 2002 and 14,514 in 2003 (Table 24.1). Among the reasons for the drop is the long distance between the UK and Ireland and Sabah, making it relatively more expensive compared with more renowned destinations in the region such as Bangkok, Bali and Phuket Island (Assistant Marketing Manager of Sabah Tourism Board, personal communication, 11 March 2004).

On the other hand, Table 24.1 shows that an increase in visitors from other countries as well as of local tourists has been noted. Many foreign visitors intending to visit the USA cancelled their plan to do so after 9/11 and looked for other holiday destinations, a decision which presented opportunities to Sabah. Travellers from North Asia such as the Japanese, Taiwanese, Koreans and even mainland Chinese avoided the USA and

Table 24.1. Visitor arrivals at Sabah from 2000–2003 by country (including Malaysia).

	2000	2001	2002	2003
Asia	353,921	354,460	472,684	472,400
Brunei	32,175	42,782	50,274	55,989
Philippines	45,887	42,133	46,897	53,865
Indonesia	116,120	120,332	233,857	208,128
Singapore	12,012	12,033	11,415	14,072
Hong Kong	12,182	14,057	12,002	15,133
China	5,232	8,387	12,505	25,165
Japan	12,124	13,943	25,569	24,500
Taiwan	111,952	94,769	65,506	49,509
Thailand	407	517	585	1,500
South Korea	5,830	5,507	14,074	24,539
Oceania	5,762	6,178	6,824	22,514
Australia	4,893	5,192	5,220	15,920
New Zealand	869	986	1,604	6,594
Europe	29,226	30,624	32,083	50,139
France	915	1,006	891	3,180
Germany	2,228	1,410	1,782	3,547
Denmark	3,638	4,363	810	1,868
Finland			291	1,378
Norway			491	2,010
Sweden			3,457	3,366
UK and Ireland	18,544	19,690	18,263	23,883
Belgium and Luxembourg	N/A	N/A	596	1,910
Italy	N/A	N/A	2,057	2,855
Netherlands	N/A	N/A	1,278	1,815
Russia	N/A	N/A	334	736
Switzerland	N/A	N/A	695	920
Others Europe	3,901	220	1,138	2,671
North America	14,185	9,717	10,466	17,781
USA	11,010	6,076	6,010	8,131
Canada	3,175	3,641	4,456	9,650
Others	5,844	5,012	6,207	6,878
International	408,938	406,009	528,264	569,712
Malaysian	365,537	512,514	579,092	681,742
Total	774,475	918,523	1,107,356	1,251,454

Source: Sabah Tourism Board (2004).
N/A = not available.

Europe. For instance, Korean visitors have increased from 5830 arrivals in 2000 to 5507 arrivals in 2001, 14,074 in 2002 and 17,793 in 2003. Unlike the Taiwanese market, which has seen a sudden fall due to saturation, the Korean market is new to Sabah as a result of the drive made by the Sabah Tourism Board, which promoted Sabah in Seoul. Local tourists outnumbered foreign tourists in terms of arrivals, increasing from 365,537 in 2000 to 512,514 in 2001, 528,264 in 2002 and 579,092 in 2003.

Tourism industry responses to 9/11

It is said that the tourism industry players are more likely to plan for disaster only after a disaster has occurred. In this sense, Sabah tourism is somewhay fortunate in that it had experienced a major crisis prior to 9/11. In April 2000, the Abu Sayaff rebels raided Sipadan, one of the top diving spots in the world and took 21 hostages including 12 foreign tourists, and Pandanan Islands, one of the tourist attractions in Sabah. The crisis management that Sabah and Malaysia undertook then was an invaluable experience for handling the 9/11 crisis.

Sabah Tourism Board has formulated specific strategies and actions plans as a response to 9/11:

1. Improve the perception and image of Sabah as a safe destination.
2. Improve the perception and image of Malaysia as a liberal Muslim country.
3. Persuade Malaysia Airlines (MAS) to lower airfares to Kota Kinabalu from Kuala Lumpur.
4. Continue to encourage, support and assist other carriers to make direct scheduled flights to Kota Kinabalu.
5. Improve cross-industry and cross-national cooperation.
6. Niche target marketing.
7. Continue to market-position Sabah as the premier nature adventure destination.

The Federal and State governments have been making vigorous efforts to ensure the safety of Sabah and its waters from terrorist threats. There is strong presence of both army and police around Sabah's coastal area now, which has made the state safer than ever.

Even though the Sabah Tourism Board together with the State government has taken steps to deflect the negative image resulting from the travel advisories of Western governments, such action clearly influenced those who intended to visit the state. The Malaysian government voiced its dissatisfaction with the advisory, stating that it is unfair simply to generalize that South East Asia is not a safe place to visit when an incident or a crisis occurred in the region (Sodhy, 2003). However, it is not only Malaysia that has been quite critical in this matter because other South East Asia countries heavily dependent on tourism, notably the Philippines, Thailand and Indonesia, also voiced their dissatisfaction with Washington.

Based on the strategies mentioned previously, the State government ensures that foreign government embassies and high commissions visit Sabah so that they can form the right impressions of Sabah's safety. Sabah's tourism industry players lobbied the American, British, German and Japanese embassies in Kuala Lumpur to ask them to avoid using words with negative connotations about Sabah in their travel advisories.

The reduction in foreign tourists brought less revenue for Sabah tourism. Therefore, Sabah has focused on domestic tourism to help cushion the impacts of 9/11. This particular market has remained untapped and the crisis has led to more intensive promotion of domestic holidays. For example, there is a 23.27 million market in Malaysia (Department of Statistics, Malaysia, 2004) alone, but only 681,724 domestic arrivals were recorded in 2003 (Sabah Tourism Board, 2004). With the hotel occupancy rate dropping after 9/11, the hoteliers quickly changed their strategies to attract more domestic visitors. Around this time, Sabah saw a variety of special offers and packages targeting families on vacation and students, not just from the local market but also from neighbouring countries including Brunei and Singapore.

Conclusion

The contribution of tourism to any country is significant, and any downturn in the industry is a cause for concern. The repercussions extend to industries related to tourism such as transportation, accommodation, or food and drink. The *Daily Express* reported that the then Prime Minister of Malaysia said that the tourism industry has recorded an encouraging performance despite the setback following the 9/11 attacks on the USA (Bernama, 2003b). The Assistant Minister of Tourism, Environment, Science and Technology of Sabah further added that the tourist influx could have been more had it not for the events of 9/11.

There were other international incidents following 9/11 that may have affected the overall tourism industry performance in Sabah. The Bali bombing which killed 187 people and the Davao bombing in Mindanao, southern Philippines (Spaeth, 2003) would have affected tourism in the South East Asian region but did not drastically affect the number of foreign tourists in Sabah. It affected Sabah because of its location in the same South East Asian region as Bali and Mindanao, which is seen as under threat from Muslim extremists. This may give an adverse impression and loss of confidence of potential tourists. However, Sabah may serve as an alternative to Bali in the meantime.

The State government has continued to promote tourism aggressively despite the safety, security and environmental incidents in neighbouring countries, which affected Sabah indirectly. Strategic marketing campaigns have been focused and implemented through the Sabah Tourism Board to attract more visitors to the State, since this sector has the potential to make Sabah the number one foreign exchange earner in the country.

Sabah, as a tourist destination, and heavily dependent on the tourism industry, has incorporated crisis management into its overall sustainable development and management strategies to protect and rebuild, if necessary, its image of attractiveness including safety, which reassures potential visitors and aids local tourism industry players in their recovery. However, exploring the possibility of developing or enhancing crisis prevention may prove more effective in the long term. Crisis management is not just concerned with terrorism; other threats such as diseases, economic instability or natural disaster, not just from Malaysia but from other countries as well, also have to be dealt with. The tourism industry has to be ready at all times to meet any contingencies and to respond to unforeseen crisis situations as expeditiously and as effectively as possible.

Note

[1] This chapter is based on a paper presented at the School of Social Science Seminar, Universiti Malaysia Sabah on 5 May 2004.

Acknowledgements

The authors would like to express their sincere appreciation to individuals who contributed their time and knowledge to this article: Sabah Tourism Board, Malaysia and Mr John Sienna of the School of Information Management, Victoria University of Wellington, New Zealand.

References

Bernama (2003a) Tourism may be affected. *Daily Express* 21 March

Bernama (2003b) Malaysia to focus on domestic tourism. *Daily Express* 1 April.

Booth, K. and Dunne, T. (2002) *World in Collision: Terror and Future of Global Order*. Palgrave MacMillan, London.

Department of Statistics, Malaysia (2000) *Sabah: Key Statistics*.

Department of Statistics, Malaysia (2004) *Malaysia: Key Statistics*.

Drabek, T.E. (1995) Disaster planning and response by tourist business executives. *Cornell Hotel and Restaurant Administration Quarterly* 36 (3), 86–110.

Economic Planning Unit (1991) *Sixth Malaysia Plan*. Economic Planning Unit, Prime Minister's Department of Malaysia, Kuala Lumpur.

Economic Planning Unit (1996) *Seventh Malaysia Plan*. Economic Planning Unit, Prime Minister's Department of Malaysia, Kuala Lumpur.

Euromonitor (2004) *Global Reports – The World Market for Travel and Tourism*. Euromonitor Plc, London.

Glaesser, D. (2003). *Crisis Management in the Tourism Industry*. Butterworth-Heinemann, Oxford.

Gonzalez-Herrero, A. and Pratt, C.B. (1998) Marketing crises in tourism: communication strategies in the USA and Spain. *Public Relations Review* 24, 83–98.

Henderson, P.G. (2002) Intelligence gathering and September 11 – what the lessons of history show. *World and I* December p. 17.

Kan, Y.C. (2001) Tourism sector must refocus. *Daily Express* 18 September.

Kong, L. (2003) Promote domestic tourism: Tham. *Daily Express* 29 April.

Kurlantzick, J. (2001) Fear moves East: terror targets the Pacific rim. *The Washington Quarterly* 24 (1), 19–29.

Larmer, B., Cochrane, J., Janssen, P., Holland, L. and Vitug, M.D. (2002) Liberty in the balance. *Newsweek International*, 18 November p. 30.

Mansfeld, Y. (1999). Cycles of war, terror, and peace: determinants and management of crisis and recovery of the Israeli tourism industry. *Journal of Travel Research* 38, 30–37.

Maskilone, C. (2003) Domestic tourism to offset loss. *Daily Express* 15 April.

Ritcher, L.K. (1999) After political turmoil: the lessons of rebuilding tourism in three Asian countries. *Journal of Travel Research* 38, 41–45.

Sabah Tourism Board (2004) *Visitor's Statistics*. Sabah Tourism Board, Kota Kinabalu.

Sodhy, P. (2003) US–Malaysian relations during the Bush administration: the political, economic, and security aspects. *Contemporary Southeast Asia* 25, 363–386.

Sonmez, S.F., Apostolopoulos, Y. and Tarlow, P. (1999) Tourism in crisis: managing the effects of terrorism. *Journal of Travel Research* 38, 13–18.

Spaeth, A. (2003) First Bali, now Davao: the bombing at an airport in the Philippines shows the threat that terrorists still pose in Asia. *Time International* 161, 17 March, p. 46.

World Tourism Organization (2001) *Tourism After 11 September 2001: Analysis, Remedial Actions and Prospects*. (No. 18). World Tourism Organization, Madrid.

25

Events in Indonesia: Exploring the Limits to Formal Tourism Trends Forecasting Methods in Complex Crisis Situations

BRUCE PRIDEAUX, ERIC LAWS AND BILL FAULKNER[1]

Reprinted with permission from *Tourism Management*. This chapter was originally published as Prideaux, B., Laws, E. and Faulkner, B. (2003) Events in Indonesia: exploring the limits to formal tourism forecasting methods in complex crisis situations. *Tourism Management* 24 (4), 511–520.

Introduction

International tourism flows are subject to disruption by a range of events that may occur in the destination itself, in competing destinations, origin markets, or they may be remote from either. The consequences may be either mild and relatively short term or have catastrophic impacts on existing industry systems. Major disruptions, also referred to as shocks, are felt in both origin and destination areas, affect both the public and private sectors and disrupt the travel plans of intending travellers. In recent years, major disruptions that have affected international tourism flows include the Gulf War, the Asian financial crisis (Office of National Tourism, 1998) and, more recently, the 11 September 2001 (9/11) terrorist attack on the USA. Commenting on disruptions suffered by the tourism industry, which he classified as either crises or disasters, Faulkner (2001, p. 136) noted that 'relatively little systematic research has been carried out on disaster phenomena in tourism, the impacts of such events on the tourism industry and the responses of industry and relevant government agencies to cope with these impacts'. Further, Faulkner stated that because of disruptions of this nature, research is required to assist the tourism industry to recover from events that are usually not forecastable. In contrast, during normal or tranquil times, forecasting has proved to be a useful planning tool for predictions of future tourism activity and is widely used by governments and the industry (Uysal and Crompton, 1985; Chu, 1998; Witt and Song,

2001). Forecasting generally uses a range of analytical techniques based on recent and current tourist flows between origin markets and destinations as well as a range of economic factors to predict future trends. However, the difficulty of predicting future economic activity, particularly in times of uncertainty, is an issue that has long bedevilled forecasters.

This chapter is concerned with various events that have the potential to disrupt established flows, resulting in subsequent tourist activity which is very different from the trends forecast in either the overall level of activity or the pattern of flows, or both. The chapter explores strategies that may be employed to improve the effectiveness of forecasting in circumstances where there are few pre-existing indicators of factors that may adversely affect national tourism flows at some point in the future. Recent events in Indonesia are used as a case study to build this discussion. The chapter develops a conceptual framework that synthesizes the issues identified but does not attempt to develop a detailed alternative forecasting model; its purpose is to suggest a direction that may offer an alternative to supplement current forecasting methods.

A Critique of Forecasting Techniques

Calantone *et al.* (1987) distinguished between four forms of forecasting. Exploratory forecasting extrapolates past trends using regression and similar techniques and is based on assumptions about relationships between variables. Normative forecasting incorporates discussion of the methods needed to attain a desired future outcome. Integrative forecasting relies on a variety of methods to determine the underlying relationships amongst a variety of forecasts, integrating these to maximize convergence of results. Finally, speculative forecasting uses techniques such as Delphic forecasting or scenario writing, and relies on the judgements of experts. In this approach, probabilities represent an assessment of the degree of uncertainty of a particular occurrence in the future. Given the frequent reliance of these methods on past experience, which in turn requires both explicit and tacit assumptions regarding the stability of relationships, the ability of forecasting to generate long-term results and account for unforseen events remains limited. Even short-term forecasting can only factor in known relationships that appear as identifiable trends, and building on these give a picture of what may occur if change occurs along predictable lines. The assumptions are basically those of equilibrium and stability, in contrast to the dynamic complexity of turbulent systems perspectives (Laws *et al.*, 1998).

A number of researchers (Song and Witt, 2000; Turner and Witt, 2001) have acknowledged the limitations of current forecasting techniques, particularly the difficulties posed by the inability to predict irregularities such as sudden changes in consumer taste and demand. To overcome these shortfalls, researchers such as Witt, Sohn and Turner have sought to improve the capability of established techniques. For example, Turner and Witt (2001) found that structured time series models incorporating explanatory variables produced the most accurate forecasts. The identification of relevant non-economic variables as determinants for future growth, and the modelling of their significance pose a high level of difficulty for forecasters. Uysal (1983 cited in Crouch, 1994), for example, noted that there were a number of limitations confronting demand forecasting including: ignoring supply factors; the omission of non-economic factors which may have long-term consequences; and the potential for the appropriateness of variables to change. To these, a range of other non-specified crises and disasters including domestic and international political factors, wars and insurrections, movements in the international economy, and natural disasters such as earthquakes, cyclones or hurricanes should be added. Although forecasters try to account for these situations by using dummy variables to allow for the impact of 'one-off' events such as the two 'oil crises' in the 1970s (Song and Witt, 2000), the problem of irregularities continues to defy prediction.

A more sophisticated approach utilizing time varying parameters (TVPs) regression to model structural change is one solution to the problem of predictive failure encountered by causal tourism demand forecasting models (Song and Witt, 2000). While the TVP approach is able to simulate a range of shocks that may influence the relationship between explanatory and dependent variables, it assumes that explanatory variables are exogenous. Where there is some doubt about the creditability of this assumption, the vector autogressive (VAR) modelling approach may be more appropriate (Song and Witt, 2000). In the VAR model, all variables are treated as endogenous.

While newer forecasting methods including TVP and VAR allow researchers to model the impact of disruptions, they are still dependent on the parameters that are selected for testing. It is at this point in the forecasting process that a major problem can be identified. Little consideration has been given to identifying the type of unexpected disruptions that should be incorporated into the current orthodoxy of forecasting. Recognizing the inability of current forecasting theory to cope with the unexpected, Faulkner and Russell (2000) put forward an alternative view suggesting that, owing to 'the certainty of the unexpected', authorities need to implement policies for coping with unexpected disruptions to tourism flows. The long-standing Newtonian paradigm of the relative stability of both internal and external environments of organizations is an inefficient theoretical basis for coping with change and crises. Yet the assumption of change along Newtonian lines underlies much of the current theory of forecasting. History has many times revealed that the tide of human events leans more to the chaotic than the ordered. If this proposition is accepted, the norm of history is change rather than equilibrium. Chaos theory talks of 'triggering events' such as a crisis or disaster. These events need not be regarded as only destructive because they may lead to new configurations or structures that are more effective than those that are replaced. A well-developed literature exemplified by journals that include *Risk Analysis*, *Risk Management*, *Disaster Planning and Prevention* and *Emergency*

Planning Digest have recognized that there is a large range of events that cannot be predicted with any certainty and which lie beyond the range of predictions that standard forecasting techniques can be expected to yield. Employment of scenarios as the basis for predicting the impact of a range of disruptions is a widely accepted method of planning for crises and disasters, including multiple environmental, economic and natural disasters. The tourism literature has not begun to investigate the rich range of techniques developed in the risk management literature, yet this literature has the potential to yield models, frameworks and theories that will assist tourism forecasters and planners to cope with a range of disasters and crises.

One direction that should be considered is a synthesis between risk specification, identification and management, and forecasting. In such a synthesis, forecasting, using current techniques, could be based on revised variables determined by forward-looking scenarios or risk analysis as an alternative to the current reliance on variables based on historical relationships. The risk literature has demonstrated the validity of scenario building as the basis for risk management. Haimes *et al.* (2002, p. 383), for example, state that '... It is clear that the first and most important step in a quantitative risk analysis (QRA) is identifying the set of risk scenarios. If the number of risk scenarios is large, then the second step must be to filter and rank the scenarios according their importance.' Ranking of risk, where the level of probability of occurrence and the degree of impact can be established, provides data that can then be used as a basis for forecasting. Of course the possible range of scenarios is large and there is some need to rank risk scenarios by the probability of their occurrence on a scale that must start with highly probable through to improbable. It is also apparent that ranking must include the flexibility to adjust the scale of probability. Prior to the 9/11 terrorist attack on the USA, an incident of this nature could be described as a highly improbable risk, but after the attack the level of risk moved to highly probable. Where then, does this leave the study of forecasting future growth trends in tourism? Where change is slow and ordered, and therefore relatively predicable, forecasting may yield a high degree of accuracy as claimed by forecasters. On the other hand, where events follow the normal course of history and exhibit a tendency to sudden, large-scale instability and unpredictability, forecasting loses its potency and an alternative form of prediction is required. Faulkner (2001) described a variety of situations that could be classified as either crises or disasters, but which were in the main single events that can be classified as either management failures (crises) or unpredictable catastrophic change (disaster). Beyond individual crisis or disaster events lie complex situations where many factors coalesce to impact on the harmony of the tourism industry. Rather than pursue a quest for definitional precision, there is a need to examine complex situations where numerous crises, disasters and political system failures act in unison to create one or more shocks on the tourism industry. Conditions in Indonesia between 1996 and 2000 created such a situation where a number of events had serious consequences for that nation's tourism industry.

By being able to determine the magnitude of the problem and identify its cause as either natural or human, or a mix of the two, actions to minimize the impact of crisis and disaster can be implemented. According to Faulkner (2001), a synthesis of the characteristics of disaster or crisis situations based on research by Fink (1986, p. 20), Keown-McMullan (1997, p. 9) and Weiner and Kahn (1972, p. 21) identified the following key factors:

- A triggering event, which is so significant that it challenges the existing structure, routine operations or survival of the organization. Trigger events may include political crises, religious or ethnic tensions, economic decline and climate change.
- Characterized by 'fluid, unstable, dynamic' situations (Fink, 1986, p. 20).
- High threat, short decision time and an element of surprise and urgency.
- A perception of an inability to cope among those directly affected.
- A turning point, when decisive change, which may have both positive and negative connotations, is imminent. As Keown-McMullan (1997, p. 9) emphasizes, 'even if the crisis is successfully managed, the organization will have undergone significant change'.

Understanding the path of the events following a shock may contribute to a methodology of identifying risk situations and thereby assist in providing some warning of when such events may occur, and how they may evolve. Faulkner's (2001) Tourism Disaster Management Framework provided one example of an operational model of this type. Once it can be admitted that current techniques have limitations, particularly in the areas of risk and uncertainty, the way is open to look for new methods that move beyond the Newtonian assumption of stability. Ignoring the possibility of disruptions in the terms stated in this discussion may lead to a prolonging of the event and exacerbation of its effects as remedial action is considered in the heat of unexpected unfolding events, rather than in the calm of prior contingency planning based on new forecasting methods.

A typical large-scale disruption precipitates complex movements away from the previous relationships which usually trend towards stability and equilibrium. During a situation of this nature, multiple events and their follow-on effects may prolong the period of disequilibrium unless there is some mechanism that can assist in re-establishing a new equilibrium situation. Chaos theory (Faulkner, 2001) provides an insightful paradigm for the investigation of changing complex situations where multiple influences impact on non-equilibrium systems. In these conditions of uncertainty, fruitful approaches to strategy formulation need to incorporate contingencies for the unexpected. Chaos theory demonstrates that there are elements of system behaviour that are intrinsically unstable and not amenable to formal forecasting. If this is the case, a new approach to forecasting is required. Possible ways forward may include political audits and risk analysis to develop a sense of the possible patterns of events allowing these to be factored into projections of future tourism activity using a series of scenarios. The latter may involve the use of a scenario building approach that may incorporate elements of van der Heijden's

(1997) strategic conversion model, elements of the learning organization approach based on a structured participatory dialogue (Senge, 1990) or elements of risk management described by Haimes *et al*. (2002). Whichever direction is taken, there are a number of factors that must be identified and factored into considerations of the possible course of events in the future.

Factors That May Influence Tourism Flows

Throughout recorded human history, it has proved impossible to predict the future, although many have tried. Faulkner (2001), for example, cites the importance of oracles in classical Greece and noted their failures. What is known of the future is that there are a number of circumstances that may exert influence on the course of events in following years. Events that disrupt the tourism industry can be divided into three groups.

Trends

Trends describe a range of possible future trends that can be identified in the present and which, unless remedial action is taken, will cause some magnitude of disruption in the future. The degree of impact of these trends will depend on how governments and industry respond to these trends to mitigate the worst of the possible range of outcomes. One example is the future impact of low fertility rates in developed countries which may see increased tensions in the future between retirees and workers (Willmott and Graham, 2001). For example, the Japanese population is projected to decline by 17.9 million between 2000 and 2050 while the number of persons aged 60 plus will climb to 42% of the population (Sayan, 2002). Population changes of this magnitude are also occurring in Korea, Italy and Spain, and in the future will have a significant impact on tourism as the national tax base falls but consumption of health services escalates.

Crises

Crises can be described as the possible but unexpected result of management failures that are concerned with the future course of events set in motion by human action or inaction precipitating the event. Events of this type include the foot and mouth outbreak on UK farms in 2001, the Chernobyl nuclear reactor and the *Exxon Valdez* oil tanker wreck. Examples of crises that may occur at some point in the future include:

● The impact of AIDS particularly in sub-Saharan Africa and potentially in the Indian subcontinent and the Russian Federation (Quinn-Judge, 2001).

- An increase in militant religious fundamentalism.
- Nuclear war in Asia.
- Financial meltdowns including global recession.
- Terrorism employed to achieve political or religious objectives.

Disaster

Disasters can be described as unpredictable catastrophic change that can normally only be responded to after the event, either by deploying contingency plans already in place or through reactive response. Durschmied (2000) cites a number of examples from history where unexpected weather turned the tide of battle, including the typhoon that saved Japan from a Mongol invasion in 1281. More recent examples include the Kobie earthquake, the 1997 El Nino climate effect and the 2002 floods in Europe and China. Events of this nature occur regularly but at undeterminable frequency, intensity and location. Examples of future disasters that the tourism industry could begin to prepare for include:

- Natural disasters of all types including floods, droughts and earthquakes.
- Long-term natural climate change separate from the current concern over human-induced global warming.
- A pandemic perhaps caused by a new strain of flu or other unknown disease.

Change in the structure of government, social organization or economic structure

To these previous classes of disruptions may be added other factors (Prideaux, 1999) that, while neither a disaster nor a crisis, may precipitate significant change in the organization of international tourism:

- Development of new blocs where nations join together in regional political and economic unions such as the European Union (EU).
- The future direction of capitalism.
- Demographic change in terms of ageing populations in developed economies as well as growing populations in many underdeveloped nations.
- A continuing search for political identity by ethnic and religious groups causing further fragmentation in a number of nations.
- Sacristy, particularly of farming lands, water, marine resources and non-renewable energy.
- Environmentalism, particularly if global warming continues.

Consideration of these trends, crises, disasters and changes to the structure of the economy or system of government is the first step to developing some capacity to factor disruptions into tourism forecasting. The concept of trends does afford some degree of predicability allowing the tourism industry to develop responses prior to the impact of the identified trend. Disasters, on the other hand, can generally only be responded to after the event, either by deploying contingency plans already in place or through reactive response. Crises may offer some scope for prediction based on the premise that after a particular type of crisis has passed, analysis of its causes should enable greater predictability of similar problems in the future. The impacts of single or multiple disruptions occurring simultaneously or in a sequence may create unexpected political, social and/or economic conditions that cause the decline of some destinations, growth of new destinations or radical disturbances to global tourism flows should also be considered.

To date, forecasts of future patterns of tourism growth have used a range of econometric demand models. However, it is apparent that there is a need to develop new techniques that identify risk and events that may cause future disruptions. Where the likelihood of disruption is small, techniques of this type are not normally required. Where history has identified areas of political disruption, use of these techniques, in conjunction with existing forecasting tools, may be an appropriate course for forecasting. For example, disruptions sometimes generate warning signs or are initiated by triggering events. Identification of warning signs and trigger events may extend warning periods and allow forecasters to produce revised forecasts using standard TVP, VAR or similar models.

Role of Government in the Unexpected

There has been limited discussion about the mechanisms that may be used to assist tourism in coping with the certainty of the unexpected, and a general criticism of the literature relating to tourism forecasting is that limited attention has been given to the impact of unforseen political and economic crises on policy development. Friedman (1999) suggested that the vulnerability of individual countries to shocks has increased exponentially as a consequence of the increase in interlocking systems associated with globalization, political alliances and modern communication technology. Examples of research include Clements and Georgiou (1998), who examined the impact of political instability on tourism flows in Cyprus, and Prideaux and Kim (1999), who analysed the impact of the Asian financial crisis on bilateral tourism between Australia and Korea. Henderson (1999) compared the impact of the crisis on Indonesia and Thailand, finding that tourism is vulnerable to outside forces such as economic conditions, and suggested that there is a need for a response strategy to cope with the unexpected. Further research of this nature can be expected from analysis of the impacts of 9/11.

Government responses to shocks are important and will often affect the rate of recovery of the tourism industry; however, we find little in the tourism literature to assist governments to prepare for the unexpected, and cope with its impact. Aside from limited use of scenario planning, governments rely on forecasts to develop budgets, policies and plans in the absence of other methods of predicting the future. Policy frameworks enacted by government provide the incentives as well as the constraints around which destinations must work as they seek to attract investment and encourage visitation. Hall (1994), for example, noted that there was a need to take into account the political context within which tourism development occurred. In an analysis of barriers to US tourism to Africa, Brown (2000) noted that political risk, defined as risks that arise from the action of governments or political forces and which interfere with or prevent foreign business transactions, can disrupt tourism flows. Risks of this nature may inhibit the flow of international tourists for a number of reasons, including the unwillingness of foreign investors to support or extend lending facilities, the inability of intermediaries to undertake financial transactions and for airlines to operate into an uncertain logistics environment. Richter (1995, 1999) has published a number of studies examining the impact of political events, including episodes of violence, on national tourism industries. In a recent article, Ritcher (1999) commented on the impact on the tourism industries of the Philippines, Pakistan and Sri Lanka caused by political disruption. It is salient to compare the consequences of political tensions in these countries with the recent situation in Indonesia. Comparisons with the Philippines are particularly relevant, as Indonesia appears to have experienced the same general course of events that occurred in the Philippines after the removal of Marcos from the Presidency in 1986. According to Richter (1999), risk assessment and political audits may be useful tools to have in place to assist nations to recover quickly from political disasters. Where there is an element of corruption evident, planning and management may be less adaptable to external shocks because of rigidities that reduce response options.

One common element that emerges from the preceding discussion is the role of governments in inadvertently creating as well as managing unforseen events. In the case of Indonesia and the Philippines during the political upheavals that heralded the demise of the Suharto and Marcos administrations, the government appeared to be the cause of the crisis. The corrupt and undemocratic nature of the Marcos and Suharto regimes eventually generated sufficient opposition that mass unrest eventually unseated the incumbent governments. In other instances, the government's response to crisis may be a critical element in the manner in which national tourism industries cope with declining tourism flows. If governments withdraw support for tourism promotion or tourism development, the impact may be exacerbated. Conversely, if governments assist the industry, as in the case of Thailand during the Asian Financial Crisis (Henderson, 1999), the impacts may be minimized. Analysis of the reactions of governments through policy mechanisms to such crises and the results of those actions appears to be important areas that warrant further research.

To illustrate the issues outlined above, this chapter presents a case study describing the main causes of disruption to the inbound tourism sector of Indonesia during 1997–2002. The difficulty of forecasting in the face of unexpected and complex disruptions to tourism flows is illustrated by analysing the projections of bilateral tourism flows between Indonesia and Australia developed by the Tourism Forecasting Council (TFC).

Case Study – Indonesia

During the 10-year period 1987–1997, Indonesia achieved a 475% increase in inbound tourism, with arrivals climbing from 1,060,000 to 5,036,000. A significant feature of the growth during this period was a shift from traditional European, US and Australian markets to intraregional travel from Asia, a result of the high and sustained growth of Asian economies. The World Tourism Organization (1994) had estimated that the growth rate throughout the 1990s would average between 13 and 15% per annum, a target that appeared achievable until a series of events disrupted the Indonesian economy from 1997 onwards. Between 1993 and 1997, total arrivals grew by 152.4% while receipts rose from US$3.99 billion to US$5.44 billion (World Tourism Organization, 1999). By 1997, foreign exchange earnings from tourism accounted for 10.2% of Indonesia's exports (World Tourism Organization, 1999).

Factors affecting Indonesian tourism during 1997–2002

In the period 1997–2002, Indonesia experienced ten major shocks that received widespread international publicity and resulted in sharply reduced activity in the tourism sector. Many of the factors listed stem from pressures that have existed in Indonesian society for many decades and which surfaced as a consequence of adverse political and economic factors.

1. *Smoke haze.* There was negative media reporting of the annual smoke haze resulting from illegal burning of forests in Sumatra and Borneo. The haze was particularly bad in 1997.
2. *The Asian financial crisis.* The crisis led to a large and rapid fall in the value of the Indonesian Rupiah, resulting in a substantial increase in unemployment, business failure and an increase in price of many imports including a number of staple food items.
3. *Political unrest.* Associated with the fall of the Suharto regime, political unrest commenced in late 1997 and reached a peak in May 1998. Much of the unrest emanated from student factions in Jakarta's universities who were pressing for democratic reforms.
4. *Ethnic unrest.* Commencing in 1997 and apparently sparked by the rapid deterioration of the domestic economy and rising unemployment, many Chinese communities and businesses in Java were targeted by rioters.

Ethnic unrest also flared in Kalimantan in 1999 between the native Dayaks and the immigrant population of Madurese, leaving 50,000 internally displaced Madurese.

5. *Religious unrest.* Commencing with the attacks on Chinese Christian communities in Java in 1997, sectarian unrest spread into a number of provinces including Ambon. The trouble continued into 2000 in the Maluku Islands where there were frequent clashes between Christians and Muslims. In some instances, religious unrest was related to ethnic tensions.

6. *Rebellion and political unrest.* Separatist movements have been active in Aceh, East Timor and Irian Jayra for several decades and subject to vigorous suppression by the Indonesian military. Suppression of the Fretilin pro-independence movement in East Timor has regularly featured in the Western media particularly after a number of reported massacres during the 1990s.

7. *East Timor.* The failure of the Indonesian military and police to control pro-Indonesian militias active in East Timor after the territory voted for self-government in August 1999 resulted in intervention by a United Nation's-mandated peace-making force. Demonstrations against Australia's leadership of the UN force (Interfet) sent to secure East Timor were prominently featured in the Australian media and were the cause of strained diplomatic relations with Australia from 1999 onwards.

8. *The Wahid administration.* Elected to the presidency as a compromise candidate in 1999 by the Peoples Consultative Assembly (MPR), President Wahid was frequently criticized during 2000 for his inability to achieve economic stability and alleged softness on corruption, particularly in relation to the Suharto family and business cronies. President Wahid was subsequently replaced by his deputy Megawati Soekarnoputri.

9. *1997 El Nino effect.* The El Nino climate shock of 1997–1998 greatly weakened Indonesia's agricultural sector (Sachs, 2002) as drought reduced farm productivity and drove up food prices. While not as obvious as the previous factors, the conditions that resulted from the impact of the El Nino climate shock appeared to be a significant background factor to the ensuing unrest.

10. *12 October 2002* night club bombing in Bali. On 12 October 2002, an unidentified (at the time of writing) terrorist group exploded a large car bomb in a popular night club district in Kuta Beach, Bali, killing an estimated 190 persons including approximately 100 Australian and 30 British tourists. The impact on the Indonesian economy will be determined by the success of the Government in arresting the perpetrators, eliminating terrorist cells and convincing the Governments of Indonesia's major generating counties that security conditions have improved to the extent that adverse travel advisory warnings can be lifted.

Combined, the factors described above generated considerable and continuing adverse publicity in the international media. Graphic images of rioting, killings, destruction of commercial districts in Java and images of mass air evacuations of expatriates from Jakarta in May 1998 made the selling of pleasure travel to Indonesia a difficult task for marketers. The ongoing and multifaceted nature of adverse events has contributed to a picture of a nation in crisis, at least to the outside observer. Terrorism and religious fundamentalism are evident in many of the recent events in Indonesia, particularly in East Timor (terrorism and nationalism) and Bali (terrorism), and religious warfare in Ambon where militant Muslim fundamentalist groups declared a Jihad on the island's Christian population. Arguably, all the factors listed are the result of crises. However, given Indonesia's history of having to deal with rebellions in disaffected provinces that were either ethnically or religiously different from the dominate Javanese culture and power structure, events 6 and 7 may also be classed as trends. These events were not factored into forecasts of tourism growth, thus confirming the need for a new approach to forecasting that moves beyond the manipulation of known variables to identification and incorporation into forecasting of other factors that may be country specific. Unfortunately, incorporation of these factors is unlikely to produce the apparent precision achieved by contemporary forecast models.

Impact of the Asian financial crisis

The Asian financial crisis exercised the first major shock on the Indonesian economy and, arguably, provided the trigger for the subsequent political difficulties that ultimately translated into reduced tourism flows (Prideaux, 1998). Following on from the Asian financial crisis was a series of events that ultimately culminated in the overthrow of President Suharto. These events received widespread coverage in the international media. The anti-Chinese sentiment of much of the earlier rioting in 1997 and the May 1998 riots was viewed with particular concern by many Asian markets and is the likely explanation for the decline of inbound tourists from Hong Kong (47.3% in 1998) and Taiwan (30.4% in 1998) (Statistics Indonesia, 2000). Continuing political uncertainty, combined with political, religious and ethnic tensions during the latter part of 1997–1998 appear to have had a cumulative effect, resulting in a substantial fall in inbound tourism particularly during 1998. In comparison, other Asian nations affected by the Asian financial crisis quickly recovered and, with a few exceptions (Singapore experienced 4.63% fewer arrivals in 1999 than 1996), recorded higher inbound tourism in 1999 than 1996, the last full year prior to the onset of the Asian financial crisis.

The net result of these series of shocks to the Indonesian tourism industry can be illustrated by comparing actual arrival data with forecast arrival figures (Table 25.1). The difficulties of forecasting tourism flows in periods of uncertainty or where the unexpected occurs is clearly illustrated by comparing forecasts with actual arrivals and departures using bilateral tourism flows between Indonesia and Australia in the period 1997–2000. The table clearly illustrates the difficulties encountered by forecasters using standard forecasting tools during times of uncertainty and the impact that unanticipated shocks can produce.

Australian outbound tourists indicating that Indonesia was their main destination of travel grew rapidly from 158,000 in 1990 to peak at 350,000 in 1998, when Indonesia was the second most popular destination for Australian outbound visitors. In 1998, prior to the adverse reporting in the Australian media from Indonesia's handling of the East Timor situation and the subsequent widespread coverage of anti-Australian sentiment in Indonesia, Australian departures were forecast to be 339,000 in 1998 and 360,000 in 1999 (Tourism Forecasting Council, 1999) but were actually 246,000 because of the unexpected political shocks that occurred in Indonesia. The significant differences in projections made during the period 1997–2000 are a reflection of the inability of traditional forecasting techniques to account for the unexpected and therefore point to the need for the inclusion of additional forecasting tools including scenario analysis.

Indonesian crisis – the limits of forecasting

Forecasts produced during the early part of the 1990s did not include an allowance for political and financial difficulties that were experienced later

Table 25.1. Comparison of forecasts and actual arrival data 1996–2002 (000s) by the Tourism Forecasting Council (TFC).

	1996	1997	1998	1999	2000	2001	2002	2003
TCF forecast of Indonesian arrivals in Australia (1997)		186	221	259	300	347	489	457
TCF forecast of Indonesian arrivals in Australia (1998)			75	75	88	97	108	121
TCF forecast of Indonesian arrivals in Australia (1999)				90	102	111	124	139
TCF forecast of Indonesian arrivals in Australia (2000)					102	111	124	139
TCF forecast of Indonesian arrivals in Australia (2001)						95	101	112
Actual Indonesian arrivals in Australia	155	160	93	91	83	94		
TCF forecast of Australian departures to Indonesia (1997)[a]								
TCF forecast of Australian departures to Indonesia (1998)		311	339	360	376	397	412	426
TCF forecast of Australian departures to Indonesia (1999)				360	376	397	412	426
TCF forecast of Australian departures to Indonesia (2000)					276	316	345	372
TCF forecast of Australian departures to Indonesia (2001)						222	242	260
Actual Australian arrivals in Indonesia	380	539	394	531	460			

[a] No forecast of Australian departures published.
Source: Based on forecasts by the TFC 1997a, 1998, 1999, 2000, 2001.

in the decade. This is not surprising as a capability of this nature is beyond the scope of current forecasting methods. However, alternative approaches including scenario development, risk analysis and/or political analysis as suggested by Richter (1999) may have concluded that Indonesia was entering the same type of domestic conditions encountered prior to the overthrow of the Marcos regime in the 1980s.

While on the surface Indonesia appeared politically stable throughout the early 1990s, a number of political pressures were beginning to build that eventually culminated in the collapse of President Suharto's New Order when he resigned in 1997. The hallmarks of the New Order period were tight control of the media, the centralization of power in the Presidency, and the ineffective nature of the parliamentary process characterized by the Peoples Consultative Council which met infrequently and had 200 of its 700 members appointed by the President. In the final years of the New Order, concerns developed over systemic corruption, the alleged wealth of the Suharto family and infringements of human rights. Importantly, there was no apparent mechanism for the succession of the Presidency or indication that thought had been given to the democratization of the parliamentary process. If these factors had been considered in the light of conditions that existed a decade earlier in the lead up to the overthrow of President Marcos in the Philippines and the ensuing years of unrest as pro-Marcos forces sought to restore the old order, the possibility of some form of internal disruption in Indonesia during the late 1990s would have at least appeared to merit consideration. Unfortunately, forecasters appear to have neglected such considerations.

There are a number of commercially available risk assessment reports that may assist, the *International Country Risk Guide* (Sealey, 2000) published by the PRS Group being one example. Based on a composite risk rating that included evaluation of quantitative indicators of political risk, economic risk and financial risk, the *International Country Risk Guide* published in May 2000 listed Indonesia as a high risk nation ranking 106 out of 140 countries evaluated. In the equivalent period in 1999, the *International Country Risk Guide* had ranked Indonesia at 130, indicating that increased stability had somewhat reduced the magnitude of risk during 1999–2000. In comparison, the risk rankings for some of Indonesia's major trading partners in May 2000 were: Singapore 1, Japan 13, Australia and Taiwan both at 15, the USA 19 and Korea 27. In a 5-year forecast of the most probable risk, Indonesia rated 62 against a 100-point index, with 100 indicating the least risk. In comparison, Singapore rated 78, Japan 85, Australia 88, Taiwan 80.5, Korea 78.5 and the USA 80.5. The discussion of the Indonesian crisis has illustrated that while unexpected events are certain to occur, traditional forecasting methods are inadequate without the incorporation of new forecasting techniques that are sensitive to signals regarding potential crises and the consideration of risk ranking that use a range of quantitative measures not usually employed in current forecasting methods. Indonesia proved not to have the institutional resilience to weather the partially self-inflicted disaster in its tourism industry. In the case of Indonesia, years of undemocratic government, cronyism and corruption have resulted in rigidities that have made its industry less adaptable and unable to respond creatively to new challenges. While not all countries face the same level of problems experienced by Indonesia in the period 1997–2002, the events such as the Asian financial crisis and the Gulf War may have significant and unanticipated impacts. Introducing new elements into forecasting, including a wide range of scenarios based on political and economic risk, may enhance managers' ability to plan for the future.

Modelling Disruptions to Tourism

A model of the factors influencing tourism flows between an origin and a specific destination was proposed by Laws (1995). The direction, frequency and intensity of tourist flows are the cumulative outcome of several influences either creating push conditions in the origin, or pulling visitors towards the destination. The approach is similar to Dann (1997), who explains that push factors are those that provide the impetus for individuals to travel, raising the question of where to go. According to Dann (1997, p. 168) 'Pull factors are the destination specific attributes which tend to determine whether the traveller will go to A or to B'. The amount of free time and disposable income of the population in tourist origin areas determine the overall volume of demand for travel from that area, pushing tourists towards destinations, while the differences in climate, culture and other attractions of the destination pull visitors towards it. Over a period of time, the flow linking one destination and one origin will stabilize, through familiarity and the institutions of tourism marketing and tour operating. However, three groups of factors can disrupt the established flow, suddenly and unpredictably, with potentially severe consequences for the destination. The groups of factors are:

1. *Inhibiting factors.* Events in the country of origin, such as an economic depression, political uncertainty or adverse foreign exchange rates, may inhibit the outflow of tourists to all destinations.
2. *Diverting factors.* Another disruption to established travel patterns is the development of new destinations (or existing destinations setting their prices at more accessible levels). This has the effect of diverting existing tourist flows.
3. *Repelling factors.* The destination may experience a natural catastrophe or civil unrest, thus repelling incoming tourists from all countries of origin. At a lower level of disruption, Governments have sometimes imposed stringent visa requirements for visitors from particular countries that are not viewed favourably for ideological reasons.

Inhibiting and diverting factors are common occurrences affecting the trends of tourism between established origin and destinations pairs, but repelling factors have different characteristics, arising with apparent suddenness, and producing rapid and significant disruption to familiar patterns of tourist activity. The triggering event may itself be the result of quite complex factors but, of significance here, there is often a cascading sequence of other events each of which has consequences for the tourism industry and the particular destination. The events outlined in the foregoing discussion of the Indonesian crisis are summarized in Table 25.2. The strength of origin push factors was reduced, particularly in Asian source markets, while the marketing tactics adopted by the Indonesian authorities were not effective in overcoming the individual and cumulative repellents to inward tourism in the short term, despite the benefits to tourists from beyond the region of the weakened Indonesian currency and improvements made to security for tourists in Java and Bali. Overall, Indonesia experienced a series of tourism shocks as the Asian financial crisis triggered further events within the country which have continued to destabilize tourism flow and revenue patterns as this chapter was being completed.

Disruptions and Forecasting the Future

History has consistently demonstrated a propensity to move beyond the expected, with unexpected shocks that disrupt the smooth and ordered unfolding of human affairs. Shocks must now be regarded as an integral feature of the tourism system and, while unforecastable in the short term, should be factored into long-term expectations. In these circumstances, the unfolding of the future as a function of past relationships ceases, and a new dynamic occurs, imposing a new set of relationships between the demand and supply of tourism services. Shocks have three major elements: (i) the cause of the shock; (ii) the magnitude of the shock; and (iii) a time element.

This is a significant observation for the tourism industry and provides a basic framework for any post-shock analysis. The time element is significant but difficult to quantify. The further we look into the future the more uncertain we can be about any relationship. For example, there is

Table 25.2. Changed influences on tourist flows to Indonesia, 1997–2002.

Origin pushes	Indonesia became more competitive as the value of the Rupiah fell during the Asian financial crisis
Destination pull factors	Asian financial crisis results in falling value of Rupiah, giving tourists greater buying power
Inhibitors	Reduced air access
Repellents	Smoke haze
	Political unrest
	Ethnic violence
	Religious violence
	Rebellions in East Timor and Ache
	Bali terrorist attack in 2002
Destination pull response tactics	Lets go Indonesia
	Discount holiday packages

evidence to suggest that California can expect a repeat of the 1906 earthquake that devastated San Francisco. The time of the next major earthquake is uncertain; it could be in the very near future or decades or even centuries away. What is certain, however, is that when the next earthquake occurs, there will be severe disruption to tourism in California.

Table 25.3 develops a framework for classifying shocks according to a scale of severity, probability, type of event, level of certainty and suggested forecasting tools for each scale of shock. Shocks are grouped into four categories according to scale, itself a reflection of the probability of these events occurring. In the table, events caused by factors such as shifts in exchange rates and inflation are classified as S1 and S2 events, and their effects should be forecastable by existing methods. S3 and S4 represent events which are more significant in their effects. S3 shocks are beyond the range of normal forecasting tools but could be included in forecasts using scenarios to identify the magnitude of the problem and then applying

Table 25.3. Classification of shocks.

Scale	Probability	Example of event	Forecasting tools	Level of certainty of forecast
S4	Not anticipated	9/11 terrorist attack in the USA, 1991 Gulf War, Asian financial crisis	Scenarios, risk assessment, Delphi forecasting and historical research may be used to identify risks of this nature and develop estimates of post-shock travel demand and supply conditions. At this point new parameters are established, allowing employment of standard forecasting techniques	Very low
S3	Unlikely but just possible	Pre-existing conditions cause major disruption, i.e. earthquakes, terrorist attacks, coups	Scenarios determine possible boundaries of the impact of shock, allowing employment of standard forecasting techniques to test tourism responses for a range of possible outcomes	Beyond current range of acceptability
S2	Possible based on worst-case scenario of past trading conditions	Upper limit of variables normally used in forecasting used, i.e. rapid rise in exchange rates	Existing forecasting techniques with allowance for sudden changes in demand and supply conditions	Medium to low
S1	Expected based on recent past trading conditions	Within the range of expected movements in exchange rates and inflation	Standard forecasting methods	High for near term, lower in the medium term

standard forecasting tools to quantify and examine the likely range of impacts based on a possibility spectrum that commences with low and moves through medium to a high level of possibility. S4 shocks are not anticipated and may be the result of a crisis or disaster. Employing a range of tools that are often neglected by current forecasting techniques will allow at least some assessment of timing, magnitude, severity and cost to be made of S3 and S4 events. Tools that are available include risk assessment, historic research, scenarios and Delphi forecasting. Using methods of this nature, Prideaux (2002) examined the impact of a range of emerging technologies on cybertourism, finding cause for alarm and indicating the need for discussion of the possible negative impacts of cybertourism on humanity likely to become apparent within 2–3 decades.

The 9/11 terrorist attack was entirely unexpected and had a significant impact on tourism, and for this reason is classified as a S4 shock. However, in the wake of the attack, further major attacks are now more likely and it has now, unfortunately, become more likely that other such shocks will occur. On the scale illustrated in Table 25.3, further terrorist attacks on civilian targets should now be classified as S3 or in some cases as S2. In the future, it is shocks on the probability scale of S3–S4 that hold the greatest potential for disrupting tourism.

A Risk Forecasting Approach

From the research conducted for this chapter, it is apparent that there are unresolved difficulties faced by forecasters. While the future will never be able to be predicted with a reasonable degree of certainty, except perhaps for the inevitability of taxes and eventual mortality, a sense of how current factors and tensions might influence the future may offer forecasters a window to the future. The need for forecasting is apparent given the long gestation periods of capital-intensive tourism investments and the need for business planning. While risk assessment based on indices and rankings offers a further tool for reducing the uncertainty of future trends, there remains a need for numerical forecasts, and it is in this area that further research is required. Future research should be directed to developing new forecasting paradigms that incorporate political risk, economic risk and a deeper understanding of the influences of history. In any future modelling, inclusion of qualitative as well as traditional quantitative methods must be considered. Perhaps the way forward lies in developing a new set of tools based on risk assessment, probability of occurrence and scenario generation which can produce new sets of variables that can then be used as the basis for forecasting.

One avenue of approach may be to attempt to bring together the quantitative elements of forecasting plus less frequently used qualitative methods to produce a series of scenarios each based on a range of possible futures. The Tourism Forecasting Council (1997b) adopted a scenario approach in 1997, when forecasts of inbound tourism to Australia were revised in the light of the Asian financial crisis. In the TFC approach, scenarios were based on possible combinations of interest rate rises and currency fluctuations. This was largely based on quantitative trends rather than qualitative trends that might be employed with risk assessment or political audits as suggested by Richter (1999). A possible method of analysis may be to produce a standard trend analysis based on the assumption that past relationships will carry on into the future. This projection could then serve as a baseline. Next, risk analysis could be employed to identify any potential non-economic problems that may destabilize the economy. These may include terrorism, racial and religious factors, land ownership disputes, changes in the level of lawlessness and political factors, and the potential for significant earthquake- or weather-induced disruption, to cite some familiar causes. Delphi techniques provide one method of assessing these types of risk and assigning to them a weighting. Using standard econometric forecasting tools, these factors could be assessed and revised trends generated as scenarios resulting in discontinuities to the baseline. Finally, a similar process could be employed to factor possible adverse political conditions identified via a political audit to produce a total probabilities forecast range.

The result would be a series of scenarios each based on a set of possible adverse or favourable outcomes in the future with a weighted probability index. While considerably more complicated than current projections, it would enable the users of the projections to have a more complete understanding of the range of probabilities in the future. While some consumers of forecasts may find added difficulty in understanding the greater detail and reduced certainty of this type of forecasting, it would give users enhanced information on which to make informed long-term business decisions and implement appropriate strategies. Ideally, however, the users should be intimately involved in the scenario generation and assessment process, rather than simply abdicating this responsibility to the technicians (Faulkner and Valerio, 1995). In developing methods for such engagement, the tourism sector would do well to draw on strategic management practices adopted elsewhere and, in particular, on methods developed by the learning organization school (Senge *et al.*, 1994) and the strategic conversion approach (van der Heijden, 1997). A culture of ongoing environmental scanning, assessment, dialogue and mutual learning is more fundamental to an informed and appropriate strategic stance than an uncritical reliance on current forecasting models.

Conclusion

The task faced by forecasters is enormous and made more difficul by deficiencies in current techniques. The problem of forecasting can be demonstrated by the following example. A forecaster, asked to develop travel projections between 1910 and 1920, would have recognized some political tensions in the Balkans but would not have been able to forecast the effect of the First World War. The forecasting problem illustrated by this example remains unresolved in the present era. Understanding the impact that unexpected disruptions may have on tourism flows is important for forecasters, planners, investors and operators. Incidents such as the Asian financial crisis (1997–1999), the break up of the USSR, coups in Fiji in 1987 and 2000, and the invasion of Kuwait by Iraqi in 1990 illustrate the manner in which seemingly unpredictable events can negate expert forecasts. The existing suite of statistical and econometric forecasting techniques is unable to deal with this type of uncertainty, and crucially they lack the ability to articulate this into the interface between forecasting and strategy. Further refinement of current methods which factor the unexpected into forecasting techniques may become possible if tourism researchers embrace new approaches to viewing the future. In particular, there is a need to use scenarios as a platform to predict the patterns and effects of events which occur during periods of disruption, perhaps brought on by multiple shocks.

From the evidence presented in the case study discussing recent events in Indonesia it is apparent that in the future forecasting techniques should incorporate recognition of the potential impacts of the underlying political, economic, social and cultural trends that affect each nation as well as the region in which that nation is situated. A thorough understanding of national history and, from this, identification of potential risk factors is essential if potential disruptions arising from these factors are to be incorporated into new tourism forecasting model.

This chapter has identified deficiencies in current forecasting techniques and pointed the way towards greater understanding of the impact of unexpected tourism shocks. Table 25.2 identified how unexpected events influence tourism flows while Table 25.3 classifies unexpected shocks by probability, examples and suggested forecasting tools. The incorporation of scenarios, risk audits and the need for a greater understanding of national history is obvious. One solution to the way forward will be to incorporate these considerations as an interface between trends to the present and forecasting of trends into the future. If the potential for these considerations to disrupt tourism flows is small, current techniques are entirely appropriate. If there is potential for a large disruption, the use of scenarios as the interface between the present and projections of the future may well be the way forward.

There is an obvious challenge for forecasters to incorporate these views into their work. Accepting this challenge and developing new methods of forecasting using wider parameters than currently employed has the potential to produce forecasting of greater accuracy in the future.

Note

[1] This paper is one of the last in which Bill Faulkner was involved before his untimely death in early 2002. Despite the illness from which he never recovered, Bill continued to advise us as this paper progressed. We wish to aknowledge the profound influence of Bill's insights into key tourism issues and emerging tourism theory, and to pay tribute to the pleasure of working with him. It was originally published in *Tourism Management* and is republished here with permission from Elsevier.

References

Brown, D.O. (2000) Political risk and other barriers to tourism promotion in Africa: perceptions of US-based travel intermediaries. *Journal of Vacation Marketing* 6 (3), 197–210.

Calantone, R., Benedetto, A. and Bojanic, D. (1987) A comprehensive review of tourism forecasting literature. *Journal of Travel Research* 27, 28–39.

Chu, F. (1998) Forecasting tourist arrivals, non linear sine wave or ARIMA? *Journal of Travel Research* 36 (3), 79–84.

Clements, M.A. and Georgiou, A. (1998) The impact of political instability on a fragile tourism product. *Tourism Management* 19, 283–288.

Crouch, G. (1994) The study of international tourism demand: a survey of practice. *Journal of Travel Research* 32, 41–52.

Dann, G. (1977) Anomie, ego-enhancement and tourism. *Annals of Tourism Research* 6 (4), 184–194.

Durschmied, E. (2000) *The Weather Factor: How Nature Has Changed History*. Hodder and Stoughton, London.

Faulkner, B. (2001) Towards a framework for tourism disaster management. *Tourism Management* 22, 135–147.

Faulkner, B. and Russell, R. (2000) Turbulence, chaos and complexity in tourism systems: a research direction for the new millennium. In: Faulkner, B., Moscardo, G. and Laws, E. (eds) *Tourism in the 21st Century, Reflections on Experience*. Continuum, London, pp. 328–349.

Faulkner, B. and Valerio, P. (1995) An integrative approach to tourism demand forecasting. *Tourism Management* 16 (1), 29–37.

Faulkner, B. and Vikulov, S. (2001) Katherine, washed out one day, back on track the next: a post-mortem of a tourism disaster. *Tourism Management* 22, 331–344.

Fink, S. (1986) *Crisis Management*. American Association of Management, New York.

Friedman, T. (1999) *The Lexus and the Olive Tree*. Harper Collins, London.

Haimes, Y., Kaplan, S. and Lambert, J.H. (2002) Risk filtering, ranking, and management framework using hierarchical holographic modelling. *Risk Analysis* 22, 383–397.

Hall, C.M. (1994) *Tourism and Politics: Policy, Power and Place*. Wiley, Chichester, UK.

Henderson, J.C. (1999). Southeast tourism and the financial crisis: Indonesia and Thailand compared. *Current Issues in Tourism* 2, 294–203.

Keown-McMullan, C. (1997) Crisis: when does a molehill become a mountain? *Disaster Prevention and Management* 6 4–10.

Laws, E. (1995) *Tourist Destination Management: Issues, Analysis and Policies*. Routledge, London.

Laws, E., Faulkner, B. and Moscardo, G. (1998) *Embracing and Managing Change in Tourism: International Case Studies*. Routledgen, London.

Office of National Tourism (1998) *Impact (August)*. Department of Industry, Science and Tourism, Canberra.

Prideaux, B.R. (1998) The impact of the Asian financial crisis on bilateral Indonesian–Australian tourism. In: Gunawan, M.P. (ed.) *Pariwisata Indonesia Menuju Keputusan Yang Lebih Baik*, Vol. 2. Bandung Institute of Technology, Bandung, pp. 15–29.

Prideaux, B. (1999) The Asian financial crisis and the tourism industry – lessons for the future. *Current Issues in Tourism* 2, 279–293.

Prideaux, B. (2002) The cybertourist. In: Dann, G. (ed.) *The Tourist as a Metaphor of the Social World*. CAB International, Wallingford, UK, 317–339.

Prideaux, B. and Kim, S.M. (1999) Bilateral tourism imbalance – is there a cause for concern: The case of Australia and Korea. *Tourism Management* 20(4), 523–532.

Quinn-Judge, P. (2001) The politics of mind over matter. *Time* 22 January, pp. 17–29.

Richter, L.K. (1995) Philippine land reform and tourism development under Marcos, Aquino and Ramos. *Crossroads* 9, 33–64.

Richter, L.K. (1999) After political turmoil: the lessons of rebuilding tourism in three countries. *Journal of Travel Research* 38, 41–45.

Sachs, J. (2002) Nature's grave warnings to our planet. *The Korea Herald* 29 August, p. 6.

Sayan, S. (2002) Globalization in an ageing world. *The Korea Herald* 20 August, p. 6.

Sealey, T.S. (ed.) (2000) *International Country Risk Guide*, Vol. XXI, No, 5. The PRS Group, New York.

Senge, P.M. (1990) *The Fifth Principle: the Art and Practice of the Learning Organisation*. Doubleday, New York.

Song, H. and Witt, S.F. (2000) Forecasting performance of econometric tourism demand models. In: Lockwood, A. (ed.) *International Millennium Conference, on Tourism and Hospitality in the 21st Century, Interchange Papers Proceedings*. 11–14 January. School of Management Studies for the Service Sector, University of Surrey, UK, pp. 138–141.

Statistics Indonesia (2000) Selected tables, <http://www.bps.go.id/statbysector/tourism> (accessed 7 August 2000).

Tourism Forecasting Council (1997a) *Forecast, 3:2*. Tourism Forecasting Council, Sydney.

Tourism Forecasting Council (1997b)

Scenarios. Tourism Forecasting Council, Sydney.

Tourism Forecasting Council (1998) *Forecast, 4:2*. Tourism Forecasting Council, Sydney.

Tourism Forecasting Council (1999) *Forecast, 5:1*. Tourism Forecasting Council, Sydney.

Tourism Forecasting Council (2000) *Forecast, 5:2*. Tourism Forecasting Council, Sydney.

Tourism Forecasting Council (2001) *Forecast. The Twelfth Release of the Tourism Forecasting Council*. August.

Turner, L. and Witt, S.F. (2001) Forecasting tourism using univariate and multivariate structural time series models. *Tourism Economics* 7, 135–148.

Uysal, M. and Crompton, J. (1985) An overview of approaches used to forecast tourism demand. *Journal of Travel Research* 23 (2), 7–15.

van der Heijden, K. (1997) *Scenarios: the Art of Strategic Conversion*. Wiley, Chichester, UK.

Weiner, A.J. and Kahn, H. (1972) Crisis and arms control. In: Hermann, C.F. (ed.) *International Crises: Insights From Behaviour Research*. The Free Press, New York, p. 21.

Willmott, M. and Graham, S. (2001) The world of today and tomorrow: the European picture. In: Lockwood, A. and Medlik, S. (eds) *Tourism and Hospitality in the 21st Century*. Butterworth-Heinemann, Oxford, pp. 29–38.

Witt, S.F. and Song, H. (2001). Forecasting future tourism flows. In: Lockwood, A. and Medlik, S. (eds) *Tourism and Hospitality in the 21st Century*. Butterworth-Heinemann, Oxford, pp. 106–118.

World Tourism Organization (1994) *Global Tourism Forecasts to the Year 2000 and Beyond*. World Tourism Organization, Madrid.

World Tourism Organization (1999*) Compendium of Tourism Statistics*. World Tourism Organization, Madrid.

26 Reflections and Further Research Priorities

BRUCE PRIDEAUX AND ERIC LAWS

The studies presented in this book analyse some of the disasters and crises that have affected tourism over the period from 1999 to 2005. Even as this chapter was being written, there are new reports of disasters including Hurricane Katrina which devastated New Orleans, more terrorist bombings in Bali and a major earthquake in Pakistan. Of even greater concern at the time of writing are reports of an increasing likelihood of a global avian flu pandemic (Osterholm, 2005) that has the potential to kill tens of millions of people. In the medium-term future, the effects of global warming are likely to create a whole series of new crises including an increase in the number and severity of wind storms (cyclones, hurricane and typhoons), rising sea levels and dramatic changes to rainfall patterns (Flannery, 2005). One impact of global warming will be rising insurance premiums which will impact on business viability. Another may be the disappearance of many reef ecosystems and the tourism industries they support.

The impact of the events reported upon in this book for the tourism industry ranged from local to global, and in each case the tourism industry suffered significant setbacks, and recovery was difficult. In the future, more crises, perhaps many times larger than those described here, may occur. The responses discussed in this book offer some strategies that might be adopted in the future. The discussion of the New Orleans hurricane disaster later in this chapter adds further lessons that should be considered by crisis planners. The chapter will also briefly consider the implications for tourism of a possible avian flu pandemic, as well as discussing the way forward in tourism crisis research.

As noted in Chapter 1, a crisis is often unpredictable and, when one occurs, it may take on a form that has not been foreseen by planners and the authorities responsible for crisis or disaster planning. As will be discussed later, the authorities responsible for protecting New Orleans expected problems to occur if a strong hurricane struck the city, but they were still unprepared for the magnitude of the ensuing disaster that resulted in the deaths of nearly 1000 persons and a cost that was measured in the high tens of billions of US dollars. At the time of writing, there was considerable discussion on the potential for an avian flu pandemic. However, unlike the pre-disaster period described by Faulkner (2001), the authorities in many jurisdictions have accepted the potential threat of a global pandemic and many governments have undertaken pro-active planning.

The last threat that was viewed as having global implications was the millennium bug (Prideaux, 1999). In that case, governments and the private sector accepted the possibility of a crisis of global proportions and responded pro-actively by investing heavily in prevention. The predicted economic collapse failed to occur and the dawn of the new millennium passed with few incidents of computer failure. The response to the potential threat posed by the millennium bug in all probability averted the occurrence of the threat. This is often not possible, particularly where the event triggering the crisis is unexpected or of a nature that was not anticipated in pre-crisis planning. This chapter draws lessons from previous chapters as well as new lessons from a brief analysis of the New Orleans hurricane disaster.

It is interesting to examine the longer term implications of specific crises on the tourism industry. The impact of the 11 September 2001 (9/11) attacks on international travel was dramatic, but some 4 years on, the scale of international travel has continued to increase. In the UK, the damage that occurred to the nation's tourism industry from foot and mouth disease was short lived, and, as has been the case with other crises, tourists returned following media campaigns to assure them that the danger had passed and that normality had been restored. It is apparent that the tourism industry has a high general level of resilience to crisis, with demand often being shifted from the affected destination to other non-affected destinations. After the 9/11 attacks, many people cancelled plans for international travel or substituted domestic destinations. After the Bali bombings of 2002, international visitors substituted other international destinations for Bali. Alternatively, where travel became impossible, as McKercher and Pine (2005) observed when the SARS (severe acute respiratory syndrome) epidemic struck Hong Kong, demand was deferred rather than extinguished. After the crisis had passed, pent up demand may result in a spurt of outbound tourism.

In the US travel trade, the term 'Teflon tourist' has emerged (Kurosawa, 2005) to describe travellers who are prepared to take advantage of the low rates offered by destinations following disasters. One example of this trend are tourists who took advantage of cheap flights to Phuket immediately after the 2004 Tsunami. Even while recovery of persons killed in the tsunami was taking place, Teflon tourists, also referred to as 'vulture tourists' by Kurosawa (2005), were arriving at the destination and recording interviews of their trip with television journalists.

Based on the findings of the discussion in this book and the statistics on recovered demand for destinations that have suffered crisis, it is apparent that provided the national economy is buoyant and there is no external military threat to the nation, demand for travel can be expected to remain high provided that there is positive consumer sentiment towards the future. In the past, when major events such as the Second World War or the Depression of 1929 occurred, demand for travel fell as consumers lost confidence and became worried about the future. Provided crises of the magnitude of global or even major regional warfare are averted and the global economy is not suffering major recession or depression, the impact of crises appears to be short term, at least on a global scale. However, for the affected destination to recover demand that has moved elsewhere, facilities must be repaired and consumers, and importantly the travel industry, must be reassured that the danger has passed and the destination is back to business as normal.

Most of the cases cited in this book relate to single crisis events that affected a destination for a specific period of time, and importantly, did not reoccur. Where multiple events separated by time but not intensity directly affect tourists in a specific destination, the long-term resilience of the destination may be less assured. The Bali bombings of 2002 had a severe impact on the destination but, through well-designed and executed market recovery strategies, demand was rebuilt. For example, the Singaporean market, responding to highly attractive package prices designed to rebuild Bali's inbound market, grew from 17,666 in 2002 to 26,881 in 2003 (Kurosawa, 2005). A second series of terrorist suicide bombings in October 2005 was a severe setback to the destination. Responding to this attack, the destination and its partners very rapidly instituted a crisis recovery campaign based on the lessons of similar campaigns used in the aftermath of the 2002 terrorist bombings and in Thailand following the tsunami. Both Garuda Indonesia and AirAsia offered free tickets to Bali, while hotels substantially reduced prices and offered extra benefits such as upgrades and free nights. The longer term implications of multiple crisis events specifically directed at tourists are unknown and will in all probability depend on the ability of the authorities to convince travellers and the travel trade that security has been significantly enhanced to prevent future attacks. If further attacks do occur, the probability of recovery in the short term is doubtful and travellers will seek alternative destinations perceived to be safer.

This trend is demonstrated by the patterns of inbound travel experienced by Fiji following the 2000 coup. In the months immediately following the coup, inbound travel almost ceased, falling from 118,517 in the third quarter of 1999 to 44,936 in the same period in 2000. However, following the restoration of a democratically elected Parliament and the removal of an adverse Australian government travel advisory, tourists returned and, by 2003, tourism arrivals had grown from 409,999 in 1999 to 480,000 (Fiji Islands, 2005). In the wake of the 2002 Bali bombings, the country experienced a massive upsurge in visitation as travellers substituted travel to Bali with travel to Fiji and other Pacific islands (Prideaux, 2005).

The value of the discussion presented in this book lies in the strategies that the authors have outlined to handle a crisis once it has occurred or the theoretical insights contributed to how crises may be more effectively managed. Given that this book only catalogues a relatively short period of time and is not exhaustive in its treatment of events that have had serious impacts for national tourism industries, it is apparent that more crises will strike and will damage tourism on a scale that may range from local to national or even global. The tourism industry cannot therefore become complacent about crisis planning and management. It is also apparent that it is not a case of 'if' but 'when' and at what scale further crises will occur.

Although not analysed previously in this volume, it is worth drawing some lessons from the events that occurred in the wake of Hurricane Katrina in the USA as indicators of the type of responses that might occur when future large-scale crises strike, the avian flu pandemic being one such possibility. Moreira (Chapter 5) suggested a model that incorporated new scales of severity that could be used for assessment and response. By using this model alongside disaster planning models of the nature suggested by Faulkner (2001), tourism managers will have available a more comprehensive range of planning tools to assist in pre-event planning and post-event recovery.

Many chapters in this book document how recovery to a long-term growth trend has been achieved following a crisis. Yet it is also apparent that after a major crisis, the underlying structure of operational relationships which the tourism industry had previously established may be changed. Furthermore, coordination with local or national government and experienced crisis response agencies may have to be established rapidly to deal with complex, unclear and rapidly changing needs, often in situations where overall leadership is lacking.

Hurricane Katrina

Built between the Mississippi River on the south and Lake Pontchartrain on the north, New Orleans has developed a substantial tourism industry based on its French heritage and the easygoing lifestyle epitomized by Jazz. While the initial settlement in the now famous French Quarter was built above flood level, the city has subsequently spread into areas that now have to be protected by seawalls and levees. Conscious of the possibility of a catastrophic event caused by either flooding of the Mississippi River or a storm surge caused by a hurricane, the US Army Corps of Engineers built and maintains several hundred kilometres of levee banks to defend the city. While the levee system had been constructed to withstand a Category 3 hurricane (*The Bulletin with Newsweek*, 2005), the possibility that even more intense hurricanes of up to Category 5 in strength could strike the city was widely acknowledged. Hurricane Katrina, with an intensity of

Category 4, struck on Monday, 29 August. The damage that occurred was far greater than planners had estimated might happen and, as a consequence, the effectiveness of the disaster plan previously developed for the city was reduced. A number of the levees were breached and seawater flooded in, inundating large areas of the city. Even after repairing the levees, it took many weeks of pumping to drain the city.

Aware of the possibility of a major hurricane strike, the city had developed a counter disaster plan to cope with a range of emergencies including breaching of the city's levee system, flooding and hurricane damage. Unfortunately, the US system of government, where power is shared by municipal, state and federal governments to create a series of checks and balances that have their origins in the US Civil War period and War of Independence, is cumbersome, particularly when a high level of coordination is required in a time of emergency. The politicized nature of US administration, based on patronage at the top levels of public administration, has resulted in many senior bureaucratic positions being filled by candidates selected for reasons other than their demonstrated public service records within the government bureaucracy. The top level of bureaucrats often owe their position to the governing party or political leader and, as a consequence, their decision making is often coloured by the anticipated political consequences of decision making rather than an apolitical appreciation of the strategies required to solve a particular problem. This is demonstrated by the incumbents in the leadership positions in FEMA (Federal Emergency Management Agency) being selected because of their political connections rather than knowledge of emergency management.

While it is perhaps too early to draw considered conclusions on a suite of issues and mismanagement that exacerbated the crisis created by Hurricane Katrina, it is possible to make a number of observations that may be critical in the management of future large-scale crises. The following discussion is based on news reports and commentary emanating from the disaster and is used to illustrate factors that have not been discussed in detail elsewhere in this book.

A major contributing cause to the disaster in New Orleans was the lack of natural seaward protection from hurricanes and the fact that much of the city was built below sea level and thus has to be protected by a series of levees. Dikes and levees have channelled silt, that would previously have contributed to the formation of a protective barrier of outer islands, into the ocean and contributed to the disappearance of wetlands along the Gulf Coast estimated to be disappearing at the equivalent of 33 football fields per day (*The Bulletin with Newsweek*, 2005). Similar observations related to the impact of redeveloping or removing natural protective coastal barriers applied in the Asian tsunami.

In New Orleans, a counter disaster management plan had been developed and practised. However, when the crisis occurred, many of the personnel responsible for administrating the crisis response plan were found wanting and either failed to implement the strategies they were assigned to administer while remaining on duty, or alternatively walked away from their responsibilities. For example, many members of the city's police force allegedly deserted, allowing looters and other criminals to gain control over large parts of the city for short periods. The city's fleet of 500 school buses were never mobilized to move residents who lacked private transport and were eventually flooded despite the city having over 24 h notice that the hurricane was possibly going to strike. Between 80,000 and 100,000 people ignored warnings to evacuate: because they wished to stay to protect their property; because of incapacity; or because of a lack of public transport (Gibbs, 2005). By the time Hurricane Rita posed a threat to Houston several weeks later, the failures of New Orleans had been recognized and a mass evacuation by public transport and private vehicles was organized in a more effective manner, though still not without some problems (CNN, 2005).

Post-hurricane rescue efforts were uncoordinated (*The Bulletin with Newsweek*, 2005), at least for the first few days. For example, the Commanding Officer of the 920th Rescue Wing of the Air Force Reserve Command spent 24 h after the hurricane had passed trying to obtain permission to commence rescue flights. FEMA was not authorized to task military units and there was confusion in both civilian and military chains of command over who was authorized to respond to requests for military assistance by civilian agencies. By Wednesday night, the Mayor of New Orleans ordered the city's police to cease trying to rescue people and to turn their attention to restoring law and order by stopping looting and arresting street gangs. Commencing on Thursday, many officers handed in their badges, unwilling to face the task of controlling looters and street gangs.

Overall control of the situation became a major issue that entailed conflicts between the Mayor, the State Governor, the US President, FEMA and the Pentagon (Federal US military forces command). Presidential advisors were reported (*The Bulletin with Newsweek*, 2005) to have argued for several days over who should take command of various military formations, basing their arguments on jurisdictional argument and not on the need to activate military resources to commence rescue efforts. Eventually, President Bush travelled to the region to work with local officials to establish a clear chain of command and, nearly a week after the disaster, Federal troops were sent to restore order and assist in rescue efforts. As a consequence of the confusion during the first few days after the hurricane, a number of elderly residents living in retirement or nursing homes perished either because they were not evacuated by the authorities, carers abandoned them or vital medical supplies were not available.

The need to develop emergency plans must be matched by the capacity to implement them, and this requires high levels of training. If emergency workers' families are at risk, they face an unenviable task of deciding between fulfilling their duty and their family suffering harm or dereliction of duty to save their familles. Plans to ensure their family safety are therefore a high priority and should be considered as part of any emergency or disaster response plan.

Clear and defined chains of command are another vital issue. Knowing who is in command and under what circumstances is of vital importance. Of equal importance are clear paths of succession for members of the command team who are incapacitated. This will become even more important in the event of a pandemic when many members of the chain of command can be expected to become ill or die. These issues are clearly understood by the military, which for combat situations must build battle damage-resilient organizations based on clear chains of command and establish a workable succession if commanders are killed, injured or captured. Unfortunately, civilian authorities often fail to develop a priori clear chains of command and succession policies and structures. Agreed strategies for handing over control to subordinates if managers or leaders in charge demonstrate an inability to discharge their required duties should also be considered. While this is a difficult matter to determine and any handover strategy is open to abuse, it is an issue that needs to be seriously debated.

To digress on this issue and illustrate these issues with a small example, Bruce Prideaux, the lead author of this chapter, who at the time was responsible for the operation of the School Bus system in Townsville Australia, was faced with having to decide if school bus services should be cancelled due to the imminent threat of a major cyclone (a southern hemisphere parallel to the northern hemisphere hurricane). The threat of the cyclone was significant, but the forecasters could not predict if it would strike the city although they stated the probability was high. The choice at 4 a.m. was to allow the bus system to operate and potentially have thousands of school students stranded at schools if the cyclone struck, or cancel the school bus service and force thousands of parents to miss a day's work even if the cyclone did not strike. The author did not have this authority. The Chief of Police was consulted but advised that he did not have the authority to order the bus service to be cancelled as his state of emergency powers only came into force after a disaster had struck. The Regional Director of Education was consulted and decided on balance that the risk of opening schools on that day was significant and cancelled classes. The bus service was then cancelled. Fortunately, the cyclone veered away and the city was undamaged. The school children enjoyed an unexpected day at home while many parent failed to report to their places of employment. In the case described, there was no formal planning or establishment of chains of command on this issue but, shortly after, clear chains of responsibility were established to deal with further incidents of this nature.

The handling of visitors or non-residents during a crisis is also a major issue for tourism managers. Pechlaner *et al.* (Chapter 12) considered the plight of visitors trapped in Galtuer, Switzerland by an avalanche and noted the mechanisms that were put in place to care for these visitors and to allow them to contact relatives. The reverse occurred in New Orleans.

Many international visitors caught in the incident gave harrowing media accounts of being accosted by thugs, being given no assistance by the authorities and of consular officials who were barred from entering the disaster area to offer assistance. Media accounts of situations such as this paint a very negative account of travel in the USA and act as a deterrent to potential visitors who may be planning to visit other areas in the USA.

The issue of media coverage is significant and needs to be considered carefully. The apparent abandonment of tourists to their fate is a perception of travel in the USA that will take some time to ameliorate. The care of foreign visitors is an important topic and, for nations wishing to build their tourism industry, the development of an effective strategy to deal with visitor needs during future crises must be given priority.

Of major concern is the picture painted of civil society collapsing under the pressure of a large but anticipated disaster. The breakdown of law and order, desertion of police, inability of citizens and authorities to care for the interest of the poorest members of society, the picture of utter selfishness of a city abandoning its weakest disabled citizens, and surrender of a major city to criminal gangs creates a terrible scenario for a world beset by a major global catastrophe of the nature of a global pandemic. How will society respond in such circumstances and what are the implications for tourism at least in the short term? Before concluding the chapter with some observations of how the tourism industry may respond to circumstances of this nature, we consider the possibilities of a global avian flu pandemic.

The Potential Avian Flu Pandemic

In 1918–1919, the world experienced a major pandemic known as the Spanish flu. The death toll, estimated to be between 50 and 100 million persons, far exceeded the casualities experienced by combatants in the First World War of 1914–1918 (Osterholm, 2005). Further flu pandemics occurred in 1957 in China when bird and human flus swapped genes, creating the Asian flu pandemic that killed 1 million people, and in 1969 when Hong Kong flu, where bird and human viruses were again swapped, killed at least 750,000 people. A fourth potential bird flu pandemic involving the same bird flu virus (H5N1) that is of current concern was effectively prevented in Hong Kong in 1997 when the authorities ordered every chicken slaughtered and disposed of after finding cases of bird flu in Hong Kong's domestic poultry flocks. In that event, casualities were limited to six deaths from 18 people infected. The current AIDS pandemic has killed approximately 25 million persons, but in a much longer timeframe and in a process that may take years. Influenza, commonly called flu, is a virus that annually causes illness and death on a global basis. In a normal year, about 36,000 people die from influenza in the USA alone (Appenzeller, 2005). In the Spanish flu pandemic, about 5% of sufferers died within 2–3 days of the symptoms appearing. In Philadelphia in the USA, 12,000 people died of

Spanish flu in October 1918 (Appenzeller, 2005). According to Osterholm (2005), if the Spanish flu mortality rate is extrapolated to the current US population, about 1.7 million persons will die. While influenza is a recurrent medical problem, its potential for causing a pandemic is very limited unless the influenza virus combines with an avian virus strain such as H5N1 to create a new and many times more deadly flu virus. The process involved is complex and difficult to predict. This is the situation facing the authorities in 2005. Vaccines able to treat H5N1 will only become available once the particular strain that affects humans has been identified and new vaccine stocks produced (Garrett, 2005).

While the authorities in many nations and the World Health Organization are treating the potential for a new flu pandemic with the utmost concern, there is no guarantee that it will occur, but there is a strong possibility that it will occur. Because of the nature of the H5N1 virus and other similar varieties that exist in the wild bird populations, the danger of it mutating and entering the human population will not disappear in the future. In a recent discussion on the potential for a new pandemic, Appenzeller (2005, p. 31) noted 'Here is what we know for sure. One day a new flu pandemic will come, and one day it will pass. And the killer strain, tamed by our immune systems and the passage of time, will fade into the background of nuisance flu's. The heir of 1918 is one of the milder flu strains around today.'

Recent development of new antiviral medications (Tamiflu and Relenza) offers some hope that a new pandemic can be averted if sufficient persons can be treated to prevent the virus spreading. Unfortunately, the demand for these drugs currently outstrips the supply, and this situation has been exacerbated by a number of governments including the USA, Germany, Australia and Britain building up large emergency stocks of these drugs.

In contrast to the millennium bug crisis when strong pro-active action by industry and government prevented the forecast disaster actually happening, government action is unlikely to prevent the development of avian flu. There will also be great difficulty controlling its spread once it is established in the human population. Until sufficient stocks of aniviral drugs can be made readily available, domestic poultry housed in a manner where they cannot come into contact with wild birds, and public health systems, particularly in parts of Africa, are more effective in identifying possible outbreaks at an early stage (as occurred in Hong Kong in 1997), the world remains at risk from another avian flu pandemic.

In October 2005, the health ministers of a number of countries met to discuss the possibility of a pandemic. In Australia, the Federal Minister for Health foreshadowed a range of measures that could be introduced if an outbreak occurred, including establishing isolation hospitals in aircraft hangers for people who entered the country with flu symptoms, requisitioning hotels for use as isolation hospitals for domestic suffers, and imposing curfews and travel restrictions on regions where outbreaks occurred. Similar measures can be expected in other countries.

For the tourism industry, the experience of Hong Kong during the SARS outbreak reported in McKercher and Pine (2005) gives some indication of what can be expected, but on a global scale rather than on a city scale. All inbound and outbound travel ceased and many people simply stayed home, hoping to avoid the risk of catching the virus through contact with sufferers in public places. Occupancy rates at hotels fell to record lows. After the outbreak was contained and after a period when no new cases were notified, travel resumed. While Hong Kong's gross domestic product (GDP) fell during the SARS crisis, it soon recovered after the SARS epidemic finished.

The reaction to a global pandemic can be expected to be much more severe than SARS was in Hong Kong (World Health Organization, 2003). A pessimistic scenario can be sketched as follows. Aside from numerous deaths, national and global economic output can be expected to decline, resulting in an increase in unemployment. The anticipated ban on international air travel will severely affect many nations that rely on air cargo for the export of high value low weight cargo and the just-in-time logistic structure used in many industries. Leaders in industry and government will die, causing further disruption. Mc Donald (2005) reported that the Asian Development Bank estimated that a bird flu pandemic could collectively cost Asia almost US$282 billion or 6.5% of its GDP. In a separate report, the World Bank estimated the loss to the global economy could be in the order of US$800 billion. If the economic downturn is severe, it will take some time for recovery to occur and, during this period, there can be expected to be a sharp fall in tourism demand. Strategies previously found to be useful in attracting tourists after a crisis has passed will probably be ineffective as total demand for tourism falls. A more positive scenario is possible. The Spanish flu, which was immediately preceded by the First World War, was followed by the so-called roaring 20s which was an era of global peace and rapid global economic growth. If this experience is repeated after a future pandemic, there is a strong possibility that the long-term effect will be small. Even in many sub-Saharan nations where the rate of infection of the AIDS epidemic is high, the economics have not collapsed as large numbers of citizens have died.

The two scenarios above indicate that recovery of the tourism industry will be dependent on the severity of the pandemic, the time it takes to pass, the impact on national and global economic growth and the rate of unemployment that emerges. If the lessons learnt in New Orleans for a clear and resilient chain of command and the need to maintain civil law and order have not been applied, the severity of the crisis might be greater.

Discussion

It is apparent that future crises will continue to occur on scales that range from localized to global in geographic impact and in severity of effect on business from minor to catastrophic. Figure 26.1 places a number of the crises discussed in the book on these scales. While a visual tool for plotting business and geographic severity is useful in understanding the range and complexity of tourism crises, it does not provide planners with help in dealing with crises and their aftermath. Faulkner's (2001) Tourism Disaster Management Framework model and its various clones and adaptations offers a useful planning tool, but it currently lacks scales of magnitude and severity. These are provided by the shock classification table developed by Prideaux *et al.* (2003) and Moreira's crises and disasters' impact scale of magnitude model (Chapter 5). Combined, the models and magnitude and severity scales provide a useful theoretical foundation for the management of tourism crises.

However, there still remain a number of gaps in the theoretical foundations outlined above. A particularly important area of theory requiring development is related to implementing resilient command structures. As demonstrated in the New Orleans hurricane and the Townsville cyclone, more attention needs to be given to this area of research. Post-disaster crises recovery, visitor care strategies and media management are other significant areas of research that require further attention. After the 9/11 attacks and the ensuing collapse of Ansett airlines, an ad hoc working committee of government and industry officials was established in Australia to investigate recovery strategies. Unfortunately, after handing in its report, the committee was disbanded. A more appropriate response from government should have been the establishment of a committee of this nature as a permeant counter crisis committee.

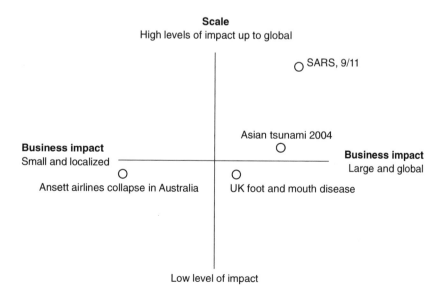

Fig. 26.1. Scale estimation of crisis impact based on business impact and geographic reach.

To handle future crises, consideration needs to be given to establishing joint industry/government coordinating committees at local, state or region and national level. Members could include representatives from various industry sectors, transport providers, police, infrastructure providers, media, health service, emergency services and defence services. Broad representation will give members of the committee access to considerable material resources as well as advice. The Alpine disaster organizations discussed by Pechlaner *et al.* (Chapter 12) indicate the usefulness of this structure in crisis situations.

The complexity of many major crises also needs to be considered in future research. Crises often develop extremely rapidly, often in ways that are not apparent beforehand, and they impose urgent demands on the people and organizations that have to manage them, often resulting in the need for individuals to take decisions and commandeer resources which are not within their usual remit. During the recovery period, existing patterns of industry networks and the relationships between tourism organizations and government or expert agencies may change. Traditional cause–effect and comparative static analysis methods appear to be inadequate to deal with these turbulent, emerging situations. Newer paradigms, particularly complexity theory, are now being applied, as several chapters in this book demonstrate.

Conclusion

This chapter has painted a sombre picture of crises, outlining very real issues that may be expected to confront the global tourism industry. It is worth noting, however, that in the past the passing of the crisis has usually been followed by a period of recovery and then, in the absence of further crisis, a return to growth. The growth of global tourism in the 20th century illustrates this observation. In spite of two major world wars, the Cold War and numerous minor or regional wars, global terrorism, natural disasters, global depression and recurrent recessions, tourism recovered after each crisis and continued to grow in line with rising global prosperity. On this evidence, it would appear that only a decline in prosperity would depress tourism demand. As prosperity returns, tourism demand can be expected to increase. The potential for long-term disruption caused by global warming will present a set of circumstances that may diverge from this pattern. If rising sea levels inundate coastal areas and changing weather patterns disrupt agriculture on a permanent basis, economic recovery may take a different path from that experienced in the past. This issue will become increasingly important in the future, and the flooding of New Orleans may have been a glimpse of the future where sea levels rise and create significant economic disruption.

It would be irresponsible for industry managers, government experts and leaders or academics to ignore the probability of future crisis situations. The academic contribution is threefold: to catalogue crisis events; to demonstrate best practice planning and responses; and to develop more effective analytical tools and advance the theoretical foundations of tourism crisis management. The issue of global warming is one issue where this response is clearly required. With increasing evidence of global warming beginning to impact on the global environment, researchers, government and industry will need to turn their collective attention to developing responses to long-term and irreversible changes in sea levels, wind storm intensity, change in rainfall and flood patterns, and the impacts of these changes on the global tourism industry.

References

Appenzeller, T. (2005) Tracing the next killer flu. *National Geographic* 208 (4), 2–31.

CNN (2005) Texans flee colossal Rita Category 5 storm is third most intense ever (September 21), <www.cnn.com/2005/WEATHER/09/21/rita/> (accessed 28 October 2005).

Faulkner, B. (2001) Towards a framework for tourism disaster management. *Tourism Management* 22, 135–147.

Fiji Islands (2005) 2003 Visitor Arrivals, <www.bulafiji.com/InfoDesk.asp?lang=EN&sub=0147> (accessed 26 October 2005).

Flannery, T. (2005) *The Weather Makers. The History and Impact of Future Climate Change*. Text Publishing, Melbourne

Garrett, L. (2005) The next pandemic. *Foreign Affairs* 84 (4), 3–23.

Gibbs, N. (2005) The aftermath. A city is failed in its hour of need. *Time* 12 September, No. 36, pp. 24–29.

Kurosawa, S. (2005) Vulture tourists. *The Australian (Features Section)* 24 October, p. 10.

McDonald, J. (2005) Bird flu to savage economies. *The Courier Mail* 5 November, p. 20.

McKercher, B. and Pine, R. (2005) Privation as a stimulus to travel demand? *Journal of Travel and Tourism Marketing* 19 (2/3), 107–116.

Osterholm, M. (2005) Preparing for the next panademic. *Foreign Affairs* 84 (4), 24–37.

Prideaux, B. (1999) The millennium bug: is the tourism industry prepared for the bug's bite? *Journal of Vacation Marketing* 5, 117–124.

Prideaux, B. (2005) Factors affecting bilateral tourism flows. *Annals of Tourism Research* 32, 780–801.

Prideaux, B., Laws, E. and Faulkner, B. (2003) Events in Indonesia: exploring the limits to formal tourism trends forecasting methods in complex crisis situations. *Tourism Management* 24, 511–520.

The Bulletin with Newsweek (2005) The lost city. *The Bulletin with Newsweek* 123 (6487), pp. 22–35.

World Health Organization (2003) Summary table of SARS cases by country, 1 November 2002–7 August 2003 World Health Organization, <http://www.who.int/csr/sars/country/2003_08_15/en/> (accessed 20 August 2005).

Index